The Strategy and Structure
of British Enterprise

ABSTRACT

The Strategy and Structure of British Enterprise

The industrial structure of an advanced economy is made up of a wide variety of different industries which in turn are composed of individual companies operating increasingly in competition with one another and with the enterprises of other nations. In reality, despite the large numbers of individual enterprises, it is a relatively small number of very large corporations which now account for the bulk of industrial production and whose fortunes determine the economic outcome of the nation.

This concentration of economic power in the hands of a relatively few corporations is a recent phenomenon. The strategies of those firms and their methods of management are therefore of significant interest for a variety of reasons, and better understanding of them is of significance to practicing executives, government planners and legislators, and teachers of business administration.

This study by Derek F. Channon focusing on the evolution of the largest 100 manufacturing companies in the United Kingdom, won the Richard D. Irwin Prize for the Best Doctoral Dissertation 1970–1971 at the Harvard Business School, where the author was a Ford Foundation European Doctoral Fellow prior to returning to the Manchester Business School, Manchester, England.

This study traces the evolution of the strategy and structure of the largest 100 British manufacturing concerns (measured by sales in 1970) over the period between 1950 and 1970. It was estimated that this group of companies represented approximately 60 percent of net assets, employed about 45 percent of the workforce, and accounted for some 60 percent of sales of the British manufacturing industry in 1970. In addition, these companies accounted for some 80 percent of the assets employed overseas by British manufacturing concerns. As such they were taken to represent the essential core of British manufacturing enterprise.

Relatively little systematic study has appeared concerning the development of large-scale British enterprise, yet the British industrial environment has undergone substantial change especially in the post-World War II period. Historically, Britain was the home of the first Industrial Revolution founded on iron and steel, coal mining, and textiles. This early industrialization was supported by Britain's position as the dominant world power, built upon naval strength and a great colonial empire which provided both markets and raw materials.

During the twentieth century this dominant position was seriously eroded by the rise of new industrial nations, the dissolution of the Empire, and two great wars. At no time in the present century was the erosion greater than during the recent postwar period. In 1946, Britain was a nation recovering from a long war with its financial resources seriously depleted. British enterprise was seriously weakened, devoted to wartime production, unused to severe competition, and seemed ill-equipped to face the challenges of the following decades which brought the loss of Empire, greatly increased competition, and rapid technological and social change.

The study therefore set out to analyze how British industry had sought to adjust its strategy in the light of new opportunities and risks presented by the environment. Further, it sought to identify what organization structural changes had taken place as a result in shifts in strategy and thus to improve understanding of the inter-relationships between strategy and structure.

The analysis begins in the first chapter which reviews previous research on corporate strategy and structure drawn primarily from American experience. From this evidence a model of the process of corporate development is presented to provide the framework for the remainder of the study. The strategy of a company is classified into four classes of diversification: single product, dominant product, related product, and unrelated product, and it is hypothesized that a company would evolve over time and in response to certain environmental conditions from an early undiversified state to a more diversified stage of development. It is anticipated that such changes in strategy would result in a subsequent revision of administrative structures which in turn would be classified into three main categories: functional, holding company, and multidivisional. In the multidivisional structure there is further subdivision to account for divisions based on geographic and product differences largely to allow for the development of multinational strategies.

Chapter 2 discusses major changes that occurred in the British industrial environment which influenced the strategies of British companies. These were considered to be primarily the changing pattern of demand, the growth of competition, and the change of technology. In addition, trends were also discussed in the factors of production, notably capital, labor, and management, together with consideration of the role of the state.

The third chapter introduces the companies, and examines and analyzes how they have undergone considerable transition since 1950. Many of the companies had clearly adopted a strategy of diversification in the post-World War II period which was subsequently accompanied by structural change leading to wide-spread adoption of a multidivisional organization structure. This structure which was almost unknown among the British companies in 1950 had been adopted by over 70 percent of them by 1970.

The pattern of strategic change was found to be gradual, with most companies moving through an intermediate stage of diversification. There was, however, a group of companies drawn from a specific series of industries which had consistently failed to diversify. The companies in these industries are discussed in Chapter 4 and their common characteristics identified.

The majority of companies which had diversified were also found to divide into two groups according to the main method by which diversification had occurred. One group was found to have diversified largely by the internal development of products related by a specific skill or technology, and their strategic and structural histories are developed in Chapter 5. The second group of companies from low technology industries had diversified primarily by acquisition, and these are discussed in Chapter 6.

Chapter 7 examines the internal characteristics of the multidivisional structures found among the three groups of companies identified in the preceding chapters and compares British and American practice.

The final chapters develop the conclusions which can be drawn. Chapter 8 develops the strengths and weaknesses which can be observed in British industry, while the final chapter summarizes the conclusions on the process of corporate development and draws out the managerial implications.

There was evidence that the main force for strategic change was increased competition. The main reaction to competitive threats in a number of industries was concentration into larger units, thus building a series of highly concentrated industries which were buttressed against competition by high entry barriers or government protection. Most industries, however, primarily elected to diversify. In 1950 diversified firms represented only about 25 percent of the largest 100 firms; by 1970, however, 60 percent of the population was relatively highly diversified. Furthermore, once adopted, the strategy of diversification tended to become institutionalized, leading to the constant search for new product markets.

The adoption of the strategy of diversification brought a dramatic change in administrative structure. A multidivisional system was found to supersede other forms of structure but frequently was introduced only after other organizational systems had failed; outside consultants were used to structure this system.

The principal implications for management deal with the process and problems of transition from a narrow product-based company to a diversified corporation and the changing role and skills required of top management in administering such an enterprise. The implications for government question conventional policies for state intervention and review some of the policy requirements brought on by a transition of corporate enterprise from a series of narrow product-based firms to a series of large diversified companies managed with a multidivisional structure.

(Published by Division of Research, Harvard Business School, Soldiers Field, Boston, Mass. 02163. LC 72–94362; ISBN 0–87584–101–5. xvii + 257 pp.; $12.00; 1973.)

The Strategy and Structure of British Enterprise

Derek F. Channon
Manchester Business School
Manchester, England

DIVISION OF RESEARCH
GRADUATE SCHOOL OF BUSINESS ADMINISTRATION
HARVARD UNIVERSITY
BOSTON · 1973

Foreword

The Strategy and Structure of British Enterprise deals with the evolution of British industrial enterprises, where each enterprise is viewed both as a "totality" and as a member of a "population" of British firms. Derek Channon's research, leading to his doctoral dissertation at the Harvard Business School, was carried on under the auspices of the school's Business Policy Area, an area whose primary focus has been that of understanding the firm as a totality.

Business Policy has long been one of the central teaching and research areas at the Harvard Business School. Given the complexity of the modern firm, much of the research in this area has consisted of case studies aimed at achieving a greater depth of understanding of the complexities of the role and functions of top management. The various Faculty members who have developed and carried forward this tradition have been sufficiently concerned with the complexity of the real world phenomena under study that, in most cases, they have been reluctant to generalize, especially about broad trends in the development of or managerial guidance of the large, modern enterprise as a "population."

In the 1960s, however, there was a shift in research emphasis, including intensive work with developmental models of the firm and the study of larger populations of companies. Inspired in no small measure by work such as Alfred D. Chandler's *Strategy and Structure*,[1] the new research thrust included not only the assessment of developmental trends in a population of approximately 50 firms in a country, but also their implications for public policy (cf. McArthur and Scott, *Industrial Planning in France* [2]).

This study of British Enterprise traces the development of a still broader population of firms, the "top 100," and over a longer time period, 1950–1970. The

---

[1] Alfred D. Chandler, *Strategy and Structure*, Anchor Books, New York, 1966.

[2] John H. McArthur and Bruce R. Scott, *Industrial Planning in France*, Division of Research, Harvard Graduate School of Business Administration, Boston, 1969.

primary emphais of the work, quite naturally, is on what has been happening and what it implies for British managers in the 1970s and beyond.

The author's initiative also became the starting point for a coordinated research project covering five countries: France, Germany, Italy, the United Kingdom, and the United States. Each of the European studies examined the strategies of development of the top 100 firms by country. In a departure from the usual doctoral dissertation research practice, the various researchers coordinated their work in terms of concepts and research methodology, as well as in terms of technical definitions. All were sponsored and coordinated through the Division of Research, under my supervision, in a project known as Industrial Development and Public Policy.

Derek Channon's was the first of the dissertations to be completed, and in many ways the trends which he found in the United Kingdom foreshadow those found on the Continent.[3] Interestingly, the trends toward diversification in related areas and management via divisions, which show up in all five studies, also show a "high performance" strategy and structure in a comparison study of "Strategy, Structure, and Economic Performance" of the *Fortune* 500 in the United States.[4] It is as if leading businessmen had discovered the high performance strategy and structure well before the academics, thus pointing out that researchers are "learners" as well as teachers.

Further work is now in progress, using the familiar case study approach, to examine not only some dramatic examples of public policy (e.g., the Canada Development Corporation and the Plan Calcul in France), but also to begin to probe for reasons for the stability of some of the low performance strategies. As a result, Business Policy now has a two-pronged approach to the study of the development of the large corporation, one based on case studies and the other on "population studies." The two are being explicitly related to one another as the search is being made both for further understanding of reality and for understanding the implications of the emerging findings.

Obviously much remains to be done, not only country by country, but also in making multicountry comparisons. This research is continuing, and I should like to acknowledge the support and encouragement of Professors Alfred D. Chandler and C. Roland Christensen who have helped in its various phases. I should also like to acknowledge the encouragement of the Dean of the Harvard Business School, Lawrence E. Fouraker, in our attempt to develop a better comparative understanding of European and American business practice.

Financial support for this project was administered by the Division of Research at the Harvard Business School by an allocation of funds from gifts to the School by The Associates of the Harvard Business School. Under the guidance of Professor Richard E. Walton, Director of the Division of Research, the School has been generous in supporting field work in Europe, and especially this study in the United

---

[3] Gareth Pooley Dyas, "The Strategy and Structure of French Industrial Enterprise"; Robert J. Pavan, "The Strategy and Structure of Italian Enterprise"; Heinz T. Thanheiser, "Strategy and Structure of German Industrial Enterprise"; all Unpublished Doctoral Dissertations, Harvard Graduate School of Business Administration, 1972.

[4] Richard P. Rumelt, "Strategy, Structure, and Economic Performance," Unpublished Doctoral Dissertation, Harvard Graduate School of Business Administration, 1972.

Kingdom. In addition, two European companies encouraged the research both morally and financially, and it is with warm thanks that, on behalf of the School, I acknowledge this support from Industrie Buitoni Perugina of Perugia, Italy, and Granges A.B. of Stockholm, Sweden.

BRUCE R. SCOTT
Professor of Business Administration

Soldiers Field
Boston, Massachusetts
December 1972

Preface

This study started when I was a Ford Foundation European Doctoral Fellow at the Harvard Graduate School of Business Administration, on leave of absence from the Manchester Business School. In its earlier form the study was the dissertation I submitted in partial fulfillment of the requirements for the degree of Doctor of Business Administration at Harvard. The intervening period between the end of 1970 and the present date has provided me with the opportunity to correct a number of the errors present in the original manuscript in the light of new information obtained both from published sources and further exposure to practicing executives from a number of the subject companies. In all, I have had the opportunity to interview managers from over 40 of the companies in the original sample. Although the results of subsequent interviews are not formally recorded in the following pages, they were found to corroborate the basic themes discernible from the more limited research originally undertaken.

Business does not stand still. Already some of the data have been overtaken by events. A number of companies discussed in my research have disappeared by merger and acquisition primarily with other companies still contained in the sample.

Seven companies, International Distillers, Watney Mann, Courage Barclay, Wiggins Teape, Carrington Dewhurst, Viyella International, and International Publishing have been acquired by others. In all cases, these new changes have supported the main findings of the research in that they have represented acquisitions by more diversified concerns than those acquired. In addition, several of the predators have taken on an increasingly unrelated diversified air with the thread of relatedness between activities becoming more tenuous. It would therefore certainly seem probable that an increasing number of unrelated diversified concerns "conglomerates," will emerge in Great Britain during the 1970s.

A further trend has been the dramatic increase in the number of executive stock option schemes being introduced which may well indicate an increasingly strong correlation between performance-related reward systems and the adoption of a divisional structure. Perhaps the most traumatic results of the widespread structural changes in the 1960s are now working themselves out. During 1972 the number of redundancies began to decline for the first time in several years, and there were somewhat fewer drastic reorganizations and subsequent executive shake-ups. British industry has still not yet trimmed down to its most efficient strategy and structure, but it is certainly a great deal better placed to face the challenge of Europe today than it was even in 1970.

Despite the changes that have occurred, however, I do not believe the new evidence indicates any real change in the basic conclusions reached from the research. As a result, no major attempt has been made to change the makeup of the sample companies which were taken as the largest 100 manufacturing concerns in 1970.

As originally conceived, the research had a number of objectives. Not least among these was a concern to make some contribution to the knowledge available on the largest British companies about which relatively little had been systematically written. This was especially true in the area of Business Policy which is concerned with the problems which affect the enterprise as a whole, and the role and responsibilities of general management. As such, the research focuses on the evolution of the strategy and structure of these large corporations and, from the data collected, an attempt has been made to distill meaningful generalizations of value to the practicing executive.

As a teacher of business administration, I am concerned that such teaching must be relevant to business practice. Frequently some businessmen have already gone well beyond the established limits of developed theory in their search for viable solutions to real problems. However, these solutions have seldom been articulated. By this collection of relevant data and analysis for useful generalizations, I hope that those who teach business administration can learn from business and so better aid practicing managers in their task. It would be extremely arrogant to do otherwise and, perhaps, too often the educational establishments have attempted to foist unsubstantiated theories on the business world to the detriment of both. A graduate school of business administration should be, if anything, a professional institution attempting to understand and theorize about the real world, not an academic institution unconcerned with the solution of real business problems.

The study would not have been possible but for the help and assistance of many others. I should, therefore, like to take this opportunity to thank all those who contributed. While it is not possible to single out all these, I should especially like to thank those members of the Faculty of the Harvard Business School who were instrumental in seeing the project through.

Professor Bruce R. Scott, who served as the Chairman of my thesis committee, was largely responsible for developing my interest in the area of Business Policy while I was at Harvard. He was involved in the project from the outset, and encouraged its development. As the work proceeded, he was a constant source of inspiration and was responsible for developing my initial ideas into a full-scale project involving similar studies in other countries. Professor C. Roland Christensen, Chairman of the Business Policy area and a member of my thesis committee from its earliest beginnings, diligently read the drafts and made many useful suggestions as to its focus and content. Finally, I was privileged to have Professor Alfred D. Chandler as my third advisor. His own classic work on the development of American industry served as a model and inspiration for my own, and his contributions both to my original thesis and its subsequent revision for publication were invaluable.

I should also like to thank many of my colleagues in the United Kingdom at the Manchester Business School who were originally responsible for developing my interest in the study of business administration. In particular, I am grateful to Professor Grigor McClelland, Director of the School, who permitted my three years' leave of absence to study at Harvard. In addition, he made valuable contributions to that part of the research conducted in Great Britain.

Although the present study started as a solo effort, it later became part of a wider project when a group of my fellow doctoral students began to conduct similar studies in other countries. Robert J. Pavan, Heinz T. Thanheiser, and Gareth Pooley Dyas, who have subsequently conducted these studies in Italy, West Germany, and France, made valuable contributions to the latter phases of my own work based on their preliminary findings in other countries. In addition, I enjoyed many hours of discussion with Leonard Wrigley, another British doctoral student at Harvard, whose discovery of a meaningful method of differentiating multidivisional corporations made an invaluable contribution to the development of a stages model of corporate growth and provided me with some basic conceptual ideas for the framework of my own work.

In addition to these people, I should like to thank the many company executives and others in Britain who entertained me and provided frank answers to my many questions. Without their help the study would have been impossible. I am also grateful to Mr. Harry Townsend, of the London School of Economics, who made available the excellent papers of his and Professor Sir Ronald Edwards' evening seminar. These papers provided a superb record of many British companies.

As originally conceived, the research dealt not only with the strategy and structure of the largest British companies, but also with the impact of public policy on their strategic development. The study also includes an analysis of certain agencies concerned with the strategies of those public bodies themselves. While these data are not reported here, the information provided valuable background material, and I should therefore like to thank Sir Frederick Catherwood and Mr. Tom Fraser together with the staff of the National Economic Development Office, Mr. Aubrey Jones and the staff of the former National Board for Prices and Incomes, and Mr. Charles Villiers and the staff of the former Industrial Reorganisation Corporation.

While I was a doctoral candidate at Harvard, financial assistance came primarily from the Ford Foundation supported by the Foundation for Management Education and the Manchester Business School, for which I am most grateful. The study itself was financed by an allocation of funds from gifts to Harvard by The Associates of the Harvard Business School, and publication of the study by the Division of Research was made possible by virtue of its having won the Richard D. Irwin Prize for the Best Doctoral Dissertation 1970–71 at the Harvard Business School. I am especially grateful to Miss Hilma Holton for her efficiency and diligence as my editor in transforming the thesis manuscript into book form.

My final thanks go to my wife, Ann, who was a constant source of strength and encouragement throughout the entire period of this study and who typed many of the earlier drafts.

Despite the valuable contribution of others, however, the responsibility for the work and any weaknesses or errors in the argument are entirely my own.

DEREK F. CHANNON

Manchester, England
October 1972

Table of Contents

List of Tables

List of Figures

CHAPTER 1

The Changing Nature
of British Enterprise

INTRODUCTION

T HE PAST FEW DECADES HAVE SEEN the rapid growth of a new social institution
—that of the giant industrial corporation. Business enterprise has undergone a
remarkable transformation from its early beginnings, when it was largely owned
and managed by its founding entrepreneurs. Today most of industrial production
is accounted for by relatively few large business enterprises which, in the main,
have outgrown their entrepreneurial family origins and become institutionalized,
thus taking on almost a life of their own. These are the new institutions capable of
transcending the constant changes in human inputs which sustain them.

In the years since the Second World War the transition of business enterprise
has perhaps shown the greatest change of all. It is the purpose of this study to
examine the change that has taken place among the largest industrial enterprises
within a specific economy, namely the United Kingdom. For, despite the fact that
Britain was the home of the first Industrial Revolution, many of its largest enterprises are of much more recent origin.

In the United States, where most research has appeared, the development of
the large business enterprise dates back to the growth of the railroads. As these
concerns grew, so they were forced to develop administrative structures in order to
manage the new complexities of widespread activities. In addition, their growth
made possible the growth of other enterprises. Chandler [1] observed that the rapid
enlargement of the market by the development of the railroads in turn permitted
and in some cases necessitated the expansion and subdivision of other manufacturing, mining, and marketing enterprises. This expansion demanded new patterns
of administration to concentrate effort on coordination, appraisal, and planning in
the work of the specialist subunits.

---

[1] A. D. Chandler, *Strategy and Structure*, Anchor Books, New York, 1966, p. 27.

By the late nineteenth century, there began to emerge a number of large, private enterprises usually engaged in a single product or market activity. These were often formed by the concentration of a number of smaller, similar companies. They were often vertically integrated, and oriented toward specific commodities such as meat, tobacco, or steel. In order to manage the enlarged enterprises, many of these concerns looked to the railroads for their model of administrative structure. They therefore usually adopted a form of organization which divided the tasks of enterprise into a series of specialized functions, such as sales, production, distribution, and finance. Other concerns remained as holding companies which lacked central direction and permitted great autonomy to the constituent subunits.

Increasing organizational size and complexity gradually produced a new breed of professional managers, who were not the owners of the enterprises. These men rapidly came to succeed the original entrepreneurs as the leaders of enterprise, bringing the prospect of continuity to the corporation. In a sense, the enterprise became an institution.

By the early years of the twentieth century, the growth of these large enterprises began causing public concern. Strong legislation was introduced to preserve competition. Another concern was voiced by Berle and Means,[2] who considered that a separation of ownership from control had developed, leading to possible impact on the performance of the enterprise.

More recently Galbraith [3] has extended this argument. He considered that where, in the past, leadership of the enterprise was identified with entrepreneurial activity, in the modern corporation built on technology and planning, with ownership divorced from control, the entrepreneur no longer existed as an individual person.

Galbraith argued that the entrepreneur had been replaced by a collective entity, the "technostructure," which participated in the formation of group decisions. As a result of the rise of the technostructure, the large enterprise was forced to depart from its original entrepreneur role. The firm isolated itself from the uncertainties of the market by seeking to control its environment. The primary goals of the technostructure were transformed from the traditional entrepreneurial concept of profit maximization into the achievement of satisfactory earnings and survival which were achieved by growth of sales. Secondary objectives of technical virtuosity and a rising dividend rate were adopted subject to the condition that they did not conflict with the achievement of the primary goals.

Galbraith's perception of the large enterprise, therefore, seemed to be that of the firm which sought to integrate its functions in an effort to stabilize its environment, thereby achieving its goals of satisfactory returns and maximum growth. This strategy did indeed seem to reflect the strategy adopted by the early large-scale enterprises which sought to grow by integrating their operations and extending their sales to similar types of customers.

Chandler,[4] however, in his classic study of the growth of large-scale American enterprise, noted two other additional strategies. He observed that growth also came as a result of a quest for new markets and sources of supplies in distant

---

[2] A. Berle and G. Means, *The Modern Corporation and Private Property*, Commerce Clearing House, Inc., New York, 1932.

[3] J. K. Galbraith, *The New Industrial State*, Signet Books, New York, 1968, pp. 81–82.

[4] A. D. Chandler, *Strategy and Structure*, p. 51.

lands, or it came from the opening of new markets by developing a wide range of new products for different types of customers.

These latter two forms of strategic growth, diversification and geographical expansion, led in turn to new types of administrative problems. Initially the firms adopting these strategies attempted to continue managing the enterprise with the functional organization or by means of a loosely knit holding company composed of virtually autonomous subsidiaries acting without central controls. However, growth in size, complexity, and information flows placed increasingly intolerable strains on the functional and holding company systems especially for those executives responsible for directing the organization as a whole. This was particularly true of firms adopting the strategy of product-market diversification where the disparate needs of the different markets rapidly escalated the complexity of managing the enterprise.

Therefore, in the early 1920s a new administrative form—a multidivisional structure—began to emerge in a few pioneering organizations notably E. I. du Pont de Nemours and the General Motors Corporation.

This new administrative form divided the enterprise in quite a different way from the previously centralized functional structure. Chandler described the four different types of executive positions within this structure as follows:[4a]

> Each of these (four) types within the enterprise has a different range of administrative activities. Normally, each is on a different level of authority. At the top is a general office. There, general executives and staff specialists coordinate, appraise, and plan goals and policies and allocate resources for a number of quasi-autonomous, fairly self-contained divisions. Each division handles a major product line or carries on the firm's activities in one large geographic area. Each division's *central office*, in turn, administers a number of departments. Each of these departments is responsible for the administration of a major function—manufacturing, selling, purchasing or producing of raw materials, engineering, research, finance, and the like. The *departmental headquarters* in its turn coordinates, appraises, and plans for a number of field units. At the lowest level, each *field unit* runs a plant or works, a branch or district sales office . . . and the like.

In the field units, managers were primarily concerned with supervising day-to-day activities. The departmental and divisional offices were concerned with some long-term decisions but their role was primarily confined to tactical or operational decisions. It was the general office which made the broad strategic or entrepreneurial decisions and controlled the allocation of the resources of the enterprise.

The adoption of this new organizational form permitted some reestablishment of the entrepreneurial functions of the enterprise. The general office, charged with responsibility for strategic decisions and the allocation of resources, could pursue a policy of long-term profit maximization for the enterprise as a whole. The general executives had no specific commitment to any one activity. Their commitment was to the total enterprise, and the divorce of policy from operations permitted objective appraisal rather than subjective and frequently factional judgment. In theory, therefore, the quasi-independent divisions could be likened to a series of portfolio investments which could be bought or sold without serious impact on the overall

---

[4a] *Ibid.*, p. 11.

corporation. The general office acted as a small, yet highly efficient, capital market with powers of direct and rapid intervention in divisional activities if and when the need arose.

The structure conceivably permitted the enterprise to transfer its resources readily to the most profitable areas or divisions and to division managers of proven ability. The development of general management skills permitted new activities to be added without serious impact to the existing structure of the enterprise. Further, it created the fund of general management skills with which to administer such ventures. The system encouraged *internal* competition as well as external market competition between the division managers,[5] since the scarce resources of the enterprise were allocated on the basis of measurable performance for each independent subunit. Profit responsibility was depressed downward to the measurable autonomous units, and performance could be rewarded or sanctioned accordingly. The individual manager of each subunit was thus motivated by a system of rewards geared directly to the profit performance of the assets in his charge. Furthermore, he was forced to compete with other subunit managers for the resources of the enterprise.

The strategy of diversification was rapidly adopted by the majority of large American enterprises and this in turn led to widespread adoption of the new structural form. A new breed of company, the conglomerate, grew up in the postwar period, and among the most successful of these concerns many deliberately incorporated the features of the new structure as an integral part of their policy. More recently, older firms which initially diversified into areas related to their original activities, have developed new ventures—divisions in new product markets to exploit their resources, not the least of which is their general management skill developed by the multidivisional structure.

In practice, clearly, some of these advantages were more difficult to achieve depending upon the actual interdependencies between divisions. Nevertheless, by 1967, it has been estimated that 86 percent of the largest 500 American manufacturing concerns were administered by a multidivisional structure.[6] As a result, the majority of enterprises have not tended to become the satisficers suggested by Galbraith's concept of the technostructure. Rather they have become profit seekers constantly engaged in the search for new competitive markets to enter. As Chandler aptly summarized: [7]

> The coming of this new strategy, and with it the new structure, is of paramount importance to the present health and future growth of the American economy. . . . The institutionalizing of the policy of diversification thus helps to assure continued production of new products to cut costs and raise the efficiency of

---

[5] This argument was first made explicit by Bruce R. Scott, who pointed out the implicit contradictions between Chandler's findings and Galbraith's contentions as to the nature of modern large industrial enterprise. See, for instance, Bruce R. Scott, "Stages of Corporate Development," Unpublished Paper, Harvard Business School, 1971; Part I for a discussion of the internal competitive system in diversified divisional firms, and Part II for a comparison with Galbraith's *New Industrial State.*

[6] L. Wrigley, "Divisional Autonomy and Diversification," Unpublished Doctoral Dissertation, Harvard Business School, 1970, p. 50.

[7] A. D. Chandler, *Strategy and Structure,* pp. 490–91.

American industry. Such a development is far more significant to the economy's overall health than production increases in the older basic industries. . . .

It has largely been these same diversified, divisionalized enterprises that have extended their operations to Europe, especially in the postwar period. The new structure not only permitted management to diversify its product line, but also facilitated a strategy of multinational operations. Commenting upon this invasion, *Fortune* stated: [8]

> During the sixties, Europeans slowly and painfully awoke to the sight of large U.S. corporations gobbling up their venerable companies by the dozen and marauding through their markets almost at will.

J. J. Servan-Schreiber termed this invasion the "American Challenge." [9] He attributed the success of the invasion mainly to the superior technology of the American concerns but he also observed that it was something else "quite new and considerably more serious—the extension to Europe of an art of *organization* that is still a mystery to us." [10]

The same organizational form that had proved so readily adaptable to changing market conditions in the United States had apparently been a primary cause for the success of the American corporations in Europe. This was due not merely to the question of economics or technology but rather to the fact that the Americans knew better how to work in Europe than did the Europeans themselves. The European gap was thus more one of methods of *organization*.

This argument provides the focus for the present study. Observers of the American business enterprise have noted the great transition of the modern corporation in the past four decades. Most of the great American enterprises have now become multiproduct, multimarket concerns managed by a multidivisional organization which permits the reestablishment of pressure for profit performance. There has yet been little examination of the evolution of the major British enterprises. The subsequent chapters, therefore, examine the strategy and structure of large-scale British enterprise as it has evolved over the postwar period.

As indicated earlier, the British industrial environment has undergone substantial change, much of it concentrated during the post-World War II period. Because, historically, Great Britain was the home of the first Industrial Revolution (founded on iron and steel, coal mining, and textiles), industrialization was supported by Britain's position in the nineteenth century as the premier world power, built upon the strength of her navy and a great Colonial Empire, which provided both markets and raw materials for her enterprise.

During the twentieth century this dominant position has been eroded by the rise of new industrial nations, especially the United States, the dissolution of the Empire, and the occurrence of two great wars which drained the nation's resources. At no time in this century has the erosion been greater than during the recent postwar period. In 1946, Britain was a nation exhausted by six years of war, with

---

[8] "Europe's Love Affair with Bigness," *Fortune*, March 1970, p. 95.

[9] J. J. Servan-Schreiber, *The American Challenge*, Avon Books, New York, 1969.

[10] *Ibid.*, p. 40.

its financial resources drained by the effort. British enterprise, seriously weakened by enemy action and concentrating on the production of war materials, seemed ill-equipped to face the competitive challenges of the peacetime consumer markets of the following decades.

Industrial enterprise, apart from damage caused by the war, was still heavily committed to the supply of overseas colonial markets in which it enjoyed a protected position. At home, much of production was covered by restrictive practices and cartels which had sprung up, often with government support, in the protectionist era of the 1930s. As a result, little rationalization of production had occurred, family firms were still very much in evidence, and industrial leadership was unaccustomed and often unwilling to engage in competition in the marketplace.

The postwar period brought enormous change. The protected overseas markets of the Empire were virtually lost following decolonization. Competition increased at the same time from other industrialized nations at home and abroad. In the domestic market, the "American Challenge" came first to Britain bringing new, aggressive competitors. Legislation was introduced to break down the old cartels. Great changes occurred in technology leading to the rise of new industries and changing the pattern of competitive advantage. Social changes such as rising affluence affected the whole pattern of consumer demand.

How then has British enterprise adapted to these great changes in its environment? Has it evolved in a similar manner to its U.S. counterpart? What strategies have been adopted and what structural responses have these brought? What are the present strengths and weaknesses of British industry? These are the questions which are considered and perhaps partially answered in the remaining chapters.

CONCEPTS AND DEFINITIONS

In order to answer these questions a conceptual framework was built to formally observe changes over time in the strategy and structure of a population composed of the largest 100 British manufacturing firms in 1969/70 as measured by sales volume. A manufacturing firm was defined as one where at least 50 percent of sales was contributed by manufacturing or processing operations. This is slightly different from the definition adopted by *Fortune* magazine [11] which includes mining alone and without processing as a manufacturing function. Thus, the National Coal Board, for example, was excluded since it did not process much of the coal it mined, but Rio Tinto Zinc, a mining company with considerable post-treatment operations for mined ores and manufacturing facilities, was included.

The conceptual framework for analyzing "strategy" and "structure" in this study has been based largely on the works of Alfred D. Chandler, Bruce R. Scott, and Leonard Wrigley. Further, in view of the very large number of companies involved, it was necessary to adopt measures of strategy and structure which were readily observable from the *outside* point of view.

Thus, the *strategy* of an enterprise was measured from the viewpoint of the out-

---

[11] *Fortune* magazine in drawing up its lists of industrial concerns defines an industrial company as one deriving more than 50 percent of revenues from manufacturing and/or mining operations.

side observer in product-market terms. These defined what business the company was in and what it had become. This concept of strategy, which had led to the observable product-market scope, did *not* define the pattern of objectives, values, purposes, and major policies derived *internally*.

Similarly the measure of structure taken was that of the *formal* administrative structure of hierarchical relationships used to administer the enterprise. This structure, therefore, did not include an understanding of the important informal system of interpersonal relationships which underlay the formal system.

Following Chandler's study of the historical development of 70 major U.S. industrial enterprises, Scott [12] devised a formalized model of the stages of corporate growth from the entrepreneurial stage to that of the large-scale corporation. Scott's central theme was that the strategy of the enterprise as observed by the consciously adopted pattern of internal/external product-flow transactions determined the characteristics of its administrative structure. He identified two types of product-market strategies for the large corporation, the first leading to an *integrated* undertaking or *closed system* requiring central coordination by functional specialists: [13]

> The first type involves an integrated sequence of operations where the aim is to relate the sequence of operations so as to facilitate the flow of the product or service from one operation to the next.

For example, such a sequence is involved in the production, refining, and distribution of oil, as shown in Figure 1.1.

FIGURE 1.1

THE INTEGRATED CORPORATION

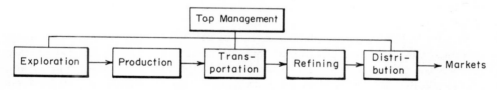

NOTE: → indicates primary direction of product flow.

The second type of strategy which represented the ultimate stage of development was that of a *diversified* corporation where divisions each served a different product market and were largely independent of each other, each operating as an *open system* thus: [14]

> In a diversified undertaking, on the other hand, the divisions are designed to stand on their own in their respective markets. Hence there is no comparable product flow to relate the divisions, as suggested in Figure 1.2.

---

[12] B. R. Scott, "Stages of Corporate Development Part I," Unpublished Paper, Harvard Business School, Boston, 1971.

[13] J. H. McArthur and B. R. Scott, *Industrial Planning in France,* Division of Research, Harvard Business School, Boston, 1969, p. 125.

[14] *Ibid.* p. 126.

FIGURE 1.2

THE DIVERSIFIED CORPORATION

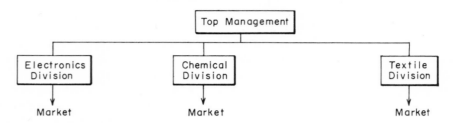

NOTE: → indicates primary direction of product flow.

. . . Strategic choice, far from aiming to relate the divisions, aims for selective use of resources in those divisions which have the highest expected economic return. . . . Thus, each division operates approximately as an open system, transacting business with its environment more than with other divisions of the company; and the parent organization treats the divisions as members of a loose confederation rather than as indispensable parts of an integrated whole.

As the corporation grew from its small entrepreneurial origins (Stage I), the model predicted that it would tend to develop from the narrow product scope, personally managed concern, first as a large integrated and/or single product firm (Stage II), and eventually evolve as a large diversified corporation (Stage III). The evolution of this product-market strategy would in turn impose change on the administrative characteristics of the corporation, leading to the transition from a functional organization to a multidivisonal structure based on product-market relationships. The internal characteristics associated with these stages are shown in Table 1–1.

Wrigley [15] conducted an analysis of 100 of the 500 largest U.S. manufacturing enterprises in 1967 and discovered that the vast majority of them had already reached the third stage of Scott's model. This led him to examine further the multidivisional population in an attempt to sort out meaningful differences between such corporations. He found that the administrative structure of such firms varied according to *the degree and type of product-market diversification strategy* they had undertaken. For Wrigley, product-market strategy was the summation of the products produced and the market served within the domestic United States and hence did not include overseas geographic diversification. Thus he found the overwhelming majority of enterprises had adopted a *multiproduct* division form of organization. In reality many of these corporations had also pursued a multinational strategy which had a significant impact on the organization structure as a whole.

Wrigley examined the various definitions of diversification adopted by previous researchers and the Standard Industrial Classification code and found these were not meaningful in terms of the managerial requirements of the enterprise. He developed a new concept of *"core skills"* which he described as the skills required

---

[15] L. Wrigley, "Divisional Autonomy and Diversification."

TABLE 1–1. THREE STAGES OF ORGANIZATIONAL DEVELOPMENT

COMPANY CHARACTERISTICS	I	II	III
1. Product line	1. Single product or single line	1. Single product line	1. Multiple product lines
2. Distribution	2. One channel or set of channels	2. One set of channels	2. Multiple channels
3. Organization structure	3. Little or no formal structure—"one man show"	3. Specialization based on function	3. Specialization based on product-market relationships
4. Product-service transactions	4. N/A	4. Integrated pattern of transactions □ → □ → □ → Market	4. Not integrated → A B C → → → Markets
5. R&D	5. Not institutionalized oriented by owner-manager	5. Increasingly institutionalized search for product or process improvements	5. Institutionalized search for *new* products as well as for improvements
6. Performance measurement	6. By personal contact and subjective criteria	6. Increasingly impersonal using technical and/or cost criteria	6. Increasingly impersonal using *market* criteria (return on investment and market share)
7. Rewards	7. Unsystematic and often paternalistic	7. Increasingly systematic with emphasis on stability and service	7. Increasingly systematic with variability related to performance
8. Control system	8. Personal control of both strategic and operating decisions	8. Personal control of strategic decisions, with increasing delegation of operating decisions based on control by decision rules (policies)	8. Delegation of product-market decisions within existing businesses, with indirect control based on analysis of "results"
9. Strategic choices	9. Needs of owner versus needs of firm	9. Degree of integration Market share objective Breadth of product line	9. Entry and Exit from industries Allocation of resources by industry Rate of growth

SOURCE: B. R. Scott, "Stages of Corporate Development," Harvard Business School, 1971, p. 7.

by a firm in order to compete within a chosen product-market area. Companies that adopted a strategy of diversification into areas related to their "core skills" were termed *related* while those which entered new product markets unrelated to past activity were considered *unrelated*. These two types of corporations he found exhibited different managerial characteristics.

Wrigley also identified a form of company which adopted a strategy of only limited diversification which he determined empirically to be 30 percent of corporate sales. These concerns he called *dominant product* companies which had the distinguishing feature that one major product line accounted for 70 percent or more of the corporate sales. The dominant product concern also exhibited different managerial characteristics to the related and unrelated diversified companies. The distinctive managerial characteristics of these three types of multiproduct division structures are shown in Table 1–2. Wrigley observed that the degree of decision-making *autonomy* in the divisions varied according to the nature and degree of the product-market diversification.

These models provided a meaningful system of categorizing three distinctive product-market growth strategies for the diversified enterprise. One significant problem arose, however, which called for revision of Wrigley's concept of "core skills." In the *dynamic* evolution of the enterprise over time it was discovered that core skills changed as a result of corporate evolution so that a static viewpoint would have placed companies in one category of relatedness whereas a dynamic viewpoint gave the opposite impression. Fortunately Wrigley developed his core-skill concept from a series of characteristic product-market *growth strategies* developed earlier by Edwards and Townsend.[16] These provided a suitable basis for consistency. Seven such characteristic growth strategies were used by Wrigley as follows: [17]

(1) *Similar Products and Processes and Markets*. Many firms produced a variety of products for one general market, and produced this variety by much the same process. The food-processing industry is an obvious example. Many food-processing firms produced canned fruit and canned vegetables, and also, frozen foods. In a few firms the relationship between products was so close that they could almost be seen as single product firms.

(2) *Complementary Products* (or *Joint Demand*). Some of the firms expanded by adding products which tended to be purchased by the consumer along with the original product.

(3) *Joint Supply* (or *By-Products*). A number of firms expanded by further processing of material produced as a by-product of the original product line. For example, steel firms often sold chemicals, which were produced through processing the gas given off in the production of coke for the blast furnace.

(4) *Existing Technology, New Market*. Expansion occurred in some firms through the application of existing technology to new markets.

(5) *Existing Market, New Technology*. A number of firms had concentrated upon a particular market, but expanded to a variety of products to service this market when quite new technologies were required.

16 R. Edwards and H. Townsend, *Business Enterprise*, Macmillan, London, 1961, pp. 39–62.
17 L. Wrigley, "Divisional Autonomy and Diversification," Chapter III, pp. 3–4.

TABLE 1-2

MULTIDIVISIONAL FIRMS—ORGANIZATION MODELS

Characteristics	Dominant Product	Related Product	Unrelated Product
Diversification	Dominant Product	Two or More Related Product Lines	Two or More Unrelated Product Lines
Product Flow	Mixed System *Dominant Area* Integrated *Other Area* Open System	Open System with Lines to Corporate Office Some Units Linked	Open System Divisions Completely Separate
Corporate Management and Staff	*Corporate* Large Specialist Staff for Dominant Product	*Corporate* Large Specialist Staff Related to Core Skill	*Corporate* Small Staff— Control and Legal Only
Organization	*Dominant Area* Weak Division or Functional *Other Area* Divisional	Product Division Plus Service Departments	Product Division
Divisional	*Dominant Area* Routine Operations *Other Area* Product Strategy	Product Strategy	Product Strategy Plus Supplies
Resource Allocation	*Dominant Area* Balance Between Units *Other Area* ROI	ROI	ROI
Control Performance Measurement and Rewards	*Dominant Area* ROI Growth Market Share Costs *Other Area* ROI	ROI Growth Market Share	ROI (Growth)

SOURCE: L. Wrigley, "Divisional Autonomy and Diversification," Unpublished Doctoral Dissertation, Harvard Business School, 1970, pp. vi–32.

(6) *Exploiting Research.* The classical pattern of expansion could be seen as the exploitation of a research effort to develop products for new markets.

(7) *New Technologies, New Markets.* Many firms, in some degree or another, expanded their activities, even though this requires new technologies and new markets. In nearly all if not, in fact, all instances, such expansion occurred through mergers and acquisitions with other firms. Many reasons could be seen for this particular pattern of expansion, but four stood out.

    (a) War Conditions. In time of war or national emergency, a government might require a firm to enter a particular market, such as the production of equipment for the air force.

    (b) Collapse of Traditional Markets. A firm might find that its traditional

market has collapsed, and, with depreciation or other funds, might plan
to enter a quite new area.
  (c) Chance. A firm might expand this way through change, through a particular opportunity, which occurred without being sought.
  (d) Strategy. Firms might expand this way as part of a strategy, for example,
because of a desire to spread their risks, say, to reduce the impact of
cyclicality.

Wrigley noted a basic difference between the first six categories above, and the
last. The first six patterns of diversification were related to the previous state of
the companies' activities whereas the seventh bore no such relationship.

In three of the first six categories there is a relatedness in the markets served by
the corporation. Those companies diversifying into similar products, processes, and
markets, complementary products, and the new technologies to serve existing
markets are all related by the *markets* they serve. Companies exploiting research
and existing technology to develop new markets are related by a *basic skill* or
technology which is transferable to meet a variety of different market needs.

Those companies diversifying by the development of joint supply or by-products,
are specific forms of vertical integration (a strategy for growth) not clearly identified by Wrigley. However, it was found that vertical integration had played a meaningful role in the growth of a number of British companies. Further, in many cases
vertical integration was clearly a mechanism for diversification. This growth strategy was, therefore, added to Wrigley's related strategies and treated as follows.
Where the product flow in a vertically integrated organization was primarily out-
ward to separate markets, then this could be diversification, but where the product
flow was primarily internal and serviced the present functions of the organization,
it was treated as integration. The test was, thus, similar to the Scott model, being
one of *market contact* which could be expected to add new managerial requirements throughout the organization. Where the strategy called for integration, it
imposed only a managerial requirement of balancing the various operations and
did not demand the development of a number of new product-market strategies.

Firms may clearly grow by adopting more than one of the three basic related
diversification strategies of market, technological, or vertical relatedness. This frequently happened, but in examining the dynamic evolution of the firm, it was readily possible to determine if a relationship existed between old and new activities.

The method used to examine the evolution of British companies was therefore
one relevant to the management of the enterprise. Companies were divided into
the four basic strategic categories based on their product-market scope with geographic market scope being treated separately. The four categories were differentiated by the proportion and the relatedness of the product-market scope of the
individual firm. These categories were defined as follows:

Single Product: Firms which grew by the expansion of one product line so that at
  least 95 percent of sales lay within this single product area. Examples of such
  companies would be British Sugar Corporation and British American Tobacco.
Dominant Product: Firms which grew primarily by the expansion of one main
  product line but which in addition had added secondary product lines making
  up 30 percent or less of the total sales volume. These secondary activities might

be related to the primary activity, for example, the chemical interests of the
Royal Dutch Shell Group or unrelated, as, for example, the food interest of
Imperial Tobacco.

Related Product: Firms which grew by expansion by means of entry into related
markets, by the use of a related technology, by related vertical activities or some
combination of these so that no one product line accounted for 70 percent of
the total corporate sales. Examples of such companies are Imperial Chemical
Industries, J. & P. Coats, and Cadbury/Schweppes.

Unrelated Product: Firms which grew by expansion into new markets and new
technologies unrelated to the original product-market scope so that no one
product line accounted for 70 percent of the total corporate sales. Examples of
such companies are Thomas Tilling and Slater Walker.

Geographic diversification, especially outside the home market, has also been
shown to affect the administrative structure of the firm significantly. John Stopford,
using a model also developed from Scott, considered this phenomenon in a study of a
sample of 170 U.S. manufacturing concerns [18] drawn from the *Fortune* 500 list
and accounting for the majority of U.S. overseas investment. He found that the
majority of these companies were already diversified to a degree and ". . . of the
170 U.S. firms considered in this research, 117 made the transition from Stage II
to Stage III; 25 Stage III firms were formed by the merger of two or more Stage
II firms; 18 remained Stage II firms." [19]

Stopford's evidence indicated that as manufacturing investment overseas increased, corporations evolved in a distinctive sequence of organizational variants.
Initially, overseas investment was supervised by an international division, but as
both overseas size in terms of sales and product diversity increased, this division
broke up to be replaced by one of three organizational variants. A relationship
existed between the degree of overseas product-market diversity (a variable similar
to one used by Wrigley although diversity was measured in a somewhat different
manner) and the relative size of geographic diversification. Stopford determined
empirically a series of boundaries within which specific administrative variants
would be expected to be adopted as indicated in Figure 1.3.

Low diversity, coupled with significant volume, led to the adoption of a series of
geographic or area divisions. This could also apply within a domestic market but
is uncommon due to the general homogeneity of the market. Size, coupled with
significant product diversity, led initially to the formation of worldwide product
divisions. Further increases led ultimately to the formation of a "grid" structure
where conflicting product and geographic demands required central coordination of
function, product, and geographic activities.

The strategy of overseas expansion has seldom led to the introduction of major
new products, although clearly, new geographic markets are being served and
minor product adjustments may be made to suit local tastes. Geographic expansion
was not, therefore, treated as product-market diversification unless it had been
accompanied by the introduction of products which added to the firm's product

---

[18] J. Stopford, "Growth and Organizational Change in the Multinational Firm," Unpublished Doctoral Dissertation, Harvard Business School, 1968, pp. 17–26.

[19] *Ibid.*, p. 16.

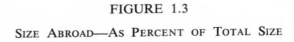

FIGURE 1.3

SIZE ABROAD—AS PERCENT OF TOTAL SIZE

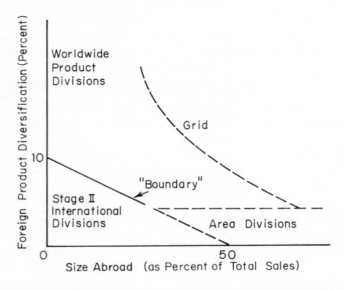

SOURCE: J. Stopford, "Growth and Organizational Change in the Multinational Firm," p. 108.

diversity. When at least six different overseas manufacturing subsidiaries had been formed, a firm was termed as multinational, and such firms were specifically identified and analyzed in the light of Stopford's model.

However, the impact of geographic diversification on corporate structure was specifically included since the total enterprise was under examination. Generally, the only concerns where the impact of geography had made a significant impact on structure was in those organizations which had been termed multinational—firms with lesser geographic diversification usually having developed their structures only as far as an overseas division.

The formal administrative structure of the total enterprise was expected to evolve with increased product-market diversity in line with the models proposed by Scott, Wrigley, and Stopford. The structure of each company was thus categorized into three basic structural forms. The first structure was the *functional form* of organization in which the enterprise was broken down into a series of specialized hierarchical functions culminating in the office of the chief executive who performed the role of coordinator and general manager of all the specialist functions. This form of organization was expected to be found associated with a low degree of product diversity, i.e., the single or dominant product categories.

Second, as product-market diversification increased, the functional structure would be expected to break down and operations divided into a series of divisions based on product, geography, or some combination of these. This *multidivision structure* was typically composed of a general office, usually divorced from operations, which serviced and monitored the operating divisions. These managed the day-to-day operations of the concern within a policy framework laid down by the general office. The divisions themselves were autonomous in that they normally possessed all the functions necessary to conduct their affairs, notably their own production facilities, sales force, and technical service function. Where the divisions were divided by product, they were defined as *product-divisional* structures, and where divided by geography, as *geographic-divisional* structures.

Overseas diversification also led to amendment of the administrative structure. Initially the change would normally have been the formation of a separate *international division* to supervise overseas activities. As these grew and passed through the boundaries delineated by Stopford, a series of geographic or product divisions would be expected according to the level of overseas product diversity. Where both high product diversity and significant overseas size occurred a *"grid" structure* would be expected. A further variation of the multidivision structure experienced in the British multinational concerns consisted of a series of product divisions in the domestic market, coupled with a series of geographic divisions to manage the overseas operations. This form was not identified by Stopford and was termed *multiproduct/multigeographic-divisional.*

A third form of structure was also experienced. It was an old one, the *holding company,* which as research on American firms indicates, has almost disappeared in the United States. It was, however, widespread during the early post-World War II years in Britain. Concerns with such a structure were clearly not functional nor multidivisional. There were, in fact, two typical types of holding-company structures, although both were normally associated with growth by acquisition. In the first, the senior executive management was composed of functional specialists generally drawn from the original parent concern, together with the general managers of a number of senior subsidiaries, which were virtually completely autonomous of the parent. In the second form, a holding-company structure had been deliberately set up and the original parent company operations were treated in the same way as those of other autonomous subsidiaries. The senior executive management was composed of a holding-company board, members of which sat on the boards of the subsidiaries and provided the only coordinating link between them.

The first of these forms had some resemblance to the functional structure, since the parent company specialists were still members of the senior executive group. However, there were no central *policy-making, coordination, or strategic* functions covering subsidiary operations, each of which operated independently and sometimes in direct competition to the parent company. The second of the variants resembled the multidivisional structure. Again, however, there was no central office for the determination of *corporate strategy, coordination, and policy,* the holding-company board was not divorced from operations, and there was no rationalization of potential conflict between subsidiaries.

The organization structures of the population were, therefore, classified into one of these three main structural variants, namely, functional, holding company, or multidivisional. The multidivisional structure, in turn, was broken down to indicate distinctions by product, geography, and international operations.

A final characteristic discovered within the sample population was a large number of "family" companies. Despite substantial share ownership dilution in many

British companies, there was a distinct tendency for many of them to continue to be managed by members of the family or families closely associated with their formation or development. The characteristics of these concerns merited some study and it became necessary to define the family company. The pattern of share ownership was not in reality an entirely meaningful measure of family control. A company was, therefore, termed family controlled if a family member was the chief executive officer, if there had been at least two generations of family control, and if a minimum of 5 percent of the voting stock was still held by the family or trust interests associated with it.

THE RESEARCH PROBLEM AND METHODOLOGY

Using the conceptual scheme just defined the strategy and structure of individual enterprises could be classified. Similarly the questions raised regarding the evolution of British enterprise were formally restated on the proposition that this evolution would possess characteristics similar to American experience. This led to redefinition of the questions raised into a number of observable hypotheses set out below:

(1) There would be an increasing proportion of the population with a diversified product/market scope during the period with a corresponding decline in the number of single product companies.

(2) Companies, having adopted the diversified product/market scope, would tend to undergo subsequent structural transformation from a functional organization to a form of multidivisional organization.

(3) The correlation between diversified product/market scope and multidivisional structures would increase over the period under investigation.

(4) Companies with multidivisional structures would tend to:

    (a) develop a substantial corporate staff in manufacturing, marketing, and research and development.

    (b) adopt control systems based on profits and return on investment measures.

    (c) use variable rewards based on subunit performance.

(5) The long history of British colonialism would be expected to give rise to substantial overseas activity on the part of British enterprise, with investment heavily concentrated in former colonial territories.

(6) The strategy of geographic expansion would be expected to lead to structural response in the parent company and the structure adopted would reflect the degree of product and geographic diversity.

(7) Pre-World War II protectionism in the British economy was expected to have sustained a significant number of family concerns. As the product/market scope of a company increased it became more difficult for a family to maintain managerial control by the family. Thus, family companies were expected to exhibit a narrower product range and those companies that diversified were expected to change to a system of control by professional managers.

In addition to the examination of these central hypotheses, an attempt was made to develop an understanding of the evolutionary path of the large industrial enterprise as a dynamic institution in the context of British society. As such, the significance of trends observed in the environment on the strategy of the enterprise were identified in an attempt to provide insights on the causation of strategic change and to evaluate strengths and weaknesses of British enterprise relevant to the future growth of the economy.

In order to examine these hypotheses, the strategy and structure of the largest 100 British manufacturing companies measured by sales of 1969–70 (as stated in the *Times 500* list *1969–70*)[20] were examined over the period 1950–70. It was estimated that these companies represented approximately 60 percent of the net assets, employed about 45 percent of the workforce and accounted for about 60 percent of sales of domestic manufacturing industry in 1970. These figures were only crude estimates. It was difficult to differentiate home and overseas figures from quoted accounts in order to make a comparison with official statistics of domestic industry. In addition, these companies accounted for some 80 percent of the assets employed overseas by British manufacturing concerns. This group of corporations, therefore, represented the essential core of British manufacturing enterprise.

The *Times* list included British subsidiaries of foreign parent companies and these were retained. The list was found to be deficient in some cases, neglecting companies which should have been included, and these were added to the best of the author's ability. Additional modification of the list was made to account for mergers and acquisitions that took place between the date of publication of the *Times 500* and January 1, 1970.

A baseline of 1950 was chosen as a starting point for observation for the following three reasons:

(1) Due to the volume of data which could be collected and collated, some choice had to be made to keep the exercise within manageable bounds.
(2) In the immediate postwar period, British industry was still subject to the system of wartime controls imposed by central government in order to allocate resources during the war emergency.
(3) The Companies Act of 1948 significantly changed the amount of statutory information required of registered companies including in particular a requirement for consolidated accounting.

Adopting a historical perspective reminiscent of Chandler's study, the strategic and structural history of the sample population was then compiled over the period 1950–70. Heavy reliance was placed on published materials in view of the large sample and the desire to collect data on each individual concern.

The principal published sources were: (1) Company publications such as annual reports (in all, well over 2,000 reports were studied), company magazines and house journals, reports of the annual general meetings, chairmen's statements, etc.; (2) newspaper and magazine articles, case histories especially from *Achievement, The Times Review of Industry, Fortune, The Manager, Management Today,* and *International Management;* (3) company histories; (4) other books and publications, in particular brokers' reports and papers given at the London School of

---

[20] *The Times 500 1969–70*, Times Newspapers Ltd., London, 1969.

Economics' evening seminar on Problems in Industrial Administration; [21] (5) government publications, in particular reports by the Monopolies Commission, the National Board for Prices and Incomes, and special reports on specific industries published from time to time by special committees of inquiry, and the National Economic Development Office.

The identification of the formal structure of each firm in any given year over the time period was based on analysis of the published materials. In approximately 95 percent of cases, one or more cross checks were available between the company data and other published sources.

To supplement the published material and validate its findings, structured interviews were held with directors or senior executives drawn from a stratified sample of 25 companies. These interviews also provided data on the internal formal organization characteristics of the corporations concerned, thus permitting some test of hypothesis 4.

It was anticipated that a significant amount of merger and acquisition activity would be observed in the sample population and that some of the concerns identified in 1970 would not have existed in 1950, since in the intervening period a new company would have been formed by merger of two or more concerns. In such cases the procedure adopted was that effort would be made to trace the history of the largest prior company.

In the case of most subsidiaries of foreign companies and some British private companies, annual reports were not available, and in these cases reliance was placed on the parent company's reports together with a search of the annual returns submitted by such a subsidiary or private company to the Board of Trade. In the case of companies which were not required to file full returns prior to the Companies Act of 1967, the amount of published data was unfortunately more limited; nevertheless, it was decided to retain such companies, since they were few, if sufficient data were available to classify them reasonably in 1970.

SUMMARY

The data thus collected were analyzed using the conceptual scheme outlined, together with information on the British industrial environment. This analysis is presented in the following chapters of this book.

Chapter 2 discusses the major changes that have occurred in the British environment, changes which have significantly influenced the strategies of British business enterprise. Three major forces were observed to have affected the pattern of supply: the changing pattern of demand, the growth of competition, and the impact of technology The supply function changed noticeably as a result of these forces,

[21] This seminar, run by Professor Sir Ronald Edwards and Mr. Harry Townsend, was started at the London School of Economics, shortly after the Second World War. It has recently become a joint seminar with the London Graduate School of Business. Many excellent papers have been given by leading industrialists on the growth and development of their respective organizations. Some of these have been published by Edwards and Townsend in *Studies in Business Organisation,* Macmillan, London, 1961; *Business Growth,* Macmillan, London, 1958; and a major definitive work *Business Enterprise,* Macmillan, London, 1961.

and influenced the changing makeup of net manufacturing output as well as increasing industrial concentration. In an examination of the factors of production, British enterprise was judged to be well served by the capital markets, but there appeared to be serious deficiencies in the system of industrial relations and management. Finally, the role of government had increased significantly, and it was considered that much of government action relevant to business enterprise may well have had some adverse effect on its progress.

In Chapter 3 the sample population is introduced as of 1970 and the transformation between 1950 and 1970 is examined. The analysis revealed that a dramatic change did occur, and this discovery helped to support a number of the hypotheses. Many of the enterprises clearly adopted a strategy of diversification in the postwar period, subsequently accompanied by the introduction of the multidivisional structure. The pattern of transition was found to be gradual, however, and most of the diversifiers initially moved through an intermediate diversification stage. However, most firms in a specific group of industries consistently exhibited a low degree of diversification. Family companies were found to be slower to adopt the new strategy and structure than nonfamily concerns.

Many British firms were found to be "multinational." Much of their investment was indeed a product of the prewar period and heavily biased to the developed Commonwealth countries. This overseas investment was found to have had an impact on the organization structure of the enterprise, but the results did not conform to the model developed for American enterprise. In particular the multi-geographic-multiproduct division structure was frequently observed as being associated with extensive overseas sales and product diversity.

Chapters 4 through 6 develop briefly the strategic and structural histories (drawn from published sources) of each of the enterprises studied. In Chapter 4 it was observed that firms in a number of specific industries, namely, drink, tobacco, power machinery, oil, and metals and materials, had by and large failed to adopt the strategy of diversification. These industries had, however, frequently adopted the multidivisional structure as appropriate but in many cases there were also close functional ties reflecting a high degree of integration. Where structural change occurred it often coincided with leadership change and there was evidence of the fairly extensive use of management consultants in effecting these changes.

Chapter 5 discusses those firms engaged in technological industries. These industries, namely, chemicals, and electrical and mechanical engineering, developed around a technology or skill which was highly transferable to a variety of product markets. The enterprises embracing these skills diversified relatively early in their history and some were among the earliest adopters of the multidivisional structure. Nevertheless, for many, structural change took place much more recently reflecting a long period of management under a holding-company or functional system. Change often occurred after a period of increased competition or adversity and, as in the less diversified industries, was also often accompanied by a change in leadership and the use of management consultants.

The enterprises described in Chapter 6 diversified mainly in the post-World War II period. They were found to be primarily engaged in low technology industries, namely, food, paper, printing and packaging, and textiles, together with a number of firms diversified into areas unrelated to their original activities. These enterprises nearly all diversified primarily either by acquisition into product markets serving similar market needs or into activities vertically integrated to the original operations.

Chapter 7 discusses the internal characteristics of a number of British enterprises based on the interviews conducted. While similarities were observed between British and American multidivisional firms, there were some distinct differences, notably in control systems where the concept of variable performance-related rewards was noticeably lacking. Also, corporate headquarters were generally less developed especially with regard to planning systems, personnel management, and clear definition of profit objectives.

The final chapters develop the conclusions which can be drawn. Chapter 8 attempts to draw together the study of the enterprises and the trends in the environment in order to develop a set of strengths and weaknesses observed in British industry. A number of such strengths and weaknesses were identified at both the level of the individual enterprise and the industry. In addition, other weaknesses were identified within the economy as a whole, notably in the political/governmental environment.

Chapter 9 develops the implications of the observations for managers, public policy makers, and teachers of business administration. An attempt is made to develop meaningful normative concepts of value to each of these groups and to suggest fruitful areas for further research.

CHAPTER 2
The British Industrial Environment

HISTORICAL PERSPECTIVE

GREAT BRITAIN REPRESENTS THE FIRST EXAMPLE of the modern industrialized state. Transition from an agricultural society began in the late eighteenth century with the expansion of trade, technological innovation, and dominant sea power. By the late nineteenth century, Britain was the greatest industrial nation in the world producing over 50 percent of the world's coal, 40 percent of the world's steel, almost 50 percent of cotton cloth, and over a third of the world's output of manufactured goods. She dominated world trade, and ruled the largest Colonial Empire in modern times.

By 1900 this industrial dominance began to fade, owing to the rise of industry in the United States and Germany. By the end of the nineteenth century, Britain's economy was suffering competitive pressures from imports and decreasing domestic profits. Nevertheless, free trade was practiced and Britain's industrialists regarded the world as their market. British capital continued to be invested in the Empire and the Americas, to some extent because of the low level of profit in the domestic market in many industries. Between 1905 and 1914 over 50 percent of total British investment went abroad. London was the world's foremost financial center and the pound sterling, backed by a gold standard, was the world's leading currency.

During the 1890s a first wave of major amalgamations occurred, concentrating certain fragmented industries partly as a result of competition caused by free trade, and partly as a result of changing markets. In cotton textiles, price competition led to a series of mergers. A combination of tobacco companies was formed to foil the threat of American invasion of the domestic market. Significant mergers also took place in brewing, chemicals, armaments, steel fabrications, and soaps. In many cases these combinations were largely protective, formed to control price and production. The constituent companies remained largely independent, still led by members of the families who brought them into the merger, but protected to some degree by an overall corporate financial umbrella. By 1914, joint stock companies represented only about 20 percent of British industry with the remainder still held by private family companies.

The 1914–18 war seriously affected the British economy: much of the manufacturing industry was converted to war production; export markets were lost, particularly in textiles; imports were drastically increased, and Britain's financial strength was significantly weakened. The war led to a contraction in domestic competition and strengthened the power of existing manufacturers. Government imposed controls on the free market and became a major consumer of production. This led to increasing cooperation between producers and to vertical integration in order to maintain the supplies of raw materials needed for production.

The world economic depression of the 1930s left still more scars on Britain's economy; the gold standard was abandoned and, to protect domestic employment, free trade was largely replaced by domestic cartels. Britain became increasingly insular. Competition diminished and restrictive practices were encouraged. A new series of combinations occurred concentrating production in chemicals, steel fabrications, banking, shipping, and aircraft. Little reorganization, however, took place in the staple industries such as textiles, iron and steel, shipbuilding, and mining, although cartel operations were set up to control prices and output. Rationalization was neglected or used mainly as a means of reinforcing cartel arrangements rather than promoting industrial efficiency.

Similarly, relationships between manufacturers and distributors were modified by the spread of branded products, the extension of resale price maintenance, exclusive dealerships, and other restrictive agreements aimed at reducing the level of competition. These were often backed by enforcement procedures such as trade boycotts to ensure conformity.

While the cartels may have had comparatively little effect on market behavior due to the deflationary conditions of the time, they did have a harmful effect on technical and commercial progress. Management skills were increasingly directed toward devising means of restricting competition rather than creating efficient enterprises able to thrive in a competitive environment.[1]

By the outset of the Second World War Britain's trading position had become increasingly dependent on the Empire. New industries had begun to assume more importance than the staple industries, although coal and textiles still accounted for 30 percent of exports. The new consumer durable industries such as automobiles, however, remained fragmented, their products custom made for the small domestic market, and they did not lead the growth of the economy as their mass production counterparts did in the United States. Nevertheless, the economy was still relatively strong, and Britain remained a major world power.

The coming of World War II encouraged further reduction in competition. The economy became subject to strict central controls on the allocation of resources. Official specifications were laid down for many classes of goods, and price controls and rationing were introduced. The Concentration of Production policy

---

[1] See G. C. Allen, *The Structure of Industry in Britain,* Longmans, London, 1970, p. 71.

caused temporary merging of some manufacturing and the trade associations and large corporations became agents of government. These same associations and companies were then the advisers to government on postwar economic reconstruction. Schooled in an era of cartelization, many businessmen disliked the thought of a return to a competitive marketplace and were ill prepared for the rebirth of competition.

The Second World War cost Britain dearly. Industry was converted to maintain the war effort; massive debts were contracted, particularly with the United States; and enemy action ravaged the domestic industry, infrastructure, and human population. To shore up the economy after the war, Britain turned to the United States and Canada for financial aid. Balance of payments pressure and lack of confidence in sterling forced devaluation in 1949. Thus, by 1950, the British economy, in the period of over half a century, had been transformed from strength to weakness. Britain stood as a nation shorn of much of its financial strength and power, attempting to rebuild a war-damaged economy. Its industrial structure, although highly developed, was still overly dependent on its former staple industries, and its leaders still unaccustomed to market competition.

This chapter, then, building on historical background, attempts to provide a brief review of the development of the forces, in the British industrial environment in the postwar era, which have subsequently guided and influenced the emerging patterns of postwar corporate strategy and structure.

THE CHANGING PATTERN OF DEMAND

The strategy of British enterprise has clearly been influenced in the postwar period by the changing pattern of demand. In part, industrial enterprise acted to influence this pattern by the growth of advertising and other marketing devices. Nevertheless, the changing distribution of incomes and the increased role of the public sector led to change in the balance of industrial production.

In 1954 almost 60 percent of the population earned less than £250 per annum and had little disposable or discretionary income. By 1968 over 60 percent earned more than £750 and, despite inflation, most people were notably better off. However, the relative growth in incomes was slow by comparison with other industrialized nations due to the slow rate of growth achieved by the British economy.

Even so, the rising trend in disposable income, together with changing levels of education and age distribution, brought significant change in the pattern of consumer spending. As consumers became more wealthy they did not simply increase their spending in like proportions but turned to new areas of expenditure, thus leading to a relative decline in some industries and a rapid growth in others. These changes are reflected in Table 2–1 which shows consumer expenditure at constant prices over the period 1951–68.

While overall expenditure rose by over 50 percent during this period, spending on food, for example, remained relatively stable and decreased from nearly 32 percent of the total in 1951 to under 22 percent by 1968. At the same time, there was considerable growth in expenditure on consumer durables especially automobiles;

TABLE 2-1

CONSUMER EXPENDITURE AT 1958 PRICES

(*Thousands of Pounds*)

	1951	1960	1968
Food	4,061	4,805	4,400
Alcoholic Drink	843	1,018	1,194
Tobacco	898	1,087	1,129
Housing	1,207	1,404	2,256
Fuel and Light	601	742	1,028
Durables	614	1,411	1,771
Other Household Goods	386	533	585
Clothing	1,171	1,616	1,837
Books, Newspapers, etc.	236	243	258
Misc. Recreational Goods	167	273	422
Chemist Goods	164	246	299
Other Goods	132	241	263
Running Costs of Vehicles	165	459	982
Travel	541	520	628
Communications Services	107	140	199
Entertainment	283	259	328
Overseas Spending	178	278	253
Other Expenditure	1,117	1,154	2,289
Total	12,871	16,429	20,121

SOURCE: *Annual Digest of Statistics*, H.M.S.O.

leisure activities such as recreational goods, entertainment, and travel; housing and clothing. Other changes also occurred, not necessarily reflected in the aggregate statistics, such as the rapid growth of convenience foods, despite the apparent stability of the food sector as a whole. Further, the choice of individual years while partially reflecting trends may also be influenced by controls over expenditure by government policy.

A further significant factor in the changing pattern of demand was the increased role of public sector purchasing. During the period of the early postwar Conservative administrations, aggregate consumption by the public sector actually declined from its peak wartime levels. However, the return of the second postwar Labour administration in 1964 brought a dramatic reversal and by 1969 public sector spending had increased by a massive 11 percent to a total of 53.6 percent of G.N.P., reflecting basic differences in the economic ideologies of the two main political parties. Public sector spending had special and increasing impact on housing, education, and social services, as well as on those enterprises producing products or services for these markets. Similarly in industries such as aircraft, energy, telecommunications, and computers, producers became heavily dependent on the demand of the public sector which, in some instances, became a monopsony buyer.

These trends led to change in the pattern of competitive advantage. Some enterprises grew naturally and were not perhaps required to seek new markets. Others, however, declined in relative terms forcing either the acceptance of such decline or the search for new product markets in order to maintain growth or even to survive.

THE GROWTH OF COMPETITION

The Impact of Public Policy

By the end of the 1940s, aided by the postwar sellers' market, restrictive practices covered a very large part of British industry. In producer goods, monopolistic practices and price fixing on both a national and international scale were common, while in consumer goods, although cartels were of somewhat less significance, collectively enforced resale price maintenance covered a high proportion of goods.

The weakened economic position of Britain and the acceptance of a full employment policy by government meant, however, that Britain could not afford policies which restricted her international competitiveness. Cartels which would check the progress of efficient firms by restricting output and maintaining the inefficient could do this, and hence, in 1948 the government passed its first monopolies legislation—the Monopolies and Restrictive Practices Act of 1948.

This Act called for the formation of a Monopolies Commission which could judge and make recommendations on monopolistic practices referred to it by the Board of Trade, monopoly being defined as control of one-third of the sales of a market. The Commission could judge the situation to determine whether or not it was against the public interest and report back to the Board of Trade. The Board, in turn, could decide in those cases found to be against the public interest, and could draw up a statutory order containing appropriate remedies, subject, of course, to Parliamentary approval. The Commission thus had no power to initiate investigations or to enforce its recommendations. Monopoly itself was not considered to be good or bad; rather, no generalization could be made and each case necessarily had to be determined on its merit.

In the next seven years various investigations were made in a cross section of British industry and the recommendations made led to the abandonment of various practices in the industries investigated, and probably in a wider sector of industry than the reports actually covered. Further, industry was subjected to the traumatic shock that legislation, which could affect restrictive practices, was now in effect.

The Commission's reports and particularly the first general report on Collective Discrimination in 1955, led to the introduction of further legislation, notably the Restrictive Trade Practices Act of 1956, which provided for the registration and judicial investigation of certain restrictive trading agreements. The Act called for the registration (with a Registrar of Restrictive Practices) of agreements between two or more parties whereby the parties accepted restrictions on the prices of goods supplied, the terms or conditions of sale, quantities produced, processes of manufacture employed, or classes of persons to whom goods were supplied. The Registrar could then bring cases before a Restrictive Practices Court which had the power to declare certain classes of agreements contrary to the public interest and therefore void. The Court also had the power, on the application of the Registrar, to issue an Order to ensure the termination of the agreements.

The most fundamental principle of the Act was that a restriction would be held to be contrary to the public interest unless the Court was satisfied that it produced one or more of seven beneficial effects. Even if such agreements did meet the requirements of the seven criteria, to be approved it was also necessary to show that the balance between the benefit thus conferred and any detriments arising or likely to arise should not be unreasonable. Restrictive practices were deemed guilty unless they could prove their innocence.

By June 1966, 2,550 agreements had been registered under the Act and, of these, 2,110 had been terminated by act of the parties, through expiration, or because all registerable restrictions had been removed by virtue of a Court order or by the parties. Less than one percent of the registered agreements was found consistent with the public interest.

Despite the Act, however, many businessmen still attempted to avoid competition. This was not altogether unnatural especially in view of the fact that most business leaders were schooled in the earlier period of legitimate cartelization.

Further, the legislation was not without deficiency: the Court operated relatively slowly, and the time allowed for case preparation was long; hence it was possible to keep operating an agreement by claiming that it would be defended, whereas the parties had no such intention and would drop the defense shortly before the case came to Court. Nor did the Registrar have an effective sanction against failure to submit an agreement for registration; hence some agreements undoubtedly went underground. In some cases, following an initial period of price competition, as for example in electric cables, a series of horizontal mergers took place with the emergence of a price leader. In addition, there was a considerable spread of "open price agreements" which were virtually unknown in Britain prior to 1956, and which the Registrar feared were being used by some for the continuance of inhibiting competition.[2]

This loophole was partially closed by the Restrictive Trade Practices Act of 1968 which called for the registration of certain types of information agreements. However, there was still discretion for the Board of Trade to exempt agreements deemed to be in "the national interest."

One area the 1956 Act failed to attack was resale price maintenance. Although collective enforcement was made illegal, the legal power of the individual manufacturer to enforce resale prices for goods was actually strengthened. Collective abandonment led in some cases, especially in food products, to much greater competition. In other trades, however, manufacturers began to invoke the law of enforcement, especially against discount retailers who were challenging the existing retail institutions. Thus until 1964 the effect of the 1956 Act on most consumer goods was marginal.

In 1964, the government passed the Resale Price Act, designed to remove individual resale price enforcement. Manufacturers were given the opportunity to apply for exemption from the general prohibition on resale price maintenance by registering particulars with the Registrar of Restrictive Practices. The effect of registration was that such goods were excluded from the ban until the Restrictive Practices Court had decided if an exemption was warranted. There was, however, only the one opportunity for registration and after February 1965 no new applications could be made and the Act came fully into effect.

The Resale Price Act caused changes in the policy of many companies—aban-

---

[2] Report of the Registrar, *Restrictive Trading Agreements,* Cmnd. 3188, H.M.S.O., 1967, p. 3.

donment by one company in an industry often caused the remainder to follow. Those companies which did apply for exemption and came before the Court were generally treated harshly, with the result that many others who had registered did abandon price maintenance. The formal dissolution, while clearly increasing competition in some areas, was not as effective as had been hoped. Manufacturers still set recommended prices and in many classes of goods these prices were adhered to. The general retailing institutions, in particular, were extremely slow to move to discount operations, and so it was left to the supermarkets, or new discount operators, to increase the level of competitive pressure.

In 1965 modified monopoly legislation was introduced extending the coverage of the 1948 Act. Under this, the Commission was given power to investigate the supply of services, and the Board of Trade was given the power to make orders enforcing the Commission's recommendations. This 1965 legislation also allowed the Board of Trade to refer to the Commission proposed mergers involving assets of more than £5 million value, as well as any likely to lead to a monopoly as earlier defined. The Board could delay all such proposed mergers until the Commission had reported and, subject to the Commission's recommendations, could veto such mergers or dissolve existing monopolies.

After the new legislation, over 200 mergers were examined by the Board of Trade but relatively few were referred to the Monopolies Commission. A degree of confusion occurred as a result, in part owing to a policy of direct intervention by the government which tended to build up monopolies by merger in some areas. These mergers were not referred to the Monopolies Commission, on the grounds that they were in the "national interest."

Thus, over the past 20 years, successive governments enacted legislation which significantly increased the degree of competition in British industry. The process was continuing and the new Conservative government in 1970 declared its intention of further strengthening the Monopolies Commission and increasing the degree of competition. Entry into the European Economic Community (E.E.C.) could also be expected to enhance such legislation. Nevertheless, as the Community moved more toward the U.S. antitrust position, although the growth of legislation undoubtedly led to substantially more competition in Britain, thus forcing business enterprise to become more effective and efficient, there still seemed to be some way to go before old traditions were finally broken down. There were still notable weaknesses in the legislation by comparison with the United States, with regard to monopoly law, and channels still remained open for enterprises to avoid competition, especially by the acquisition of weaker competitors.

The Rise of U.S. Investment

American investment in Great Britain was also a force for increased competition. Next to Canada, Britain had the largest share of any country of U.S. direct investment. By the end of 1966 there were 1,600 U.S. firms operating in the United Kingdom with a cumulative investment of $5,625 million.[3] This represented 10

---

[3] J. Dunning, *The Role of American Investment in the British Economy*, PEP Broadsheet 507, 1969, p. 119.

percent of all U.S. foreign investment, 33 percent of investment in Europe, and 66 percent of all nonresident investment in the United Kingdom. The majority of this investment was concentrated in manufacturing industry.

Companies from the United States had a considerable history of investment in Britain dating back to the nineteenth century. Further, during the interwar period, British restrictionist policy encouraged many U.S. companies to commence local operations. By 1940 there were over 600 U.S. subsidiaries operating in Britain. By 1950 the U.S. capital stake had risen to $847 million, but it was in the next 20 years that the major growth of U.S. investment occurred. The growth slackened after 1960, however, due to declining British economic growth rate, failure of an early U.K. bid to enter the E.E.C., and increased direct investment by U.S. companies in the E.E.C.

Nevertheless, by 1965 U.S.-owned companies supplied 10 percent of the total goods produced in Britain. However, this percentage of production was much greater in specific sectors of industry particularly those with a high technological input such as pharmaceuticals, computers, and office machinery, and in differentiated consumer goods such as automobiles, cosmetics and toiletries, packaged foods, and appliances. This is indicated in Table 2–2.

These companies brought to the United Kingdom improved exploitation of technological innovation and the extensive use of marketing techniques, both of which

TABLE 2–2

APPROXIMATE MARKET SHARE BY NORTH AMERICAN FINANCED COMPANIES IN 1966

Percent	Industry
80 or more	Boot and shoe machinery, carbon black, color film, custard powder and starch, sewing machines, tinned baby foods, typewriters.
60–79	Agricultural implements, aluminium semi manufactures, breakfast cereals, calculating machines, cigarette lighters, domestic boilers, potato crisps, razor blades, spark plugs.
50–59	Cake mixes, cosmetics and toiletries, electric shavers, electric switches, ethical drugs, foundation garments, pens and pencils, motor cars, pet foods, petroleum refinery construction equipment, tinned milk, vacuum cleaners.
40–49	Computers, locks and keys, photographic equipment, printing and typesetting machinery, rubber tires, soaps and detergents, watches and clocks.
30–39	Abrasives, commercial vehicles, floor polishes, instant coffee, elevators and escalators, portable electric tools, refined petroleum products, refrigerators, washing machines.
15–29	Greeting cards, industrial instruments, materials handling equipment, medicinal preparations, mineral drinks, mining machinery, paperback books, petro-chemicals, synthetic fibers, telephones and telecommunications equipment, toilet tissues.

SOURCE: J. Dunning, *The Role of American Investment in the British Economy*, PEP Broadsheet 507, 1969, p. 178.

permitted market segmentation and product differentiation. They also brought an attitude of market competition since they were subsidiaries of corporations which grew in an environment where competition had long been legally guarded. There were few examples where the U.S. subsidiaries had been involved in cartel-type operations, and in the main their presence tended to increase competitive activity. The parent companies who made these investments were overwhelmingly of the multidivisional type which encouraged internal, as well as market competition. As a result, perhaps, the growth of U.S. subsidiary companies was consistently much faster than that of their British competitors.

The Growth of International Competition

In addition to changes in the domestic environment, the postwar period produced a marked increase in international competition. This affected both the domestic market, where considerable growth occurred in imports of manufactured goods, and export markets, where it became increasingly difficult to obtain overseas sales, especially in the staple industries.

Britain's import bill grew dramatically. In 1952 manufactured goods, including chemicals, represented £701 million or 22.5 percent of imports. By 1968 these had grown to £3,358 million or nearly 50 percent of total imports. At the same time, the value of crude materials imported, which provided the ingredients for conversion into high value-added production, remained almost constant. While some growth of manufactured imports was to be expected with increased liberalization of trade due, for example, to the General Agreement on Tariffs and Trade (GATT) negotiations and British entry into the European Free Trade Association (E.F.T.A.), there was no doubt that much of the increase was due to a relative decline in the competitive advantage of British producers. By comparison with other industrialized nations, British wage costs per unit of output rose more rapidly and productivity less rapidly, thus resulting in reduced international price competitiveness.

In addition, other factors have been cited for the reduced level of competitiveness of British production vis-à-vis other nations including "quality of products (including design and durability), reliability and speed of delivery, marketing, and after sale services." [4]

Further, the dissolution of the Empire, the weakening of Imperial Preference and the lack of large industrial markets in the Commonwealth forced a dramatic shift in the geographic distribution of imports, and exports as well (see Table 2–3).

In 1952 the Commonwealth nations were the source of 45.8 percent of Britain's imports, but by 1969 the importance of this source had declined to only 23.2 percent of the total. At the same time, imports from the E.E.C., E.F.T.A., and the United States had risen dramatically from a combined total of 30.6 percent to 47.9 percent.

Great Britain held 21.5 percent by value of world trade in manufactures in 1952. This share progressively declined and by 1969 had fallen to 11.2 percent. Some

---

[4] R. E. Caves and Associates, *Britain's Economic Prospects*, Brookings Institution, Washington, D.C., 1968, p. 284.

TABLE 2–3

VALUE OF BRITISH EXPORTS AND IMPORTS BY DESTINATION AND SOURCE

Destination and Source	Imports					Exports				
	1952	1955	1960	1965	1969	1952	1955	1960	1965	1969
Commonwealth	1,588	1,750	1,754	1,704	1,933	1,242	1,209	1,323	1,353	1,601
Latin America	177	239	312	283	356	151	113	171	162	248
European Economic Community	426	485	662	995	1,611	292	375	563	980	1,526
European Free Trade Area	320	371	464	783	1,248	263	344	433	687	1,081
Middle East	304	244	344	388	660	n.a.	159	202	272	486
Soviet Bloc	84	105	139	220	332	15	37	77	117	232
United States	315	420	567	671	1,124	146	183	322	514	903
Japan	29	24	42	78	105	n.a.	n.a.	29	53	129
Rest of the World	222	222	273	629	955	617	457	528	763	1,132
Total	3,465	3,860	4,557	5,751	8,324	2,726	2,877	3,648	4,901	7,338

SOURCE: Annual Abstract of Statistics.

special factors were also at work which went against Britain in export markets. In 1952 the largest single market was the Commonwealth countries which, with the exception of Canada, formed the Overseas Sterling Area. Trade with the Commonwealth accounted for over 55 percent of Britain's export trade despite the fact that as a trading bloc the Commonwealth only accounted for about 20 percent of world trade. In these markets Britain enjoyed preferential tariff treatment over a wide range of goods under the principle of Imperial Preference. By 1968 trade with the Commonwealth had fallen to less than 27 percent of Britain's export trade. In addition, Britain's share of the Commonwealth market fell much more than did her share of other markets. Between 1960 and 1966 Britain lost 27 percent of her share in Overseas Sterling Area markets as compared with only 14 percent of her non-O.S.A. markets.[5]

At the same time, Britain substantially increased her export trade with the higher growth and developed nations of Western Europe and the United States, although her absolute market share of these markets declined. In 1952 trade with what is now the E.E.C. and E.F.T.A., and the United States, only amounted to 24.5 percent and 6.4 percent of total exports, respectively. By 1968 this trade had grown to 39 percent and 16 percent, respectively. The transition was, therefore, even more marked than the change in import sources.

Nevertheless, this was a poor performance. While some loss was to be expected, the United States in a somewhat similar position managed to maintain its share of world trade in the face of competition, especially from Japan and West Germany. This poor British export performance, coupled with rising imports, was a primary cause of the stop-go economic policies which in turn seriously held back postwar economic growth.

Thus, in both import and export markets, Britain was forced to readjust her trading pattern considerably. Reliance on the relatively protected Commonwealth markets diminished and Britain was forced increasingly to compete in the industrialized markets where both internal competition and tariff disadvantage were generally greater.

Changes in Market Institutions

Significant institutional changes occurred in the domestic marketplace especially in consumer goods, which also increased the level of competition. In retailing, there were relatively few self-service stores operating on high turnover and low profit margins in 1950. Half of the retail trade was handled by small independent shopkeepers serving a small local catchment area. Moreover, although the rationing of consumer goods was progressively swept away, it did not actually end until 1954. In 1951 about 70 percent of consumer expenditure was subject to governmental price control and in 1954 the figure was still as high as 40 percent. The population of retail outlets underwent dramatic change especially in the 1960s, due to the growth of self-service stores, supermarkets, and multiple stores. In 1950 it was estimated there were less than 500 self-service stores; by 1957 the number had grown to 4,000. By 1966 the estimate was over 17,000. In addition, supermarkets

---

[5] *Ibid.*, p. 215.

began operating in Britain in 1956, there were about 870 by 1961, and they were estimated at 3,000 in 1966.[6]

Multiple stores selling specialist products began discounting from list prices in the early 1960s, and the appearance of private label and fighting brands (low-priced version of a producer's main branded product) also occurred. Private label multiples, such as Marks and Spencer, acted as price and quality leaders much like Sears, Roebuck in the United States, but over a narrower range of products. However, there was at that time little development of U.S.-style discount department stores despite the recent abandonment of resale price maintenance. In general goods, although discounting had become widespread, some further increase in competitive pressures seemed necessary. Advertising also grew, and the advent of commercial television in 1954 led to increased use of branding and the development of national markets where local markets were previously common. By and large Britain's retail institutions became a relatively efficient and effective competitive force, and any gaps in the system were expected to be remedied in the near future.

In summary, therefore, Britain's industries experienced a considerable increase in competitive pressure during the two decades 1950–1970. This was caused by significant changes in legislation, the invasion of foreign, especially American, direct investment, changes in the pattern of international trade which brought British industry into increased competition with other industrialized nations, and changes in domestic market institutions leading to increased retail competition. Furthermore, the evidence suggested that these pressures were increasing rather than decreasing. American investment had accelerated in the postwar period, the transition of foreign trade had been greater during the 1960s than the 1950s, and legislation enforcing competitive pressure was of recent origin. Furthermore British entry into the E.E.C. in the 1970s could be expected to increase competition still further as British enterprise faced up squarely to the developed economies of Western Europe.

THE IMPACT OF TECHNOLOGY

Since World War II there has been a rapid growth of industries based on technology. It was a successive theme of British political leaders that industry must exploit what Mr. Harold Wilson called the "white hot technological revolution." This growth of technology did have a visible impact on both the structure of British industry and the individual enterprise. There was very significant growth in areas such as synthetic fibers, chemicals, and electronics, which produced new markets, products, and processes. Those companies exploiting technology entered into existing markets to provide new competition for traditional producers and often increased the degree of competitive substitution possible between products. Traditional industries were transformed by the adoption of new techniques such as the discovery of float glass or the development of basic oxygen steel.

---

[6] Central Office of Information, *Britain 1969: An Official Handbook,* H.M.S.O., 1969, p. 401.

The exploitation of technology generally substituted capital for labor and, once adopted, the process tended to be cumulative and irreversible. It became profitable to invest not only to exploit existing knowledge but also to pursue innovations. This pursuit of innovative knowledge in turn led to institutionalization of the process. Companies which did institutionalize began to seek new markets or products as a conscious goal, thus becoming diversified away from their original, possibly narrow, area of interest.

Research activity in Britain expanded after 1950 but, even before the war, research intensive industries were providing a substantial and increasing share of G.N.P. In 1955, British R&D expenditure was approximately £300 million or 1.8 percent of G.N.P. at factor cost; by 1967–68 this had risen to 2.7 percent. Government provided the major source of finance for research in Britain supplying 51.3 percent of funds in 1967–68, while private industry provided 37.5 percent.

As a nation, Britain alone among the major industrialized societies approached the United States in terms of the percentage of its G.N.P. devoted to research. Further, the distribution of expenditure was also similar to that of the United States, with a heavy emphasis on aircraft and aerospace research where funding was primarily provided by government (see Table 2–4). Herein, however, lay a

TABLE 2–4

COMPARISON OF NATIONAL R&D EFFORTS IN MANUFACTURING INDUSTRIES

Industry	Percent Distribution of Manufacturing Research & Development			
	United Kingdom	United States	France	West Germany
Aircraft	35.4	36.3	27.7 ⎫	
Vehicles	3.0	7.4	2.6 ⎬	19.2
Machinery	7.3	8.2	6.4 ⎭	
Electrical Machinery	21.7	21.6	25.7 ⎫	
Instruments	2.3	3.9	n.a. ⎭	33.8
Chemicals	11.6	12.6	16.8	32.9
Steel and Metal Products	2.9	2.0 ⎫		
Non-Ferrous Metals	1.2	0.6 ⎭	3.2	6.6
Stone, Clay, and Glass	1.3	1.0	1.2	0.8
Rubber	1.2	1.1 ⎫		⎧ 1.0
Paper	0.9	0.6 ⎭	Included	⎩ 0.6
Food and Drink	1.9	0.9 ⎫		⎧ 0.6
Other Manufacturing	3.4	2.0 ⎭	Elsewhere	⎩ 1.9

SOURCE: Central Advisory Council on Science and Technology, *Technological Innovation in Britain*, H.M.S.O., 1969, p. 32.

significant disadvantage since this expenditure did not produce an adequate return due to the lack of an adequate domestic market for such products. By contrast, France and especially West Germany devoted a greater percentage of research expenditure to areas such as chemicals, electrical machinery, and instruments which had a much greater prospect of a commercial return on investment. As a result, therefore, it would seem there is a case for the redistribution of some British research funding, and especially that part provided by government, into more commercially promising areas which might produce a payoff in economic growth and employment for the funds invested.

Further, while British researchers proved very adept at initiating new discoveries, they performed poorly in the exploitation of innovation. American corporations were much more proficient. In the past 20 years some two-thirds of the successful innovations came from the United States.[7] One reason for Britain's comparative failure has been attributed to a national shortage of suitable engineers capable of developing the ideas generated by primary research. This shortage of qualified engineers inevitably led to the substitution of pure scientists less well-equipped to exploit discoveries.[8] Further, managerial deficiencies have been claimed as a contributory cause especially in the aircraft industry.[9] In Britain there has been a tendency for management to produce products with advanced engineering or design for its own sake, rather than to cater to market needs and/or products which would show an adequate return on investment. These factors, coupled with private industry's failure to invest sufficient capital for new plants, were cited [10] as possible explanations for a general lack of competence in exploiting the comparative strength of Britain's wide technological base.

THE CHANGING PATTERN OF SUPPLY

Although suffering a slight decline over the past 20 years, Britain's manufacturing industry was still the largest contributor to Gross Domestic Product in 1969. In 1950 manufacturing accounted for 36.7 percent of G.D.P. and by 1969 had only declined slightly to 35 percent. The role of manufacturing and the enterprises which it entailed were thus vital to the well-being of the economy.

The internal structure of the British manufacturing industry underwent significant change in response to the stimuli of the changing pattern of demand, increased competition, and technological innovation. By 1950, despite its relative international decline during the early part of the twentieth century, Britain was a highly developed industrial nation with a well-established capital market and system of industries. As wartime shortages eased and pent-up demand was released, Britain entered the age of mass consumption. Reliance on the former staple industries was still apparent but declining. In 1954 mining and quarrying (mainly coal mining) represented 3.6 percent of employment and 7.0 percent of net output from the production industries; metal manufacture (mainly iron and steel), 2.4 percent of employment and 8.5 percent of manufacturing net output; textiles, 4.2 percent of employment and 10.3 percent of manufacturing net output. Agricultural employment was already very low representing only 5.0 percent of total. The newer industries of chemicals, vehicles, and electrical engineering were established. Service industries already represented 30 percent of employment.

[7] Report of the Third International Conference of Ministers of Science of O.E.C.D. countries, *O.E.C.D. Observer,* April 1968.

[8] R. E. Caves, et al., *Britain's Economic Prospects,* pp. 448–84.

[9] *Ibid.,* pp. 448–49.

[10] Central Advisory Council on Science and Technology, *Technological Innovation in Britain,* H.M.S.O., 1969, p. 9.

Considerable change occurred in the postwar period (see Table 2–5). The relative importance of food, chemicals, electrical equipment, and engineering, other metal goods, and paper and publishing, all increased, reflecting changes in the pattern of demand and the growth of technological industries. Decline continued in metal manufacture, shipbuilding, textiles and clothing, and leather goods, while other industries remained approximately the same. Vehicles grew in importance until 1963 when, due to governmental constraints on domestic demand, they subsequently slipped back to their position of 1954.

Apart from a widely distributed industrial structure, British industry has been found to compare favorably by comparison with other nations in the scale of its operations at both the plant and enterprise level. Similarly, Britain contained a large number of firms of significant size by international standards. Of the largest 200 non-U.S. firms in the free world ranked by sales in 1969, over 20 percent were British. Of the largest 300 manufacturing firms in Western Europe in 1969, approximately one-third were British. The companies studied all had sales of almost $150 million or more. They employed nearly 4 million people in Britain alone—some 44 percent of the total number employed by the whole of the manufacturing industry. Thus, the British industrial structure did not suffer from overfragmentation in most industries.

Indeed, British industries had become increasingly concentrated during the postwar period. A major study of some 220 different trades conducted for 1951 [11] showed that high concentration (where over 66 percent of net output was held by the three largest firms) existed in 50 trades but that these only accounted for some 10 percent of the labor force. Medium concentration (between 34 and 66 percent of net output held by the largest firms) was found in 69 trades representing 24 percent of employment, while low concentration was most common, existing in 101 trades containing 66 percent of the labor force.

This low concentration did not result in a high level of competition due to the large number of restrictive agreements and collusion existing in British industry at this time, as discussed earlier. Rationalization was forestalled permitting the survival of many smaller, less efficient firms. However, the growth of competition in particular speeded the process of rationalization and concentration, especially during the 1960s. Much of this was accomplished by mergers. Over the seven years from 1952 to 1958 cash purchases of other company securities totaled only about £550 million—2 percent of total expenditure by companies. However, between 1959 and 1965, the figure rose to some £2,000 million, nearly 5 percent of total expenditure.[12] After 1965 mergers became even more important and in the peak year of 1968 alone, £1,208 million of net assets were acquired by mergers.

This large-scale merger movement further increased concentration. The Monopolies Commission, concerned about the increasing wave of merger activity, studied concentration by broad industrial classification between 1957 and 1967.[13] The survey covered all quoted companies mainly operating in the United Kingdom with

[11] R. Evely and I. M. D. Little, *Concentration in British Industry,* Cambridge University Press, 1960, p. 51.

[12] "Company Finance 1952–65," *Bank of England Quarterly,* March 1967, pp. 29–38.

[13] Monopolies Commission, *A Survey of Mergers 1958–69,* H.M.S.O., 1970.

TABLE 2–5

PRODUCTION INDUSTRIES (NET)—OUTPUT AND EMPLOYMENT, 1954–68

Industry	1954				1958			
	Net Output (£M)	Net Output Per Person (£)	Output of Total Mfg. (%)	Number Employed (Thousands)	Net Output (£M)	Net Output Per Person (£)	Output of Total Mfg. (%)	Number Employed (Thousands)
Food, Drink & Tobacco	645	982	10.3	657	917	1,263	11.7	726
Chemicals and Allied Products	538	1,316	8.6	409	736	1,656	9.4	444
Metal Manufacture	533	968	8.5	550	689	1,213	8.8	568
Engineering and Electrical Equipment	1,308	819	21.0	1,598	1,743	1,006	22.2	1,733
Shipbuilding	187	660	3.0	284	227	825	2.9	275
Vehicles	636	856	10.2	742	818	1,047	10.4	782
Other Metal Goods	358	755	5.7	474	439	931	5.6	472
Textiles	640	655	10.3	977	615	723	7.8	851
Leather Goods	45	676	0.7	66	43	796	0.6	54
Clothing and Footwear	279	483	4.5	578	308	583	3.9	529
Bricks, Glass, Etc.	252	785	4.0	321	297	975	3.8	304
Timber and Furniture	185	671	3.0	276	211	835	2.7	254
Paper and Publishing	445	894	7.1	499	577	1,065	7.4	542
Other Manufacturing	184	756	3.0	243	227	718	2.9	248
Total Manufacturing	6,234	813	100	7,672	7,849	1,009	100	7,781
Mining	575	690	—	832	726	872		832
Construction	933	596	—	1,567	1,245	792		1,573
Gas, Electricity, and Water	438	1,155	—	379	621	1,625		383
All Industries	8,180	783	—	10,450	10,441	988		10,568
Agriculture				1,164				1,090
Distribution				2,802				3,000
Other Services				4,149				4,335
Transport and Communications				1,744				1,733
Local and National Government				1,359				1,334
Total Civil Employment				23,148				23,607

TABLE 2–5 *(Continued)*

Industry	1963				1968			
	Net Output (£M)	Net Output Per Person (£)	Output of Total Mfg. (%)	Number Employed (Thousands)	Net Output (£M)	Net Output Per Person (£)	Output of Total Mfg. (%)	Number Employed (Thousands)
Food, Drink & Tobacco	1,269	1,679	11.7	756	2,002	2,485	12.5	806
Chemicals and Allied Products	1,058	2,388	9.7	443	1,571	3,585	9.8	453
Metal Manufacture	830	1,449	7.6	573	1,098	1,958	6.9	561
Engineering and Electrical Equipment	2,507	1,307	23.1	1,919	3,745	1,905	23.1	1,966
Shipbuilding	215	1,060	2.0	203	286	1,587	1.8	180
Vehicles	1,154	1,455	10.6	793	1,639	2,078	10.2	789
Other Metal Goods	618	1,218	5.7	508	999	1,765	6.2	566
Textiles	804	1,060	7.4	758	1,104	1,574	6.9	701
Leather Goods	59	1,105	0.5	54	77	1,551	0.5	50
Clothing and Footwear	382	771	3.5	497	524	1,102	3.3	476
Bricks, Glass, Etc.	429	1,354	3.9	309	610	1,986	3.8	307
Timber and Furniture	299	1,138	2.8	263	482	1,776	3.0	271
Paper and Publishing	846	1,449	7.8	584	1,252	2,041	7.8	614
Other Manufacturing	392	1,301	3.6	302	623	1,852	3.9	336
Total Manufacturing	10,851	1,363	100	7,960	16,012	1,984	100	8,076
Mining	772	1,190	—	649	748	1,672	—	448
Construction	1,819	1,076	—	1,691	2,850	1,745	—	1,634
Gas, Electricity and Water	982	2,417	—	406	1,569	3,859	—	407
All Industries	14,423	1,347	—	10,705	21,179	2,005		10,565
Agriculture				566				423
Distribution				2,965				2,832
Other Services				4,977				5,669
Transport and Communications				1,711				1,610
Local and National Government				1,374				1,440
Total Civil Employment				23,060				23,125

SOURCES: Census of Production 1958, 1963; *Board of Trade Journal*, Jan. 30, 1970; Annual Abstract of Statistics.

net assets of greater than £0.5 million in 1961, in all a population of some 2,024 companies. In 14 of the 22 industrial classifications an increase in concentration clearly occurred, in 2 a reduction, and 6 remained the same. At the same time, the percentage of total net assets held by the largest companies increased considerably. In 1957 the top 120 companies in this sample held 50 percent of the total assets but by 1968 this proportion had climbed to 71 percent. By 1968 the original 2,024 companies had been reduced to 1,253 by mergers and acquisitions. In the manu- facturing sector, 600 companies (40 percent of the number at the end of 1957) were acquired or merged, and concentration increased in most industry segments both in terms of concentration within industry sectors and in asset concentration by the largest companies.

Five industries in particular, namely, electrical engineering, drink, vehicles, tex- tiles and paper, printing and publishing, accounted for more than 75 percent of the total net assets absorbed within the same industrial classification. Mergers within the same industrial classification accounted for 66 percent of the total asset transfer while 26 percent of mergers were between firms in different industrial classifications. Thus, concurrent with this increasing concentration, a substantial element of diversi- fication took place even allowing for deficiencies in the system of Standard Indus- trial Classification (SIC) coding.

Analysis over the 10-year period showed that the net assets of the 1,253 remain- ing companies studied increased by 165 percent of which more than a quarter came from acquisition. The 10 largest companies achieved a higher growth rate of 194 percent, but more than 40 percent of this growth was derived from acquisitions.

Thus, the British industrial system, already highly developed in 1950, underwent substantial change in the postwar period in response to changing patterns in de- mand, technology, and competition. The relative importance of different industrial sectors changed and overall concentration increased substantially, especially as the result of sustained merger activity during the 1960s.

SOURCES AND USES OF CAPITAL

A recent Organization for Economic Cooperation and Development (O.E.C.D.) report on Western European and United States capital markets concluded that the British market met all the various tests of market efficiency.[14] Large enterprises generally experienced little difficulty in raising new capital. Gross corporate invest- ment amounted to over £2,000 million per annum during the 1960s, with net new capital issues accounting for about £500 million per annum. Bank borrowing accounted for about half of this, with new capital issues by quoted companies some- what less.

Almost 75 percent of new finance was internally generated from retained earn- ings and depreciation.[15] Further, this heavy reliance on internal funds was perhaps accentuated by the 1965 Finance Act, which effectively increased taxes on dis- tributed income while reducing the rate on retained earnings. Nevertheless, over

---

[14] O.E.C.D., *Capital Markets Study,* Paris, 1968, see particularly Volume 3, pp. 567–610; Volume 4, pp. 445–88.

[15] "Company Assets Income and Finance," 1963 *Board of Trade Journal.*

the past 20 years the portion of G.N.P. arising from corporate profits declined relative to personal incomes. Further, for much of the period, corporate taxation tended to increase, especially on corporate income derived from overseas investment. The heavy reliance on retained earnings, coupled with falling profits and higher taxation perhaps provided some explanation of the low investment rate in British industry.

Interest rates on loans were set generally in relation to the British bank rate, which was under government control and used frequently as a tool of monetary policy. Such changes in interest rates were often accompanied by the use of credit controls, while special deposits and reserve ratios were applied to the main clearing banks. Indeed, short-run changes in monetary policy were a conspicuous and frequently used aspect of governmental economic policy in the postwar period, leading to increased uncertainty in the investment climate for corporate enterprise.

British financial institutions, which were well developed, increased in relative importance as sources of corporate capital and, by 1969, the assets of life assurance funds totaled some £12,740 million while pension fund assets were £7,383 million.[16] Mutual funds and investment trusts were also growing and totaled some £4,700 million.[17] The low liquidity requirements and strong income needs of pension and life funds meant that they provided a prime source of long-term capital. However, differences in portfolio balance were such that pension funds were the largest corporate equity investors, having increased their equity holdings from 38 to 51 percent of their portfolios between 1963 and 1969.[18]

The institutions had been traditionally passive in their requirements for corporate performance although recently this had been changing due to competition for funds and pressures from agencies such as the government-sponsored, Industrial Reorganisation Corporation (I.R.C.). It was with pleasure that the I.R.C. in its 1970 report noted a recent statement by an institutional chairman which promised to use its weight to revitalize "flagging managements." [19]

The uses of capital by companies tended to place more emphasis on capital investment relative to current expenditure over the period 1952–65. This rise was associated with official encouragement of capital investment by capital allowances against taxable profits. By 1965 expansion of depreciation, initial and investment allowances, removed tax liability on nearly £2,000 million of gross trading profits compared with £400 million in 1952.[20] Investment allowances were replaced by investment grants in 1966, which were designed to reduce the time between realization of tax incentives and investment decisions.

Capital investment accounted for over half of corporate expenditure and showed a strong cyclical pattern reflecting government fiscal and monetary policy. Dividend payments increased rapidly from 1952 due in part to a rise in merger rates and increased shareholder interest in the growth of share values. In 1965 tax changes

---

[16] "The Financial Institutions Part I," *Bank of England Quarterly,* December 1970, p. 419.

[17] "Investment Trusts and Unit Trusts: Assets and Transactions," *Bank of England Quarterly,* March 1969, p. 62.

[18] "The Financial Institutions Part I."

[19] "Industrial Reorganisation Corporation," *Report and Accounts 1970,* H.M.S.O., 1970, p. 6.

[20] "Company Finance 1952–65," pp. 31–34.

again tended to reverse this trend. As would be expected, capital expenditure on acquisitions grew substantially as concentration and diversification took place.

Despite an apparently high level of expenditure on fixed assets, however, Britain's comparative position was poor. In a study of nine industrial nations, Britain ranked eighth between 1950 and 1962 with respect to both investment in capital stock of enterprises and fixed capital alone.[21] The average British worker was thus supported by an exceptionally small amount of capital—a factor that has been noted as a cause of the relatively poor economic growth performance.

THE ROLE OF INDUSTRIAL RELATIONS

The British system of industrial relations contained a number of significant deficiencies which had led to both direct and indirect consequences on the development of British enterprise. Inefficiencies caused by overmanning and restrictive labor practices, coupled with high wage inflation led to a relative decline in the unit output per man and the international price competitiveness of British goods. By comparison with most other industrial nations, labor productivity in the British manufacturing industry had shown slower growth than in France, Germany, Italy, and Japan. At the same time, there had been significant wage inflation resulting in the wage costs per unit of output rising faster in Britain than elsewhere, as shown in Table 2–6.

TABLE 2–6

WAGE COSTS PER UNIT OF OUTPUT
(INDEX 1963=100)

	1956	1960	1965	1969
United States	105	103	99	110
West Germany	78	86	105	105
France	80	92	102	107
Italy	85	87	100	110
Japan	82	85	104	107
United Kingdom	88	94	106	118

SOURCE: *National Institute Economic Review.*

Apart from the direct consequences of decreased price competitiveness of British goods, the high level of domestic inflation which appeared evident more in wages than in prices, resulted in continual pressure on sterling and continuous government intervention in the economy. In no small part, these problems were due to a fragmented structure of trade unions and weaknesses of both management and men in dealing with problems of industrial relations.

In 1968, although declining, there were still 534 trade unions in Britain, the largest 10 percent of which accounted for 90 percent of union membership. By comparison there were only 189 national unions in the United States covering a

---

[21] R. E. Caves, et al., *Britain's Economic Prospects,* pp. 248, 271.

nonagricultural workforce of 64 million. Despite the obvious strength of the union movement in Britain, however, only 41 percent of the workforce were members.

There were basically three types of union: craft, general, and industrial. The craft unions were built around a specific skill: they controlled supply by restricted entry and sought to maintain skill-pay differentials. The general unions catered more for unskilled and semi-skilled workers and were willing to recruit nearly anyone, anywhere. The industrial unions were specific for a given industry and covered a broad range of skills. The fact that these three types of unions were often found in the same industry and that there were large numbers of unions overall led to serious structural causes of industrial inefficiency. Interunion disputes, such as the craft unions attempting to maintain pay differentials and avoid skill dilution, resulted in inflated wage costs, inefficient manning, restrictive practices, and demarcation disputes in a variety of industries especially automobiles, engineering, shipbuilding, printing, coal mining, and chemicals.[22]

A further serious weakness occurred within the structure of individual unions. A recent report of the Royal Commission on Trade Unions and Employers Associations noted that there were essentially two industrial relations systems in Great Britain.[23] The first of these was the formal system with a keystone of a national collective agreement negotiated between the trade union executive and the industry employers association. Such collective agreements established national rates of pay, hours of work, and other conditions appropriate to regulation by agreement. The second system was informal and created by behavior at the plant or enterprise level which conducted bargaining on such items as piecework and incentive earnings.

These two systems were found to be frequently in conflict with one another and actual wages drifted far apart from the national agreements. The elements of local plant and enterprise bargaining were not controlled by the union executive or even the local full-time union hierarchy, but by the shop stewards on the shop floor. Local bargaining resulted in competitive sectional wage agreements and agreed dispute procedures were frequently ignored.

The Commission found the trade unions to be lacking in the number of full-time officials available to maintain official control of local events. The full-time officials at present were insufficient in many cases for the volume of work, hence resulting in a loss of contact between the executive and the shop floor. A serious need for training was also noted for both full-time and part-time officials. Most full-time officials and two-thirds of the 175,000 shop stewards had received little or no formal training in industrial relations.

Apart from criticism of the unions, however, the Commission was critical of management. It was found that, despite the decline in the authority of the employ-

---

[22] See, for example, *Financial Times,* October 10, 1967, which deals with overmanning on the docks; see also The Economist Intelligence Unit, *The National Newspaper Industry: A Survey 1966,* p. 99; Ministry of Labour, *Final Report of the Committee of Inquiry into Certain Matters Concerning the Port Transport Industry,* Cmnd. 2734, H.M.S.O., London; National Economic Development Office, *Manpower in the Chemical Industry,* H.M.S.O., 1967, pp. 46–50; *Royal Commission on Trade Unions and Employers Associations, 1965–68. Report,* H.M.S.O., 1968, paragraphs 396–399.

[23] *Royal Commission on Trade Unions and Employers Associations 1965–68. Report,* H.M.S.O., 1968.

ers associations which negotiated national agreements on behalf of individual firms, most companies had not developed suitable systems for regulating the terms and conditions of local plant bargaining. While there had been a growth in numbers of personnel specialists, it was found that many companies had "no effective personnel policy to control methods of negotiation and pay structures, and perhaps no conception of one." [24] The increased power of the shop stewards and local work groups had been augmented by the attitude of management which was criticized for its preference for keeping many matters out of national agreements, for the inadequacy of its methods of control over payment systems, for its preference for informality, and its tolerance of custom and practice.

The result of this conflict led to increased unofficial and unconstitutional strikes and other forms of workshop pressure. Official strikes, which although individually serious, were relatively infrequent and showed no consistent tendency to grow. Unofficial and wildcat strikes, however, accounted for 95 percent of industrial stoppages and were becoming more common. About half the wildcat strikes concerned wages and over 40 percent concerned "working arrangements, rules, and discipline," and "redundancy, dismissal, suspension, etc.—all matters usually dealt with at the level of enterprise." [25]

The distribution of such stoppages was narrowly confined to a small number of industries, notably mining, motor vehicles, docks, and shipbuilding. Other industries with poor records were iron and steel and engineering, and in all these industries work group organization was high, fragmented bargaining had been the rule, and wage structures notoriously anarchistic. Changing needs in the industrial relations system had not been met by changes in the institutions of labor or management and the unofficial strikes were symptomatic of this failure.

The British system of industrial relations, therefore, had a considerable impact on the efficiency and performance of the enterprise especially in those industries with poor records for industrial strife. The deficiencies of the system did not merely lead to the inefficient use of labor, but to slow acceptance of change, resistance to innovation, inefficient use of working capital caused by stockpiling, lack of confidence in the marketplace, poor production planning, and a continuing high rate of wages and inflation.

THE ROLE OF MANAGEMENT

The key resource for the successful development of any firm is its management, who chooses and allocates the mix of resources and determines the strategy of the enterprise. The relative ability of British managers has come under much criticism from many quarters in recent years. While it is difficult to measure the quality of management, the available evidence has tended to support the conclusion that by comparison with the United States, especially, British management has been, in general, less proficient.

The first criterion of managerial ability is corporate performance. Dunning [26] has

---

[24] *Ibid.*, p. 262.
[25] *Ibid.*, p. 266.
[26] Dunning, *The Role of American Investment in the British Economy.*

provided perhaps the nearest direct comparison of relative corporate performance between the British and the Americans. He found that American firms operating in Britain consistently earned a higher rate of return on capital than their British competitors. The American concerns were on the whole more capital intensive, paid more attention to marketing, demanded higher academic and technical qualifications from managers, and evaluated risks and planned more professionally. Dunning summarized his argument as follows: [27]

> First and perhaps most important, U.S. firms in Britain have access to more *knowledge* and *expertise* . . . than is used by U.K. competitors. . . . Second, they tend to use such knowledge and expertise as is available (not only from their parent companies, but throughout the world) more effectively. These two considerations give them the *power* to be more efficient. Third, U.S. subsidiaries would appear to have a more dynamic and professional attitude to management and decision taking. They are usually under considerable pressure from their parent companies which encourage a spirit of competitiveness among their offshoots. This is reflected in their greater *will* to be efficient.

It would appear, then, that it has been not merely a question of technical competence that has made the American concerns different, but rather a question of basic attitude—the *will* to be profitable and efficient.

Other observers have made similar criticisms of the technical competence and attitude of British managers. Hugh Parker, the managing director of the London office of McKinsey & Company, has commented on the underdeveloped nature of marketing in British companies,[28] the low degree of professionalism and effectiveness, the lack of a tradition of competitive managements, the weakness of the educational system and the lack of profit motivation.[29] Dubin also noted the difference in British managers' will to achieve, which he attributed to a reluctance to change and innovate, the low level of educational attainment, the persistent emphasis on social class and age grading, and the expectation of indefinite service within the same organization.[30]

An examination of the wool textile industry revealed that only 7 percent of the industry's directors were university graduates, few modern managerial techniques were used, most companies were run on an ad hoc basis, planning and control systems were underdeveloped, there was too much emphasis on production and too little on marketing, and there was a tendency to resist innovation.[31] In the shipbuilding industry deficiencies were noted in marketing, production planning, management of the labor force, and an attitude which regarded shipbuilding as an art remote from the general run of engineering and management development.[32]

---

[27] *Ibid.*, pp. 135–36.

[28] H. Parker, "Government Regulation: Tampering with the Mainspring," *McKinsey Quarterly*, Winter 1968, pp. 10–13.

[29] H. Parker, "Can British Management Close the Gap?" *McKinsey Quarterly*, Summer 1967, pp. 38–44.

[30] R. L. Dubin, "Management in Britain—Impressions of a Visiting Professor," *Journal of Management Studies*, May 1970, pp. 183–98.

[31] National Economic Development Office, *The Strategic Future of the Wool Textile Industry*, H.M.S.O., 1969, pp. 30–31, 211.

[32] *Shipbuilding Inquiry Committee Report*, Cmnd. 2937, H.M.S.O., 1967, p. 51.

A comparative study of the printing industry in five countries revealed that the British companies studied were relatively deficient in marketing, technical skills, and general managerial proficiencies.[33] A report on the British process plant manufacturers judged the quality of management to be poor, and found that men were promoted to responsible positions without adequate training despite the availability of suitable educational courses.[34] A study of 47 firms in 6 industries including machine tools, electronics, domestic appliances and earth-moving equipment, revealed that many firms did not apply even comparatively simple techniques that would improve productivity and indicated "almost complete indifference to modern managerial practice in the widespread strata of British industry." [35]

A survey of the Institute of Directors of 10,000 company directors indicated the low level of educational attainment by British directors.[36] The average number holding a university degree was only 14 percent, although in large companies with issued capital greater than £5 million, the figure rose to 27 percent. Other professional qualifications, especially that of chartered accountancy, were important, however, and about 10 percent of all directors possessed such qualifications with the percentages again higher among the larger corporations. This survey also revealed that over 40 percent of British directors received their secondary education at a public school despite the fact that such schools educated only about 4 percent of the school population.[37]

Some further comments are appropriate relative to the British educational system and managerial attitudes to education in general. A survey of 100 firms in Essex found that "attitudes to professional qualifications were prejudiced, and in some firms the possession of academic or professional qualifications was regarded as a handicap." [38] However, one survey has evaluated the professional and academic qualifications of company directors in a group of industries having 12 or more firms with either net assets of more than £1 million or more than 2,000 employees. The results showed a significant correlation between directorial qualifications and profit performance over time, which held for both the sample as a whole and for specific industries.[39]

There was still evidence that many directors had been educated at public schools and at one of the two traditional universities, Oxford or Cambridge—a factor which has given rise to a claim of British "amateurism." The high element of public school-educated executives reflected the relative immobility of the British social structure, which was partially perpetuated by the ability of the privileged to provide their children with public school education.[40] In 1969 the great majority of children in Britain

[33] National Economic Development Office, *Printing in a Competitive World*, H.M.S.O., 1970, p. 19.

[34] *Report of the Process Plant Expert Committee*, H.M.S.O., 1969, p. 17.

[35] PEP, *Attitudes in British Management*, Penguin Books, Hammondsworth, 1966.

[36] Institute of Directors, "The Anatomy of the Board," *The Director*, January 1965, pp. 87–91.

[37] A. Sampson, *Anatomy of Britain Today*, Harper Colophon, New York, 1965, p. 196.

[38] J. Woodward, *Industrial Organisation: Theory and Practice*, Oxford University Press, London, 1965, p. 14.

[39] R. Betts, "Characteristics of British Company Directors," *Journal of Management Studies*, February 1967, pp. 71–88.

[40] Public schools in Britain are comparable to private schools in the United States.

still left school at the age of 15 or 16, and, although some might receive additional vocational training subsequently, many were initially undereducated and unskilled. Meanwhile, Britain educated a lower percentage of its population at university level than most industrialized nations. Furthermore, the relative level of technical education was even lower than average and again a class division existed between the old traditional universities and the new "Redbrick" institutions.[41]

The educational system thus tended to reinforce class barriers which seemed very prevalent in British society by comparison with those in the United States. Deficiencies in exploiting the full potential within the population, especially among the lower classes, tended to inhibit the rate of upward social mobility, which was much lower than in the United States; to perpetuate upper class elite and perhaps "amateurism" in management; and to foster negative attitudes in worker-management relationships, characterized by a "them" and "us" dichotomy.

In the late 1960s there were some signs that attitudes had been changing in recent years and the belief that managers could only learn from experience was less widely held. However, it has been pointed out with regard to business education that a tendency persisted to discount the value of longer comprehensive courses as compared with short specialized ones, and a stubborn tendency in many firms to believe that their management processes and problems were unique.[42]

The low degree of interfirm mobility, low compensation, and to some extent the attitude of maintaining the status quo, could be largely attributed to the system of personal incentives in Britain. A high level of personal taxation which reached marginal rates of $88\frac{1}{4}$ percent, at income levels about £15,000 per annum, precluded the possibility of salaried executives accumulating personal capital in order to maintain an independent posture which might encourage risk taking and improved efficiency. A study of the personal wealth of directors[43] showed that for those who had not inherited wealth, a third possessed negligible personal assets beyond their homes and consumer durables. Less than a third had disposable wealth of more than twice their pre-tax income at the end of some 30 years of service. Other evidence suggested that remuneration of directors in the late 1960s was in fact worse than it was before the war,[44] due to the personal tax system which was aimed to redistribute income on an egalitarian basis.

Despite the high rate of tax on personal income, many companies paid directors high gross salaries which was found to be related to the sales of the corporation rather than to its profits.[45] The reason for this was not the almost negligible impact on net salary, but rather because some individuals were apparently motivated by gross income levels and, more practically, were concerned about the impact on pensions.

Pension rights provided the probable key to the lack of interfirm mobility and

[41] A. Sampson, *Anatomy of Britain Today*, Chapters 12–13.

[42] National Economic Development Office, *Management Education in the 1970's*, H.M.S.O., 1970, p. 7.

[43] A. Merrett, "How Well Off Are Directors?" *The Director*, January 1968, pp. 60–63.

[44] L. Coulthard, "Directors' Salaries: The Aftermath of Disclosure," *The Director*, March 1968, pp. 398–401.

[45] "Boardroom Salaries: The First A.I.C.—Director Reports," *The Director*, October 1969, pp. 78–81.

perhaps the attitude of maintaining the status quo. A study of directors' pension rights [46] indicated that in large firms from 60 to 70 percent of concerns offered what were known as "Top Hat" pension schemes. These schemes, which were largely paid for by the firm, offered the senior executive a pension of up to two-thirds of the salary achieved in the latter years of employment. More important in some respects, they contained a feature which allowed the individual to take a lump sum, tax-free commutation of 25 percent of pension salary upon retirement. The pension rights of most executives were not transferable despite repeated government statements of intention to make them so (but new legislation proposed that this would be corrected by 1975). Hence, the net salary gain for an executive wishing to transfer jobs was negligible, due to the high level of taxation, whereas the loss of pension rights was very substantial. Pension security depended on an individual's maintaining his/her present position and no other financial security was available. The individual was, therefore, unlikely to take risks which might potentially jeopardize this security, and was unlikely to move to another firm, for this same reason.

Other incentives such as stock options were rare in Britain and although a number of such schemes began in the early 1960s, they were effectively ended by the 1966 Finance Act. Since 1966 a number of new schemes of stock purchase had begun to appear in increasing numbers. These schemes basically allowed the individual to purchase shares at or below market price using money loaned by the firm via a specially established trust. Profits on the sale of the shares at some time in the future were then only subject to long-term capital gains tax. As of 1970 such schemes were still uncommon, and were not normally linked to achievement of specific profit targets, but were often related to the gross salary level of the individual. There was evidence that such schemes could well become more widespread, however, provided future fiscal policy permitted them.

British management has been criticized for its attitudes and its level of technical competence. The research evidence reported has supported these criticisms and it would appear that the causes of these lie in the level and type of education received, questions of attitude and motivation within the wider society, and a system of personal reward which effectively locks the individual into the position of remaining within the same firm and maintaining the status quo. The evidence of American corporations in Britain suggests that these attitudes and skills are capable of being changed and, given the will, the management of British corporate enterprise could and should improve efficiency and profit performance.

THE ROLE OF GOVERNMENT

Government has had a significant impact on many aspects of the enterprise. This impact increased during the post-World War II period as successive governments intervened in an attempt to manipulate the domestic economy and the market system. Many of the influences of government have been mentioned previously but, in

---

[46] L. Coulthard, "Directors' Salaries."

addition, the public sector was also a major employer and a substantial part of the British industrial system was in public ownership. Nationalization had been extended in the postwar period to cover much of the utility and transportation industries and, in 1967 in the manufacturing sector, the steel industry was nationalized for the second time since 1950.

The two main British political parties, Labour and Conservative, were ideologically different. Labour had been the proponent of state ownership and had adopted a posture of much greater state intervention in industry as well, while the Conservatives placed more emphasis on the market system. In addition, Labour had been initially responsible for the introduction of many of the features of the British Welfare State. Labour was greatly concerned with a more egalitarian distribution of personal wealth and as such favored (more so than the Conservatives) the continuation of regressive taxation on high levels of personal income. As a consequence of such ideological differences, the potential threat of a Labour administration served to undermine business confidence relatively frequently at election periods.

Further, the government's management of the macroeconomy had a major impact on business confidence as well as directly affecting specific industries by the use of fiscal and monetary measures. The primary responsibility for economic management rested with the Treasury, which manipulated the pressure of demand in the light of economic forecasts, in particular those of short-term national income and balance of payments. In the light of the government's economic objectives, an annual budget was prepared which manipulated demand over the short term, primarily in relation to the balance of payments situation and the level of unemployment. In addition to this budget, economic policy interventions were also often made in the light of short-term fluctuations in the principal variables. However, the influence of constant changes in short-term policy on the long-term development of industry was apparently not given great weight.[47]

As a result, continuous short-term responses to changes in these primary indicators resulted in a series of stop-go policy decisions. The fiscal and monetary tools of economic management were alternatively applied and relaxed, causing sharp fluctuations in economic growth.

The pattern of stop-go had been dysfunctional to industry, sharpening the cyclical movement of capital investment and undermining confidence in general. Within specific industries, especially consumer durables, the rapid changes in monetary policy had almost certainly had a deleterious effect on the long-term potential of these industries.

The pattern had also seemingly been affected by the timing of general elections. Since the incumbent party had the right to select the timing of elections, these tended to occur during most favorable economic periods, to be preceded by relatively inflationary policy and be followed by deflationary packages. Recognition of the dysfunctions of stop-go resulted in an attempt, by both parties, at national planning during the 1960s, but this was poorly implemented and proved abortive. Some observers, therefore, considered that the economic policy makers had accentuated

---

[47] S. Brittan, *Steering the Economy,* Secker and Warburg, London, 1969, p. 63.

Britain's economic problems by the misuse or mistiming of their policy interventions.[48]

In addition to its other policies, government on occasion intervened directly in the affairs of specific industries. These interventions, apart from nationalization, were usually in those industries in decline, notably textiles, aircraft, and shipbuilding. The use of public funds to prop up areas of the economy unable to compete did not improve industrial efficiency or overall economic performance. More recently the 1966 Labour administration attempted systematic rather than spasmodic intervention by the creation of an Industrial Reorganisation Corporation (I.R.C.). This agency was charged with the task of restructuring areas of British industry where it felt that rationalization and modernization would improve efficiency and competitiveness.

The I.R.C. addressed its attention primarily to the engineering and electrical industries and its activity led to a significant number of mergers, some of them large, which led to concentration in many segments of these industries. The pattern normally adopted was to concentrate the manufacturers of specific products, such as ball bearings, together into large relatively narrow product-range units. In so doing, I.R.C. sought to achieve synergistic effect by the rationalization of resources, the economies of large-scale operations, and the achievement of critical size sufficient to support professional management, and research and development. A lack of conspicuous success and ideological differences led the incoming Conservative administration to disband the I.R.C. in 1971.

The direct and indirect impact of government on industry and the enterprise was, therefore, widespread and increased during the period studied. Criticisms have been raised about the effectiveness of much of this policy, both in macroeconomic management and elsewhere. The divergent economic ideologies of the two main political parties have contributed to the problems of the enterprise. Some reconciliation of short-term aims of political policy makers, with the long-term strategic needs of industrial enterprise, seemed necessary if British industry is to achieve the economic goals the policy makers have set.

Conclusion

This chapter has attempted to sketch briefly the environment within which British enterprise has developed. Within the domestic market, rising affluence, the redistribution of incomes, changing social characteristics, and the role of government all served to effect change in the demand function. Similarly, technology was a significant agent for change, despite deficiencies observed in the transformation of discoveries into successful product innovations. Perhaps most important, however, was the rising level of competition due to the breakdown of restrictive agreements by legislation, the invasion of foreign investment, especially American, and changes in international trade. These factors each served to influence the distribution and scale

---

[48] R. E. Caves, et al., *Britain's Economic Prospects*, pp. 42–43; see also A. Madison, *Economic Growth in the West*, W. W. Norton, Inc., New York, 1967, p. 115; J. C. R. Dow, *The Management of the British Economy, 1945–60*, Cambridge University Press, 1964, pp. 210–11, 391; *Report on the Working of the Monetary System*, Cmnd. 827, H.M.S.O., 1959, paragraph 472.

of British manufacturing industry. Concentration and rationalization, delayed by restrictions on competition, occurred with increasing rapidity during the 1960s, increasing the relative importance of the largest enterprises.

The strategy of an enterprise evolves in response to and in anticipation of trends in its environment. The trends discussed in this chapter were frequently observed in the strategic development of the largest British enterprises. For some, certain influences were more important than others, but the most common cause of strategic change was clearly from pressures within the marketplace which transformed the pattern of competitive advantage. In turn, strategic changes frequently brought structural transformation, and the magnitude and characteristics of these changes, the identification and analysis of which form the bulk of this study, have significant implications for policy makers in both industry and government.

CHAPTER 3

Diversification and Divisionalization

INTRODUCTION

THIS CHAPTER INTRODUCES AND ANALYZES the company data in terms of the development of diversified corporations and their corresponding organization structures. The companies are first introduced and classified, as of the beginning of 1970, by the degree of diversification and organization structure exhibited. Companies were assigned into the relevant categories of product-market diversity and structure previously defined in Chapter 1.

The changes that have taken place in the population over time are examined by observation of the transitions of companies between the diversification categories and the changing numbers of companies adopting some form of multidivisional structure. Comparison of the population has been made at three points in time, 1950, 1960, and 1970. A further comparison has been made with a similar breakdown of the population of the largest 100 manufacturing companies measured by asset value as of 1953, the earliest year for which such a list was available. This comparison illustrates the similarity between the 1970 population as it was in 1950, and the population of the largest firms at about that time. In any event, the present-day largest concerns in the early 1970s were slightly more diversified in 1950 than were the largest 100 companies in 1953.

In addition to an examination of the static scene at each of three points in time, a detailed study has also been made of the dynamics of strategic and structural transitions between the three static review points. This analysis highlights the main types of transitions that occurred, especially the growth of the diversified enterprise and the widespread adoption of the multidivisional organization structure. The results also raise some questions regarding the dominant product companies which are the subject of brief discussion.

Some observations have been made on the role played by family-controlled companies over this time period. Their degree of diversity and the degree of adoption of the multidivisional structure have been examined in some detail.

An examination has also been made of the overseas market diversification by that group of English companies which have become multinational concerns. The distribution of the assets of the major British companies operating internationally has been examined by industry and by geographic dispersal to determine which industries have invested overseas and where the investments have been made. In addition, the structural forms adopted by these multinational companies have been examined. A test has been made of the boundaries in terms of size and diversity of foreign operations suggested by Stopford (see Chapter 1, footnote 18), with comments on the findings.

The chapter concludes with a brief comparison of the differences between the development of British large-scale corporate enterprise in the early 1970s and its United States counterpart as examined by Wrigley (see Chapter 1, footnote 6).

THE LARGEST BRITISH INDUSTRIAL ENTERPRISES

The population examined was the largest 100 manufacturing companies by sales volume operating or registered in Great Britain, taken from the *Times* 500 list of 1969–70. The *Times* list was modified in three main respects. First, those companies which did not qualify as manufacturing companies as defined in Chapter 1 were excluded—a total of some 50 companies engaged in retailing, shipping, or other nonmanufacturing activities. The smallest company included was the 147th company, according to the *Times* list, with sales of £64 million ($154 million [1]). Second, the *Times* list excluded two international companies, Nestle and Phillips, which had U.K. subsidiaries of sufficient size to justify inclusion, and these companies were, therefore, added. Third, the list was corrected for mergers which took place during 1969 and companies such as General Electric Company/English Electric were treated as a single corporate entity.

The sample population thus chosen was classified into four classes of product-market diversity, namely: single product, dominant product, related product, and unrelated product, as defined in Chapter 1. Those companies with foreign parents were classified according to the product-market scope of the parent company but the list of products manufactured included only those produced in the United Kingdom.

The organization structure of each company was classified into four main structural classes, namely: functional—F.; holding company (H.C.); multiproduct divisions (M.D.); and multigeographic divisions (M.G.), as previously defined. Those companies with multinational (M) manufacturing operations in six or more overseas countries were further classified according to the organization of their overseas operations into the above categories where applicable or into additional categories, such as multiproduct/international divisions (M.D./I); multiproduct/multigeographic divisions (M.D./M.G.). Companies with foreign-owned parents were classified according to the organization structure of the parent company rather than that of the British subsidiary. There were a small number of cases where a form of

---

[1] The prevailing official sterling exchange rate of £ = $2.40 was adopted. This made the companies examined of near-equivalent size and range to the *Fortune* 500 U.S. companies.

hybrid structure occurred indicating a state of transition. In these cases the direction of the change was used in classifying the structural form.

The results of this classification are shown in Table 3-1 which lists the sample companies according to the diversification class into which they fall, indicates the organization structure, foreign or domestic ownership, and multinational status. Two companies which had Anglo-Dutch parents, namely, the Royal Dutch Shell Group and the Unilever Group, were treated as British in view of their close connections with the United Kingdom and despite the fact that their shareholders were partly Dutch.

TABLE 3–1

THE 100 LARGEST BRITISH MANUFACTURING ENTERPRISES, 1969–70

Product	Structure	Sales (1969–70) (Millions of Pounds)	Products
SINGLE PRODUCT			
British American Tobacco (M)	M.G.	1,467[a]	*Tobacco products* (97%) perfumery and cosmetics, packaging, foods.
British Sugar	F.	64	*Beet sugar.*
Carreras—F.	H.C.	132	*Tobacco products.*
International Computers	F.	115	*Electronic computers* and data processing equipment.
International Distillers and Vintners (M)[b]	F./H.C.	100	*Wine and spirits*, manufacture and distribution.
Watney Mann[c]	F.	144	*Brewing*, public houses, hotels, entertainments.
DOMINANT PRODUCT			
Metals and Materials			
Alcan Aluminium (F.M.)	F.	67	*Aluminium*, mining, refining, fabricating.
Associated Portland Cement (M)	F.	145	*Cement*, cement products, sand, and gravel.

KEY: F. = Functional.
    M.D. = Multidivisional by product.
    M.G. = Multidivisional by geography.
    M.D./I = Multiproduct divisions plus an international division.
    M.D./M.G. = Multidivisional by product and geography.
    H.C. = Holding company.
    (M) = Multinational—the definition of "multinational" used here is that the company must possess six or more manufacturing subsidiaries overseas.
    (F.) = Subsidiary company controlled by a non-British parent company. In these cases the product range shown is that of the British subsidiary or subsidiaries while the structure shown is that of the parent company.

NOTE: Two companies, Shell and Unilever, have been treated as British companies in the analysis, but in fact are both Anglo-Dutch owned.

a Including excise duty on tobacco goods.
b IDV has since been acquired by Watney Mann.
c Watney Mann (including IDV) has since been acquired by Grand Metropolitan Hotels.

Table 3–1 (Continued)   53

Product	Structure	Sales (1969–70) (Millions of Pounds)	Products
British Insulated Callenders Cables (M)	M.D.	404	Refining and processing of nonferrous metals, capacitors, insulated, power, supertension and winding wires, telephone and general cables, electric power cable contracting.
British Steel Corporation (M)	M.D./I		*Iron and steel*, special steels, steel strip, tubes, construction engineering, chemicals.
Johnson Matthey (M)	H.C.	148	Refiners and dealers in *precious metals*, rare earth extraction, colors, glazes, transfers, copper alloys.
Pilkington Bros. (M)	M.D.	98	*Flat glass*, safety glass, fiberglass, optical glass, pressed glass.
Ready Mix Concrete (M)	M.G.	126	*Ready-mixed concrete*, aggregates, precast concrete claybricks, roofs and suspended ceilings, fuel distribution, plant hire, builders merchants.
Drink			
Bass Charrington	M.G.	315	*Brewing*, soft drinks, public houses, wine and spirit distribution, hotels.
Courage Barclay[d]	M.G.	115	*Brewing*, public houses, wine and spirit distribution, whiskey blending.
Distillers	H.C.	382	*Whiskey and other spirits*, glass containers, yeast, canned foods, carbon dioxide.
Guinness	H.C.	163	*Brewing*, confectionery, pharmaceuticals, soft drinks, plastic moldings.
Scottish & Newcastle	H.C.	117	*Brewing*, public houses, hotels, whiskey distilling
Whitbread	M.G.	174	*Brewing*, public houses, soft drinks, wines, and spirits distribution.
Food			
Farmers Meat Company	M.D.	133	*Meat slaughter and distribution*, poultry, bacon, sau-

[d] Courage Barclay has since been acquired by Imperial Tobacco.

Product	Structure	Sales (1969–70) (*Millions of Pounds*)	Products
			sages, fellmongery and by-products.
Rowntree Mackintosh	M.D./I	113	*Confectionery products*, biscuits, dessert and snack foods, pickles.
Tate and Lyle (M)	M.D.	228	*Sugar production and refining*, molasses trading, alcohol distillation and trading, sugar machinery, concrete building blocks.
United Biscuits	H.C.	83	*Biscuits*, snack foods, prepacked cakes, bakeries, and retail outlets.
Tobacco			
Gallaher—F.(M)	H.C.	447	*Tobacco products.*
Imperial Tobacco	M.D.	1,120[a]	*Tobacco products*, paper board and packaging, canned foods, snack foods, frozen foods, poultry, seafoods, sauces.
Oil			
British Petroleum (M)	M.D.	2,243	*Petroleum products*, distribution, petrochemicals natural gas.
Burmah Oil (M)	M.D.	243	*Petroleum products*, distribution, oil additives, retail car accessories, wax blending, building products.
Esso Petroleum—F.(M)	M.D.	563	*Petroleum products*, distribution, petrochemicals.
Shell Transport and Trading (M) (Royal Dutch Shell Group)	M.D.	2,352	*Petroleum products*, distribution, natural gas, petrochemicals, nonferrous metals
Power Machinery			
British Aircraft Corporation	M.D.	184	*Civil and military aircraft*, aerospace engineering.
British Leyland Motors (M)	M.D./I	970	*Automobiles*, trucks, buses, construction equipment, foundry products, and general engineering.
Chrysler U.K.—F.(M)	M.D./I	165	*Automobiles*, trucks.
Ford Motor—F.(M)	M.D./I	488	*Automobiles*, trucks, tractors.
Massey-Ferguson—F.(M)	M.D.		*Tractors* and agricultural machinery, engines, indus-

Table 3–1 (Continued)   **55**

Product	Structure	Sales (1969–70) (Millions of Pounds)	Products
			trial and construction equipment, leisure equipment.
Rolls-Royce	M.D.	299	*Civil and military aero engines*, industrial diesel and locomotive engines, automobiles.
Swan Hunter	M.D.	86	*Shipbuilding*, marine engineering, and ship repairing.
Vauxhall Motors—F.(M)	M.D./I	204	*Automobiles*, trucks.
Other			
British Printing Corporation	H.C.	69	*Printing*, periodicals, books, packaging products, chain libraries.
Burton Group	F.	68	*Men's tailoring* and retailing, women's fashion retailing.
International Business Machines (U.K.)—F.(M)	M.D./I	125	*Computers*, office equipment, typewriters, time clocks.
RELATED PRODUCT			
Drink			
Allied Breweries	M.D./I	346	Brewing, public houses, hotels, wines and spirits distribution, wine, cider, soft drinks.
Food			
Associated British Foods	M.D./I	503	Flourmilling, bakeries, packaged cakes, biscuits, tea, coffee, animal feeds, snack foods, retail and wholesale food distribution.
Brooke Bond Liebig (M)	M.G.	209	Tea growing, packing and distribution, meat extracts, canned meats, seafoods, sauces, wholesale meat, cheese.
Cadbury/Schweppes (M)	M.D./I	262	Confectionery, cakes, soft drinks, preserves, canned foods, convenience foods.
H. J. Heinz—F.(M)	M.G.	72	Soups, babyfoods, sauces, convenience foods, dairy products.
J. Lyons	M.D.	155	Bakery products, packaged cakes, tea, coffee, ice

Table 3–1 (Continued)

Product	Structure	Sales (1969–70) (Millions of Pounds)	Products
			cream, restaurants, hotels, food franchising.
Mars (F)	M.D.	97	Confectionery products, canned petfoods.
Nestle (F.M.)	M.G.	76	Milk products, instant coffee, chocolate and sugar confectionery, soup mixes, canned vegetables and convenience foods, infant cereals, seasonings, instant drinks.
Rank Hovis McDougall (M)	M.D./I	359	Flourmilling, bakeries, packaged cakes, seasonings, packaged flour, petfoods, breakfast foods, pastes and spreads, animal feedstuffs, agricultural merchandizing.
Spillers	M.D.	174	Flourmilling, bakeries, packaged cakes, retail distribution, animal feedstuffs, wholesale meat, spices, wire products.
Unigate	M.D./I	301	Milk processing, wholesale and retail distribution, ice cream, cheese, dairy products, infant foods, wholesale and retail food distribution, retail fashion stores, reinforced plastics, garage management.
Unilever (M) (Anglo-Dutch)	Grid	1,145	Edible fats and oils, soaps and detergents, animal feedstuffs, ice cream, packaged foods, dairy products, frozen foods, toiletries, seafoods and meat products, chemicals, packaging, retail distribution.
Chemicals			
Albright and Wilson (M)	M.D./M.G.	121	Phosphorus and phosphorus chemicals, detergent intermediates, plasticizers, silicones, flavors and essences, fine chemicals, cosmetics.

Table 3–1 (Continued)   57

Product	Structure	Sales (1969–70) (Millions of Pounds)	Products
British Oxygen (M)	M.D./H.C.	161	Oxygen, industrial gases, vacuum equipment, engineering products, chemicals, melamine resins, cryogenics, gas welding equipment, food products.
Dunlop Rubber (M)[e]	M.D.	495	Tires, wheels, precision rubbers, foam rubber and plastic, brakes, aviation accessories, hose, suspensions, belting, general rubber products, plantations, sports goods, footwear, flooring materials, tire distribution.
Fisons (M)	M.D./I	82	Fertilizers, agricultural and horticultural chemicals, chemical intermediates, foods, pharmaceuticals.
Imperial Chemical Industries (M)	M.D./M.G.	1,355	Inorganic and organic chemicals, fertilizers and agricultural chemicals, synthetic fibers, dyestuffs, paints and wall coverings, explosives, pharmaceuticals, nonferrous metals.

Pharmaceuticals and Toiletries

Product	Structure	Sales	Products
Beecham Products (M)	M.D./M.G.	161	Ethical, veterinary and proprietary pharmaceuticals, cosmetics and toiletries, health foods and drinks, soft drinks, animal feedstuffs.
Glaxo (M)	H.C.	140	Ethical and proprietary pharmaceuticals, infant foods, laboratory chemicals, medical equipment, · drug wholesaling.
Wellcome Foundation (M)	H.C.	75	Ethical pharmaceuticals, veterinary products, chemicals, household products, industrial and animal nutrition products, hospital equipment.

Metals and Minerals

Product	Structure	Sales	Products
Rio Tinto Zinc (M)	M.G.	338	Metals and minerals, mining and refining, chemicals,

[e] Dunlop has since merged with Pirelli to form Dunlop-Pirelli.

Table 3–1 (Continued)

Product	Structure	Sales (1969–70) (Millions of Pounds)	Products
			steel, hydroelectric power, metal fabricating, and stockholding.
Turner & Newall (M)	H.C.	113	Asbestos mining and distribution, brake linings, asbestos cement and building products, belting, insulation, asbestos textiles, glass fiber, gaskets, plastic molding powders, synthetic resins.

Materials and Glass

Product	Structure	Sales (1969–70) (Millions of Pounds)	Products
Marley Tile (M)	F.	71	Concrete roof tiles, concrete fabrications, P.V.C. flooring, plastic extrusions, foam plastic moldings, carpets, retail stores.
Tarmac Derby	M.D./I	113	Roadstone, coated aggregate, asphalt, stone powder, civil and process engineering, contracting, bitumen, roofing felt, mining equipment, malleable castings, concrete products.

Engineering
Heavy Engineering

Product	Structure	Sales (1969–70) (Millions of Pounds)	Products
Babcock and Wilcox (M)	H.C.	104	Steam generating plant, heat exchangers, chemical and metallurgical plant contracting, construction equipment, truck mixers, road rollers, earth moving equipment, shell boilers, air heaters, valves, castings and forgings, bulk handling systems.
John Brown	H.C.	78	Machine tools, cutting and hand tools, plastic processing machinery, vehicle bodies, heavy chemical engineering and contracting.
Guest Keen & Nettlefolds (M)	M.D./H.C.	512	Steel, rolled and bright steel, screws and fastener bolts and nuts, machine tools, plastic machinery, brewery machinery, automatic vending machines, auto components and

Table 3–1 (*Continued*)   **59**

Product	Structure	Sales (1969–70) (Millions of Pounds)	Products
			transmissions, castings and forgings, building supplies, store fittings.
Hawker Siddeley Group	H.C.	402	Civil and military aircraft, guided missiles, automatic vending machines, navigation and guidance systems, electrical engineering, alloy extrusions and castings, diesel engines, compressors, agricultural machinery, road tankers, sewage treatment plant, power stations, railway rolling stock, steel fabrications.
Henry Simon	M.D.	75	Flourmilling and food machinery, heavy industrial machinery, pneumatic and mechanical bulk handling contracting, chemical engineering contracting, boiler and oven plant, antipollution plant, hydraulic platforms.
Tube Investments (M)	M.D./I	294	Steel tubes, cycles, gas and solid fuel appliances, machine tools, flexible tubes, auto components, spring making and grinding machinery, bending and shearing machinery, electrical components, domestic appliances, lighting equipment, primary aluminium, extrusions and fabrication.
Vickers (M)	M.D.	166	Shipbuilding, heavy engineering, armaments, forgings and castings, printing machinery, office duplicating equipment and furniture, chemical engineering.
Light Engineering			
Associated Engineering	M.D./I	90	Bearings, pistons, engine components, machine tools, castings and auto components.

Table 3–1 (Continued)

Product	Structure	Sales (1969–70) (Millions of Pounds)	Products
Birmid Qualcast	M.D.	72	Automotive and aircraft castings, foundry products, wrought metal products, lawnmowers, agricultural irrigation equipment, plastic products, kitchen furniture and household appliances.
Delta Metal (M)	M.D./I	172	Refined, rolled and drawn nonferrous metals, brass and copper rods, sections, castings, electric cables, water fittings, turned components.
Joseph Lucas (M)	M.D.	251	Auto and aircraft electrical accessories and components, electronic components, servo controls, brake systems, hydraulics, precision engineering.
Smiths Industries	M.D./I	67	Instruments and controls for autos, aircraft, marine, industrial and domestic appliances, auto accessories, spark plugs, industrial ceramics, clocks and watches, building supplies.

Electrical and Electronic Engineering

Electrical and Musical Industries (M)	M.D./M.G.	176	Records, music publishing, cinemas, T.V. and cinema, films, T.V. entertainments, magnetic tape, record players, industrial and defense electronics, hearing aids, record stores, fire alarms and fire prevention equipment, microwave and power tubes.
General Electric/ English Electric (M)	M.D./M.G.	898	Electronics, telecommunications systems, automation and telemetry, electric power engineering, diesel engines, electrical components, cable and wire domestic appliances.
Plessey (M)	M.D./M.G.	179	Radar, telecommunications, electronic compo-

Table 3–1 (Continued)

61

Product	Structure	Sales (1969–70) (Millions of Pounds)	Products
			nents, record players, aerospace equipment, numerically controlled machine tools.
Phillips (U.K.)—F.(M)	M.D.	152	Radio and T.V. sets, telecommunications, electronics, control systems, instruments, domestic appliances, T.V. equipment, radar systems.
Reyrolle Parsons (M)	H.C.	84	Turbine generators, transformers, rotating plant, switchgear, light engineering, instruments, high voltage bushings.
Thorn Electric (M)	M.D.	267	T.V. sets, radio production and rental, domestic appliances, lighting products, heating systems, general engineering.
Textiles and Clothing			
Carrington & Dewhurst[f]	H.C.	69	Natural and synthetic fiber processing and finishing, woven and knitted fabrics, men's and women's clothing, industrial fabrics, textile engineering.
Coats Patons (M)	H.C.	268	Industrial and retail knitting yarn and thread production, knitwear and clothing, precision die castings, retail yarn and garment distribution.
Courtaulds (M)	M.D./H.C.	627	Rayon and synthetic fibers, textile processing, household textiles, hosiery and clothing, textile wholesaling, paints, plastics, chemicals, chemical and textile engineering, packaging films and materials.
English Calico (M)	M.D./H.C.	152	Thread, textile fiber processing, fabrics, household textiles, knitwear and garments, retail clothing and textiles.

[f] Carrington and Dewhurst and Viyella International have now been acquired by I.C.I. forming a new company Carrington Viyella.

Table 3–1 (Continued)

Product	*Structure*	*Sales (1969–70)* *(Millions of Pounds)*	*Products*
Viyella International[f]	M.D.	76	Natural and synthetic fiber processing, woven and knitted fabrics, household textiles, men's and women's clothing.
Paper and Packaging			
Bowater (M)	H.C.	268	Pulp, newsprint, general packaging, coated papers, tissue products.
Dickinson Robinson (M)	M.D./I	124	Paper and board, stationery, general packaging, bulk packaging, plastic film, gummed paper and adhesive tapes, packaging machinery, mechanical handling plant.
Metal Box (M)	M.D./I	194	Cans, metal containers, paper and plastics packaging, packaging machinery.
Reed Paper (M)[g]	M.D./I	314	Pulp, paper and board, packaging, stationery, wrapping and specialty papers, wall coverings, paints, retail and wholesale paint and wall covering distribution, building products, plastic extrusions, paint brushes, cellulose fillers, household textiles.
Wiggins Teape (M)[h]	M.D./M.G.	116	Speciality papers, packaging, stationery, carbonless copy paper.
International Publishing Corporation (M)[i]	M.D.	156	Newspapers, magazines, business publications, exhibitions, book publishing, printing.
Thomson Organisation (M)	M.D.	95	Newspapers, magazines, publishing, directories, exhibitions, general printing, package tour operations.
UNRELATED PRODUCT			
Rank Organisation	M.D.	237	Movie production and distribution, cinemas, hotels,

[g] The name of this group has been changed to Reed International.
[h] Wiggins Teape has been acquired by British American Tobacco.
[i] International Publishing Corporation has been acquired by Reed Paper.

Table 3–1 (Continued)   63

Product	Structure	Sales (1969–70) (Millions of Pounds)	Products
			dance halls, gambling clubs, bowling alleys, scientific instruments, electronics, T.V.s and radios, xerographic equipment and distribution.
Reckitt & Coleman (M)	M.D./M.G.	157	Ethical and proprietary pharmaceuticals, toiletries, mustard, soft drinks, shoe polish and accessories, household polishes, cleaners and disinfectants, blueing agents, convenience foods, industrial polishes and equipment.
Sears Holdings	H.C.	277	Footwear production and retailing, department stores, hosiery and machinery, mining quarrying and contractors plants, industrial pumps, electric transformers, pipework fabrication and installation, automobile distribution, jewelry stores, laundries, knitwear.
Slater Walker Securities[j]	M.D.	92	Investment banking, unit trusts, insurance, rubber goods, optical products and retail opticians, window frames and building products, textiles, engineering, tanning extract.
Standard Telephones & Cables—F.(M)	M.D./M.G.	107	Electronics, telecommunications, aerospace components, cables T.V. and appliances, insurance, car hire.
Thomas Tilling	H.C.	190	Laboratory glassware, oven glass, hosiery, printing, aerosol products, light engineering, insurance, building materials, builder merchants, electrical wholesaling, automobile distribution.

[j] Slater Walker Securities has since divested its industrial operations and is now a financial services corporation.

Examination of Table 3-1 reveals that, by 1970, 94 percent of the population had diversified to some degree and 60 percent of the companies had moved into the related or nonrelated product classes. In terms of structure, some form of multidivisional structure was the predominant organizational form, being found in 71 percent of the population. There were a number of variations of this structure which in large part depended on the degree of overseas activity of the parent company. Four main variants were examined of which the most common was the multiproduct-division structure of which there were 30 examples. There were 32 examples of multiproduct divisional variants where, in addition to product divisions, some form of geographic divisionalization also occurred. There were 22 cases of a domestic product-division structure with an additional international division and 9 cases of a multiproduct/multigeographic form. Only one example of a "grid" structure was observed where both product and geographic responsibilities were clearly divided. Finally, 9 examples of purely multigeographic divisional structures were observed which tended to be either regional breakdowns of the domestic market or breakdowns of world markets. This type of structure was more commonly found associated with a low degree of diversification, for example, in brewing, cement, and tobacco companies, but a number of multinational concerns exhibiting quite high product diversity maintained this form.

The population contained 14 companies with non-British parents of which 9 were American, 2 Canadian, 1 Swiss, 1 South African, and 1 Dutch in origin. This number excluded the two Anglo-Dutch companies and also excluded Associated British Foods and the Thomson Organisation. The majority of the shares in Associated British Foods were held indirectly by the Weston family; similarly the majority of the shares in the Thomson Organisation were held by the Thomson family. Both these families were Canadian but were domiciled in Great Britain, and the British companies were not directly linked to other holdings the families held in Canada. They were, therefore, treated as British companies.

These foreign-owned companies had nearly all adopted a multidivisional structural form; only 3, Alcan, Carreras and Gallaher, having nondivisional parent structures. Two of these companies, both in tobacco, had been acquired relatively recently by their new parents and were still single product companies in the United Kingdom. The parent concerns were also basically tobacco companies, although American Brands Inc. (formerly American Tobacco) had recently diversified somewhat and some 20 percent of sales were in nontobacco products. Alcan also retained a functional structure although its marketing operations were divided into geographical divisions. The remaining 11 companies were multidivisional and, with the exception of Massey-Ferguson, had been so for some time. Eight of the 14 companies were categorized as dominant product and, apart from Alcan and American Brands, consisted of the big three U.S. automobile manufacturers (Ford, General Motors, and Chrysler); one oil company (Standard Oil); an agricultural equipment manufacturer (Massey-Ferguson); and International Business Machines, a company where the growth of one product line converted a diversified company into a dominant product firm. These foreign-owned companies were mainly multinational in their operations, only two failing to manufacture in at least six countries.

The British resident companies also reflected a high degree of multinational activity, 50 of them having manufacturing operations in at least 6 countries. The more diversified companies had a greater tendency to operate overseas also, and

74 percent of the British related products companies were multinational compared with 42 percent of the dominant product companies and two of the five single product companies. There were six nonrelated product companies in the population and only two of these were multinational. However, both Slater Walker and Sears Holdings were increasing their geographic spread, and the Xerox division of Rank Organisation did operate extensively outside the United Kingdom. A small number of companies, while adopting a multidivisional structure in the domestic market, still maintained a holding-company structure for their overseas subsidiaries.

The largest British companies had by 1970, therefore, largely become diversified both by product and geography mainly into areas of related activity to their original chosen product-market scope. Further, they had tended to adopt a multidivisional structural form in managing the diversified enterprise. The process over time whereby this situation came about was considered and the results are dealt with below.

THE EVOLUTION OF STRATEGY AND STRUCTURE

Analysis of the change in product-market strategy and organization structures over the period 1950–70 was made to test the following hypotheses restated from Chapter 1:

(1) There would be an increasing proportion of the population with diversified product/market scope during the period with a corresponding decline in the number of single product companies.

(2) Companies having adopted a diversified product/market scope would tend to undergo subsequent structural transformation from a functional to a form of multidivisional organization.

(3) The correlation between diversified product/market scope and multidivisional structures would increase over the period under investigation.

The first of the above propositions implied that a substantial shift should have occurred over the period from less to more diversified enterprises. In terms of the four categories of diversification in which companies were classified, the main transitions which were expected to occur are indicated by the arrows in Figure 3.1.

FIGURE 3.1

THE EXPECTED ROUTE OF CORPORATE DEVELOPMENT

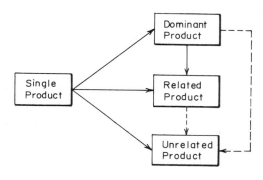

The second proposition indicated a relationship between product-market strategy and organization structure which suggested that, with increasing diversity, structural change would occur with functional structures being superseded by other structures particularly the multidivisional form, the latter being split into divisions by product, by geography, or by some combination of both.

The third proposition implied that diversification would ultimately lead to widespread adoption of the multidivisional form as the specific organizational choice to manage the diversified enterprise and that this form would gradually supersede other forms. The correlation between the numbers of diversified concerns and those with a multidivisional structure was thus expected to increase over time.

In order to test the above propositions, the companies were classified at three specific points in time, 1950, 1960, and 1970, according to product-market diversity and organizational structure. Data were available on a total of 92 companies for the entire period 1950–70 and for 96 companies for the period 1960–70. The data were incomplete for all or part of the period basically because some companies were not operating in the United Kingdom over this period; this restriction applied to British Aircraft Corporation, British Printing Corporation, British Steel Corporation, Farmers Meat Company, Ready Mix Concrete and Slater Walker. British Steel Corporation represented an unusual case of the amalgamation of 14 major steel companies by nationalization. Therefore, British Steel was excluded from the sample before its formation, since it was considered that the earlier substitution of one or more of its constituents would be unrealistic. One company, Viyella International, was excluded for the period 1950–60, since the present company did not possess a logical antecedent. The Wellcome Foundation was also excluded for lack of data until 1967, since this company as a charity was not required to make a full annual return until the 1965 Companies Act came into effect.

For comparison purposes, using the same classification, an analysis was made of the largest British-owned or operating manufacturing companies as of 1953 as measured by assets (sales figures were not mandatory under British company law until 1965). This list was drawn from a classified list of large companies drawn up by the National Institute of Economic and Social Research (N.I.E.S.R.) [2] and provided the earliest known suitable list available.

The results of this analysis are shown in Table 3-2 which indicates the number and percentage of the total of companies in each category of diversification and the number and percentage of the number of companies in a diversification category with a multidivisional organization structure. This table reveals that significant change took place in the two decades between 1950 and 1970.

The N.I.E.S.R. listing of the largest 100 British manufacturing companies as measured by assets was roughly similar in degree of diversification to that of the *Times* population as of 1950. This was not altogether surprising, since some 60 of the companies were common to both lists. The N.I.E.S.R. sample was on balance slightly less diversified, a factor basically explained by the inclusion of the major steel companies. These were still in private hands in 1953 and tended to be either dominant product or single product companies. These companies were all combined into the British Steel Corporation in the *Times* population allowing perhaps the in-

---

[2] N.I.E.S.R., *A Classified List of Large Companies Engaged in British Industry 1955.*

TABLE 3-2

Diversification and Multidivisional Structure, 1950–70

	N.I.E.S.R. Sample		Col. 3		1950		Col. 3		1960		Col. 3		1970		Col. 3	
	Col. 1 No.	Col. 2 %	No. with M.D. Structure	Col. 4 % of Col. 1	Col. 1 No.	Col. 2 %	No. with M.D. Structure	Col. 4 % of Col. 1	Col. 1 No.	Col. 2 %	No. with M.D. Structure	Col. 4 % of Col. 1	Col. 1 No.	Col. 2 %	No. with M.D. Structure	Col. 4 % of Col. 1
Category																
Single Product	33	34	1	3	31	34	2	6	18	20	1	6	6	6	1	17
Dominant Product	43	45	3	7	38	41	4	11	35	35	8	23	34	34	24	70
Related Product	19	20	4	21	21	23	6	29	39	41	19	49	54	54	43	78
Unrelated Product	1	1	0	0	2	2	0	0	4	4	1	25	6	6	4	67
Total	96ᵃ	100	8	8	92	100	12	13	96	100	29	30	100	100	72	72

(The N.I.E.S.R. Sample occupies the first group of columns; the three groups headed 1950, 1960, and 1970 are the Times 500 Sample.)

ᵃ Data unavailable on four companies.

clusion of a number of more diversified concerns. By 1970, over 30 percent of the N.I.E.S.R sample had been acquired by or merged with other companies which appeared in the *Times 500* sample. It is perhaps significant that this mortality rate was highest among the dominant product companies where 17 were acquired, followed by the absorption of 10 single product companies. Only three related product companies were acquired. This small evidence suggests the relative staying power of the related product companies.

The constitution of both samples thus indicated that in 1950 the corporate population was composed largely of companies exhibiting relatively little diversification and only about a quarter were classified as diversified. The largest single category was then the dominant product category in both cases, representing 45 percent of the N.I.E.S.R. companies and 41 percent of the *Times* companies. Single product concerns formed the second largest category, being 34 percent in both cases. Unrelated diversification was almost unknown in both lists, only one case being found in the N.I.E.S.R. companies and the same company plus one other in the *Times* set. The *Times* population thus probably reflects fairly accurately the makeup of large-scale British industry over the period in terms of its degree of diversification. The large numbers of dominant product companies suggested that some modest degree of diversification had been adopted long before 1950, and that many of the population found in this category might be expected to move on beyond it to increased diversification. The 1970 population was, however, somewhat more diversified than would have been the case if the sample had been taken in 1967 before the vesting of British Steel Corporation, which removed 14 dominant product companies and replaced them with a single dominant product concern.

One further comparison between the largest companies shown in the N.I.E.S.R. population for 1953 and the 1970 population is of interest. An examination was made of the net asset distribution by class for both groups. This revealed some changes in order of magnitude between the classes. In 1950 the dominant product class represented 43.6 percent of the net assets and 45 percent numerically of the population. In 1970 this group still represented 47 percent of the net assets despite a decline in the numbers to 34 percent of the population. In 1950 the related product companies represented only 20 percent of the population by number but 28.4 percent of net assets. By 1970 this class was numerically the greatest with 54 percent of the population, but represented only 44.6 percent of net assets—slightly less than the dominant product group. The single product group declined from 28.4 percent of net assets to 4.1 percent confirming the substantial numerical decline, while the unrelated group rose from 0.6 to 4.3 percent of net assets.

This suggested that some at least of the dominant product group were very stable in their degree of diversity and also very large in terms of assets invested. The group might well represent "heavy" companies in capital intensive industries which do indeed exhibit different properties to the more diversified companies. Table 3–1 reveals that these companies fell mainly within the power machinery, oil, and drink industries, which all conform to the proposition of high capital intensity (in the case of the drink companies, heavy capital investment was basically in distribution, property assets, or stocks, not manufacturing, plant, and equipment).

The multidivisional structural form was almost unknown in British companies in 1950 being found in only 8 percent of the N.I.E.S.R. concerns and in a slightly higher 13 percent of the *Times* companies. It was found mainly in the related product companies, in 22 percent of the N.I.E.S.R. group and in 29 percent of the *Times* companies. Despite the large numbers of dominant product companies, very few had adopted the multidivisional structure—7 percent of companies in the N.I.E.S.R. sample and 11 percent in the *Times* companies. Further, 8 of the 12 companies in the *Times* list using a multidivisional structure were foreign owned, mainly with U.S. parents, and one of the indigenous companies was Unilever, the multinational, Anglo-Dutch concern. There did not appear to have been as many great organization innovators in the British industrial system as Chandler had found emerging in the 1920s and 1930s in the United States. The failure of British companies to either develop or import the multidivisional form may perhaps be attributed to the relative protection and isolation of the British environment in the interwar period.

The predominant structures to be found in British industry in 1950 were, therefore, either functional systems or the loosely held holding-company structure both of which were to be found in all classes of diversification. The holding-company form was, however, mainly associated with a degree of diversification, although some loose associations of companies manufacturing the same product were observed.

The situation in 1960 indicated that considerable change occurred during the 1950s. The largest single category of product-market diversification was by now the related product group representing 41 percent of the total. An additional 18 companies had diversified to the related product category. The four additional companies on which data became available by 1960 were either single or dominant product companies.

The number of dominant product companies actually showed little decline, which could tend to indicate stability in this class of company. Or, it could indicate loss by diversification of some number of companies which were largely replaced by additions from single product companies that had partially diversified. Wrigley implied that these companies were essentially stable in that one major product line continuously dominated attempts to diversify, as was the case in the American automobile or oil companies.

Considerable decline occurred in the number of single product concerns which fell to 19 percent of the sample. An actual reduction of from 31 to 15 companies occurred; this was disguised by the addition of three of the four new entering companies falling into this category.

The number of unrelated product companies remained extremely small although a small increase did occur, the numbers increasing from two companies to four.

There was a considerable expansion in the number of companies adopting a multidivisional structure, and 30 percent of the total population had such a structure. In the individual product-market categories, 49 percent of the related product, and 23 percent of the dominant product companies had found and adopted a multidivisional organization. Some of the new adopters were still in a transitional phase, where the multidivisional structure was somewhat of a hybrid form frequently containing elements of a prior functional form represented in particular by the presence of a line marketing function at board level. The structure was also not adopted in a random fashion, but concentration occurred by industry, the structure appearing first in the electrical and chemical industries, two of the earliest diversified industries.

The situation in 1970 represented further considerable gains in the numbers of diversified companies and a decline in the number of single product companies. The related product company had become the major corporate form, with 54 percent of the total. The dominant product category remained very stable, declining only slightly to 34 percent. The number of single product companies again fell heavily and by 1970 represented a mere 6 percent of the population. Little growth, however, was observed in the number of unrelated companies, thus reflecting the failure of any manufacturing industry conglomerate movement to appear in the United Kingdom during the 1960s.

The growth of the multidivisional structure was even more dramatic; it more than doubled in 10 years. By 1970 this structure was clearly the dominant organizational form: 72 percent of all corporations had adopted it; the functional structure was essentially confined to concerns with little or no diversification; and the holding-company structures also exhibited sharp decline. These results clearly tended to support the initial hypothesis, but at the same time as they revealed dramatic change over time, they raised several questions concerning the dynamics of the change. First, did companies move directly from a single product strategy to a related product strategy or did they pass through an intermediate dominant product stage? The sharp decline in single product companies from 34 percent in 1950 to 6 percent in 1970, coupled with relative stability among the dominant product group, which only declined from 40 percent to 34 percent, suggested the former route. Second, were all the structural changes that occurred during the 1960s coupled with a corresponding strategic change, or was there change independent of strategic change? The numbers of companies adopting the multidivisional form suggest that adoption of the multidivisional structure might be associated with the strategic change of the 1950s, or even earlier. This being the case it would provide valuable insights on time lags between strategic and structural change and would support Chandler's contention that structure follows strategy. These questions prompted the examination of the actual transitions that occurred in diversification strategy and organization structure during the two decades 1950–1960 and 1960–1970.

Transition matrixes were prepared for each of the two decades which depicted each of the following four possible states of nature:

- No change in diversification strategy or structure—this state would be expected to be the largest single state.
- Change in strategy with no change in structure—a significant number of such transitions would imply a long lag between strategic change and structural change.
- Change in structure with no change in strategy—a significant number would again indicate a lag between strategy and structure and the appearance of large numbers of transitions to the multidivisional form would support the third proposition.
- Change in both strategy and structure—the appearance of a large number of such observations predominantly in the direction of increased diversification and accompanied by adoption of the multidivisional structure would support the propositions.

In order to keep the number of variables within manageable limits, only three organization forms were included—the functional, holding-company, and multi-divisional structure. The multidivisional category thus contained both multiproduct, multigeographic, and combined forms of this structure, and transitions which might have occurred between one multidivisional form and another were discarded. The use of three organizational forms allowed the possibility of six transitions, together with three stable states. The four classes of diversification were used allowing a possible twelve transitions plus four stable states. In any event, the transitions from nonrelated company to any other class of diversification were discarded as being highly unlikely and, indeed, no such transitions occurred. The results of this analysis are shown in Tables 3–3 and 3–4.

Table 3–3 reveals that more than half the population of 92 companies under-went some form of transition over the period 1950–60. The 50 transitions that occurred involved 10 diversification transitions without a corresponding structural change; 21 structural changes without a diversification change; and 19 transitions involving a change in both diversification and structure.

All of the 29 strategic transitions, whether or not involving a structural change, were in the direction of increased diversification. There were 16 transitions by single product companies of which 9 were moves to the dominant product category, 6 to related product diversification and 1 to unrelated diversification. This implied that diversification took place gradually and that while there might be a number of stable dominant product companies, many such companies were merely being observed in an intermediate stage of diversification. The transitions by the domi-nant product companies tended to confirm this viewpoint. There were 13 such transitions, 12 of which were from dominant product to related product. There were no cases of transition by related product companies to a less diversified form or into the area of unrelated diversification.

The structural transitions revealed one major surprise. There were 40 such transitions of which 21 occurred without a significant change in diversification. This implied a long lag between strategic change and corresponding structural reform. Approximately half of the structural transitions involved adoption of a multidivi-sional structure, 13 by companies which did not increase in diversification and 7 by companies where the structural change was accompanied by a strategic transi-tion. For the 13 companies which adopted the multidivisional structure without in-creased diversification, 9 were related product companies. This indicated the dis-satisfaction of managing the diversified enterprise with either a functional or hold-ing-company structure and supported the proposition that the multidivisional form superseded other structures as an organizational form for managing the diversified enterprise.

At the beginning of the period in 1950 the predominant organizational form was the functional organization which was found in 52 of the 92 companies. During the 1950s, however, there were 31 transitions from the functional organization to either a holding-company or multidivisional structure. Fifteen of these transitions involved strategic changes while seven companies diversified yet retained their functional structure. The 16 transitions which did not involve a change in diversifi-cation strategy were mainly among companies which were already somewhat diver-sified, 8 of which adopted the multidivisional structure and 8 of which adopted the holding-company structure. By 1960 the predominant structure had become the

TABLE 3-3

DIVERSIFICATION AND STRUCTURAL TRANSITIONS, 1950–60

	No Change					Change in Strategy										Total
	S	D	R	N	Subtotal	S→D	S→R	S→N	D→S	D→R	D→N	R→S	R→D	R→N	Subtotal	
No Change																
F	9	4	1	0	14	4	1	0	0	2	0	0	0	0	7	21
H.C.	3	8	5	2	18	0	0	0	0	3	0	0	0	0	3	21
M.D.	1	3	6	0	10	0	0	0	0	0	0	0	0	0	0	10
Subtotal	13	15	12	2	42	4	1	0	0	5	0	0	0	0	10	52
Change in Structure																
F→H.C.	2	6	0	0	8	3	4	1	0	2	0	0	0	0	10	18
F→M.D.	0	2	6	0	8	1	0	0	0	4	0	0	0	0	5	13
H.C.→F	0	0	0	0	0	0	0	0	0	0	0	0	0	0	0	0
H.C.→M.D.	0	2	3	0	5	0	1	0	0	0	1	0	0	0	2	7
M.D.→F	0	0	0	0	0	1	0	0	0	0	0	0	0	0	1	1
M.D.→H.C.	0	0	0	0	0	0	0	0	0	1	0	0	0	0	1	1
Subtotal	2	10	9	0	21	5	5	1	0	7	1	0	0	0	19	40
Total	15	25	21	2	63	9	6	1	0	12	1	0	0	0	29	92

NOTE:

Structure

F = Functional structure
H.C. = Holding company structure
M.D. = Multidivisional structure
F→H.C. = Transition from functional to holding company structure, etc.

Diversification

S = Single product
D = Dominant product
R = Related product
N = Unrelated product
S→D = Transition from single product to dominant product, etc.

holding company and 40 companies had such a structure of which 35 were at least partially diversified and 18 were related or unrelated product diversified. In 1950 there had been 28 holding companies and, during the 1950s, 7 companies had changed from this structure all by adoption of the multidivisional form, but this loss was more than made up by the addition of 19 new companies which adopted a holding-company structure. This implied that much diversification was initiated by a process of acquisition leading to the formation of a functional/holding-company hybrid structure.

During the 1950s the predominant trends observed were of increased diversification, which was a gradual process accompanied in the main by the adoption of the holding-company structure and a decline of the functional organization. There was also a significant number of structural rationalizations, the most important of which was the further spread of the multidivisional structure especially among diversified companies with a functional structure.

Table 3–4 reveals that the number of overall transitions during the 1960s was somewhat higher than in the 1950s but not significantly so. In all, some 59 of the companies adjusted diversification strategy, structure, or both.

There were 32 companies which changed their degree of diversification, 29 of which were in the predicted direction of increased diversification but 3 of which showed decreased diversification. This compared with 29 cases all of increased diversification during the 1950s. There was thus no significant difference between the two periods in terms of the total numbers of strategic transitions. The largest category of strategic change was among the dominant product companies, 14 of which became diversified to related product companies adding further support to the concept that this category was in the main merely a transitional phase in the development of a strategy of diversification. The numbers of dominant product companies in the population remained high due to the entry of 11 former single product companies which embarked on a strategy of diversification.

Only 13 companies changed their degree of diversification without a structural change, while 19 companies did have changes in both strategy and structure, 13 of these adopting the multidivisional structure. Indeed, the predominant structural change was the widespread adoption of the multidivisional form; of 46 structural changes no fewer than 36 involved the adoption of a divisional structure. The largest number of such transitions occurred among holding companies, 27 of which switched, including 17 companies which did not change their degree of diversification. The remaining 9 transitions to the multidivisional structure occurred among functionally organized companies, 7 of these transitions occurring among companies which did not change their degree of diversification but were already somewhat diversified.

The multidivisional structure had become the predominant structural form by 1970 being found in 68 of the 96 companies and in 72 of the overall 100 population. During the 1960s the number of holding companies declined from 40 to 20, there being 8 new holding-company structures appearing mainly by the diversification of single product companies. The number of functionally organized companies declined from 23 to 8 caused either by diversification with structural change or structural change alone.

The 1960s, therefore, repeated the trend of the 1950s in terms of increased cor-

TABLE 3-4

DIVERSIFICATION AND STRUCTURAL TRANSITIONS, 1960–70

	No Change					Change in Strategy										
	S	D	R	N	Subtotal	S→D	S→R	S→N	D→S	D→N	D→R	R→S	R→D	R→N	Subtotal	Total
No Change in Structure																
F	1	1	1	0	3	2	0	0	0	0	0	1	0	0	3	6
H.C.	0	3	3	2	8	1	0	0	0	0	3	0	0	0	4	12
M.D.	1	6	18	1	26	2	0	0	0	0	2	0	1	1	6	32
Subtotal	2	10	22	3	37	5	0	0	0	0	5	1	1	1	13	50
Change in Structure																
F→H.C.	1	1	0	0	2	2	3	0	0	0	1	0	0	0	6	8
F→M.D.	0	5	2	0	7	1	0	0	0	0	1	0	0	0	2	9
H.C.→F	1	0	0	0	1	0	0	0	1	0	0	0	0	0	1	2
H.C.→M.D.	0	4	12	1	17	3	0	0	0	0	7	0	0	0	10	27
M.D.→F	0	0	0	0	0	0	0	0	0	0	0	0	0	0	0	0
M.D.→H.C.	0	0	0	0	0	0	0	0	0	0	0	0	0	0	0	0
Subtotal	2	10	14	1	27	6	3	0	1	0	9	0	0	0	19	46
Total	4	20	36	4	64	11	3	0	1	0	14	1	1	1	32	96

NOTE:

Structure

F = Functional structure
H.C. = Holding company structure
M.D. = Multidivisional structure
F→H.C. = Transition from functional to holding company structure, etc.

Diversification

S = Single product
D = Dominant product
R = Related product
N = Unrelated product
S→D = Transition from single product to dominant product, etc.

porate diversification as well as in terms of the numbers of structural changes which occurred without change in diversification. However, the 1960s were marked by the rapid and widespread adoption of the multidivisional organization structure, which superseded other structural forms especially in companies adopting a strategy of widespread or even partial diversification.

The observations in general tended to support the proposition that there would be an increasing proportion of the population with diversified product-market scope during the period coupled with a decline in the number of single product firms. The number of strategic transitions was found to be about the same in both periods. The evidence, therefore, suggested that the tendency to diversify was rapid over the whole period and while earlier periods were not studied, the composition of the *Times* and N.I.E.S.R. populations around 1950 suggested that a strategy of diversification was much less common in earlier periods. The choice of two 10-year periods may have affected the analysis, since the diversification could have occurred at the end of the 1950s. This may be true to some degree, but detailed consideration of individual strategies did not seem to justify increasing the number of periods considered.

The evidence in general tended to support the second and third hypotheses. Clearly a relationship existed between diversification and structure, but the lag between the adoption of a strategy of diversification and a new structure could be long and to some degree extended by the adoption of a holding-company structure which permitted diversification to continue but without central strategic control. The growth of the multidivisional structure was found not only among newly diversified companies, but also among those companies that had shown diversity for some time. This supported the propositions that the multidivisional form would be adopted as a consequence of diversification and that the correlation between this strategy and structural form increased over time. It is interesting to note that many firms underwent two structural transitions in pursuit of the strategy of diversification. Many initially adopted a holding-company structure which was apparently quite stable until the 1960s both among early diversifiers and many new diversifiers. However, this structure proved increasingly unstable during the latter period and was superseded by the widespread adoption of the multidivisional structure. The reasons for this are discussed in subsequent chapters which deal in more detail with the individual corporations.

A further factor to explain the initially slow adoption of a multidivisional structure may well have been the relatively large number of family-controlled companies present in the sample in 1950. In total, 50 out of 92 companies were controlled by families at this time.

This number fell progressively but not substantially so that, by 1970, 30 of the 100 companies still contained significant elements of family control. The family-controlled companies consistently proved to be less diversified than the nonfamily companies, as shown in Table 3–5.

The distribution of family-controlled companies showed a higher percentage of companies present in both the single and dominant product categories and a correspondingly smaller percentage in the two diversified categories than the nonfamily-controlled companies. This indicated that the family companies were perhaps less willing to diversify and, since these companies *were* controlled by the family, they

TABLE 3-5

PERCENTAGE DISTRIBUTION OF FAMILY AND NONFAMILY COMPANIES BY
DEGREE OF DIVERSIFICATION

	1950		1960		1970	
	No. of Companies		*No. of Companies*		*No. of Companies*	
Category	F[a]	Non-F[b]	F	Non-F	F	Non-F
	(Percent)		*(Percent)*		*(Percent)*	
Single Product	36	31	24	15	7	6
Dominant Product	44	36	41	33	40	31
Related Product	18	31	33	45	50	56
Unrelated Product	2	2	2	7	3	7
Total	100	100	100	100	100	100
Sample Size	50	42	42	54	30	70

χ^2 significant at .001 level.

[a] F = Family
[b] Non-F = Nonfamily

were less subject to market forces than those companies without major management shareholdings.

Within each category of diversification, the family companies also showed somewhat less readiness to adopt the multidivisional organization structure. This was true especially when a company had only diversified to the dominant product stage. By the time it had reached over the 30 percent diversification level, however, the family firm seemed as willing as the nonfamily concern to adopt a divisional form. Transitions to a multidivisional structure, however, did tend to occur at the same time as there was either a change in the generation of family leadership, or as delegation of greater authority was given to nonfamily management, or as the existing family leadership neared retirement. The results of this analysis of the distribution of multidivisional structures are shown in Table 3–6.

TABLE 3-6

DISTRIBUTION OF FAMILY AND NONFAMILY COMPANIES AND NUMBER WITH
MULTIDIVISIONAL STRUCTURES

	1950		1960		1970	
	No. (M.D. No.)		*No. (M.D. No.)*		*No. (M.D. No.)*	
Category	F[a]	Non-F[b]	F	Non-F	F	Non-F
Single Product	18(0)	13(2)	10(0)	8(3)	2(0)	4(1)
Dominant Product	22(2)	15(2)	17(2)	18(6)	12(8)	22(17)
Unrelated and						
Related Product	10(3)	14(4)	15(8)	28(13)	16(13)	44(34)
Total	50(5)	42(8)	42(10)	54(22)	30(21)	70(52)

[a] F = Family
[b] Non-F = Nonfamily

The above evidence offers support to the proposition that "as the product-market scope of a company increases, it becomes more difficult for a family to maintain managerial control by the family. Thus, family companies might be expected to exhibit a narrow product range and those companies that diversify might be expected to change to a system of control by professional managers." The family companies tended to exhibit a lower degree of product-market diversity than the nonfamily companies, and those that did diversify underwent significant dilution of family control by the addition of an increased number of nonfamily managers as the multidivisional structure was adopted. The newly created divisions were usually managed by nonfamily managers who became a significant voice on the corporate board. Diversification also tended to dilute family financial holdings, larger percentage shareholdings being retained in the less diversified companies. Diversification appeared to be resisted by the family in an attempt to retain control, and the limited experience of a number of companies that moved to nonfamily control, followed by rapid diversification, supported this. The family companies showed, however, a significant capacity to survive—only 20 of the 50 moving to nonfamily control and, in the majority of cases, the survivors were now controlling diversified enterprises. Many of these diversified family companies were of recent origin, however, and it remained to be seen if the family could successfully accommodate the transition without the loss of managerial control.

The evidence of the transition observations in Tables 3–3 and 3–4 raised some questions regarding Wrigley's finding of the existence of the dominant product category of company with its own characteristic management style. While a number of the British companies did clearly fall into this category and could be expected to remain there, for many others it was found that this category was merely an intermediate step toward greater diversification. The largest single number of transitions, 27 in all, were moves by dominant product companies on to increased diversification. The numbers of all such strategic transitions are depicted in Figure 3.2.

The number of transitions between the dominant product and diversified forms was clearly the largest. It was mainly composed of single product companies which passed through a dominant product stage, there being only 10 direct transitions from single product to a diversified form.

The companies which passed through the dominant product category tended to be in industries where expansion within the industry did not involve heavy and continuous commitment of financial resources to maintain the existing business. Funds were, therefore, available for initially limited diversification into areas where there were relatively low capital requirement barriers to entry. Those companies which did not diversify further were from industries requiring heavy and continuous capital inputs such as the oil, automobile, steel, brewing, and aircraft companies. These companies were similar to those in Wrigley's sample but it would be predicted that some others of the British companies presently classified as dominant product would indeed move on. Three companies, Tate and Lyle, Associated Portland Cement, and the Burton Group had recently modified or were modifying their structure to a multidivisional form for the express purpose of diversifying. These companies represented relatively unusual examples of structural change being made as a prerequisite of strategic transformation.

FIGURE 3.2

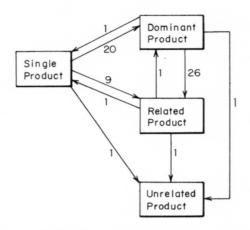

One special factor present in the United Kingdom was the absorption into the British Steel Corporation of the major steel companies. The presence of these companies in the 1970 sample would have made the dominant product category even more stable. Nevertheless, some of the companies currently labeled as dominant product were considered to be in an intermediate state and as such their management systems might well not reflect significant differences between either a single product company at one extreme or a highly diversified company at the other.

THE GROWTH OF MULTINATIONAL DIVERSIFICATION

In addition to the adoption of the strategy of product diversification, there had been increased adoption of market or geographic diversification. In 1950, 29 of the 92 companies on which data were available, were operating at least 6 overseas manufacturing subsidiaries and of these 7 were subsidiaries from the subpopulation of 11 companies with foreign parents. The 23 domestic multinational concerns in 1950 grew to 30 by 1960 and by 1970 a dramatic increase occurred with 50 of the domestic companies now operating at least 6 overseas subsidiaries. The percentage of British "multinational" companies thus rose from 29 percent of the domestic population to 58 percent in the 20-year period.

Some exploration of this apparently dramatic rise in the 1960s is necessary. Many of the companies now termed "multinationals" were actually operating some number of overseas subsidiaries, less than six in prior periods. Thus a relatively small amount of new subsidiary formation transformed the population. In the 1960s there was little greenfield development of new foreign subsidiaries. The new multinational status of the majority of companies came about either by direct acquisition of overseas subsidiaries or, more frequently, by acquisitions within the United Kingdom of companies that brought their own overseas subsidiaries into the combined system.

The data available on the sample population did not permit a detailed breakdown of the distribution of overseas assets but aggregate data on the asset values of overseas subsidiaries of a sample of companies were available in the Reddaway Report.[3] This report provided aggregate data on asset values by industry and by location for the main British multinational corporations which with only slight differences reflected the actual multinational companies contained in the population under review.[4]

The report classified the companies by the main industry in which they were engaged and provided aggregate figures on the value of overseas assets and profitability for each industry as of 1955 and 1964. These data are reproduced in Table 3–7.

The companies in the Reddaway sample included only those companies registered in Britain without a foreign parent and excluded holdings in overseas companies of less than 50 percent. The coverage of the Reddaway sample of some 50 major British

TABLE 3–7

DISTRIBUTION OF OVERSEAS INVESTMENT AND PROFITABILITY
BY INDUSTRY

Industry	Total Net Assets[a]	Total Pre-Tax Income[b]	Nine-Year Addition to Net Operating Assets	Profitability
	(Millions of Pounds)			*(Percent)*
Building Materials	68.0	15.2	49.0	22.4
Mining	137.8	21.9	153.8	15.9
Food, Drink, Tobacco and Household Products	517.7	85.1	197.0	16.4
Textiles	87.7	11.6	37.1	13.3
Metals and Metal Products	179.7	22.2	174.4	12.4
Chemicals	172.2	21.5	118.9	12.5
Nonelectrical Engineering	21.3	2.5	11.0	11.6
Electrical Engineering	61.3	6.8	44.2	11.0
Vehicles and Components	116.0	12.5	90.4	10.8
Paper	141.0	14.1	124.2	10.2
Total	1,502.6	213.5	1,000.0	14.2
Oil[c]	918.9	119.7	NA	13.0

[a] Annual averages 1955–63, and of the mid-years 1956–64 for the oil companies.
[b] Annual averages 1956–64. The oil figures are not completely comparable.
[c] The oil company figures deal with the U.K. Groups Stake and not the total net assets.

SOURCE: W. B. Reddaway, *Effects of U.K. Direct Investment Overseas.* Interim Report, pp. 37, 38, 42.

---

[3] W. B. Reddaway, *Effects of U.K. Direct Investment Overseas,* 2 vols., Cambridge University Press, 1967–68.

[4] *Ibid.,* pp. 146–47. The list of companies contained in the Reddaway sample is, with only minor differences, the same as those companies identified in the sample population as multinational.

corporations represented some 75–80 percent of the total direct overseas investment by British industry as identified by the Board of Trade.[5] A survey conducted by the Board of Trade also revealed that the majority of the British investment occurred prior to 1946.

The results indicated that the major British overseas investment was in food, drink, and tobacco products representing 34 percent of the total, excluding oil, of which British American Tobacco and Unilever account for a large part. This investment had been growing only slowly, however, and its size reflected the longevity since its formation. This dates back to the days of the British Empire, and much of the investment was in overseas sources of raw materials for the production of finished products elsewhere.

The most rapidly growing areas of overseas investment were again in the low technological areas of paper, metal and metal products, and represented some further pursuit of raw material bases. Surprisingly perhaps the high technological industries, such as electrical engineering and chemicals, were only of moderate importance and moreover had not exhibited dramatic growth. Thus, it appeared that a strong tendency existed for the less diversified, *integrated* corporations engaged in oil, paper, and metals and materials to become international because of the lack of domestic natural resources.

The distribution of British investment by country of investment was also provided for the same period although a matrix by industry and by country was not available, since this would reveal too clearly the relative value of an individual company's assets. The geographic distribution was given for 15 major countries identified by Reddaway and the results are shown in Table 3–8.

The dominant location of the direct investment made by the major British companies had clearly been the former Empire territories of the developed "White Commonwealth" countries representing nearly 41 percent of the total excluding oil and mining. These investments, however, had not been particularly profitable for the U.K. parent companies. The United States had been the second largest investment area with 19 percent of investment and average profitability. Investment was also made in the developing Commonwealth countries, where the profitability was somewhat higher, perhaps due to relative political instability. Western Europe proved to be the area avoided the most for direct investment. Although the Reddaway Report provided the most complete available financial data on overseas investments, more recent information on overseas direct investment revealed that somewhat more investment was now being directed to North America and Western Europe, while at the same time investment in the "White Commonwealth" areas also remained high.[6]

The growth trends over the period did indicate a slight shift to Western Europe with the main percentage increases in assets taking place in West Germany, Italy, and Denmark. However, growth had also remained very high in Australia and Canada, whereas it had been low in the United States.

These data provided clear evidence that British overseas investment followed the pattern of colonial expansion. Much of the present investment had a long history of

---

[5] *Ibid.*, p. 140.

[6] Board of Trade, "Book Values of Overseas Investments," *Board of Trade Journal,* September 23, 1970, pp. 644–49.

TABLE 3–8

DISTRIBUTION OF OVERSEAS INVESTMENTS BY COUNTRY AND THEIR RELATIVE PROFITABILITY

Country	Net Operating Assets (Annual Averages)	U.K. Stake (Annual Averages)	Nine-Year Addition to Net Operating Assets[a]	Post Tax Profitability to U.K. Group (Annual Averages)
	(Millions of Pounds)			(Percent)
Australia	199.3	154.5	170.6	7.9
Canada	287.6	166.4	201.8	5.5
South Africa	97.2	96.7	34.9	10.5
White Commonwealth	584.1	417.6	407.3	N.A.
Ghana	22.1	21.3	−0.1	10.6
India	90.7	70.3	70.4	8.6
Jamaica	8.3	5.2	7.0	8.4
Malaysia	24.0	19.7	13.5	26.9
Nigeria	51.2	49.5	14.5	4.7
Other Commonwealth	196.3	166.0	105.3	N.A.
U.S.A.	279.4	207.6	101.9	8.3
Denmark	5.5	4.4	6.3	5.3
France	23.3	14.5	16.6	1.9
W. Germany	29.6	27.8	44.8	22.8
Italy	8.2	6.0	8.0	12.3
Western Europe	66.6	52.7	75.7	N.A.
Rest of World	315.9	263.3	N.A.	N.A.

[a] Excludes the effect of revaluations. No oil or mining companies are included.

SOURCE: W. B. Reddaway, *Effects of U.K. Direct Investment Overseas*, pp. 43–44.

formation prior to World War II when the Commonwealth nations were part of the Empire, ruled and administered from London. Since the dissolution of the Empire, investment growth tapered off in the developing Commonwealth countries but remained high in the main White Commonwealth countries. The lack of investment outside the Commonwealth, with the exception of the United States, tended to suggest a language-related pattern which was not a true seeking of multinationality but was rather a strategy heavily influenced by domestic cultural values.

The early nature of the bulk of the investment was also reflected by the industrial distribution. The majority had been made by the older industries, especially those with a relatively low technological content, and primarily represented investment in sources of natural raw materials. The main technological companies of the postwar period while perhaps adopting a multinational strategy, had not invested overseas to the same degree as the lower technology companies. This pattern may reflect the fact that the Empire countries did not generally constitute a favorable market for such manufactured products since these countries were either still developing and were, therefore, economically and technically lagging, or were already developed but had only small domestic markets.

An examination was made of the structural characteristics of the British multinational population. Stopford indicated that overseas expansion as well as product diversity [7] had an effect on corporate structure. He suggested that the size of overseas operations and the degree of their diversity were the primary causal determinants of structure. This argument was, therefore, similar to the domestic market case, except that in multinational operations the degree of diversification might be expected to be smaller, as new products were introduced first in the home market before being introduced in foreign markets. Stopford deduced boundaries from his sample data, and suggested that within the boundaries particular structural forms would most likely be found. His data were somewhat limited, since relatively little of his sample had reached the stage in its development where major new structural forms had appeared. This was almost certainly due to the relatively large size of the domestic market of the United States. Britain with a small home market was considered to have a sample potentially exhibiting a greater degree of overseas operations.

In view of the expected high degree of overseas operations by British companies, it was decided to examine the hypothesis that British companies which had adopted a strategy of market diversification would follow the pattern outlined by Stopford. It was possible to arrive at data in terms of the percentage of overseas sales to total sales and degree of product diversity for 39 companies with multinational operations. Some estimates were necessary where the weight of overseas sales by product was not always available. However, it was possible to eliminate products not manufactured overseas and arrive at a reasonable approximation of overseas diversity.

These results are shown in Figure 3.3 together with the boundaries suggested by Stopford. While the sample of U.K. companies was not as large as that of U.S. companies, distribution tended to reflect the smaller domestic market, more companies having a high percentage of overseas sales. The three British oil companies were omitted, since they did not even segregate their domestic sales, but divided the world by continental areas. Their addition would have added to the number of companies with a very high percentage of overseas sales.

While Stopford's 170 firms were still mainly in the stage of having an international division (observed in 108 cases as of 1966), most of the British companies had moved beyond the stage of the international division (observed in 13 of 42 cases). There were thus 26 observations of other structures in the British sample compared with 62 observed by Stopford.

It was found necessary to modify some of the structural forms which Stopford had identified. His category of "mixed" divisional form was abandoned since none of the sample really fitted it and two new forms were introduced, namely the holding company and the multiproduct/multigeographic divisional form, both of which

---

[7] J. Stopford, "Growth and Organizational Change in the Multinational Firm," p. 108.

FIGURE 3.3

FOREIGN SALES (AS PERCENTAGE OF TOTAL SALES)

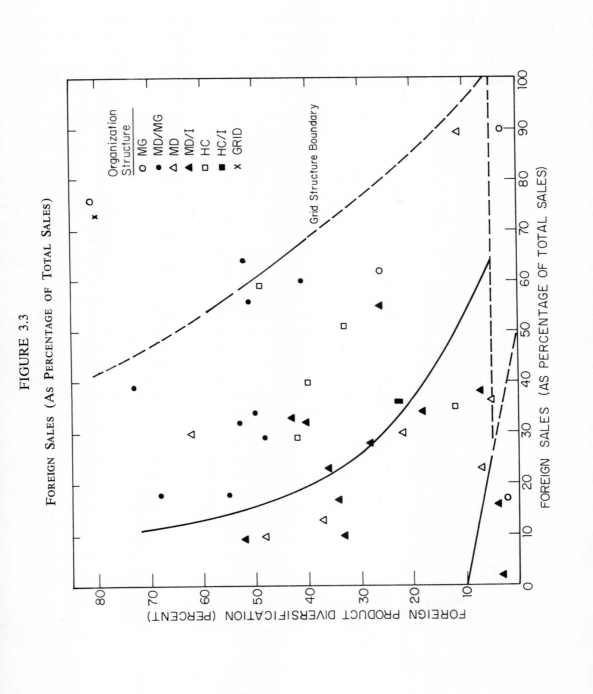

were defined in Chapter 1. Stopford's "mixed" form did incorporate both area and product divisions but with reference to the structure of a firm's overseas operations, whereas the multiproduct/multigeographic structure refers to the structure of the total enterprise and implies a system of multiproduct divisions within the domestic market and a series of geographic divisions for overseas operations. To ignore the structure of the total enterprise and to label such companies as having an area structure fails to differentiate them from companies which may possess an area organization overall as would be expected with a narrow product range. There were 9 examples of such a structure, which was generally associated with a fairly high degree of diverse overseas activity. Indeed, all these companies fell within the boundary Stopford denominated for his "grid" structure.

The holding-company structures were generally of two types: first, subsidiaries were found overseas with almost complete autonomy from the parent and a local board of directors who held control over the strategy of the subsidiary reporting to a single board member in the parent; second, the parent company itself had a holding-company structure within which individual subsidiaries managed the affairs of their own overseas subsidiaries. There were six cases of holding-company structures among the population.

The remaining structural forms examined by Stopford were accepted and 12 examples of multiproduct division structure with an international division were found: 7 examples of firms with worldwide product divisions, together with one "grid" structure, and 3 area divisional structures.

The distribution of companies with an international division did not conform well to the proposed boundaries—10 of the 12 companies with this structure were operating much greater product diversity and/or overseas sales than would be predicted. The explanation of this phenomenon may be in the weight distribution of the overseas investments of these companies. Since British overseas investment was heavily committed to relatively few countries possessing characteristics similar to the United Kingdom, the weight of investment might be predominantly in these areas. This would provide greater stability for the international division structure.

Companies with worldwide product divisions did lie predominantly in the area predicted—5 of 7 cases conforming to the model. It was not possible to really check the boundaries of the area or grid structures, due to lack of suitable examples, although 2 of the 3 area structures lay well outside the predicted boundary.

The most curious phenomena were the widespread adoption of the multiproduct/multigeographic divisional companies which did not appear in Stopford's sample. These companies all fell within Stopford's boundary for the "grid" structure and yet they clearly did not have such a structure. The companies adopting this structure had generally exhibited a long period of overseas operations during which the overseas activity had conformed to a holding-company structure and the adoption of a multidivisional structure within the parent was relatively recent. The natural form of organization of the overseas operations was, therefore, to allow them to retain their relative autonomy but to now treat them as geographic divisions. Further, the prior reporting arrangements were usually personal with no significant central office control staff. The stability of the structure might thus be strengthened initially by divisionalization which divided the domestic operations into divisions of a size similar to some area operations, neither dominating the other. This was unlike the U.S. experience where the domestic divisions were frequently very large, relative to the overseas operations, and a large central staff was available to coordinate overseas activity, leading to less autonomy for the area general managers. In addition, however, the recent development of trading blocs, such as the E.E.C., had clearly led to change from a system of national operating companies, or worldwide product divisions, to one of geographic area divisions in a few cases. This tendency might be expected to increase with growing market homogeneity and lead to reduced autonomy for either product-division or national company managers.

The observations suggested that Stopford's model might need modification depending on the size of the domestic market and that in the British case the boundary for a grid structure, if such a structure was indeed practicable, should be shifted to the right as indicated in Figure 3.3.

Further, the observations clearly demonstrated that many large enterprises have not merely diversified their product line but have also pursued a strategy of multinational expansion. This strategy has, like that of product diversification, significantly affected organization structure. Where the two strategies have been pursued simultaneously, a new degree of complexity has been added to the task of management. Little evidence was seen for the "grid" structure advocated by Stopford as a means of reconciling the conflicting demands of function, product, and geography. However, geography had clearly become an extremely important variable in a number of companies and could be expected to grow in importance as overseas operations outgrew the relatively small British domestic activities.

In general, transnational operations placed significant new tasks on central management adding to the staff advisory, strategic, and coordination functions. There was a tendency to upset the relatively easy decentralization and measurement of quasi-autonomous domestic product divisions. Further, worldwide product divisions did not seem completely adequate as overseas activities outgrew domestic. Apart from corporate strategic considerations, there were frequently legal reasons for forming geographic centers, and these could often lead to conflict with product division requirements. In addition, there was a serious tendency toward increased centralization not only of finance, taxation, and the like, but in marketing, in such areas as trademarks, advertising, and quality control, in production especially in integrated transnational operations or capital intensive industries, and in research in technologically intensive industries. A number of companies were therefore forming small, overseas-based secondary central offices on an area basis to provide coordination and/or control over groups of national subsidiaries.

COMPARISON WITH THE UNITED STATES

In Table 3–9 a comparison is shown between the population of U.K. companies and their U.S. counterparts, as identified by Wrigley. The U.K. population is revealed as still not as diversified as its U.S. counterpart. There was still a greater percentage of single product and dominant product companies in the United Kingdom than in the United States, although the trend in Britain had clearly been in the direction of the position reached by the U.S. population.

TABLE 3–9

PERCENTAGE DISTRIBUTION OF THE LARGEST U.K. AND U.S.
COMPANIES BY DIVERSIFICATION AND STRUCTURE

	500 Largest U.S. Companies to 1967		100 Largest U.K. Companies—1970	
Category	Computed (Percent)	Percent with Multidivisional Structures by Class	Computed (Percent)	Percent with Multidivisional Structures by Class
Single Product	6	0	6	1
Dominant Product	14	9	34	25
Related Product	60	57	54	43
Unrelated Product	20	20	6	3
Total	100	86	100	72

SOURCE: Data on U.S. companies have been drawn from L. Wrigley, "Divisional Autonomy and Diversification," Unpublished Doctoral Dissertation, Harvard Business School, 1970, Chapter III, p. 50.

The number of unrelated product diversified companies in the United States reflected the strong conglomerate movement in that country during the 1960s. These companies were not observed by Chandler in his analysis of the major U.S. corporations around 1960, and represented a relatively new type of organization. Wrigley's sample was taken using 1967 data, and despite market reverses for the conglomerates, it is possible that this group may have become still larger by 1970. In Britain no such conglomerate movement occurred in the manufacturing industry, and government authorities seemed unfavorable to its appearance.[8] Only two of the U.K. unrelated product companies resembled the U.S. conglomerates, the remaining three, while somewhat acquisitive, did not. However, there was evidence of a number of British conglomerates operating in nonmanufacturing sectors especially connected with property and services, and it was estimated that some of these companies would act as predators for the acquisition of some of the manufacturing concerns during the 1970s.

The growth of the multidivisional structure had been very rapid in the United Kingdom and was approaching the overall percentage reached in the United States. Some differences did, however, occur especially in the strength of geography as a form of divisional stratification. For example, the United Kingdom had nine multigeographic divisional structures and nine concerns with a multiproduct/multigeographic structure. Geographic divisionalization was very uncommon in Wrigley's classification due probably to his failure to deal with the structure of the total enterprise by neglecting international operations.

A higher percentage of the dominant product companies in the United Kingdom had adopted the multidivisional structure than in the United States. Those com-

---

[8] See, for example, the Monopolies Commission reports on the proposed mergers between *Rank Organisation and De la Rue; Allied Breweries and Unilever Limited,* H.M.S.O., London, 1969.

panies which had adopted such a structure did appear in the main to have a logical reason. For example, some of them were probably in a transitional stage toward further diversification.

Five, however, seemed likely to revert to the functional form. British Steel's present structure seemed logical but a return to a functional form was possible, as large integrated steel works superseded the present specialized works system. British Leyland appeared to represent a somewhat illogical system with far too much autonomy for the volume of output within its car divisions, and centralization of styling and major components production seemed probable eventually. The brewery companies were also moving to a functional system from the multigeographic divisions they tended to use following the adoption of a strategy of geographic expansion by acquisition. Further, a number of these concerns although classified as multidivisional did retain a high degree of functional coordination within the central office, and the multinational oil companies were only multidivisional due to their chemical interests. The dominant oil product area was generally either functional or divided into multigeographic divisions with strong central functional coordination. Strong functional ties also seemed to be present in some of the power machinery concerns especially the foreign-owned companies.

The related product groups were rapidly approaching parity in each sample, there being only slightly more such companies in the United States. Fewer British companies had as yet accepted the multidivisional structure but its rapid spread during the 1960s promised there would be little difference between the two populations by the mid-1970s.

CONCLUSION

This chapter has introduced and examined the evolution of the population of the largest 100 British manufacturing companies, over the 20-year period 1950–1970. Analysis of the evolutionary trends revealed a substantial growth in strategies of diversification within the population since 1950.

An analysis of the route to diversification revealed that most companies moved initially through a transitory stage of becoming a dominant product company before further diversification occurred to make them highly diversified. A number of companies did clearly appear to remain in the dominant product category. For these companies further transition was inhibited by their difficulties in either readily transferring their resources or creating sufficient new resources to both maintain their existing business and undertake the major investments necessary for diversification.

The adoption of a strategy of diversification was associated with a change in structure from a traditional functional form of organization to either a holding-company or multidivisional structure. The holding-company structure was found to be initially the prevalent form of organization probably due to a lack of ability to innovate the more sophisticated control and planning mechanisms which form a necessary ingredient of a multidivisional system. However, especially during the 1960s, the multidivisional structure was rapidly adopted and superseded many of the holding-company structures, some of which had existed for a long time. The holding company which represents extreme decentralization thus gave way to a structure that at least in strategic decision making recentralized the enterprise. This movement was still under way and appeared about a decade after its major adoption in the United States. It had still to be institutionalized, and remnants of the former system lingered on. Nevertheless, by 1970, 72 percent of the population had at least partially adopted this structure compared with 86 percent in the United States.

An inhibiting factor to the growth of both the strategy of diversification and the adoption of the multidivisional structure appeared to have been an initially high percentage of family-controlled companies in the British population. These companies which were slower to diversify and to adopt the multidivisional structure, still formed a significant part of the population in 1970.

The British population, in addition to increasing product diversity, exhibited a significant level of overseas investment. Much of this investment had its origin in earlier periods than that under study and was concentrated in low technology industries. The location of the overseas investment tended to be concentrated in the English-speaking areas of the world, particularly the White Commonwealth and the United States.

Structurally the organizational forms adopted by British companies with substantial overseas investment tended to emphasize geographic rather than product divisions. This may be due to the longevity of the investment and the corresponding autonomy accorded to the overseas subsidiaries.

A final significant difference between the British and United States corporate populations was the failure of a British conglomerate movement to materialize, and this may well be a phenomenon that will appear during the 1970s.

CHAPTER 4

The Undiversified Enterprises

INTRODUCTION

THE NUMBER OF SINGLE PRODUCT FIRMS had been reduced to only 6 percent of the population by 1970 and, since most of these firms were found to have some characteristics similar to other dominant product concerns, it seemed appropriate to consider the two categories together.

The companies in these two classes accounted for 51 percent of the net assets controlled by the largest 100 firms in 1970, yet numerically they represented only 40 percent of the population. The average size of these firms was therefore greater than that of the more diversified concerns, and clearly size was not the determining factor in their low degree of diversification. By dividing the total population into broad industrial categories, it was found that by 1970 over 75 percent of these companies were in five main industry groups. Further, the migration by companies to classes of greater diversification within these industries had been minimal over the postwar period—only six such companies entering more diversified categories. This is illustrated in Table 4–1.

The five industry groups were identified as drink, tobacco, power machinery, oil, and metals and materials. Further, the evidence would have been even more striking if data had been included on the major steel companies which only entered the sample in 1970 as a single entity, the British Steel Corporation. It is interesting to note that these same industries are identical to those identified by Chandler [1] in his study of U.S. enterprise as exhibiting low product diversity.

By 1970 there were only nine concerns outside the identified industries exhibiting a low degree of product diversity. Five of these were engaged in food manufacture, two in electronic data processing, and one each in printing and clothing. The majority of the firms in these industries had diversified and it seemed reasonable to examine the reasons why those remaining had not.

First, family influence was high—six of the concerns still had, or had until re-

---

[1] A. D. Chandler, *Strategy and Structure*, Chapter VII.

TABLE 4–1

SINGLE AND DOMINANT PRODUCT CONCERNS BY INDUSTRY

| | 1950 | | 1960 | | | 1970 | | |
Industry	S	D	S	D	Net Migration	S	D	Net Migration
Drink	5	4	3	6	0	2	6	−1
Tobacco	4	0	4	—	0	2	2	0
Power Machinery	1	7	0	7	−1	0	8*	0
Oil	2	2	1	3	0	0	4	0
Metals and Materials	5	4	2	6*	−2	0	7*	−2
Other	14	21	8	13***	−17	2	7	−14
Total	31	38	18	35	−20	6	34	−17

NOTE: Each * denotes one new addition to the sample population data.

     S = Single product.

     D = Dominant product.

cently, a significant degree of family management. Second, most of these firms were major producers within their field and/or may have enjoyed some degree of protection from competitive forces. For example, there were two sugar companies which operated in an area where competition was restricted; the British computer company enjoyed some government protection while the other was the world market leader; the one meat company was partly owned by the livestock producers; and the clothing company owned its own retail outlets. Third, the growth rates for the industry segments in which these concerns were engaged had been relatively low—the computer concerns were an obvious exception. In one such case it was the rapid growth of computers which made the company a dominant product concern, since it was also active in other product markets. Fourth, again with the exception of computers, the level of technology was very low.

There was some similarity between these characteristics and those of the five main industry groups. First, there was still significant family influence among the drink companies, and this influence was also evident until recently in some of the tobacco, metals and materials, and power machinery concerns.

Second, these industries were highly concentrated by 1970 and the companies were market leaders. For example, there were only two airframe manufacturers and one aero engine manufacturer in Britain; approximately two of the automobile companies, three oil companies, and one tobacco company, accounted for two-thirds or more of their respective industries' output. In steel, one company accounted for approximately 90 percent of total output; in cement the leading company accounted for 66 percent of production; two companies accounted for nearly all the agricultural tractors produced; and one company had a monopoly in the output of flat glass.

While some of these industries such as glass, tobacco, and cement had been concentrated for a long time, for most, concentration was recent. In general, however, these industries often increased in concentration in the postwar period in response to domestic and international market pressures. Rather than diversifying, companies attempted to reduce competitive pressures by amalgamation with like concerns.

Third, in addition to concentration, there were also high entry barriers to new competition within these industries. Such barriers took a variety of forms. Thus, it was difficult to enter the brewing, automobile, and oil industries due to the controls held by the present companies over the channels of distribution. In oil, steel, and automobiles there were high threshold levels of capital investment required for new entry and it was difficult to adopt a strategy of narrow market segmentation due to the relatively low degree of product differentiation. In the tobacco industry the investment required was not in plant and equipment but in advertising, to build up brand identity and image due to the extremely dispersed distribution system. In steel, cement, automobiles, drink, tobacco, shipbuilding, and aircraft, some constraints were imposed by government intervention which tended to either concentrate the industries or affect market prices.

Fourth, with the exception of oil and to a lesser extent automobiles, the growth rate and/or profitability of these industries was not particularly attractive to new potential competitors. This factor in turn may have provided some reasons for the lack of diversification by those already engaged in these industries, since insufficient cash flow may have been generated both to sustain existing activities and launch new ones. Even where growth had been higher, the capital requirements of, say, oil were mainly provided internally, and insufficient cash had been available to maintain existing business and launch extensive diversification.

Finally, these industries were largely without a high degree of *transferable* technology or skills which would ease entry into other markets. The aircraft industry, for example, was clearly a major investor in research, but this expenditure was so specialized it provided little that could be spun off into new enterprises. Similarly, the automobile companies' research was heavily committed to the next generation of automobiles and not to new products for new markets. The tobacco, drink, and metals and materials industries generally spent little on research which might lead to the development of new product markets. Only in the oil companies had significant technological diversification really occurred, and this was due to the extreme flexibility of the raw material which could be exploited for a wide variety of applications.

Indeed, the characteristic which was true of several of these undiversified industries was the concentration on the processing of a specific *material* such as oil, steel, glass, alcohol, and tobacco. This concentration led to the formation of an *integrated* chain of functions whereby new product markets tended to be developed only at the end of a chain of linked operations. To some extent the analogy could be extended to the power machinery concerns but in a somewhat reverse manner, with a large number of diverse components providing the inputs which were eventually integrated into a single end product.

The structural implications of these activities reflected the degree of integration. Thus, in the single product concerns, the primary structural form was still functional (found in four of six cases). In the dominant product concerns most companies had adopted a multidivisional structure by 1970 (found in 24 of 34 cases), but where divisional interdependency was high, the divisional form was accompanied by a strong tendency for central functional coordination of many operational activities.

The oil companies, for example, were formed into product divisions basically by a split between oil products and chemicals due to significant market differences.

However, within the oil division the main differentiation then tended to be by geography, although one company remained purely functional until 1970. Strong functional coordination was found at the center of the three main multinational oil companies to coordinate the flow of products between geographic divisions restricting the autonomy of the divisions which were seldom self-sufficient in both crude oil and market opportunity. Similarly in the automobile concerns, disregarding nonautomobile activities which accounted for the multiproduct divisional classification, the automobile sector was divided by geography where independent self-sufficient units existed. In the U.S. concerns, a high degree of interdivisional flow of key components necessitated increasingly strong central control and reintegration of the former, largely autonomous automobile divisions. This was less apparent in overseas subsidiaries which were normally more self-contained and concentrated on a specific, relatively small, national market. A recent trend, however, had been the increasing interdependency of proximate overseas subsidiaries and the creation of geographic center management groups as markets became more homogeneous.

The brewing companies which grew by geographic expansion had also begun to recentralize to some degree, as the initially geographic divisions built around large local breweries gave way to new, larger brewing units and markets became more homogeneous. In steel, the product divisions seemed likely to be reintegrated under central functional control as new integrated units were built. Aluminum and glass had become multidivisional only at the point of market differentiation—a functional system ensured the integration of prior activities. It seemed, therefore, that economies of scale at some stage or stages within the production function necessitated central functional coordination, while it was the significantly different requirements of separate markets that led to divisionalization.

A further tendency observed among the British concerns was that in many of the firms a significant element of their growth had been achieved by horizontal concentration within an industry. Initially this concentration tended to result in holding-company structures accompanied by little or no consolidation of production or markets. It was only in recent years when changes occurred in patterns of demand, technology, and competition that rationalization took place, often accompanied or closely followed by the introduction of a multidivisional structure. Where diversification did occur, it was usually initiated by acquisition, since the skills required for entry into new product markets were not available internally. Further, such diversification was frequently hindered by the overriding influence of the dominant activity to which the organization and its management were primarily committed.

These characteristics can be best observed by an examination of the strategic and structural evolution of the individual concerns, and these are considered in the following sections.

THE DRINK COMPANIES

There were nine firms engaged in the production and distribution of alcoholic beverages in the population. Seven of these companies were producers of beer, while two were concerned primarily with wines and spirits. The seven beer companies and one of the spirit concerns exhibited a significant degree of vertical integration forward to command a major part of their distribution network. The other spirit company was formed as a combination in the latter part of the nineteenth century and was the dominant producer of Scotch whiskey, the largest volume spirit sold in Britain. Many of the drink firms were similarly combinations embracing a number of smaller, usually family concerns, and family influence still strongly pervaded throughout the industry. The main barrier to new competition in the brewery industry was the existence of a tied distribution system, while in the case of the whiskey distillers it was the large amounts of capital invested in stocks which needed to be aged and the cost of advertising to build brand identification. Industry growth rate in the main, and return on capital, had not been very high throughout much of the industry, and the level of technology was very low. A major element of growth strategy, especially among the brewers, had been geographic expansion by acquisition, and one of the wine and spirit concerns had also been active in mergers.

Diversification within the industry had been low, only one concern diversifying beyond the dominant product category. The modest diversification which had moved most concerns into the dominant product category, was usually by the expansion of the wine and spirit, mineral water, and hotel operations of the brewing companies. The dominant strategy was rather one of increased concentration largely in response to competitive pressures. This was especially true among the brewing concerns, since combination had occurred much earlier in the distilling industry. The adopted strategy reflected, among the brewers, a production orientation, and only in recent years had any real attention been devoted to marketing or recognizing that the bulk of corporate investment was in retailing establishments. Some 80 percent of the brewing companies' assets were commonly tied up in public house and hotel real estate— a factor which made the brewers potential prime targets for acquisition by non-brewing companies that were better equipped to exploit these extensive property assets.

Structurally the drink companies tended to adopt a holding-company pattern as they grew by acquisition. The degree of central control was limited, and considerable autonomy was allowed within the subsidiaries. Some holding companies still persisted in 1970, but many of the brewing companies had reorganized to adopt a system of multigeographic divisions, regrouping their subsidiaries into regional management companies usually centered around the major local brewing units. Of late the degree of central control had been extended in some of the drink companies indicating a return to a functional form of organization caused by recognition of scale production economies and the need to develop a corporate marketing image.

There were six brewing companies, all of which had a similar history; but the seventh was somewhat unique. The six main brewers varied slightly in their degree of diversification: four were dominant product concerns, namely, Bass Charrington,[2] Courage Barclay and Simmonds,[3] Whitbread,[4] and Scottish & Newcastle.[5] One,

---

[2] "Something Old—Something New," *Times Review of Industry,* May 1963, pp. 44–46; G. Turner, *Business in Britain,* Eyre and Spottiswoode, London, 1969, pp. 278, 280–82; W. Mennell, *Takeover,* Lawrence and Wishart, London, 1962 pp. 44, 161–63.

[3] G. Turner, *Business in Britain,* pp. 273, 279–81; W. Mennell, *Takeover,* pp. 44, 161.

[4] G. Turner, *Business in Britain,* pp. 223, 224, 278–82; W. Mennell, *Takeover,* pp. 44, 46, 161–63.

[5] W. Mennell, *Takeover,* pp. 44, 163.

Watney Mann,[6] was a single product concern, while the last, Allied Breweries,[7] had diversified. The strategy and structure of these concerns had been formed by changes within the industry brought about by a number of specific forces.

The structure of the British beer market was such that most beer was consumed in public houses, many of which were owned or managed by the brewing companies, and these assets represented the vast majority of the companies' fixed investment. These public houses formed what was known as "tied estate" where the brewery determined the brands of beer to be sold. Beer was also distributed via joint agreements between the companies which covered, in particular, the distribution of bottled beer. Finally, a limited number of "free houses" existed, were independently owned and, therefore, free to sell the beer of their choice.

After the Second World War there were two types of brewing companies: local brewers serving a small geographic area via their tied estate, and a limited number of companies specializing in bottled beers which could travel, centered on Burton-on-Trent and London. This latter group had little tied estate investment and sold their products by agreement through the tied estate of local brewers or in the free-trade market.

In the late 1950s several forces came about almost simultaneously, thus causing much restructuring of the industry from 1957 onward. First, the advent of commercial television made it easier to build up national brand identities. Second, the local brewers became aware of a threat of take-over bids from outside the industry by those interested in exploiting their significantly undervalued tied estate assets. Third, the high degree of family ownership meant that estate duties could cause a serious threat to survival. Fourth, there was a change in consumer taste in favor of light beers, and new keg beers were developed which were better able to travel. Finally, there was a threatened invasion of the British market by Edward Taylor's Canadian Breweries Group.

These forces led to a flurry of aggressive and protective acquisitions which served to concentrate the industry. A number of large groups were formed by the main London and Midland brewers so that by 1969 seven major groups controlled 70 percent of the beer production in Britain. The number of licensed breweries declined from 358 in 1960 to 211 by 1969. Of these, some 70 were owned by the seven largest groups which together accounted for almost 75 percent of U.K. production.

The common elements of the brewing companies' strategy were to expand their areas of geographic coverage and to build national brand identities. Thus Ind Coope, a bottling company which already had the nucleus of a national brand, acquired tied distribution by merging with Ansells and Tetley Walker to form Allied Brew-

---

[6] H. James, *The Red Barrel*, John Murray, London, 1963; see also M. G. T. Webster, "How Watney Mann Plans Its Profit Strategy," *Business Administration,* May 1970, pp. 45–47; G. Turner, *Business in Britain,* pp. 279, 282; W. Mennell, *Takeover,* pp. 44, 48, 161–62; M. G. T. Webster, "The Development and Organisation of Watney Mann Ltd.," private paper given at the London Business School, November 1971.

[7] Monopolies Commission, *Unilever Ltd. and Allied Breweries Ltd.—A Report on the Proposed Merger,* H.M.S.O., London, 1969; E. H. D. Thompson, *The Development and Organisation of Allied Breweries Ltd.,* private discussion paper, London School of Economics, November 1965; A. Sampson, *Anatomy of Britain Today,* p. 543.

eries. A local brewer like Mitchell and Butler, strong in the Midlands but unknown outside it, acquired Bass Radcliff and Gretton, a national brand brewer known for bottled beers. A subsequent merger with Charrington United to form Bass Charrington increased the geographic coverage.

The main London brewers developed their own brand names and expanded geographically. Watney Mann, for example, was formed in 1958 by the merger of two family companies, Watney Combe Reid and Mann Crossman and Paulin. This merger occurred shortly after Watney had defeated an attempted takeover by Sears Holdings, anxious to obtain Watney's undervalued property assets. Subsequent mergers in the early 1960s extended the new company's sphere of influence north into the Midlands and north of England, and eastward into East Anglia.

Whitbread tried to some extent to stem the tide. For protective reasons to ensure distribution of its products, it acquired small shareholdings in a number of local family breweries to build a "family of brewers." However, in time it proved necessary to acquire these concerns outright and to integrate them slowly by closing many of the smaller breweries. Courage Barclay and Simmonds alone did not extend its sphere of influence much beyond the heavily populated southeast.

The English brewers were relatively slow to enter Scotland where the major force remained Scottish Brewers, a combination of two large family brewers. This company did not extend its operations much, except for a move into the northeast of England to acquire the main brewery in Newcastle to become Scottish & Newcastle.

Initially the brewing companies adopted a loose holding-company form of organization structure, being content to leave local family management in control of the newly acquired assets. The products chosen for national distribution were merely added to the new outlets. This occurred partially because there was little geographic overlap in most cases and, in addition, close familial bonds existed between many of the brewing companies. Many of the old trade names were still to be found in their former local areas of interest, and the names of the surviving brewing companies themselves often attested to their origin by association.

Gradually, however, rationalization came to the structure when small brewing units became more uneconomic and were closed down. A new structure of geographic divisions was created and this encompassed all the main groups except Scottish and Newcastle. Nonfamily management appeared to speed the consolidation. At Bass, Mitchell and Butlers, and Allied Breweries, where this happened, the companies were often the industry aggressors and amalgamated their newly acquired assets more rapidly than others.

More recently the trend to rationalization had quickened as the brewing companies recognized the need to exploit their own property assets; the result was the closing of unprofitable outlets. Most expanded and consolidated their wine and spirit merchandising activities because of the higher growth element in this sector and introduced "Housebrands" with higher margins than other proprietary products. Some developed hotel operations, but these in general remained small. Several of the brewers had recently turned their attention to Western Europe in order to further their strategy of geographic expansion. Recent acquisitions, especially in Belgium and Holland, gave Watney Mann and Allied Brewers significant stakes in Europe where the brewers hoped to duplicate the British pattern of tied house distribution.

In 1969 a further structural shift occurred simultaneously in Whitbread, Bass

Charrington, Courage Barclay, and Watney Mann, giving increasing weight to central functional specialization and reducing the autonomy of the regional groups. Production was becoming more centralized as new, large breweries were built to exploit economies of scale, and national brands were developed requiring coordinated manufacture and common quality standards. The introduction of selective national brands, heavily backed by promotional expenditure, caused an increased need for central marketing. The important property assets were also often placed under central control to ensure their best exploitation and a common corporate image. Activities such as wine and spirit distribution, hotels, and soft drinks, however, tended to be hived off as separate subsidiaries and probably formed the nucleus of future product divisions. The corporate management in the future seemed likely to be composed of functional specialists from the brewing activities coupled with general managers for the related activities.

Watney Mann and Allied Brewers had gone further than the others but in somewhat different directions: Watney Mann completed a reorganization in 1969 which centralized much of its operations into a functional system divided for overall planning and control into production, marketing, tied estate development, finance, and personnel. The boards of the five regional companies were, however, retained to manage operations and implement the policies laid down centrally. The company's interests in wine and spirit distribution and soft drinks were separated from the company by absorption into other concerns in exchange for investment shareholdings. Allied on the other hand diversified its product line by extending its wine and spirit operations. Acquisition of cider, sherry, and wine-producing interests, together with significant brewing acquisitions in Europe, led it to adopt a multidivisional structure in 1970 following advice from P.E. Consultants. This was the only brewing concern to migrate from the single or dominant product group.

One brewing company, Guinness,[8] had adopted a markedly different strategy from that of the other major brewers. It did not own any tied estate in England but sold a distinctive product nationally through a wide network of public houses. It operated only one brewery in London which produced stout, a dark, heavy, bottled beer which traveled. The lack of a tied estate allowed Guinness to operate with a much smaller fixed asset base than the other main brewers, and the distinct nature of its product led other brewers to accept the company's dependent distribution policy.

The London brewery was responsible for sales and distribution in Great Britain, while the other main Guinness brewery in Dublin also produced stout for Ireland, export markets, and a small part of Great Britain. The company was family owned and controlled at board level but there was apparently little family intervention in management. The two main breweries in London and Dublin operated mainly as independent units, and an overseas company was set up to supervise the export sales and the five overseas Guinness Breweries which had been opened.

The shift in consumer taste toward light ales caused Guinness to partially di-

---

[8] Viscount Boyd of Merton, "Guinness—10 Years On," in a private paper delivered at the London School of Economics, April 1963. See also "What's Good for Guinness," *Management Today,* December 1967, pp. 51–57, 118, 120, 122; B. Sterling, "The Goodness of Guinness," *International Management,* April 1967, pp. 41–43.

versify. It developed lager beer, and three lager breweries were set up together with a marketing company in Great Britain and Ireland. Guinness owned 50 percent of this venture, the remainder being held by Courage Barclay and Scottish and Newcastle. In Ireland, the company moved into ale brewing in conjunction with Ind Coope, and to soft drinks in joint ownership with Showerings Limited; and it also acquired a limited number of licensed properties.

More interestingly, the group also undertook limited protective diversification into confectionery products, pharmaceuticals, and plastics moldings. This strategy led to the adoption of a holding-company structure with the boards of the subsidiary companies exercising full control over activities, subject only to the requirements that matters of major policy should receive prior consultation with the parent company board. Again, unlike the other brewing companies, Guinness had long enjoyed a reputation for research, from agronomy to beer dispensing. The group consistently recruited science graduates for its future management, developing some transferable technological and managerial skills which eased the diversification program. It did not impose great pressures on its management. Blessed with a majority family shareholding, the company seemed prepared to forego outright pursuit of profits maintaining, instead, a paternalistic sense of duty to the community. Nevertheless, its rate of return remained substantially higher than that of any other brewing company due to its low fixed asset base.

The largest of the two wine and spirit concerns was the Distillers Company,[9] founded as an association of whiskey distillers in the late nineteenth century. By 1970 the company still accounted for some 50 percent of the whiskey distilled in Britain. The company extended its interests into the production and distribution of industrial alcohol and, after the Second World War, this part of the business developed into a significant chemical interest. Overseas potable interests were also developed, mainly in the White Commonwealth areas, by the construction of gin distilleries. The chemical interests of the group were expanded mainly via the formation of joint ventures, since Distillers did not possess the necessary technological skills, but chemicals' profitability was low relative to the potable beverages. Whiskey sales, particularly exports, grew rapidly especially in the United States, but the two industries proved increasingly incompatible—the whiskey business was being required to finance the capital intensive chemical interests which were not very profitable and, at the same time, to provide the funds for an ever-increasing whiskey stockholding.

This combined cash drain, coupled with an unfortunate entry into pharmaceuticals, proved too much for the management, which was drawn predominantly from the liquor interest, and in 1967 the company sold nearly all its chemical interests to British Petroleum. Since then the company had shown modest diversification into food products, and in 1969 moved vertically to acquire United Glass, a large manufacturer of glass containers, many of which were used in-company.

9 "A Blend of Interests," *Times Review of Industry,* July 1964, pp. 28–30; see also "The Destiny of Distillers," *Management Today,* May 1968, pp. 67–73, 138, 146, 150; "Johnny Walker—The Hard Sell Pays Off," *International Management,* September 1966, pp. 40–43; "Chemical Company With a Whisky Base," *International Management,* December 1964, pp. 79–82; Evely and Little, *Concentration in British Industry,* pp. 121–22; A. Sampson, *Anatomy of Britain Today,* p. 537; G. Nicholson, "The Scotch Giants' Quiet Comeback," *Management Today,* May 1966, p. 76.

Structurally the company never really consolidated the main whiskey and gin distillers' companies and these remained highly independent; however, the chemical interests were formed into product divisions until they were sold. An extensive committee system provided coordination, and some 36 separate gin, whiskey, and vodka companies reported to a system of central committees. Central services were minimal, and no skills appeared evident in corporate planning, marketing, and management accounting. The marketing function, for example, was decentralized in the individual companies and, while such items as advertising budgets were approved by the management committee, they were spent at the distilling companies' discretion. The heads of the larger distilling companies then reported formally to a marketing subcommittee, of which they were members. There remained a considerable measure of family continuity on the boards of the subsidiaries, and the main board contained a number of distilling family members.

The outstanding production position of Distillers, to a degree, shielded it from outside competition in the United Kingdom. More recently, however, competition had significantly increased with the abolition of resale price maintenance, the entry of supermarkets into wine and spirit trading, and the major brewers' utilization of their control over tied-off licenses and licensed premises. Further, new well-promoted brand names appeared, increasing the competition by such concerns as International Distillers, which had also moved vertically to acquire a chain of retail outlets. As a result, Distillers steadily lost ground in the 1960s, and its whiskey market share fell from 75 percent in 1959–60 to about 50 percent in 1966–67.

International Distillers and Vintners [10] (IDV), the second wine and spirit company, was a recent entrant to the marketplace, having been incorporated in 1952 as United Wine Traders, a holding company set up to acquire the assets of two private, old, established wine merchants. These small companies built their reputation by the distribution of certain brands of whiskey, brandy, and champagne. The company grew rapidly owing to the development of overseas whiskey sales and, in 1962, integrated backward with the acquisition of Gilbey's, a gin and vodka distiller with some overseas distilleries. Expansion of wine merchandising in the United Kingdom also occurred by the acquisition of a number of wine distribution chains; hence the adoption of the company's ultimate name. A loose corporate structure was replaced in 1966–67 with a basically functional organization of production, purchasing, and home and overseas marketing divisions, although the identities of the various trading companies were preserved because of the value of their trade names. An attempt to acquire the company led to a partial merger with Watney Mann, whereby that company transferred its own wine and spirit interests to IDV in exchange for a major shareholding in IDV. Subsequently, wine merchandising activities in the United Kingdom were coordinated under a common name and the corporate marketing team strengthened. By 1970 the company was partially vertically integrated at home, being engaged in both the production and distribution of liquors, while overseas operations consisted of some wine production and local distilling together with an extensive export trade from the United Kingdom.

The strategic and structural histories of the brewing companies thus had much

---

[10] A. Robertson, "New Spirit in the Wine Trade," *The Manager,* April 1965, pp. 43–45; D. T. Thomas, "IDV Takes It Neat," *Management Today,* December 1971, pp. 51–59.

in common. They responded generally in a similar manner to the changes in environment brought about by perceived threats in the late 1950s. The primary strategy was one of concentration and geographic expansion with little attempt at diversification. The slow rate of structural adaptation to changing strategy was perhaps indicative of the relative lack of aggressive competition and perhaps low-order management skill in the industry. Structural adaptation was also slow in the largest distilling company despite increased competition, and it seemed likely that some change might occur if market share continued to decline. Until recently the industry appeared production-oriented; it has only been in relatively recent times that more emphasis has been placed on marketing and property development. Family management, often stretching back over many years, was perhaps a significant factor in this slow rate of change in the industry.

As the traditional family shareholdings and power positions declined, the drink companies entered the 1970s looking increasingly vulnerable to acquisition by more rapidly growing predators from outside the industry. By the end of 1972 three of the companies had already been absorbed into other groups and the smaller remaining companies seemed likely to suffer a similar fate.

THE TOBACCO COMPANIES

The four tobacco companies were all primarily engaged in the production of tobacco products, although only three of them were active in the British market. By 1970 two of these concerns were still in the single product category while two were dominant product concerns. Diversification was beginning, however. There were signs that one of the single product companies would shortly diversify to the dominant product stage. Further, one of the dominant product concerns seemed to be diversifying toward an unrelated product concern.

Family elements played a role in the development of three of the tobacco companies. The largest company, Imperial Tobacco, also held substantial shareholdings in two of the other concerns until recently. Two of the firms had been acquired by foreign parents in the period under examination.

The industry was already highly concentrated before 1950, with the three largest firms together accounting for virtually all tobacco products sold in Britain, and this position was maintained. By 1970 Imperial Tobacco alone held over two-thirds of the cigarette market, with its nearest rival (Gallaher) holding just over 25 percent.

Although not capital intensive, substantial investment in stocks of tobacco was a necessary ingredient in the industry. The level of technology was very low and such diversification as had occurred was by acquisition into fields basically unrelated to tobacco, such as food products, paper and packaging, and cosmetics. Thus, the lack of growth in demand which became apparent during the 1960s effectively stimulated search for opportunities outside the industry. Fortunately, the cash flow characteristics of the tobacco industry meant that financial resources could be made available for such diversification despite the high capital costs of entry into the industry.

Competition within the industry was controlled mainly by heavy brand advertising and, because of the heavy excise duty, a variety of market price segments developed. The presence of restrictive agreements created during the 1930s in part reduced competition until the Restrictive Practices Act. Further, the use of Resale Price Maintenance restricted retail price competition until the late 1960s.

Structurally the tobacco companies traditionally adopted a holding-company or functional system of management. The functional pattern still remained in two of the concerns, although these were now part of wider foreign-owned holding-company systems. Two companies had developed multidivisional structures—one undiversified company had a system of geographic tobacco products divisions, while the other had adopted a multiproduct divisional system in response to different market needs brought on by diversification.

The largest British tobacco company, the Imperial Tobacco Company,[11] was formed as an association of family companies to repel (around the turn of the century) the invasion of Winston Duke's American Tobacco Company. An outcome of this rivalry was the subsequent formation of the British American Tobacco Company, formed to handle the export business of both American Tobacco and Imperial in exchange for shareholdings in the new company.

Imperial soon came to dominate the British market, especially in the rapidly growing cigarette sector. By 1920 the group controlled over 90 percent of the cigarette trade, and nearly 75 percent of the total tobacco market.

During the interwar period further steps were taken to consolidate Imperial's position. Together with British American, the company acquired Ardath Tobacco and interests in the Mollins Machine Company—the major supplier of cigarette machinery. Interests in retailing were added and, in 1932, Imperial acquired a controlling interest in Gallaher's. Imperial thus developed a near-monopoly position in the tobacco market with interests in both retailing and the supply of packaging and machinery. In addition, a series of restrictive trading agreements were made in the 1930s between the major tobacco manufacturers, agreements which persisted until the Restrictive Practices Act in the late 1950s. Individual resale price maintenance was not finally abolished until the late 1960s.

For over 50 years Imperial contained a strong element of family management. Initially composed of a loose federation of family concerns, with the Wills family outstanding among them, a system of "branches" remained intact until 1964, although the number of branches was gradually reduced as smaller units were merged together. Internal rivalry between the branches was encouraged, resulting in the rise to parity with Wills of the Players Branch. Each branch was largely autonomous, being responsible to the central office only for capital expenditure, pricing, and advertising. These were closely supervised by a central staff and executive committee of the main board.

By 1961 family representation on the board had largely disappeared, and the first tentative diversification into foods began with the acquisition of a potato chip company as growth in the sales of tobacco products began to decline. Development also took place in the packaging interests which had originally been set up or ac-

---

[11] D. Clark, "Imps: Reorganisation for Reality," *The Manager,* November 1964, pp. 31–35; see also D. T. Thomas, "What Marketing Means for Imps," *Management Today,* April 1968, pp. 78–83; J. Partridge, "Imperial Tobacco Group Ltd.—Retrospect and Prospect," private paper given at the London Business School, March 1969; "The Ever Spreading Imps," *The Director,* August 1968, pp. 232–35; Monopolies Commission, *Report on the Supply of Cigarettes and Tobacco,* H.M.S.O., July 1961; A. Sampson, *Anatomy of Britain Today,* pp. 534–35.

quired to provide for the internal needs of the tobacco branches. In 1964 a divisional structure was adopted which divided the group into three divisions: tobacco, paper and board, and general trade, the latter containing the potato chip and retail tobacconist interests of the company. Further extensive diversification by acquisition occurred in foods, and the divisional structure was later modified to account for the change. A major food acquisition in 1969 led to the formation of two new food divisions, a distributive trade division covering wholesale and retail distribution of primarily tobacco products, and a general trade division with minor interests in glass bottles, molded plastics, and woolen textiles. The company seemed to be moving rapidly toward a diversified company where only limited relationships existed between the new and old activities. However, the problems of integrating these new activities into a system where central management was still mainly composed of former tobacco company men had yet to be resolved.

British American Tobacco [12] (B.A.T.), which was still classified as a single product company, was somewhat unusual because of its early history. It had grown to become the largest tobacco company in the world, yet it did not compete in the British market.

Following the invasion of the British tobacco market in 1902, after a short trade war, agreement was reached between American Tobacco and Imperial Tobacco whereby each would operate exclusively within its respective domestic markets. The result was the creation of the British American Tobacco Company, formed to handle their export interests. British American's main assets were, therefore, the trademarks and brand names of American Tobacco and Imperial Tobacco outside of the United Kingdom and the United States. The American Tobacco Company's shareholding in B.A.T. was sold in 1911 following U.S. antitrust action, but Imperial Tobacco still owned 28.5 percent of B.A.T.'s stock. The subsequent acquisition of a majority holding in Gallaher's by Imperial in 1932 also gave B.A.T. the non-British trademarks of that company. British entry into the E.E.C. severely threatened the long-established relationship between British American and Imperial and, due to European antitrust law, the two companies agreed to terminate their agreements in 1972 and in the future to compete with one another.

British American was, therefore, a British company with only minor trading interests in Britain. By 1970 it operated in over 100 other countries and its largest subsidiary, Brown and Williamson, was in the United States, which B.A.T. entered after the antitrust action against American Tobacco. Its activities were concentrated in tobacco products which represented 97 percent of 1969 sales. The company manufactured widely for local consumption and produced the brands of its former founders in the United Kingdom and the United States, products for sale in export markets.

The company had been very slow to diversify but did invest in modest vertical integration such as paper, printing and packaging, and tobacco machinery. In the

---

[12] G. D. Cuthbert, "Interview With the New Chairman," *Achievement,* May 1966, pp. 6–7; Sir Duncan Oppenheim, "The Growth and Organisation of British American Tobacco Company Limited," private paper for the London School of Economics, May 1961; "B.A.T.—the Empire Built on Smoke," *International Management,* August 1966, pp. 26–28; "The Bold Bet of British American Tobacco," *Duns Review,* July 1969.

late 1960s it began to diversify more seriously by acquiring food products and cosmetics which, it hoped, would have marketing characteristics similar to tobacco. Part of this recent diversification strategy was being conducted centrally and part by the local geographic companies. In 1970, anxious to build up U. K. operations in view of changes in British taxation rules, the company acquired Wiggins Teape, a large specialty paper and packaging manufacturer. Further diversification seemed inevitable and, indeed, in 1972 several acquisitions were in hand to extend the company's interests in retailing.

Structurally British American had a multigeographic divisional system, as might be expected with its low degree of product diversity. Local companies enjoyed considerable autonomy but were responsible to central office area divisional directors. The central office provided a wide range of service functions which were available on request to the overseas subsidiaries. Due to the varied characteristics of different markets, the geographic divisions enjoyed somewhat more autonomy than the branches of Imperial. Nevertheless, strict central control was maintained over the primary assets of British American, notably its brand names. The current program of diversification seemed almost certain to cause British American to change its single product classification in the near future. A corresponding structural transition would then be expected to give more emphasis to product divisions.

Imperial Tobacco's main domestic rival in the post-World War II period was Gallaher's.[13] This company, formed by Thomas Gallaher in 1857, did not merge with other British concerns, despite the threat from Winston Duke. Initially Gallaher's market was localized mainly in Northern Ireland, the company having entered the cigarette market relatively late. In 1928, however, shortly after the death of its founder, the company became public and rapidly expanded its share of the cigarette market. In 1932, fearing that American Tobacco would purchase Gallaher's, Imperial acquired a 51 percent controlling interest. Imperial, however, did not apparently take any part in the management of Gallaher's and, in 1946, its holding was reduced to $42\frac{1}{2}$ percent.

In the postwar market, after decontrol of tobacco in 1954, Gallaher expanded rapidly. By 1962 when it acquired J. Wix, another small cigarette manufacturer, Gallaher's had succeeded in acquiring 37 percent of the U.K. cigarette market. Imperial began to react to this competition and, capitalizing on the change in consumer taste to filter tipped cigarettes, succeeded in reducing Gallaher's market share to 27 percent by 1968.

Gallaher did not diversify its product line at all and shortly after Imperial Tobacco sold its shareholding in 1968, seven years after a recommendation by the Monopolies Commission, Gallaher was acquired by the American Brands Company. This acquisition represented a return to Britain by part of Duke's old American Tobacco Group and marked the successful completion of the maneuver contemplated in 1932 which had led to the original acquisition of the Imperial shareholding. Prior to this acquisition, American Brands had already begun to diversify into food products in the United States, and Gallaher was therefore classified according to the product mix of the overall group. The British company was still largely independent

---

13 *Gallaher Ltd. 1857–1956,* Company Publication 1956; see also Monopolies Commission, *Report on the Supply of Cigarettes and Tobacco.*

of the U.S. parent but a limited diversification program was under way. Further, the new parent called in the consultant firm of McKinsey & Company to reorganize Gallaher's management structure which was divided into four clearly defined functional areas of marketing and sales (divided in turn into a system of product managers), manufacturing, finance, and distribution rather than the somewhat looser treatment of Gallaher's subsidiaries in the past.

The fourth tobacco company, Carreras, was again wholly engaged in tobacco products and held about 7 percent of the British market. First established in 1788, the present company was registered in Great Britain in 1903, when it became associated with the Barron family. The company was relatively successful in the prewar period but after decontrol of tobacco in 1954 it rapidly lost its market share. In 1958 the company was in difficulty and was acquired by the Rembrandt Group, a South African-based tobacco group which also owned Rothmans of Pall Mall, another small British producer. After the acquisition the former family management was soon replaced and Carreras and Rothmans were merged. The corporate structure remained functional within the framework of a wider holding-company structure for the group as a whole. In 1972, following advice from McKinsey & Company, the Rembrandt Group underwent a major reorganization into a series of geographic divisions.

The tobacco companies were not subjected to many new competitive pressures during the postwar period, although the relative strength of the smaller companies was potentially enhanced after their acquisition by strong foreign parent companies. The real impact on their strategic development came from a reduction in the growth rate for tobacco products, coupled with increased awareness of the health dangers of tobacco, which in the future threatened legislation against the industry. By a process of acquisition the companies had begun to diversify. The companies had attempted to move into new product-market areas where it was hoped they could capitalize on their marketing skills. This had not really succeeded well because, despite some structural modification in the case of American Brands and Imperial, the overall corporate mentality still reflected the dominance of the tobacco interests, and marketing skills were not found to be as transferable as had been anticipated. Nevertheless, the tobacco companies possessed the financial resources to pursue a policy of diversification, and it seemed probable that they would develop as conglomerates by the acquisition of other low-technology consumer market interests.

THE POWER MACHINERY COMPANIES

This somewhat broad industrial classification embraced firms engaged in four basic industries: automobiles, aircraft, agricultural machinery, and shipbuilding. In 1950 there were eight such companies in the sample population, seven of which were classified as dominant product concerns. By 1970 the British Aircraft Corporation had been added to the number of power machinery corporations. Only one company in this group had diversified beyond the dominant product category in the past 20 years. The single migrant was the Hawker Siddeley Company, one of the two surviving British airframe constructors, which had diversified into a wide range of other engineering and electrical interests causing it to be reclassified.

The four industries represented were all relatively concentrated by 1970; the two largest automobile manufacturers accounted for nearly 70 percent of the domestic market. There were only two airframe and one aero engine manufacturers in Britain, two concerns accounted for most of the agricultural machinery, and recently shipbuilding had been concentrated into a few major groups. Much of this concentration occurred in the postwar period in response to competitive pressures often from outside the domestic environment.

Competitive entry into these industries involved a substantial amount of capital expenditure in all cases. Nevertheless, the level of competition increased. This came mainly from other large firms outside the domestic economy and resulted in significant change. In aircraft, the joint impact of rising technological costs and competition from the United States led to increased dependence on government. In shipbuilding, Japanese and German competition in particular had the effect of government-sponsored concentration. In automobiles, the global strategies of the U.S. concerns and the impact of other European manufacturers again resulted in concentration of the British-owned sector. Growth and profitability were both low in aircraft and shipbuilding. In automobiles after initial high growth there was a subsequent decline due to governmental constraints on the growth of the domestic market and rising costs. These industries to a greater or lesser degree were also characterized by high labor unrest which served to enhance their problems.

The level of technology was variable, being very high in aircraft and very low in shipbuilding. However, the level of transferable technology appropriate for entry into other activities was generally low.

By 1970 the basic structural form of the concerns was that of a multidivisional system. Four of the companies were local subsidiaries of North American parents which were divisionalized. The four British concerns tended to have a more recent history of divisionalization. Within the multidivisional systems of the North American firms, however, the level of autonomy had been reduced over time and an increasing degree of central coordination became necessary as divisional interdependency had increased. The companies all therefore developed central staff units with responsibilities which significantly controlled and coordinated the affairs of the operating divisions. By contrast the British firms had divisionalized more recently and their central staff functions were still weak and ill-defined. There also seemed to be unfamiliarity with the mechanisms of an effective divisional system in the British companies and a reluctance to enforce central controls over what had been "federal" or holding company structures.

The British automobile and agricultural machinery companies clearly reflected the narrow market base of the United Kingdom. The automobile industry in Britain never developed as a major mass production industry before the Second World War as it did in the United States. None of the domestic companies grew to a large size, their production remaining relatively small and specialized. Two of the U.S. major automobile companies, General Motors and Ford, established plants in Britain before World War II, and the third, Chrysler, acquired one in 1967 after a period of association with Rootes. No major agricultural machine companies developed indigeneously, and the main companies in this field in 1970 were Ford and Massey-Ferguson, both North American.

The formation of large mass production companies in the United Kingdom was really a post-World War II phenomenon despite the prewar presence of Ford and General Motors subsidiaries. After the war, rising affluence led to considerable expansion in demand which called for the high output and economies of scale of mass production. The initially rapid postwar expansion as raw materials became available meant that diversification outside the main product lines was slight, and the small British automobile companies were continuously forced to concentrate to meet the competitive challenge, especially from Ford.

By 1970 the only remaining major British-owned automobile company was British Leyland.[14] In 1950 this company still consisted of a plethora of small companies. Amalgamation began in 1952 when the two largest British-owned car producers, Austin Motors and Morris Motors (both ruled by dominant personalities, Leonard Lord of Austin and Lord Nuffield of Morris), merged to form the British Motor Corporation. In 1953 Fisher and Ludlow, a body pressings company, was acquired. These three companies continued their almost separate existence under the same corporate title much as did the divisions of General Motors in its early years. The rivalry that had existed before the merger between Austin and Morris was indeed intensified under Lord's leadership of the new group and persisted even after Lord retired.

The company was production and engineering oriented, but neglected the development of managerial skills. In 1959 the group introduced the first of a series of front-wheel-drive cars (the mini-car) designed to be a cheap mass market car, well engineered but utilitarian. Each company produced its own version, together with variants attributable to other small subsidiaries, which had been earlier absorbed within the group, resulting in duplication and intergroup competition for the same market. The high initial success of this model subsequently brought larger variants of the same car. The model range so produced then remained basically unchanged for the next 10 years. However, growing affluence caused consumer tastes to change to larger and less austere cars, a phenomenon successfully exploited by Ford. The result was a declining market share for the British Motor Corporation. In the early 1960s this forced some closer cooperation between Austin and Morris, but serious internal frictions still remained. In 1965 the British Motor Holdings Group acquired the Pressed Steel Company to increase its body-building facilities and introduced new management to the group. Further expansion occurred in 1966 with the acquisition of Jaguar Cars. This company produced more expensive specialty cars and was ruled by another strong personality, Sir William Lyons, who insisted on maintaining Jaguar's autonomy as the price for joining the British Motor Holdings Group.

---

[14] Sir Donald Stokes, "The Development and Organisation of the Leyland Motor Company," private paper for the London School of Economics, January 1967; Austin Motor Co., *Our First 50 Years—Longbridge 1905–55*, Austin Motor Co., 1955; see also A. Sampson, *Anatomy of Britain Today*, pp. 545–46; A. Sampson, *Anatomy of Europe*, Harper Colophon, New York, 1968, pp. 130–32; "Reorganising a Car Empire," *International Management*, September 1969, pp. 18–21; R. Hill, "British Leyland Chases Bigger Profits," *International Management*, December 1965, pp. 33–36; G. Turner, *Business in Britain*, pp. 307–08, 379–88; R. Winsbury, "The Labours of British Leyland," *Management Today*, October 1969, pp. 67–72; R. Winsbury, "How Exports Powered Leyland," *Management Today*, June 1966, p. 60; G. Turner, *The Leyland Papers*, Eyre & Spottiswoode, London, 1971.

Financial problems brought on by the declining market share led to a merger with Leyland Motors in 1968. Leyland had entered the automobile market in 1961 by acquiring the small and almost bankrupt Standard Triumph International. Leyland's primary interest was the heavy truck and bus market where it had been very successful and had already acquired several other major British heavy vehicle manufacturers. By 1968 Leyland had increased its stake in automobiles with the acquisition of the Rover Company, another small specialist car producer.

Following the merger with British Motors, the combined group was placed under the control of Sir (later Lord) Donald Stokes, a former Leyland export salesman with a highly personal management style. The group adopted a multidivisional structure initially in 1969 and in modified form in 1970. Financial controls were improved by the appointment of a former Ford senior financial executive, and a very small central office was built up. However, by the early 1970s, the group still remained largely unconsolidated. It was disturbed by the declining market share, by its fragmented and, in some cases, antiquated production units, by the low turnover dealer network, by labor problems, and by the lack of a strategically balanced yet excessive product range with which to compete. The style of management remained mainly personal, and the power of the divisions and subunits, especially Jaguar and Rover, still semed paramount. Meanwhile, the key production unit, the mass production Austin Morris division, remained in serious financial difficulty and much depended on the success of the new range of conventionally engineered automobiles to be introduced in the early 1970s. There were signs that the Group was belatedly tackling its problems. By 1972 significant improvements were becoming apparent in coordinating the divisional activities and improving financial controls following the injection of new managerial talent primarily trained by the company's U.S. competitors.

Perhaps the main force which caused the restructuring of the British industry was Ford's British subsidiary. The Ford Motor Company [15] initially was built upon the concept of the mass-produced motor car developed by Henry Ford. The successful development of the model range concept by General Motors eventually forced Ford to change from his dogmatic single model principle, but he never recaptured the dominant position he had once enjoyed. When he was succeeded by his grandson, Ford left behind him a company in crisis with a functional organization that had been almost totally dominated by his own personality.

In the early 1950s when Henry Ford II took over, he began to decentralize within the company along the lines of the General Motors company, and a number of relatively autonomous, functionally integrated automobile divisions were set up in the U.S. market each of which designed, assembled, and marketed its own product line. Similarly, the two main overseas subsidiaries in Britain and Germany enjoyed a

---

15 "Ford Motors Managing Machine," *Management Today,* February 1968, pp. 4, 52–59, 120; see also H. Stieglitz and C. D. Wilkerson, *Corporate Organization Structures,* National Industrial Conference Board, New York, p. 56; J. Ensor, "How Ford Has Invested in World Market Freedom," *Financial Times,* February 25, 1971; G. Turner, *Business in Britain,* pp. 379–80, 385, 388–93; Sir Patrick Hennessy, "The Development and Organisation of the Ford Motor Company," private paper given at the London School of Economics, November 1964; A. D. Chandler, *Strategy and Structure,* pp. 462–64; E. R. Corey and S. H. Star, *Organization Strategy,* Division of Research, Harvard Business School, Boston, 1971, pp. 261–88.

considerable degree of local autonomy. Ford manufactured tractors in the United States under the Tractor and Implement Division, while in the United Kingdom a separate model line was made and sold by the British subsidiary.

By the late 1960s this structure had undergone substantial change. In the United States the consolidation of automobile activities took place in order to integrate production of essential components, especially body shells and engines. All cars and trucks were designed, manufactured, and sold by a single, functionally organized division, North American Automobile Operations. Consumer electronics products were added as a separate division in 1961 when the Philco Corporation was acquired. In 1962 a worldwide Tractor Division was formed to design, manufacture, and distribute tractors and implements. Overseas operations, especially in Western Europe, were increasingly integrated and, in 1967, a European subdivision was formed to increase this integration.

The British subsidiary of Ford expanded rapidly after the Second World War and, in 1947, it was the largest single British auto manufacturer due mainly to the splintered nature of the other domestic producers. Heavy capital expenditure, based on the assumption of a rapidly growing market, coupled with the introduction of modern styling, increased Ford's production nearly threefold during the 1950s. British Ford initially enjoyed considerable local autonomy as far as Detroit was concerned, but in the 1960s this independence was significantly reduced.

In 1960 the U.S. parent acquired the local shareholding, and the influence of Detroit became more apparent. By relatively frequent model changes and recognition of changing market taste, Ford improved its British market share. In 1967 Ford became the first of the major U.S. companies to adapt its multinational strategy and structure from a national to a continental market concept. Increasing homogeneity within Europe led to the development of a European Area Division responsible for European Operations. Models were being introduced for which interchangeable production was possible in both Germany and the United Kingdom, thus reducing the threat of serious labor disputes in one country or another and making possible the introduction of models for which a single domestic market was inadequate. The scale of these operations could also help sustain more frequent model changes like the domestic U.S. pattern, thus increasing the threat to companies like British Leyland, still largely confined to a single national market.

The remaining two major U.S. automobile manufacturers, General Motors [16] and Chrysler,[17] were the other two main automobile producers in Britain, both with

---

[16] F. Donner, *The Worldwide Industrial Enterprise,* McGraw-Hill, New York, 1967; see also A. P. Sloan, *My Years With General Motors,* Doubleday, New York, 1964; L. Wrigley, "Divisional Autonomy and Diversification," Unpublished Doctoral Dissertation, Harvard Business School, Boston, 1970; P. W. Copelin, "Development and Organisation of Vauxhall Motors Ltd.," in R. Edwards and H. Townsend, *Studies in Business Organisation,* Macmillan, London, 1961; G. Turner, *Business in Britain,* Chapter 3; H. Stieglitz and C. D. Wilkerson, *Corporate Organization Structures,* pp. 65–68.

[17] J. Ensor, "The Mass Market Avenger," *Financial Times,* February 17, 1970; see also G. Turner, *Business in Britain,* pp. 379, 395–97; Lord Rootes, "The Development and Organisation of the Rootes Group," private paper for the London School of Economics, November 1965; A. D. Chandler, *Strategy and Structure,* pp. 462–64; H. Stieglitz and C. D. Wilkerson, *Corporate Organization Structures,* pp. 35–37.

small market shares. General Motors, formed by William Durant, was initially a collection of small U.S. automobile producers. An expansionist rather than administrator, Durant was removed from the organization in the early 1920s (following a financial crisis), and the company shortly became associated with the Du Pont family. Durant was succeeded by Alfred P. Sloan—one of the earliest innovators of the multidivisional system. Sloan introduced a cohesive policy and administration into the divergent elements of General Motors and, within a few years, the company surpassed Henry Ford's company as the leading contender in the American market—a position it has maintained ever since.

Sloan divided General Motors into a series of semi-autonomous product divisions and introduced a product policy dividing the market into segments, each catered to by a specific division. A large central staff was built up to determine future policy and to coordinate and monitor the affairs of the divisions. While these boundaries have since been broken down by degrees and divisional autonomy significantly reduced, there is no doubt that the success of General Motors owed much to the strategy and structure forged by Sloan.

Shortly after the advent of Alfred Sloan in 1925, General Motors began operations in the United Kingdom by purchasing the small Vauxhall Motors Company. This was administered by the parent company through its International Division. Although Vauxhall enjoyed fairly close ties with Detroit regarding styling, operationally it was left mostly decentralized along the lines laid down by Sloan for the divisions of General Motors. While the U.S. operating divisions were partially reintegrated to allow for economies of scale in such items as body-shells, the overseas subsidiaries of General Motors remained more independent, each developing, within policy limits, its own product range, tailored to specific local needs.

General Motors had not made a major effort to capture the market share in Britain. It introduced a small low-priced model in 1963 to fill out its product line but the company had not really attempted to increase its penetration much since that time. The relatively static British market, upset by frequent fiscal measures to curtail demand, and harassed by poor labor relations, may have deterred such expansion. General Motors was, however, much more active in developing its German subidiary where these problems seemed less evident. Late in 1970 a European area organization was set up similar to that of Ford. Thus, a closer liaison seemed likely between the European subsidiaries, and this might lead to a European strategic product policy as the market became more homogeneous.

Chrysler, the last and weakest of the big three American manufacturers, was formed by Walter P. Chrysler, who had previously successfully helped build the Buick Division of General Motors. In 1920 Chrysler was asked to reorganize the bankrupt Maxwell Motor Corporation which, in 1926, became the Chrysler Corporation. It was not until 1967 that the company came to Britain, at which time it acquired the Rootes Group, after having purchased an initial stake three years earlier. Rootes, a family company, was on the verge of bankruptcy in 1967 due largely to its late entry into the very small car market. A large new plant was built to produce this small car with which Rootes hoped to rebuild and increase its declining market share. However, Rootes had misjudged the market: the car was introduced at a time when demand had already begun moving toward larger, more powerful models.

The Chrysler acquisition led to the introduction of improved management systems and most of the Rootes family management was replaced. Nevertheless, the company remained a weak contender in the market. As in the United States, Chrysler was the weakest of the big three American automobile producers in Europe, but it, too, recently adopted a European area organization to coordinate the activities of its European subsidiaries.

The majority of concerns in the British automobile industry were controlled from Detroit by 1970, and this development has had repercussions on the strategies of British subsidiaries and potentially on the British economy. At a time when Japanese and German manufacturers enjoyed a boom in automobile exports, particularly to the United States, British exports from Vauxhall to the United States were stopped completely, and neither Chrysler nor Ford had sold many British small cars in the United States. British Leyland, with its poor marketing and distribution, had been consistently outmaneuvered by others, especially the Germans and Japanese. The U.S. corporations, with multiple overseas subsidiaries, exported across geographic boundaries to maximize their own advantage, subject only to placating the constraints applied by national governments, but their strategy did not appear promising for the long-term development of the British automobile industry.

Closely allied to automobiles, in many respects, agricultural machinery in Britain had a history similar to that of the development of automobiles. The rapid mechanization of British agriculture was born of wartime necessity during the First World War. A number of agricultural machinery producers developed, but these were generally small and remained so. The engineering genius of Harry Ferguson did, however, evolve and it made a major British contribution to the development of agricultural equipment.

Ferguson developed the three-hitch system which led to a revolution in tractor design. Unable to get satisfactory cooperation from British manufacturers, Ferguson eventually formed a gentleman's agreement with Henry Ford whereby the highly successful Ford-Ferguson tractor was to be introduced in the United States in 1939. The agreement between Ford and Ferguson continued until it ended in acrimonious dispute in 1947, shortly after the accession of Henry Ford II.

In the United Kingdom the board of Ford U.K. had little use for the Ferguson tractor, and Harry Ferguson therefore persuaded the Standard Motor Company to produce it for the Eastern Hemisphere. However, the serious problems in the United States after the breakdown of the Ford-Ferguson agreement led Ferguson to agree to a complete merger with the Canadian company, Massey-Harris, in 1953. This resulted in the formation of the Massey-Ferguson Co.[18]

Massey-Harris itself, a long-established agricultural machinery manufacturer, was very successful in the late 1930s with the development of self-propelled combine harvesters. It was, however, weak in tractors. From its early beginning the company had been export conscious and by the Second World War had established manufacturing facilities in France and Germany to combat rising tariffs and, in 1945, it began to manufacture implements and combines in Britain.

Britain soon became a major manufacturing center after the merger with Fergu-

---

[18] "Massey Ferguson's Global Strategy," *International Management,* September 1968, pp. 44–50; "Massey Ferguson," Case Study, BP 866, Harvard Business School, Boston, 1966; "Massey Ferguson's British Dollar Battle," *Management Today,* October 1968, p. 66; E. P. Neufeld, *A Global Corporation,* University of Toronto Press, 1969.

son. In 1959 the company acquired the British Perkins Diesel Company as its first internal source of engines for its line of machinery, and in 1960 purchased the tractor manufacturing facilities of the Standard Motor Company.

The merger with Ferguson created serious problems for the company due largely to the personality of Ferguson and the perpetuation of a policy of twin product lines. In 1956, after a financial crisis in North America, the president, J. V. Duncan, was replaced by W. E. Phillips, and a new organization structure and control system were immediately introduced. Until 1956 the company had been run in a very informal, ad hoc fashion but, since a new system was needed badly, the consultant firm of McKinsey & Company was brought in and they advised introducing a system of clearly defined geographic divisions, to be coordinated and monitored by a largely new corporate staff responsible for specific functional areas. The need for such coordination became greater as a policy of interchangeability of components between the international manufacturing centers·became more widespread.

As more international operations developed, further expansion of the number of geographic divisions was needed. Moreover, in 1966, following the expansion of industrial equipment and then later of leisure products, the company again revised its structure into a series of worldwide product divisions to provide for the stresses created by the diversity of product lines, superseding the divisional boundaries previously created by geography.

The two remaining industrial sectors concerned with power machinery, namely, aircraft and shipbuilding, were somewhat different from the mass production automobile and agricultural equipment producers. Nevertheless, a similar pattern of concentration occurred in an attempt to achieve economies of scale, especially in technology and managerial skills.

By 1970 the British aircraft industry had been reduced to two airframe manufacturers and a single aero engine manufacturer. In 1950 the industry had consisted of a number of companies many with histories extending back to the pioneering age of aviation. Over the years these companies had progressively amalgamated, with the active encouragement of government and in response to rapidly escalating development costs and overseas competition. Two of the three remaining companies were almost exclusively engaged in the aircraft industry and relied heavily on government support. The British government (by the late 1960s) supplied the bulk of the research fundings for technical development and also provided the primary market for military and civil aircraft, since the firms' own resources were inadequate to support the necessary heavy development expenditures.

The British Aircraft Corporation (B.A.C.) [19] was formed in 1960 at the request of the British government, because it wanted to concentrate the British airframe industry on the grounds that size was a prerequisite of survival in the face of soaring development costs, of fewer military orders, and because of competition in the com-

---

[19] J. Fielding, "Britain's Airmen on a Foggy Flight Path," *The Times,* London, September 8, 1968; see also D. Thomas, "How BAC Fights For Its Future," *Management Today,* August 1968, pp. 77–81, 122; G. B. Cuthbert, "Piloting BAC's Management Into the Supersonic Age," *Achievement,* March 1967, pp. 7–17; *Report of Committee of Inquiry Into the Aircraft Industry,* Cmnd. 2853, H.M.S.O., London, 1965; G. Turner, *Business in Britain,* pp. 370, 372–77.

mercial market from the United States aircraft industry. The company combined the airframe interests of three former rivals: the English Electric, Vickers Armstrong, and Bristol Aeroplane companies; and its shareholding was held by these three parent companies. A loose, federal division structure was adopted which in reality merely reflected the locations of the former main factories of the parent concerns. Thus, Weybridge Division was the main Vickers Armstrong (Aircraft) works; Filton Division was the former Bristol Aeroplane Company, and Preston Division the central works of the English Electric aircraft division. A guided weapons division was set up which incorporated the interests of all three parents.

The forerunners of British Aircraft Corporation had enjoyed mixed fortune in the post-World War II period. After initial success with turboprop civil aircraft, Vickers committed itself to the expensive and unprofitable V.C.10, a pure jet competitor to the Boeing 707. Bristol Aeroplane was in serious difficulty with no major aircraft in production, while the English Electric Company was still doing well with military aircraft. These divisions of British Aircraft were initially highly autonomous, and loyalties centered on the individual divisions rather than on the corporation as a whole. The managing director, Sir George Edwards, was the only direct link between all the divisions and the parent company board which consisted of representatives of the three shareholding parents. He was also made the chairman of each of the operating divisions; thus all divisional policy decisions were coming through the same man. At this stage the company structure was more akin to a holding company than to a multidivisional form.

In 1964 a new corporate entity was formed—British Aircraft Corporation (Operating)—which provided an intermediate management group. The executive board of this operating company consisted of the chairman and managing directors of each of the divisions, together with a number of functional specialists.

Since its foundation, B.A.C.'s fortunes had been mixed, with profitability generally low. After a political decision to drop the company's main military aircraft prospect in 1964, it was forced to rely more on sales to the competitive civil market. This loss of government support on B.A.C.'s main military contract, however, did tend to weld the company together somewhat in the interests of mutual survival. By 1970 the Weybridge Division concentrated on civil aircraft but at that time had no major new product for the 1970s. Preston concentrated on military aircraft and again lacked a major product of its own, the main military work by now being under joint development with the French. The Filton Division represented the largest area of activity since it was the British center for the Anglo-French government-funded Concorde—the problematic supersonic civil aeroplane whose success still seemed far from guaranteed. The most profitable division was the small guided weapons division which had concentrated on small defensive missiles with some success.

The future of British Aircraft seemed heavily linked to government support in one form or another, but it looked almost certain to survive as a "national champion." It had had little chance to pursue a policy of diversification even if it had wished to, since the method of its formation virtually precluded alternative product markets. Technological skills were not readily transferable, and internal capital requirements were such that there were no available funds to develop other interests.

While a duopoly still existed in airframe manufacture, aero engine manufacture in

Britain was reduced to a single concern by 1970, the Rolls-Royce Company.[20] Although it produced a number of luxury automobiles, the company's main product line consisted of aircraft power plants. Rolls-Royce was the world's third largest aero engine manufacturer with engines representing some 95 percent of sales in 1970. Originally the company had primarily produced automobiles, but the aero engine interests grew rapidly during and after the Second World War due in part to capitalization on British development of the jet engine. The company subsequently added to its product line other engines for use in military vehicles and diesel engines. In 1958 each of these activities was carried on mainly at separate works; this situation naturally led to the adoption of a formalized product divisional structure.

The size and cost of aero engine development increased reliance on this product and with it came a closer dependency on government funds to assist with development costs. In 1966, with the support of government, Rolls-Royce acquired the only other remaining British aero engine group, Bristol Siddeley, thus creating a virtual monopoly. However, despite the acquisition of Bristol, the two aero engine divisions were not subsequently integrated.

Lacking a large enough domestic market for aero engines, Rolls-Royce was forced to try to sell to the U.S. civil airframe producers, and in 1968 obtained a contract to supply a new generation engine for the Lockheed airbus. This contract proved expensive for the company, and led to major cost overruns which, together with general financial and technical overcommitment, resulted in bankruptcy in February 1971.

The final power machinery company, Swann Hunter, was engaged in the shipbuilding industry. Once the world leader in shipbuilding, the British industry had been declining, due to increased foreign competition, especially since the late 1950s. The position was exacerbated by unimpressive management and serious industrial relations problems. The British government attempted to support the industry by the use of special financing arrangements and by encouraging modernization. But finally, in 1966, after the industry's continued weak performance, a government committee of inquiry encouraged the industry to concentrate into a small number of large units in an attempt to achieve economies of scale in production and hopefully to improve the level of management.

The biggest of the enlarged units created was Swann Hunter,[21] an old established company of shipbuilders based at Tyneside and the Clyde. Like most British ship-

---

[20] "The Whisper of Power," *Times Review of Industry,* October 1964; see also R. Winsbury, "Rolls-Royce Faces Current Squeeze," *Financial Times,* March 19, 1970; D. Smith, "Success With Quality," *International Management,* December 1968, pp. 22–26; G. Turner, *Business in Britain,* pp. 360–71; J. M. Mecklin, "Rolls-Royce $2-Billion Hard Sell," *Fortune,* March 1969, pp. 123–28, 136–40; G. B. Cuthbert, "How Rolls-Royce Is Managed," *Achievement,* December 1965, pp. 4–9, 15, 17; Sir Denning Pearson, "The Development and Organisation of Rolls-Royce Limited," private paper given at the London School of Economics, November 1964; A. Bambridge, "The Real Thrust at Rolls-Royce," *Management Today,* November 1966, p. 56; Department of Trade and Industry, *Rolls-Royce Ltd. and the RB 211 Aero Engine,* Cmnd. 4860, H.M.S.O.

[21] S. Hunter and W. Richardson, *Launching Ways,* Swann Hunter, Wallsend, 1953; see also Sir John Hunter, "The Development and Organisation of Swann Hunter and Wigham Richardson, Ltd.," private paper delivered at the London School of Economics, March 1966; "Swann Hunter Sails Through," *Times Review of Industry,* April 1964, pp. 24–27.

builders, the company enjoyed the boom period after the Second World War and showed itself to be more progressive than most by adopting a major modernization program to build ships by prefabrication methods. It was, therefore, more ready than most British shipbuilders to face competition from overseas, but its technological reconstruction was still not as great as that of the German, Swedish, and Japanese yards. In addition, the industry's antiquated craft union system remained a serious weakness in attempting major modifications of construction methods.

Swann Hunter, as one of the more efficient groups, became one nucleus for the government-inspired concentration and undertook a series of horizontal acquisitions in 1967–68. The strategy of the group remained centered on shipbuilding and its ancillary activities of ship repairing and marine engineering, despite one attempt to diversify into civil engineering, without much success. By 1969, despite its concentration, Swann Hunter was again in serious trouble with heavy losses reported from shipbuilding operations.

Structurally, the company was traditionally a holding company for a group of shipbuilding and marine engineering concerns, with the subsidiary companies enjoying a high degree of autonomy. In 1966 a shipbuilding division was set up to incorporate and consolidate all the shipbuilding activities of the group. The subsequent acquisitions were incorporated into this division and thus operated under unified management control. The estimating and marketing functions were centralized to a considerable degree in an attempt to improve the marketing skills which the government inquiry had found to be underdeveloped. Other activities (mainly in marine engineering and ship repairs) which were not so geographically dispersed were also concentrated in a similar manner.

Thus, despite the disparate nature of the power machinery industries, a number of common characteristics can still be observed. The primary strategic development was one of concentration. The causation was primarily the increasing level of competition from non-British companies, especially American, operating both inside and outside the United Kingdom. Whether this concentration would in turn lead to the formation of viable internationally competitive enterprises still remained to be seen.

However, there seemed little prospect that any of these concerns would attempt to diversify beyond the dominant product category within the near future, and increasing dependency on government protection seemed probable.

Structurally, concentration often led initially to the formation of a holding-company structure which prevented the achievement of many of the objectives of the initial concentration. As this became recognized a multidivisional system frequently emerged based on the disparate market needs of the limited product range.

THE OIL COMPANIES

There were four oil companies in the sample population, three of which were among the world's largest integrated oil concerns. The fourth concern was much smaller and, until the early 1970s, its area of operations was confined to a specific geographic area.

The oil industry was still to some extent dominated worldwide by a relatively few, giant, integrated concerns, although during the 1960s an increasing number of small nonintegrated concerns had entered the industry. Worldwide influence of the integrated majors had been declining and the level of competition increasing. Nevertheless, the three main oil companies operating in Britain still maintained about two-thirds of the gasoline market in 1970.

The major oil companies were of necessity highly integrated. Crude was usually produced in a variety of places, in differing political climates, and the crude streams themselves usually had differing properties. Markets and refining capacity, on the other hand, were usually remote from the sources, and these characteristics necessitated careful coordination of production, supply, and refining. The capital intensity of oil operations was very high and therefore largely financed from operations, thus presenting a barrier to major new competitors, but also making it difficult for companies in the industry to diversify. Further, the distribution of products, especially gasoline, was often directly controlled by the oil companies. However, during the 1960s the environment for the industry tended to increase the pressures on the majors. Apart from the growth of small operators there were increasing threats from the governments of the producing countries including that of equity participation, and in many consuming countries governments were actively encouraging the growth of nationalized oil products concerns.

The oil companies had only undertaken limited diversification, although the flexible properties of oil had caused the industry to develop a variety of refined products after the stabilization of the initial growth of the automobile market. During the Second World War the rapid growth of petrochemicals led to some diversification into downstream chemical activities. However, the main diversification within the industry was one of geographic expansion which led to the rise of the large multinational concerns. The changing environment at the end of the 1960s did cause a number of new diversification ventures to be considered; these were for the first time perhaps outside the mainstream of oil operations. However, the impact of this activity was still small and was not yet a significant ingredient in the strategy of the majors.

The technology of the industry was moderate and the entry into petrochemicals, together with the discovery of new uses for oil, perhaps led to an increasing level of technology. All the major oil companies maintained large research and development facilities often in several countries, and this diffusion created a further need for central coordination.

The growth rate of oil consumption had remained high due, no doubt, to increased demand for energy products, the rapid growth of petrochemicals, and the development of new demand for new product innovations.

Structurally the large oil companies were complex. Chandler classified the U.S. concerns he examined as multidivisional, due largely to the division of oil operations by geographic area and the development of chemical activities which were usually separated from oil as they reached significant size. A multiproduct divisional classification was made of those concerns in the British sample, but this was to some extent a misnomer and largely due to the presence of separate chemical divisions. The companies also contained highly developed central functional departments possessing considerable operational responsibilities due to their coordination and integration role over the high level of internal product flow between product divisions and the geographic divisions into which these were further subdivided. This role made measurement of divisional performance difficult, since many of the ingredients of independent divisional operations were missing and determined centrally in relation to the total corporate viewpoint.

The Royal Dutch Shell Group,[22] was one of the earliest oil companies. The company was formed by the amalgamation of two parent holding companies, one Dutch, Royal Dutch Petroleum, the other British, Shell Transport and Trading. The company was formed in 1907 when the two founding companies merged under the leadership of Henri Deterding. The Dutch were senior partners in the new enterprise, thanks to the initiative of Deterding who dominated the company until shortly before his death in 1939. The company grew rapidly but, like so many of the great builders of enterprises, Deterding did little to build a suitable administrative structure.

Until 1959 the group was managed through two main operating companies, centered in London and The Hague, which usually held the shares in the large numbers of subsidiaries operating throughout the world. The two central offices performed a coordinating role, provided policy recommendations, and monitored the activities of the subsidiaries. They each had their own geographic spheres of interest and specialist functional responsibilities, although there was some duplication. The group's growing interest in petrochemicals was treated as a functional area engaged in the production and distribution of oil by-products. The growing complexities of rapid postwar expansion and the subsequent organizational confusion initially remained hidden by a complacency born of a seller's market where mere possession of oil almost ensured profits.

By 1959 the organization problems had become apparent, and growing world competition had reduced complacency. McKinsey & Company, consultants, after reorganizing the group's activities in Venezuela, were brought to Europe to restructure the central offices. As a result, these were unified and the duplication was ended. Four new central service companies were created out of the original two holding companies. Regional boundaries were redrawn and control was decentralized to geographic regions which were to operate autonomously within broad lines of central policy and budgets, and subject to the advice of a newly appointed set of regional coordinators. Chemicals were divorced from oil operations, and a separate chemical division was set up with its own central service functions. The seven group managing directors were each given both functional and area responsibilities to ensure that each part of the world received the attention of a managing director, who at the same time maintained a global view by the supervision of a functional area.

This structure persisted in 1970 but, with improved management information systems, sophisticated coordination, and so on, the functional departments had

22 A. Engle, "Organisation and Management Planning in the Royal Dutch/Shell Group," in *Business Enterprise*, pp. 342–53; see also A. Sampson, *Anatomy of Britain Today*, pp. 480–89; "General Management Practice in Companies of the Royal Dutch/Shell Group," Presentation by Shell International Petroleum for the British Institute of Management, November 29, 1968; G. Turner, *Business in Britain*, pp. 109–23; P. Ferris, "Shell After McKinsey," *Management Today*, May 1966, pp. 98–103; C. Tugenhat, *Oil the Biggest Business*, Eyre & Spottiswoode, London, 1968, pp. 43–58.

tended to become more powerful again, and the area coordinators less autonomous. London still handled the marketing, finance, marine and supply functions, with the technical departments such as exploration, production, and manufacturing, handled mainly in The Hague. Structurally, oil companies are complex; they are perhaps best described as hybrid with clear divisionalization by product between the oil and chemical interests. However, within these broad product groups both area and functional departments coexist. It is interesting that the Shell's chemical division perhaps reflected its oil company ancestry in that it, too, was divided functionally with product divisions within the functions. Marketing was centered in London, manufacturing in The Hague, and research was under a separate research function. This was different from the structure of most chemical companies which had organized into self-contained product divisions.

Shell, one of the earliest oil companies to invest heavily in petrochemicals, took its first major step into diversifying away from oil in 1970 by acquiring a large Dutch metals and mining concern. A new ventures operation was also set up indicating a continued search for further new potential product markets to enter.

The largest British-owned oil company, British Petroleum [23] (B.P.), began in 1909 as the Anglo-Iranian Oil Company, formed to develop the newly discovered oil deposits in Persia. As a means of safeguarding the supply of fuel oil to the British navy, the British government acquired a majority holding in the company in 1914, and this was essentially maintained. Unlike the nationalized industries, however, the company operated completely independent of government and grew to be a major multinational oil company. The British government still had the power to appoint two directors with a veto on strategic issues, but this veto had never been used. After the Second World War the company's main refining capacity remained in Iran, and its sphere of operations restricted mainly to the United Kingdom and Western Europe. In 1950 the Abadan refinery was nationalized by the Persian government, a move which had a notable effect on the company and, indeed, the entire industry. Restoration cost the company part of its monopoly in the rich Persian oil fields. As a result of the Iranian action, refining capacity was rapidly developed near the main markets of Western Europe, and other sources of oil were earnestly sought.

British Petroleum was very fortunate in oil exploration, and major resources were discovered in the Persian Gulf, giving the company the largest proven crude reserves of any oil company. While the company spread its geographic area of activity after the war, it lacked an entry in the lucrative, highly protected U.S. market enjoyed by Shell. In 1968, however, the company discovered a major new oil field in Alaska which made entry into the United States' domestic market possible by the acquisition of refining and distribution assets from Atlantic Richfield and Standard Oil of

---

[23] British Petroleum, "Fifty Years in Pictures," company publication, 1959; see also A. Sampson, *Anatomy of Britain Today,* p. 534; "Jersey, Texaco, Gulf, Meet B.P.," *Forbes,* April 1, 1969, pp. 32–36; C. Mansell, "B.P.'s Biggest Oil Change," *Management Today,* March 1971, pp. 86–93, 138, 142; H. E. Snow, "Planning, Budgeting, and Control in British Petroleum, Ltd.," paper given at the London School of Economics, May 1959; D. Palmer, "B.P.'s Management Changes," *Financial Times,* October 9, 1970; G. Foster, "B.P.'s Continental Breakthrough," *Management Today,* February 1967, p. 60; British Petroleum, "Our Industry—Oil," company publication, 1970.

Ohio. In the marketing of oil products, British Petroleum was a relatively slow starter and preferred close association with Shell in several areas such as the United Kingdom where joint marketing and distribution organizations were formed. More recently, however, the company had been more aggressively attempting to develop its own market image, and the old relationships showed signs of being terminated.

British Petroleum entered petrochemicals relatively late, due to a lack of refining capacity in industrial markets but, as this capacity grew, entry into chemicals followed mainly by joint ventures. In 1965 the acquisition of the Distillers Company's chemical interests gave B.P. a large direct chemical interest in the United Kingdom. Chemicals became separated from oil in the United Kingdom in 1967 by the formation of a separate subsidiary which seemingly preferred direct investment to additional joint ventures.

Structurally the company was for a long time managed with a functional organization, six of the seven managing directors holding responsibility for the key functions. The functional groups were internally subdivided on a regional basis, and the only formal coordinating body in B.P. was at the main board level. This situation lasted until October 1970 when a major structural change occurred which shifted line responsibilities to an area division basis. A new committee, the B.P. Trading Executive Committee, was set up to serve as a permanent formal body for coordinating functional and regional activities worldwide. Four regional directors were appointed to provide the line of authority between the B.P. Trading Board and the trading companies, with the regional directors responsible for the performance of companies within their region. Four functional directors remained responsible for "operations," such as crude oil sales and shipping for which the regional directors were not responsible, "finance and planning," "technical," and "administration." Ironically, therefore, B.P. was moving in somewhat the opposite direction from Shell in modifying its structure toward a hybrid functional/divisional system.

Of the remaining oil companies Esso Petroleum, the British subsidiary of Standard Oil, New Jersey,[24] had a structure similar to that of Shell except there was only one central office and it did not form a separate chemicals division until somewhat later.

The final oil company, the Burmah Oil Company,[25] was much smaller and, until the early 1960s, confined its operations to India, Pakistan, and Burma, although it had played a role in the development of Anglo-Iranian which led to a major shareholding in B.P. maintained even in 1970. The company's main crude fields in Burma were expropriated by the Burmese government forcing the company to undertake major strategic change.

By 1970 the company still operated in India and Pakistan partially in conjunction with Shell, in which it also held a substantial investment. In addition, however, the company developed new oil interests in North and South America, and in the

---

[24] N. Biggs, "The Development and Organisation of Esso Petroleum Company," private paper given at the London School of Economics, November 1963; see also G. Turner, *Business in Britain*, pp. 209–11; A. D. Chandler, *Strategy and Structure*, Chapter 4; C. Tugenhat, *Oil the Biggest Business*, pp. 13–34.

[25] C. Mansell, "The Burden of Burmah Oil," *Management Today*, May 1970, pp. 70–81; "Management on the Move," *Management Today*, March 1969; "Burmah Oil = Another B.P.?" *Duns Review*, August 1969.

United Kingdom it developed, by acquisition, some manufacturing and marketing interests especially in motor lubricants. Acquisition was also used to enter new markets in industrial and building products, but the company's search for what it called a "heavy nucleus" had proved elusive.

Burmah with its original narrow geographic concentration, subsequently lost, was a very unusual oil company. This was reflected in the structural system which had evolved. In part this structure reflected the needs of an oil company with some central functional coordinating departments, but the newly acquired interests in nonintegrated product markets were organized into divisions in a manner more reminiscent of a highly diversified concern.

The post-World War II period resulted in increased competition in the oil industry. This was caused mainly by the increased expansion of other international oil groups and the rise of independent operators especially those of U.S. origin. The British market alone was thus very small by comparison with world markets in which these concerns generally fought for position. It was this international characteristic of the major oil companies which had been the main force in the development of their structures. While the differing needs of dispersed geographic markets had generally forced some form of divisionalization, the need to integrate supplies and markets had also demanded strong central functional coordination. Only the development of what were, in the early 1970s, relatively minor chemical or other interests had led to formation of product divisions.

THE METALS AND MATERIALS COMPANIES

Seven of the 11 concerns engaged in metals and materials production still remained within the dominant product category by 1970. These concerns were engaged in steel, aluminum, copper, fine metals, glass, and cement. Only two of the four concerns that migrated to the related product category were strictly comparable to the less diversified dominant product concerns which were generally heavily oriented to a specific metal or material. The limited diversification activity observed was mainly confined to the expansion of downstream activity based on the dominant product.

Similar trends were observed in many cases in terms of high concentration, (true in steel, aluminum, metal cables, precious metals, glass, and cement), relatively low growth and profitability (true especially of steel and cement), low technology (here the glass company was an exception), and high capital barriers to new competitive entry (true of steel, aluminum, and glass). Family influence had been high in steel, glass, precious metals, and to a lesser extent in cement. At least an element of integrated processing was observed in all the industries represented although nowhere was it as significant as in the oil companies.

The metals and materials concerns had mainly adopted the multidivisional structure by 1970 basically in response to the disparate market demands of recently developed downstream activities. The adoption of the multidivisional structure had generally been of recent origin with all such structural changes occurring within the 1960–1970 decade. Again only slight differences occurred between the British companies in this group, and those found by Chandler in the United States which also exhibited low diversification. The British paper makers and the main can maker were not classified in this industrial group, unlike the two companies Chandler observed in these product areas, whereas two of the British companies were engaged in the cement and concrete industry for which there were no equivalent large U.S. companies.

The British steel industry had twice been nationalized, first in 1950 when it was almost immediately denationalized in 1951, and more recently in 1967. The first nationalization was total, incorporating all those companies engaged in steel making, but their nonsteel activities were not nationalized, thus companies with small captive steel-making capacity were able if they so desired to give up what were probably uneconomic units. Upon denationalization, however, most companies advocated reclaiming their original assets. In 1967 the total activities of the 14 largest steel makers were absorbed into the British Steel Corporation. This situation was difficult to deal with, and the steel industry was not, therefore, represented in the sample until 1967. In the interim period of independence some government control still continued over the pricing policies of the steel companies with the result that a fully competitive environment did not exist.

Most of the old steel companies absorbed in 1967 were long established and frequently had grown by a process of horizontal acquisition and expansion in line with demand. Some had developed processing or by-product industries, such as Dorman Long which had structural steel-making and chemical subsidiaries. Others, such as Stewarts and Lloyds, were processors which had integrated backward into metal making.

In many of the companies there was a history of family continuity which presented problems during the period between the two nationalizations, preventing further consolidation and concentration which might well have prevented the second state take-over within the industry.

The steel companies were either structured along functional lines or were holding companies, depending on their ancestry. None, apart from the smaller steel makers which really produced for captive usage, had diversified much beyond steel or its immediate converted products.

In 1967 the British Steel Corporation[26] was formed against a background of great protest by the industry. The assets acquired were generally of poor quality—the independent steel makers had not built any large new integrated works such as those appearing in Japan and the United States, and many of the existing works were too small and badly located for modern steel making. The political goal of early nationalization caused the new corporation initially to adopt a structure of four regional divisions to which the facilities of the fourteen companies were allocated.

---

[26] Lord Melchett, "The British Steel Corporation: Its Task and Problems," private paper given at the London Graduate School of Business Studies, May 1969; see also British Steel Corporation, *Report on Organisation 1967*, Cmnd. 3362, H.M.S.O., 1967; British Steel Corporation, *Second Report on Organisation*, H.M.S.O., 1969; British Steel Corporation, "They're Looking After Our Overseas Interests," *Steel News*, November 19, 1970; "The Drastic Surgery at British Steel," *The Director*, March 1970, pp. 382–86; British Steel Corporation, *Third Report on Organisation*, H.M.S.O., 1970; C. Pratten, "Getting British Steel Right," *Management Today*, January 1966, p. 56.

These geographic groups were based around four of the largest original companies, and the new group managing directors appointed had previously been chief executives of the old steel companies. In general terms these men had been bitterly opposed to nationalization, but in the new corporation they were given larger empires to manage. It was not long, however, before a power struggle broke out as the corporation attempted to build up a central office with functional specialization thus threatening the power and autonomy of the group managing directors. A period of attrition followed during which the old group managing directors left the organization, and a subsequent structural change was then implemented. The regional divisions were broken into separate product divisions and the power of the central office was increased. The product divisions in themselves seemed logical self-contained units, but corporation spokesmen indicated that the development of large integrated works would cause increasing reliance on a functional organization based on a strong central office.

Britain did not possess large indigenous metal production industries apart from steel. Aluminum smelting was being developed following incentives by the British government to develop it but, by 1970, no smelters were yet in operation. Alcan Aluminium,[27] a Canadian company, had been active in fabricating and in the sale of ingot aluminum produced in the group's smelters outside the United Kingdom. The company was an international group which had vertically integrated forward from mining to fabrication. Competitive pressures led Alcan to erect a local smelting operation in Britain in order to protect its dominant local position, despite the lower operating efficiency of such an operation.

The need to integrate mining, smelting, and fabricating operations meant that Alcan had a strong similarity to the oil companies. Raw bauxite, often mined at considerable distance from the final market, was usually converted to alumina before shipment to a smelter. Electrolytic reduction of alumina to metal required access to cheap electrical energy; hence smelters were often sited in areas of cheap electricity. Alcan's main smelting facilities were situated in Canada and Norway, and the metal produced was then distributed to local marketing concerns and fabricating interests. During the 1960s some smaller smelters had been erected in some consuming countries often due to political pressures similar to those in the United Kingdom.

In order to coordinate the production flow from mine to market, Alcan had developed a structure reflecting the need for central integration together with the disparate requirements of different markets. The central staff was divided into a series of functional areas of which the key operating functions were raw materials, smelting, and fabricating and marketing. The fabricating and marketing function was further subdivided into five geographic divisions which handled local fabricating operations, metal sales and, in some cases, local smelting operations. The smelting function was concerned with major smelters. In particular it included all Canadian operating companies, although Canadian fabricating and sales were still under the strategic direction of the vice president of fabricating and sales.

----

[27] Aluminium Limited, *Aluminium Panorama,* company publication, Montreal 1953; see also R. Winsbury, "Alcans British Shake Up," *Management Today,* January 1970, pp. 56–63; C. Tugenhat, *The Multinationals,* Eyre & Spottiswoode, London, 1971, pp. 96–103.

The British Insulated Callenders Cables Company [28] was formed in 1946 as a combine of two major cable companies with prior histories dating back to the late nineteenth century. This company was engaged essentially in the production of a wide variety of cables together with a number of accessories in the United Kingdom and overseas where its main investments were in Australia and Canada. It was grouped with the metal companies because it had integrated backward into copper refining and fabrication and was presently in partnership with others to erect an aluminum smelter. The company also had a construction group for the installation and erection of cables. Little diversification had developed outside of the production of cables; the group had grown by market expansion and by the acquisition of other cable companies. Initially, the structure of the group was essentially a holding company, but a central office was gradually built up and was based on functional specialisms which eventually led to consolidation of the product line. A number of manufacturing divisions, with their own boards, existed in the cables group, but all sales were made through a common sales organization. The increasing complexity of operations gave rise in 1967 to a reorganization which divided the company into three divisions: the cables, metals, and overseas and construction groups, each under a group managing director responsible to the corporate managing director. A small advisory committee was set up to work on overall strategy and policy, and the managing director became divorced from operational responsibilities. Once again the divergent needs of differing markets led to the formation of a divisional structure, which was advocated and introduced with the help of outside consultants.

The final metal company, Johnson Matthey, specialized in precious metals which still represented 82 percent of sales by 1970. The company refined metals which it sold as bullion and fabricated products for industrial and jewelry usage. Apart from these activities modest product diversification had taken place in colors and pigments, transfers, and semi-conductors. The company remained highly traditional and was ruled by H.W.P. Matthey as chairman for 47 years until his retirement in 1960. After the departure of Matthey some decentralization was gradually introduced and in 1966–67 three operating companies were formed to supervise the activities of the parent company and its subsidiaries in three main product areas, metals, metallurgical products, and chemicals, with a separate banking company concerned with bullion dealing.

Apart from the metal companies there were three materials producers engaged in the cement and glass industries. The youngest of the group was Ready Mix Concrete, [29] which was incorporated in London in 1961 as the subsidiary of an Australian parent company, which it soon outgrew to become independent in 1964. The company expeditiously built a national coverage for the supply of ready-mixed concrete by establishing small mixing plants to serve the needs of local markets. These local

---

[28] Sir William McFadzean, "The Development and Organisation of British Insulated Callenders Cables Limited," private paper given at the London School of Economics, January 1963; National Board for Prices and Incomes, *Pay of Staff in BICC Ltd.*, Cmnd. 4168, H.M.S.O., 1969; Monopolies Commission, *B.I.C.C. and Pyrotenax Limited—A Report on the Proposed Merger*, H.M.S.O., 1967; Lord McFadzean, "The Key Tasks of a Company Chairman," *International Management*, January 1972.

[29] See *Strata*, Ready Mix Concrete, various editions.

plants were grouped into area divisions. Expansion of these plants in the United Kingdom had been fairly rapid, owing to an internal building program and to the extensive acquisition of other small local operations. There had also been a strategy of geographic expansion overseas with operations being built up mainly in Western Europe. Some diversification took place by forward integration into concrete products and backward into the supply of aggregates where regional groupings had again been adopted.

By contrast, the second cement company, the Associated Portland Cement Company,[30] had an older ancestry. It was formed in 1900 as an association of 24 cement manufacturers in an attempt to stabilize cement prices. After some 20 years of internal problems, a common marketing company was set up to sell the group's products under a single brand. This action formed the basis for centralization under a functional structure. Amalgamation occurred elsewhere in the industry, and a cartel had persisted to the 1970s with the price of cement being legally controlled by the cartel in conjunction with government. Overseas, production of cement had been built up in former Empire areas particularly Australia, and also in Mexico. Diversification had been only modest with moves into specialized cement products and, in recent years, by acquisition into gravel. Recent growth had been slow and this, coupled with price controls, had resulted in a serious decline in return on capital. The company represented a fine example of the problem associated with attempting to diversify with a rigidly delineated functional structure. In 1970 the lack of growth in cement forced the company to call in McKinsey & Company to attempt to break down the functional boundaries and provide a management system which would allow it to undertake diversified expansion.

The glass company, Pilkington Brothers,[31] was the world's fourth largest glass maker and until late 1970 was a private company owned by the Pilkington family since its foundation in 1825. It had a monopoly in flat glass manufacture in the United Kingdom, built by expansion and acquisition, and also supplied the majority of the toughened glass used in British automobiles. Foreign subsidiaries operated mainly in the former colonial territories, especially Canada. Until 1969 authority was concentrated within a small family caucus and only limited delegation was allowed, mainly to the overseas subsidiaries and the nonflat glass interests.

The company had traditionally spent heavily on research, an unusual phenomenon in the glass industry, and in 1959 produced the float glass process which had revolutionized flat glass manufacture. Unable or unwilling to find the funds to invest in markets such as the United States, Pilkington licensed its process to the

---

[30] J. A. E. Reiss, "The Development and Organisation of the Associated Portland Cement Manufacturers Ltd.," private paper for the London School of Economics seminar, December 1965; see also "What Shook Up APCM," *Management Today,* October 1970, pp. 78–81, 164, 168, 170; Evely and Little, *Concentration in British Industry,* pp. 117–18.

[31] T. C. Baker, *Pilkington Brothers and the Glass Industry,* Allen and Unwin, London, 1960; see also Monopolies Commission, *A Report on the Supply of Flat Glass,* H.M.S.O., 1968; "The Glass Revolution," *Times Review of Industry,* December 1963, pp. 18–21; W. M. Pilkington, "The Development and Organisation of Pilkington Bros. Ltd.," private paper for the London School of Economics seminar, November 1952; G. H. Wierzyrisk, "The Eccentric Lords of Float Glass," *Fortune,* July 1968, pp. 90–94; "Management Face Life for Pilkington," *Financial Times,* May 6, 1969; L. B. Pinnell, "The Development of Long-Term Corporate Planning at Pilkington," *Long Range Planning,* June 1969, pp. 14–19.

other major glass producers. The advent of float glass created considerable opportunity for growth which, together with increased diversification in related forms of glass such as glass fiber, had in turn caused structural change. In 1969, with the advice of consultants, the company adopted a multidivisional structure with worldwide product divisions. As a result of expansion and diversification, the influence of the family was slowly waning enhanced by a lack of new generations of family management. In 1970, to raise further funds, the company became a public company, although the majority of the stock still remained in family hands. However, the lack of suitable family successors and the gradual dilution of stock ownership seemed likely to result in an eventual loss of family control and to give rise to the formation of another institutionalized corporation.

This group of companies, despite the different types of products, exhibited similar trends both between the companies themselves and the other industry groups associated with low diversity. Strategic and structural change had been slow, with diversification low, integration high and structural change was primarily associated with the needs created by widespread interests in the marketplace.

OTHER SINGLE AND DOMINANT PRODUCT CONCERNS

Apart from firms engaged in the five industrial groups discussed above, there were nine firms remaining in the single and dominant product category engaged in four other industry groups. Five of these firms were engaged in food products, two in computers and one each in clothing and printing. The majority of the concerns engaged in these industries had diversified beyond the dominant product category and in most cases the remaining firms could be considered as laggards. The computer manufacturers did represent a different phenomenon where the growth of one product line had been so great that it had completely overshadowed any other activity.

As observed at the beginning of this chapter, these firms frequently exhibited characteristics similar to those commonly associated with the most significant low diversification industries. Save for the computer concerns, there was often evidence of family influence, low competition, high concentration, low technology, and low growth.

The two computer concerns were exceptions in terms of low growth and low technology. The first such company was the British subsidiary of International Business Machines (I.B.M.).[32] Formed originally as a diversified holding company in 1911 with interests in accounting machines, time recording equipment, and weighing machines, the company expanded under the direction of Thomas Watson. Using techniques learned at the National Cash Register Company, Watson built a successful, market-oriented enterprise. By the Second World War rapid growth of usage for accounting machinery and successful sales techniques led I.B.M. to

---

[32] E. R. Corey and S. H. Star, *Organization Strategy*, pp. 108–11; see also G. Turner, *Business in Britain*, pp. 211–12; W. Rogers, *Think: A Biography of the Watsons and I.B.M.*, Signet Books, New York, 1969; C. Tugenhat, *The Multinationals*, Chapter 9; "I.B.M. After Watson: Tougher Than Ever," *Business Week*, January 22, 1972; H. Stieglitz and C. D. Wilkerson, *Corporate Organization Structures*, pp. 77–79.

dominate the North American market. During the latter part of the war, electronic computers began to develop. Watson encouraged this development and, by the time of his death in 1956, I.B.M. was well placed to take advantage of and subsequently dominate perhaps the greatest product innovation since the automobile. It was this rapid growth of computers that caused the company to be reclassified as a dominant product company.

Watson's death brought new leadership to I.B.M.: his two sons. The functional, somewhat ad hoc structure built by the old patriarch was found unsuitable for the enterprise and, following advice from the consultant firm of Booz, Allen & Hamilton, a multidivisional structure was introduced in the mid-1950s. Overseas operations started in France and Germany before the Second World War and were extended into a rapidly growing worldwide operation controlled by the I.B.M. World Trade Corporation which coordinated all non-U.S. activities. With the rapid growth of computers, the key function in I.B.M. perhaps changed from selling to research and development and it was in this area that the most careful control links existed between the overseas operations and the U.S. parent. With this exception international operations were divided into seven relatively autonomous geographic divisions. Individual national companies specialized in specific products or components which were allocated between the production centers on a competitive basis.

Operations in Britain began with the production of time recording equipment but, as computers began to grow, domestic manufacture in Britain was extended. I.B.M. was initially restricted in Britain due to the exclusive license to make and sell its products held by British Tabulating Machine Company covering Britain and the Commonwealth. In 1949, therefore, I.B.M. offered the British company a non-exclusive license, free of charge, on products then in the I.B.M. line and on patents still pending. In return I.B.M. was to be allowed to compete against British Tabulating. The British concern agreed and thus I.B.M. began competing with itself by selling against its own sales agency in Britain and the Commonwealth.

A separate British company was formed which initially had a 38 percent British shareholding. This was the only time I.B.M. allowed foreign ownership of part of an I.B.M. company, although this shareholding was subsequently bought out by the I.B.M. World Trade Corporation. The British subsidiary rapidly overhauled British Tabulating, as computers grew in importance, and was only held in check in the British market by government sponsorship of the British-owned industry.

British Tabulating Machine itself eventually evolved into International Computers,[33] the second computer company, but still a single product concern and representing a further example of government involvement found in several of the British-owned dominant product concerns. This involvement led to the formation of a "national champion" concentrating all the British interests engaged in computers in order to stave off foreign (in this case American) competition.

After the termination of the agreement with I.B.M., the company developed its own punched card machines and also entered the computer industry which began to threaten the punched card product line. Electronic equipment became the main

---

[33] C. Mansell, "I.C.L.'s Uphill Fight," *Management Today,* August 1970, pp. 74–85; see also A. Robertson, "I.C.T.—Born of the Age We Live In," *The Manager,* March 1965, pp. 52–54; P. Siekman, "Now It's the Europeans Versus I.B.M.," *Fortune,* August 15, 1969, pp. 87–91, 174, 77, 78, 180; G. Turner, *Business in Britain,* pp. 322–28, 334–38.

development interest by the late 1950s when the cost of development, coupled with the small size of the company, led to a merger with Power Samas Accounting Machines in 1958. A new company was formed from the merger—International Computers and Tabulators. This merger left the Vickers Company with a major holding in the new group, since Power Samas had been a Vickers subsidiary.

International Computers was still relatively small compared with I.B.M. and initially was forced to concentrate on small, low-cost, general-purpose computers. The group was also unable to finance its growing rental commitments and a special acceptance credit facility was formed. Purchases of U.S.-made equipment was used to supplement the product line. In 1962 further concentration occurred when the computer interests of Electrical and Musical Industries were absorbed in exchange for shares. Computers were by now replacing many of the conventional punched card operations which shortly became a minor activity. Competition from I.B.M. was considerable, and I.C.T. was not making sufficient profits to undertake the necessary research and development to keep up with I.B.M. Additional technical inputs were, therefore, added by the acquisition in 1963 of the computer interests of Ferranti Limited for cash and shares, adding large computers to the product range and another major shareholder to the ranks.

By 1966 the company was devoted almost entirely to making electronic computers and was in head-on competition with I.B.M. Government was showing significant interest in the sustenance of a strong, indigenous computer industry and introduced incentives favoring the domestic companies. In 1968 the company became the British "national champion" when the only other major British computer interests—those of the English Electric Company—were absorbed. At the same time, a joint venture was formed with Plessey in exchange for shares, and the Ministry of Technology took a shareholding. The company became International Computers (Holdings) Limited with a board which contained representatives from most of the main British electronic manufacturers. This board in turn delegated the running of the company to the board of International Computers Limited.

Apart from the untidy nature of the Holdings board, the structure of I.C.L. throughout its development remained essentially functional and, unlike any of its competitors, it had no real diversification outside of computers. Nor did such development seem likely since, apart from financial considerations, much of the shareholding was held by other major electrical groups. Due to the number of acquisitions, its product range at times contained a large number of incompatible and obsolescent systems which were concentrated into two main systems. I.C.L. held about $2\frac{1}{2}$ percent of the world computer market by 1970 but held most of the British market, in part due to governmental preference over I.B.M. The future of I.C.L. seemed difficult without continued government assistance, international growth, or a combination with other activities which could provide the funds flow required to enable it to continue to compete head-on with I.B.M.

The remaining companies within the single and dominant product categories were mainly engaged in food. The two exceptions were the Burton Group [34] and British

---

[34] Monopolies Commission, *United Draperies Ltd., and Montague Burton Ltd.—A Report on the Proposed Merger,* H.M.S.O., 1966; see also "Management on the Move," *Management Today,* August 1969, p. 54; D. Palmer, "How Fast Can Rice Run," *Financial Times,* May 28, 1971; "The Burton Group," Case Study, Manchester Business School, 1972.

Printing Corporation.[35] The first of these companies was originally a family-owned concern built up by Sir Montague Burton as a gentlemen's tailoring company. Retail operations led to backward integration into garment and cloth production. A subsequent merger transferred management control to the Jacobsen family and added a separate chain of men's retail tailoring stores. In the late 1960s, following a further management succession crisis, nonfamily management was introduced which, in 1970, was completely redirecting the company from its traditional production orientation. The company had undertaken modest diversification into women's fashion retailing and the new direction the company was taking was to exploit its retailing and extensive property strengths in a variety of new directions. Structurally the company was still essentially functional, in its major activity, although the new market orientation seemed likely to lead to a series of different retail divisions based on diverse market segments. The new management was actually deliberately breaking up the integrated production and retailing operations forcing both activities to become profit centers and autonomous. The possible loss of the advantages of integrated operations were accepted as a viable cost in the complete reorientation of the company. The Burton Group thus represented a second relatively uncommon example of a company where structural change had been seen as an essential precursor to a transformation in strategy.

The British Printing Corporation, on the other hand, was primarily engaged in a variety of printing activities. This company had been rapidly put together during the mid-1960s by a series of acquisitions. Some of these dealings were somewhat suspect and led to a managerial shakeup, as well as the appointment of a new board of directors. Nevertheless, despite management changes, the company remained structured as a holding company apparently in need of organizational reform.

Among the food companies, two were engaged in sugar production. There were two sections to this industry: the first was concerned with the manufacture of raw sugar from beet; the second was concerned with refining raw sugar from either beet or cane. The factories producing raw sugar from beet also undertook some refining, and in 1936 the 18 sugar beet factories then operating in Britain were merged under an Act of Parliament into a single concern, the British Sugar Corporation,[36] in order to consolidate the industry. This corporation, protected by government, enjoyed a monopoly position on the processing of raw sugar from beet. Its structure had remained functional with a number of central services such as personnel, information, and accounting. The emphasis was on production, and the key personnel were the factory general managers.

The beet sugar factories were also refiners of raw sugar, and the competition between them and the orthodox refiners had become so crucial by 1932 that the

---

[35] "The Man Who Put Planning Into B.P.C.," *Director,* July 1968, pp. 86–91; see also H. Johannsen, Editor, *Company Organisation Structure,* British Institute of Management, 1970, pp. 18–19; R. Winsbury, "How Head Office Changed B.P.C.," *Management Today,* September 1968, p. 50.

[36] British Sugar Corporation, *Home Grown Sugar,* company publication, London, 1961; see also Evely and Little, *Concentration in British Industry,* pp. 243–47; Sir Allen Saunders, "Development and Organisation of the British Sugar Corporation Ltd.," private paper delivered at the London School of Economics, January 1957.

government persuaded the parties to negotiate an agreement whereby factories and refiners would be allocated specific quotas. The principal refiner was Tate and Lyle,[37] which refined over 80 percent of the sugar in Britain from both beet and cane raw materials. The company's market share had been increased substantially by buying up smaller refiners in order to obtain their quota rights.

The company was still largely family controlled and operated in a somewhat protected environment by virtue of government controls on the industry. The company was vertically integrated, operated extensive cane plantations in the West Indies, and had its own fleet of sugar carriers. Refining was also conducted overseas. The narrowness of its product range and shrinking profit margins led the company in 1965 to acquire United Molasses, a company trading in molasses and alcohol. The group, still dissatisfied by performance and growth, employed McKinsey & Company in 1968 to reorganize its structure so that the company could develop a strategy of diversification by acquisition. An essentially multidivisional grouping was set up in 1969 to replace the former holding-company structure. This company, therefore, provided another of the very few examples observed where structural change had been deliberately introduced prior to the evolution of a new strategy.

The remaining food companies were primarily engaged in meat products, confectionery, and flour confectionery. The first of these concerns, the Farmers Meat Company (F.M.C.),[38] was formed in 1954 by the National Farmers Union as a new meat marketing organization for farmers. This Union still owned 36 percent of the stock by 1970. F.M.C. was then known as the Fatstock Marketing Corporation and came into operation at the end of government control of meat and livestock marketing. The company became public in 1962 and integrated forward into meat processing and bacon curing. It was divided into divisions by types of meat such as poultry and pigs, together with divisions dealing with meat processing and by-products. Profits were very low due to a system of government agricultural subsidies, which meant that there was neither complete competition nor effective government control within the industry.

The second company, United Biscuits,[39] was initially an association of four old, established, family biscuit manufacturers, the first two of which came together in 1947. Initially the constituent companies continued to operate independently but by 1965 competitive pressures forced integration. Growth was slow, and modest diversification was attempted internally into packaged cakes and by acquisition into snack foods. Limited vertical integration into bakery and cake distribution also occurred by acquisition. By 1970, the group consisted of three operating companies each with its own board still essentially in a holding-company structure.

---

[37] P. Lyle, "The Development and Organisation of Tate and Lyle Ltd.," private paper delivered at the London School of Economics, November 1951; see also Sir Peter Runge, "Tate & Lyle Ltd., Fifteen Years On," private paper for the London School of Economics seminar, January 1966; Evely and Little, *Concentration in British Industry*, pp. 243–47.

[38] G. Nicholson, "Saving F.M.C.'s Bacon," *Management Today*, September 1967, pp. 81–83, 142, 146, 150, 154; *F.M.C.—A Brief Guide*, F.M.C. Ltd., 1969.

[39] H. Johannsen, Editor, *Company Organisation Structure*, pp. 88–92; Evely and Little, *Concentration in British Industry*, pp. 273–77.

The final essentially undiversified food company was Rowntree-Mackintosh,[40] formed by merger in 1968–1969 between Rowntree and the family-owned John Mackintosh after an abortive take-over bid for Rowntree by General Foods. While Rowntree had diversified somewhat into foods from its primary interest in chocolate confectionery, Mackintosh was still wholly engaged in confectionery products. In 1966 consolidation of its activities caused Rowntree to adopt a new structure incorporating a number of product divisions and an international division. However, certain specialist functions such as transportation were also classified as divisions. This structural form was subsequently introduced into the merged company and it seemed likely that this structure would gradually move to a product divisional system if the group continued to diversify.

Conclusion

This chapter has described briefly the strategy and structure of the single and dominant product companies in the population as of 1970. It was found that, essentially, these concerns could be grouped into five main industrial groups as of 1970. Furthermore, the firms in these industries have remained very stable in the degree of diversification exhibited over the time period studied.

The industries concerned, namely, drink, tobacco, power machinery, oil, and metals and materials, were virtually identical to those identified as exhibiting low product diversity by Chandler in his study of U.S. enterprises. Chandler identified one group of agricultural processors—the food companies—which had diversified, and the majority of British food companies had undertaken a similar strategy.

Within the industries identified, and to some extent in the undiversified firms outside these industries, a number of general characteristics were observed. By 1970 concentration within specific industry segments tended to be high; there were significant barriers to the entry of new competition; growth rate and profitability tended to be low; the level of transferable technology seemed to be low; and most of the concerns were engaged primarily in processing a specific raw material. It was observed that by comparison with the diversified concerns, there was a significant degree of government involvement in many of the industries.

As a result of environmental conditions, strategic change had been slow. The primary form of such change had been the concentration of production within specific industries by the acquisition of weaker competitors in an effort to reduce the effects of competition in low growth markets. In many cases such concentration had been recent and had notably occurred with the arrival of new competitors in the United Kingdom or in world markets. The impact of North American companies was particularly notable in some industries. Acquisition had also provided the primary mechanism for such limited diversification as had occurred, reflecting the lack of internal development and managerial skills for entry into new product markets.

---

[40] D. Thomas, "How Rowntree Matched Mackintosh," *Management Today,* September 1970, pp. 103–07, 154–56; see also W. Wallace, "The Development and Organisation of Rowntree and Co. Ltd.," private paper given at the London School of Economics, February 1957; R. Falk, *The Business of Management,* Penguin Books, 1970, pp. 195–202.

Structurally, most of the companies had adopted multidivisional organizations by 1970, as a result primarily of the needs of different market segments. However, most of the firms also contained significant elements of interdivisional dependency and product flow, and this integration necessitated the inclusion of strong central functional coordination. Further, Scott's model predicted that the Stage II firm would be either a large single product or integrated concern. The evidence of the British companies suggested that for the integrated concern diversification was uncommon or extremely slow. This was perhaps caused by the choice of the strategy of integration which could provide protection against competition and also require extensive financial investment in all components of the business whenever a change was made in any one component. In addition, the concentration on a specific dominant activity tended perhaps to produce a narrow concept for the corporations. This concept was reflected in central management's treatment of diversification activities as peripheral, somewhat haphazard, and primarily adopted in order to sustain or provide outlets for the dominant product. Indeed, a few firms had been forced to restructure their organization before undertaking major strategic change, in an attempt to change the narrow concept of themselves held by the participants in the firm.

Many of the British firms which had often reached their present size by some degree of combination to concentrate production within an industry, remained as holding companies for long periods. In recent years these associations had tended to become consolidated by changes in demand, technology, and competition. The need to combine also provided a significant force for adoption of a multidivisional structure. However, in a significant number of cases, this structural transition had only been introduced with the assistance of management consultants often after financial difficulty or a change in corporate leadership.

Finally, a further feature which became apparent and which appeared again many times in the diversified enterprises was the significant impact of individual leadership. While it was not the purpose of this study to examine the personalities of business leaders, certain observations appeared with some consistency.

In the family firms where a dynastic system built up over time, this often led to stagnation and maintenance of the original product market scope of the enterprise, as in the case of the brewing concerns. In other firms, such as I.B.M. and Ford, which had been built by autocratic entrepreneurs, the task of the second generation leaders was different, since they were forced to administer the enterprise, and formal structural reform was vitally necessary.

This was also true of many of the nonfamily enterprises. Leadership by dominant personalities such as Deterding, Durant, Ferguson, and Nuffield, built great enterprises. Their death or retirement often left a vacuum and brought a need for serious structural reform. These men whose personal characteristics created the great enterprises frequently lacked the skills to administer them. Where new leaders with different personalities attuned to administration did not quickly materialize, long periods of stagnation seemed to occur, as at Standard Oil and British Motors. These observations suggest that further study on the personality of leadership is needed to enable the enterprise to select the executive body most relevant to its specific stage of development.

CHAPTER 5

The Technological Diversifiers

INTRODUCTION

IN 1950 THERE WERE 21 FIRMS which had diversified into related product markets. The great majority of these concerns came from three industry groups: electrical and electronics engineering, chemicals and pharmaceuticals, and mechanical engineering. By 1970 all the firms in these industries, except the two computer manufacturers discussed in Chapter 4, and one company that had become a conglomerate, were diversified and in the related product category. This is illustrated in Table 5–1, which shows that in 1950 the firms in these three industries accounted for over 70 percent of the diversified concerns.

Two of these industries were identical to the early diversifiers observed in Chandler's study of U.S. enterprise. The third, mechanical engineering, was not

TABLE 5–1

DISTRIBUTION OF THE TECHNOLOGICAL INDUSTRIES, 1950–70

Industry	1950			1960			1970		
	S	D	R	S	D	R	S	D	R
Electrical Engineering	2	1	6	1	—	8	1	1	6[a]
Chemicals	1	3	3	—	2	5	—	—	8[b]
Engineering	3	3	6	—	2	10	—	—	12
Other	25	32	6	17	31	16	5	33	28
Total	31	39	21	18	35	39	6	34	54

[a] One company became unrelated diversified.
[b] A new company entered the sample.

NOTE: S = Single product.
　　　　D = Dominant product.
　　　　R = Related product.

included in Chandler's sample but did exhibit some characteristics similar to the other two.

The firms in these industries were characterized by the central theme of a technology or skill, which was applicable to a wide variety of end products serving the needs of many markets. The continuous evolution of that skill or technology led naturally to the development of new product markets. In chemicals and electrical engineering, the level of research expenditure was relatively high. However, it was moderate to low in mechanical engineering. Nevertheless, the skill of metal manipulation was readily transferable to a wide variety of different end uses which tended to explain the diversity of such concerns.

There had been a degree of family influence in a number of these technologically related firms and this still persisted in a few. However, by comparison with a number of the low technology industries, large family companies were comparatively rare.

While overall concentration and capital intensity was high in specific segments, the wide market scope of these industries had not precluded new competitive entries. Further, the constant rapid change of technology frequently transformed the pattern of competitive advantage. For example, the development of electronics profoundly affected the electrical engineering industry. In chemicals, the growth of petrochemicals brought new competition from the oil companies. And engineering machinery underwent drastic change due to automation. The breadth of the product markets served by these industries thus permitted the adoption of specialist "niche" strategies and obviated the necessity of direct competition with the dominant producers.

In general the degree of integration between the different corporate activities was low. There were cases where one unit supplied raw materials or components to another but usually all activities had a direct interface with outside markets. Therefore, while some central coordination of interdependent activity might be necessary, this was usually low relative to the product flow of the corporation as a whole.

Growth rates and profitability within the industries had been variable and dependent upon the product markets chosen for concentration. In aggregate, however, all three industries had increased their share of the total net output from manufacturing industry. Profits were highest in pharmaceuticals, with rates well above the manufacturing industry average, and lowest in heavy engineering, which had shown below average profitability. While there had been some growth by acquisition, especially during the 1960s many of these firms also reflected a high degree of internally generated growth.

A structure containing both product and geographic divisionalization was therefore common but with some tendency toward dominance by the product over the geographic divisions. The level of direct government interest in these industries had been relatively low, although in recent years some noticeable concentration occurred in electrical engineering as a result of state intervention.

Many of the companies in these industries had been early adopters of the multi-product divisional structure due to the significantly different needs of the product markets served. Many were also multinational in their scope of activities. Dependent upon the size and spread of such overseas activity, many firms tended to adopt geographic divisions to organize their international interests.

The multidivisional structures had often been introduced by management consultants, especially McKinsey & Company, who were extremely active during the 1960s. Further, structural change had often been associated with declining fortunes or a change in leadership. In many companies, especially those that changed their structure during the 1960s, declining profits preceded structural change.

Such change also tended to be resisted. This was not unnatural since transition to a multidivisional system called for the creation of new managerial roles and revision of the old power structure. Thus, in the functionally organized concerns, the functional specialists lost control over operations which were delegated to the division level. The new role for functional specialists was that of staff adviser, while change brought with it the need for a whole new level of general managers. The leaders of the specialist functions were often ill-equippd to fill this role, hence change often necessitated the departure of older executives. Within holding-company structures resistance was also encountered. This was due to the consolidation of like activities which usually accompanied divisionalization. Thus, the degree of autonomy of subsidiary company managers was reduced, as these managers were made to conform to greater central control or to operate under new, division general managers. The process of structural transition to a multidivisional system was, therefore, often painful, and this factor may well account for the lag between adoption of a strategy of diversification and structural change.

THE ELECTRICAL AND ELECTRONICS COMPANIES

There were originally nine electrical and electronic manufacturers in the population, seven of which were diversified, although one had become a conglomerate by 1970. The remaining two companies had been diversified at one time, but the runaway growth of one product line, computers, caused them to be classified as less diversified. Six of these concerns were already diversified by 1950. At the same time five were already engaged in extensive overseas operations and, by 1970, eight of the firms were classified as multinational.

The electrical and electronics companies were engaged in activities revolving around a common technology that was highly transferable to a wide range of related consumer and industrial markets. Since the Second World War there had been considerable technological and market changes within the industry. For example, the growth in ownership of both large and small consumer appliances; the advent of computers; and the development of electronics, all served to change the product mix of manufacturers and make them increasingly diversified. Many companies, therefore, concentrated on specific market segments where they were able to maintain a competitive position despite the presence of a few large, full line manufacturers. New competitive entry was relatively easy in the ever-expanding number of market segments which allowed time for the build-up of the necessary technical skills and financial resources to permit further diversification. Indeed, the breadth of market was such that the full line manufacturers were increasingly forced to concentrate in order to remain competitive.

Three of the companies exhibited a degree of family influence although the scope of activities concentrated this influence at the top. The breadth of operations also meant that many general management positions had long been filled by professional managers drawn from outside the ruling family.

The level of competition within the industry had increased. In 1950 restrictive agreements covered many product markets, especially those where product differentiation was low, such as in light bulbs and components. These restrictions were gradually broken down, although some remained. During the 1960s increased competition came from foreign manufacturers, especially from Japan, Italy, and the United States. These competitors concentrated on the markets for consumer products and electronic equipment. Subsequently, as a result, within the appliance and electronics sectors some attention was given to the achievement of economies of scale, in order that the British concerns could remain competitive.

Growth rate and profitability within the industry was generally above average. Two of the full line manufacturers and one specializing in heavy electrical machinery were less successful, due in large part to fluctuations in the demand for heavy electrical machinery. This market and that for telecommunications equipment was dominated domestically by the public enterprise sector which in some areas was a monopsony buyer.

The electrical companies were early adopters of a multiproduct division structure. New structures became widely accepted during the 1950s and, by 1960, six of the nine concerns had adopted this organization form. Earlier, organizations tended to be functional, and this form was observed in seven of the firms in 1950.

The largest of the British electrical companies, General Electric/English Electric,[1] was of very recent origin (late 1960s) in its present form. Inspired by the government-sponsored Industrial Reorganisation Corporation (I.R.C.), the General Electric Company of Great Britain (G.E.C.), absorbed in successive years the other two full line British electrical manufacturers, Associated Electrical Industries[2] and English Electric.[3] In backing the General Electric Company, the I.R.C. was proclaiming its faith in one man, Sir Arnold Weinstock, the chief executive of G.E.C., who had dramatically improved the fortunes of that company after a period of financial crisis in the early 1960s.

It is interesting to note that the recent successful merger of these three companies

---

[1] R. Heller, "The Total Transformation of G.E.C.," *Management Today,* April 1966, pp. 129–32; see also A. L. G. Lindley, "The Development and Organisation of General Electric Co. Ltd.," private paper given at the London School of Economics, March 1962; "How G.E.C./E.E. Tackles Research Problems," *Financial Times,* December 8, 1969; Monopolies Commission, *Report on the Supply of Electric Lamps (Part I and II),* H.M.S.O., London, 1968; R. Jones and O. Marriott, *Anatomy of a Merger,* Cape, London, 1970; G. Foster, "How English Automated G.E.C.," *Management Today,* August 1970, pp. 66–73; G. Turner, *Business in Britain,* pp. 308–17, 323–25.

[2] Sir Joseph Latham, *Takeover,* Iliffe Books, London, 1969; see also G. Walker, "The Development and Organisation of Associated Electrical Industries Ltd.," private paper given at the London School of Economics, May 1957; R. Jones and O. Marriott, *Anatomy of a Merger;* "The Gentle Shake Up at A.E.I.," *International Management,* July 1966, pp. 33–36; G. Turner, *Business in Britain,* pp. 317–20.

[3] Lord Nelson, "The Development and Organisation of the English Electric Co. Ltd.," private paper given at the London School of Economics, May 1964; see also "English Electric's Growth Challenge," *Management Today,* April 1968, pp. 67–73, 154, 156, 158; R. Jones and O. Marriott, *Anatomy of a Merger;* G. Turner, *Business in Britain,* pp. 320–23.

had an unsuccessful precedent in the 1920s. Gerard Swope, then president of the General Electric Company of America, had attempted to merge the four largest British lamp and heavy electrical companies in such a way that they would be under his effective control. This scheme formed part of a wider attempt by the American company to build a worldwide electrical cartel operated through the international division of General Electric. Swope's plan came close to succeeding, and resulted in the formation of the Associated Electrical Industries (A.E.I.) by the merger of British Thomson Houston, a company controlled by Swope, and Metropolitan Vickers, a company in which Swope had clandestinely acquired control of a majority holding. An attempted merger with the British General Electric Company failed and, in the 1930s, Swope withdrew from the United Kingdom under pressure from the Bank of England. Nevertheless, although financial control was impossible, a complex system of pricing arrangements, restricted trading areas, and information agreements was built up which persisted until antitrust action was taken against General Electric by the United States government.

After World War II, the three main full line producers initially enjoyed the boom of postwar reconstruction. Rapid expansion took place internally and by acquisition, and during the early 1950s profits rose accordingly. Associated Electrical Industries, the company which expanded the most, was perhaps the worst hit, as profits began to decline because of increased competition and overcapacity in the late 1950s. The organization of A.E.I. was ill-suited to its strategy. In 1954 it had been formed into five main subsidiary groups, the original British Thomson Houston and Metropolitan Vickers companies, together with the domestic appliance subsidiary Hotpoint, the Siemens-Ediswan Group, and an overseas group. The chairman of A.E.I. was the chairman of all these groups which were allowed to maintain their independence. The result was wasteful duplication and ineffective central policy making. The links between the operating companies were a series of functional committees under an executive committee composed of the chairman and group managing directors, and the director of central services.

In 1958–59 a series of product divisions was formed but there was latent conflict between the new divisional general managers and the functional members of the boards of the group management companies who were accustomed to exercising power and who intended to continue doing so. Performance continued to decline, and shortly before 1963 the system of collective responsibility began to give way to a system of individual general managers responsible for a group of product divisions. In 1964 Sir Joseph Latham became chief executive, and he attempted to revitalize the company's flagging fortunes. An attempt was made to build up the central office, new control and financial procedures were introduced, and a number of the old senior executives were retired. By 1967, however, the company was still in trouble and, after much internal resistance, it was agreed in September 1967 to call in McKinsey & Company to examine the situation. This was not to be, however, for on September 28, 1967, the General Electric Company of Great Britain, encouraged by the Industrial Reorganisation Corporation, made its successful bid for the Associated Electrical Industries.

General Electric itself had not been without its difficulties and, despite a lesser emphasis on heavy electrical products, profits declined by the late 1950s. Structurally G.E.C. was a contrast to A.E.I. A functional organization was in existence until 1958–59, with manufacturing based on a series of geographically separated works, while marketing was conducted through a large central office, and a series of over 30 wholesaling branches scattered throughout the United Kingdom. Although close connections existed between the main departments in the central office and like departments in the branches, there was no central control, since each branch manager was responsible to the sales director.

Some of these trading departments were amalgamated in 1958–59 to form divisions, with the head of the division being given overall responsibility for both production and marketing. However, the latter was still based on the branch system, thus creating divided responsibility in the branches. Urwick Orr, a consulting firm, was engaged to introduce more central controls on financial resources, and this work was continued until 1960.

In 1961 G.E.C. acquired Radio and Allied (Holdings), a highly successful T.V. manufacturer built up by Michael Sobell, and his son-in-law, Arnold Weinstock (later knighted). These two men joined the main G.E.C. management committee, holding some 15 percent of the G.E.C. equity. In 1961–62 profits declined to £2.9 million before taxes, leaving the company in serious financial difficulty. Shortly thereafter Weinstock was made managing director and many changes soon followed.

The entire system of wholesale branches, including the head office, was closed down and disposed of. The company was then broken up into a series of product divisions, each of which could develop, manufacture, and market its own products. Joint costs and shared services were eliminated, and the manager of each of the separate business divisions was held responsible for performance. The head office staff, reduced to less than 200 in total, moved to modest premises and retained responsibility only for personnel, finance, and overseas coordination. A number of factories were closed down, and part of the company's interests in the less profitable heavy electrical engineering were sold. Pressure to perform was applied from the streamlined central office, performance was closely monitored by a system of detailed financial controls, and stock options were introduced for senior executives. As a result, profits rose rapidly from £4.1 million before taxes in 1962, to £19.5 million in 1965.

In 1967 G.E.C. acquired the foundering A.E.I. After the acquisition, consolidation proceeded as it had in G.E.C. The A.E.I. central office was immediately closed down and sold, several layers of management were discarded, and the complex A.E.I. organization structure was disbanded and its business divided into measurable product groups, which were either combined with similar units in G.E.C., formed into new groups, or closed down.

English Electric, which merged with G.E.C. in 1968, was certainly not in as bad condition as A.E.I. at the time of its merger. English Electric, too, had done well in the 1950s and had lost ground subsequently, but it did progressively better than A.E.I. as far as competing for heavy electrical plant markets. English Electric also diversified into aircraft and, when this interest was absorbed into the British Aircraft Corporation, the company was still doing well. English Electric also invested heavily in the high growth areas of electronics and automation equipment.

In the 1950s English Electric was organized geographically by manufacturing works and not products, thus reflecting the original creation of the company in 1918 as a merger of four separate companies in different locations. The board was composed of the area works managers together with functional specialists for sales, research, and engineering. Until 1956, however, the company's affairs were dominated by the first Lord Nelson who had played a major role in the company since 1930. He was succeeded in 1956 by his son who reorganized the structure, setting up a number of product managers. This move was only partially successful, since the new product managers remained subordinate to the powerful area general managers. Declining profits in the early 1960s caused the company to seek the advice of McKinsey & Company and, in 1965, four main product divisions were set up, each responsible to an executive director of the group.

In August 1968, prompted by the G.E.C./A.E.I. merger, the Plessey Company made a bid for English Electric. The Industrial Reorganisation Corporation, having already held discussions with G.E.C. and English Electric with a view to a possible merger between the two, declined to support Plessey's bid for English Electric. Instead, it supported an agreed merger with G.E.C. on the grounds that this would better serve the purposes of rationalizing the heavy electrical industry. The reshaping of the electrical industry thus owed much to the activities of the I.R.C.

After merging with G.E.C., the English Electric assets were divided up by products and, where possible, grouped with the corresponding activities in G.E.C. Since the merger was agreed upon between the parties, the retrenchment was less drastic; even so, English Electric's head office was disposed of and the number of employees significantly reduced. The new company, G.E.C./English Electric, still had a central office staff of less than 200 and looked distinctly different from its U.S. counterpart in this respect. Research and development, marketing, and production were all handled within the product divisions. The overseas activities were being regrouped and backed by personnel in each of the main product divisions, the central office maintaining special responsibility for exports. It seemed possible that a system of worldwide product divisions might well materialize as the links between the product groups and the geographic divisions overseas became more closely integrated.

The structure Weinstock had imposed on G.E.C./English Electric was closely akin to that expected in a well-managed unrelated product concern. The very small central office with its emphasis on financial controls, and the lack of central operations planning and coordinating functions was very unlike that found in the corresponding American General Electric Company with its large central office function. Although some doubts remained as to the long-run viability of G.E.C.'s structure, Weinstock's results to date gave no hint of structural deficiency, a fact which could cause reconsideration of the structures of many other related product concerns.

The second main electrical concern, the Plessey Company,[4] the original bidder for English Electric, was not a full line electrical company, but it had concentrated in the fields of telecommunications, components, and electronics. This concentration in rapid growth areas was reflected in a very high rate of corporate expansion, although much of this came through acquisitions. Sales expanded from £19.4 million in 1956, to over £200 million in 1969–70. In the early 1950s the company

4 "Why Plessey Acts Tough," *Management Today,* January 1970, pp. 43–47, 98, 100; see also G. Turner, *Business in Britain,* pp. 328–34, 307–08; D. Palmer, "How the Clarks Drive 'Em," *Financial Times,* November 30, 1971; D. Palmer, "Where Plessy Went Wrong," *Financial Times,* December 1, 1971.

concentrated on the production of a multiplicity of electrical components, performed only modest research, and depended for its technology largely on licenses from U.S. companies. The company was built up and managed in a highly personal manner by Sir Allen Clark, and when he died in 1962 a managerial vacuum remained to be filled.

Just before his death, Clark acquired two major telecommunications companies, which were to be major growth areas in the 1960s, and the highly successful Garrard Company, manufacturer of record changers. The two telephone companies, which had previously been rivals, continued to operate as separate entities, thus resulting in considerable duplication.

After Clark's death, his two sons, who had been groomed to succeed him, took over after a board room struggle resulting in a number of resignations. A policy of decentralization was introduced, and an attempt was made to build up the short supply of managerial skill. No real marketing organization had existed, for example, because Clark had mainly handled selling. In 1964 McKinsey & Company was called in to reorganize the structure, and in 1965 a series of product divisions was set up, including a telecommunications division to combine the two telephone companies. Overseas divisions were also set up in Australian and South Africa, together with an international division which handled other overseas manufacturing and sales. A central staff was built up and consisted of functional specialists in charge of research and development, finance, marketing, management services, and personnel. In 1969, following further overseas expansion, a new geographical division was added to cover the United States following the acquisition of Alloys Unlimited, a concern engaged mainly in semi-conductor work. Following serious reported losses at Alloys in 1970 and dissatisfaction with the decentralization of the McKinsey structure, a measure of recentralization took place in 1971 which subdivided the product groups and brought the two Clark brothers back into closer contact with operations.

Like Plessey, the other British electrical and electronics companies also adopted a strategy of concentration within specific niches of the industry. Electrical and Musical Industries (E.M.I.),[5] formed in 1931, grew from a merger which consolidated a major portion of the world's phonograph record manufacture. The company diversified into the manufacture of appliances before World War II, a move that laid the groundwork for the subsequent development of electronics. In 1955 E.M.I. reentered the U.S. market by acquiring Capitol Records. It had sold the Columbia record concern in 1932. This enabled E.M.I. to dramatically exploit the growing U.S. record market in the mid-1960s, although serious managerial problems developed at the end of the decade.

In 1956 the company was divided into product groups in the United Kingdom. In 1957 radio and T.V. production ceased, but appliance production was later increased by the acquisition of Morphy Richards. The large number of overseas

---

[5] J. E. Wall, "The Development and Organisation of Electrical and Musical Industries Ltd.," private paper given at the London School of Economics, May 1964; see also N. Travers, "What's Happening Now at E.M.I.?" *The Director*, May 1969, pp. 257–261; "Record Maker, Record Breaker," *Times Review of Industry*, August 1964, pp. 20–24; "Cassettes, Profits—and EMI," *Duns Review*, October 1969.

subsidiaries, engaged mainly in the production of records, began to be divided into area groups in 1959, and additional overseas activities were gradually built up.

The early 1960s saw a period of static profitability but, in 1964, thanks largely to the discovery and worldwide popularity of the Beatles, profits recovered dramatically and provided the funds for further growth. The poorly performing appliance activities were hived off in 1966, and a series of acquisitions took place to aid in reshaping the company. Major moves were made to extend the company's interest in leisure industries by acquiring the Grade Organisation (1967) and the Associated British Picture Corporation (1969). These acquisitions resulted in a further structural refinement into four main product groups in the United Kingdom: records, entertainment, electronics and industrial operations, and television, together with four overseas area divisions, North America, Australia, Europe, and the rest of the world.

Thorn Electric [6] was also a specialized producer in light electrical products. The company was built up and, by 1970, still largely owned and controlled by Jules Thorn, a Viennese emigré who came to Britain in 1926. Starting from virtually nothing, Thorn built a highly successful corporation by the shrewd handling of entrepreneurial opportunities. He had been personally responsible for choosing each new product market the company had entered, had made all the major strategic decisions, and was responsible for every principle which the company endorsed.

In 1928 Thorn set out to break into the international lighting cartel by price-cutting. After having his lamp supplies cut off by the cartel, he built his own factory. In 1936 he entered the market for radio sets, again undercutting the majors, and during the Second World War obtained government contracts for both lighting and radio items, in view of the efficiency of his production units.

His company still being very small at the end of World War II and threatened with the loss of government contracts, Thorn went to the United States in search of a new product which would give him a competitive advantage. This he found in fluorescent lighting, and he made a long-term agreement for know-how and distribution rights with Sylvania Electric. In 1949, again based on information gathered in the United States, Thorn began the manufacture of T.V. sets which were launched at competitive prices. Thorn's fluorescent lamp and T.V. business grew rapidly during the 1950s, and he added to this prosperity by further shrewd acquisitions and the decision to integrate forward into the market for rental T.V.

In the late 1950s the company entered the domestic appliance market, concentrating initially on the production of stoves. During the 1960s a major series of acquisitions took place making Thorn the largest T.V. rental company in Britain and ensuring a continuous captive market for much of the company's T.V. production capacity. Other new activities were added in general engineering, and the range of appliances was extended.

Structurally the company reflected the patriarchal personality of Thorn the entrepreneur. There was little formal organization and head-office personnel were

---

    [6] Monopolies Commission, *Thorn Electrical Industries Ltd., and Radio Rentals Ltd.—A Report on the Proposed Merger,* H.M.S.O., 1968; Monopolies Commission, *Report on the Supply of Electric Lamps (Part I and II),* H.M.S.O., London, 1968; D. Palmer, "The House That Jules Thorn Built," *Financial Times,* November 24, 1970; D. Palmer, "What Future for Thorn," *Financial Times,* November 25, 1970.

kept to a minimum. Thorn himself made most of the marketing decisions, while production, which used the biggest and best plant and equipment available, was delegated to two long-standing executive board members. The growing complexity of the business, coupled with Thorn's age, led to some structural modification in 1970, as the problem of succession became imminent. The finance director, who had worked for Thorn for over 25 years, was designated as the nominal successor, and he divided the company into a series of profit-centered product groups, each the direct responsibility of an individual managing director. It remained to be seen, however, if and when Thorn retired, if the company was well-equipped to survive the transition from the personal guidance of the entrepreneurial corporation builder to the guidance of an administrator over the empire that had been built.

In contrast to the above companies, Reyrolle Parsons [7] had remained largely undiversified. The present company was only formed in 1967 as part of the rationalization of the heavy electrical industry stemming from the G.E.C./A.E.I. merger. Reyrolle acquired control of C. A. Parsons by purchasing G.E.C.'s holdings. The Reyrolle and Parsons companies had been closely associated for many years, and a financial association already existed. Both, however, had remained independent and an attempt to merge in 1959 had proved impossible. Reyrolle had concentrated on the production of switchgear; Parsons on turbogenerators and transformers. In 1967, the two companies finally merged following declining fortunes for the heavy electrical industry. In 1969, the combined group acquired Bruce Peebles, another transformer company, to rationalize further and reduce overcapacity in British transformer manufacture. After this agglomeration, however, the group remained largely unconsolidated with the individual companies still retaining much of their original identities.

The two remaining concerns were both subsidiaries of foreign parent companies. The first of these, Standard Telephone & Cables, was the British subsidiary of International Telephone & Telegraph (I.T.T.), a U.S. company that became a conglomerate during the 1960s. This company is dealt with in Chapter 6.

The other, Phillips N.V. of Eindhoven,[8] was one of the earliest examples of a European company with a multiproduct divisional structure that was adopted just after the Second World War. Originally a lamp maker, Phillips was founded by Anton Phillips and expanded from lamp making by integrating vertically back to the manufacture of glass and metal filaments for the lamps. This initial integration was followed by modest diversification within the lamp department into X-ray tubes and radio valves. In the period between the First and Second World War, widespread geographic manufacture was forced on Phillips by the development of pro-

---

[7] H. H. Mullers, "Development and Organisation of C. A. Parsons & Co. Ltd., and A. Reyrolle and Co. Ltd.," private paper given at the London School of Economics, March 1960.

[8] B. William Powlett, "Phillips," *The Times*, London, January 7, 1970; see also R. Winsbury, "What Phillips Did for Pye," *Management Today*, May 1969, pp. 75–77, 150; Monopolies Commission, *Report on the Supply of Electric Lamps (Part I and II)*; R. Clark, "Phillips: The Enigmatic Giant," *The Director*, June 1969, pp. 452–55; F. Harmon, "Why Phillips Stresses Teamwork," *International Management*, October 1969, pp. 42–44; A. Erikson, "How Phillips Hopes to Double in Size Within 10 Years," *International Management*, March 1965, pp. 17–20; A. Sampson, *Anatomy of Europe*, pp. 95–96; P. Catx and R. Heller, "Profitless Progress at Phillips," *Management Today*, November 1966, p. 70.

tective trade barriers in export markets. This led to the formation of a number of departments at Eindhoven with responsibility for the geographic subsidiaries outside of Holland, even though reliance was placed on the Eindhoven factories for semi-finished components and machinery.

The Second World War caused dramatic change in Phillips. Following the German invasion of Holland, the parent organization was cut off entirely from its overseas subsidiaries, and Anton Phillips and his son-in-law moved to New York to maintain the subsidiaries in the non-Nazi occupied territories. By foresight the war had been anticipated. In the early summer of 1939 two trusts were formed, one in Britain incorporating the British and Empire subsidiaries, and one in the United States covering the rest of the free world. These trusts prevented the overseas subsidiaries from being lost to the company. In addition, many of the Dutch research staff also left Holland to escape the Nazis and went to the subsidiaries. For example, the Mullard Valve Company in Britain was built up largely by Dutch research personnel during the wartime period.

After World War II the overseas management returned to the Eindhoven plant, which had been left in charge of Anton Phillips's son, Fritz Phillips (president of the company in the 1970s). During the war the overseas subsidiaries had developed many new products, such as radar, and had been virtually autonomous of their parent. Management was thus faced with the task of reconsolidating the corporation which had become fragmented by the war. At that same time, a change in leadership occurred when Anton Phillips stepped down. To allow for these changes, a form of multiproduct division organization was introduced as a means of maintaining some autonomy in the subsidiaries and of easing the task of ramification.

Expansion and rapid technological change, after the Second World War, led to rapid diversification in electronics and consumer appliances, yielding the present highly diversified, multinational concern. By 1970 the founding family was still well represented at Phillips. The family held the power to appoint the board of directors and the executive board of management. This management body determined the overall corporate strategy as well as the policies for the product divisions. It also monitored the series of national companies that supervised the affairs of all local overseas subsidiaries. These national companies, which might infer a grid structure, were apparently subordinate to the product divisions, although from time to time some conflict was apparent between the geographical and product organizations.

A well-developed central office provided assistance to the board of management as far as policy making and monitoring the affairs of the product divisions. These divisions were charged with responsibility for operations and product strategy within their spheres of influence. Each product division had two general managers— one commercial and one technical—a system which reflected Anton Phillips's original organization when he handled technical matters and his brother commercial affairs. By 1970 a system of "concern supply centers" had become increasingly important where particular national companies became responsible for the development, manufacture, and sale of specific products to supply a large geographic area. For example, Pye in the United Kingdom was responsible for gas chromatography and T.V. transmission equipment. Despite a recent accelerated trend of growth by acquisition, the predominant growth of the group had come from the extensive internal development of new products.

Examination of these corporate histories revealed that strategically the electrical companies were early diversifiers. Technological development insured that the full line companies were all diversified prior to the Second World War and had already institutionalized the search for new products by the development of extensive internal research capabilities. Acquisition had also proved a significant element in initial strategic diversification especially among the newer concerns, such as Thorn and Plessey, and among more recently diversified concerns, such as Reyrolle Parsons and I.T.T. The growth of competition in the postwar period was also a significant cause of a major series of acquisitions in the late 1960s and had led to considerable restructuring of the British electrical industry.

The structural change within the electrical companies frequently came much later than the adoption of the strategy of diversification. Consultants, especially McKinsey & Company, were sometimes used to introduce the new structure, but change most frequently occurred with a change in leadership. A multidivisional structure did not come to G.E.C. until Weinstock, to A.E.I. until Latham, to English Electric until the second Lord Nelson, and to Plessey until the succession of Sir Allen Clark's sons. There was the tendency in some cases for this leadership change to be one also of a transition between a strong entrepreneurial personality, which had built the organization, and a new managerial personality. This was true at A.E.I., English Electric, Plessey, and Phillips, and seemed a future possibility at Thorn.

THE CHEMICAL AND PHARMACEUTICAL COMPANIES

Eight firms were classified as belonging to the chemical and pharmaceutical industry. This classification included one rubber company which, prior to the Second World War, was a processor of a natural raw material. In the postwar period, however, the growth of synthetic materials, produced as chemical polymers, transformed the rubber industry, and it became more closely related to the chemical industry.

Like the electrical concerns, firms engaged in chemicals and pharmaceuticals developed their activities around a common technology, which was readily adaptable and transferable to a wide variety of product markets. The systematic research and development common to these companies thus led naturally to the continuous evolution of new products and diversification of the product line.

The period of the late 1930s and the Second World War proved very fruitful for technological development in the chemical industry. It included the early development of the petrochemical industry, discovery of new polymers such as the polyolefins, new synthetic fibers such as nylon, and new routes to the production of heavy organic chemicals. In pharmaceuticals major innovations were made, for example, in antibiotics. These advances led to wholly new product markets as well as to rapidly increased demand for the more established products of the industry. The discoveries transformed the product mix of many companies and increased the degree of diversification. In 1950 there was only one single product chemical concern out of seven on which data were available. By 1960 five of the seven were related product concerns, and all had diversified by 1970.

The level of competition within the industry appeared to increase in the postwar period. This was due to the entry of new competitors in many markets. Several major oil companies and American chemical firms entered the British market. Some increase in foreign competition during the 1960s also occurred from West Germany and spasmodically from Eastern Europe, Japan, and Italy.

One company, Imperial Chemical Industries (I.C.I.), clearly dominated the remainder in sheer size, but there were few specific segments where this dominance went unchallenged. Other firms specialized within specific market segments where they were able to build plants of a similar size and achieve economies of scale similar to I.C.I. In pharmaceuticals, I.C.I. itself was a newcomer and was weak by comparison with the specialist pharmaceutical manufacturers. The breadth of the chemical industry thus provided adequate scope for specialist manufacturers to pursue a niche strategy. Further, the continuous evolution of technology often changed the balance of competitive advantage.

The chemical and pharmaceutical firms showed a low level of family influence. There were only two family companies in 1950, both of which exhibited low product diversity. By 1970 none of the chemical firms contained any family influence.

The chemical companies were somewhat slower than the electrical concerns in adopting a multidivisional structure. In 1950 only I.C.I. had a crude form of multidivisional organization which divided up the diverse production activities. By 1960 three firms had adopted a product divisional structure, and by 1970 this number had grown to six, largely with the help of management consultants.

Like the electrical concerns again, all of the chemical companies had developed overseas operations. Five of seven companies were already multinational in 1950, with overseas operations generally concentrated in the White Commonwealth countries. In 1970 all the chemical companies were multinational and were extending their operations, especially in Europe and North America. The structural impact of overseas operations had generally resulted in the formation of geographic divisions, to supplement domestic product divisions.

The largest British chemical company, Imperial Chemical Industries,[9] dominated the British chemical industry and was one of the world's major chemical groups. It was formed in 1926 as a result of the merger of four leading British chemical companies and was run in a highly autocratic fashion by Lord McGowan, until he retired as chairman in 1950 at the age of 76.

The original emphasis of the company was on heavy inorganic chemicals based on alkali, explosives, and dyestuffs. By 1950 some heavy organics, paints, pharmaceuticals, and fiber activities had been added, but these still represented less than 20 percent of sales. The company entered the fiber industry during the Second

---

9 "Imperial Chemical Industries," *The Times,* London, May 30, 1961; see also M. J. Grant, "The British Company That Found a Way Out," *Fortune,* August 1966, pp. 104–06, 179–85; R. Edwards and H. Townsend, *Business Enterprise,* pp. 66–67, 152–55; A. Sampson, *Anatomy of Britain Today,* pp. 497–505; G. Turner, *Business in Britain,* pp. 139–59, 404–09, 416; S. P. Chambers, "The Financial Control of Imperial Chemical Industries," paper given at the London School of Economics, February 1953; P. T. Menzies, "Top Level Organisation and Management in I.C.I.," private paper given at the London School of Economics, March 1962; M. Johannsen, *Company Organisation Structure,* pp. 38–42.

World War, with the manufacture of nylon in conjunction with Courtaulds and, in the 1950s developed polyester fibers after their discovery by Calico Printers Association. Polyethylene was discovered as part of the research of the Alkali division, which retained initial control of its development. The company developed some overseas activities under a cartel-like arrangement with the American Du Pont company, which also gave I.C.I. access to Du Pont's nylon technology. These overseas activities were mainly in the White Commonwealth areas and in South America. Antitrust action against Du Pont (in the United States) caused the relationship between the companies to be broken, and the joint overseas activities were then divided up. Basically I.C.I. obtained the operations in the British colonial territories, while Du Pont held those primarily in Latin America. No major investments were made in the United States as part of the agreement with Du Pont, and another agreement with the German company, I. G. Farben, was partially responsible for I.C.I.'s strictly limited investment in Western Europe.

During the 1950s the company continued to be managed basically by scientists. McGowan was succeeded by J. Rogers, who in turn was succeeded by Alexander Fleck (later Lord Fleck) in 1953, a chemist of some distinction who had little knowledge of finance or commercial matters. Fleck was, however, less authoritarian, relying on the formation of consensus opinion. Investments were stepped up in fibers, organic chemicals, and plastics, and the product mix of the group began to change, bringing Imperial Chemical into increasing competition with the oil companies who were pursuing their own downstream diversification in petrochemicals.

In 1960 Fleck was replaced as chairman by Paul Chambers, an ex-civil servant who had become finance director in 1948. Chambers provided the break from the production and scientific emphasis of the past. The company at this time was still largely a British operation, its overseas interests were weak, many of its plants were small, its product line was still heavily entrenched in traditional lower growth inorganics, and its structure was unsuited to its strategy.

The structure that I.C.I. had developed was somewhat curious, especially, perhaps, in view of its close association with Du Pont. In 1950 the company's manufacturing activities were divided into 12 product divisions, each with its own chairman and board of directors. Each division was responsible for all operations necessary for the development of its product interests, and was concerned with the sale and pricing of these products. The actual operation of selling and overall control of commercial policy, however, was still a central functional responsibility in the hands of the commercial director. The main board was composed of functional and operational directors who were the central liaison directors for a group of product divisions. This system led to attempts by the operational directors, who were usually from the divisions, to continue to try to manage their old empires from within the central office.

In 1962 McKinsey & Company was retained to review I.C.I.'s structure, and McKinsey's recommendations were partially adopted leading to greater delegation of authority. The chairman of each division, and not the collective division board as had formerly been the case, was made personally responsible for the division's affairs. A system of control groups was set up, each consisting of a deputy chairman and three other executive directors. The control groups each had three operating divisions assigned to them and were responsible for the general direction of the divisions, for monitoring performance, and coordinating activities. In addition, a control group was set up for the head office departments. A system of overseas policy groups developed as overseas interests expanded, and by 1970 there were eight such groups. These consisted of two or more directors, including a territorial director who gave guidance to the overseas subsidiaries in the eight territorial areas. A full set of central functional responsibilities was retained, and the functional directors were retained and assigned specific powers, together with coordination responsibilities for each function on a companywide basis. The executive directors each fulfilled a number of these roles. Thus, the finance director might also be a territorial director and sit on a control group as a division liaison director. No director could serve as liaison director for a division of which he had previously been chairman. The large central office function in I.C.I., therefore, contained a plethora of interlocking committees which were, perhaps, partially necessary to coordinate the extensive product flows between some of the product divisions. However, this extensive system did seem in need of some streamlining.

With Chambers at the helm, I.C.I. became more aggressive and its character underwent considerable change. Heavy capital investment was made in fibers, organics, plastics, and fertilizers all of which dramatically shifted the balance of products. The company moved closer to the consumer-developing interests in pharmaceuticals, wallpaper, and horticulture. In 1961 I.C.I. made an unsuccessful take-over bid for Courtaulds, the main British rayon manufacturer. As a result, I.C.I. ultimately exchanged the stock it had accumulated in return for Courtaulds's share of the joint venture (between the companies) in nylon fibers. Subsequent heavy investment in nylon and polyester fibers eventually led I.C.I. to attempt major changes within the textile industry. Early in 1970 it acquired two of the leading textile companies, Viyella and Carrington & Dewhurst, in order to integrate them and improve their efficiency. Finally, heavy new overseas investments were made especially in Europe and North America.

The structure that developed, apart from a lack of performance-related reward systems, was very similar to the expected form of the related-product concern that had evolved in the United States. There was a large central office, a well-developed series of support functions and systems, and a series of central coordinating activities to deal with interdivisional dependency.

While I.C.I. might, therefore, be considered the dominant British full line chemical company, the multiplicity of chemistry-related product markets still permitted the development of many smaller companies which had specialized in particular market segments.

An example of this strategy was Albright and Wilson [10] which grew from a family-owned, narrow product based company in phosphorus and phosphorus compounds in 1950 to enter the areas of fine chemicals, flavors and essences, silicones, and detergent intermediates. Growing mainly by acquisition, the company adopted a holding company structure until 1967 when it called for advice from McKinsey &

---

[10] "U. K. Chemical Firms Revamp Command Chains," *Chemical and Engineering News,* April 17, 1967, pp. 36–38; see also Sir Sydney Barratt, "The Development and Organisation of Albright and Wilson Ltd.," private paper given at the London School of Economics, March 1964; *Albright Magazine,* company publication, various editions.

Company and subsequently organized into a system of product and geographic divisions.

Similarly, the British Oxygen Company [11] built a near-monopoly in Britain and had extensive overseas interests in the supply of oxygen and industrial gases; when faced with new competition from the American Air Products Company, it expanded into melamine resins, engineering equipment, cryogenics, vacuum equipment, and food processing. In so doing it changed its structure from a functional form to the multidivisional structure. However, the overseas operations, which still consisted primarily of industrial gases, remained only loosely coordinated at the center.

The Dunlop Rubber Company [12] was the only full line British rubber company. Its main product was tires, but Dunlop was an early diversifier into the production of a wide range of other rubber goods. The company's main competitors in Britain were local subsidiaries of American or European parent companies. Dunlop, despite its widespread product and geographic spread, persisted with a functional form of organization until the internal and external pressures of rapid postwar growth brought change.

In the early 1960s Dunlop sought the aid of McKinsey & Company to introduce a decentralized product-divisional system. Like I.C.I., Dunlop, an early diversifier, had built a large central office which was retained and, by 1970, consisted of functional departments for coordination and the setting of central policy objectives to guide the activities of the divisions.

Toward the end of 1969, Dunlop announced that it intended to merge with Pirelli SpA the leading Italian tire and rubber goods producer which was still led by the Pirelli family. This union was one of the first of what will probably be an increasing number of major transnational mergers in Western Europe. In 1970 the two concerns formally began administrative restructuring to manage the new enterprise. Broadly this consisted of a series of senior committees charged with coordinating the new Dunlop-Pirelli group activities. The key committee was the central committee which would make policy for the union, although for fiscal reasons it was only advisory. It was composed of executive board members from both concerns and was to be chaired in alternate years by the two respective chairmen.

By the end of 1970 little real integration had occurred, the merger remaining in name only. For fiscal, legal, and chauvinistic reasons such mergers seemed very difficult to implement and, while the intent of the Dunlop-Pirelli union was to produce a truly multinational enterprise such as Royal Dutch Shell or Unilever, this

---

[11] "Profits from the Air," *Times Review of Industry,* May 1960, pp. 25–27; see also "B.O.C.'s Human Formula," *Management Today,* April 1970, pp. 82–89, 158, 160; J. S. Hutchinson, "The Development and Organisation of the British Oxygen Co. Ltd.," private paper given at the London School of Economics, January 1963; Monopolies Commission, *Report on the Supply of Certain Industrial and Medical Gasses,* H.M.S.O., 1956.

[12] P. Jennings, *Dunlopera,* Dunlop Rubber Co. Ltd., London, 1961; see also R. Edwards and H. Townsend, *Business Enterprise,* pp. 218–20, 286, 288; A. Sampson, *Anatomy of Britain Today,* p. 542; "Devolving to Prosper," *Times Review of Industry,* July 1963, pp. 46–50; R. Geddes, "Decentralising at Dunlop Rubber," *The Manager,* July 1965, pp. 31–35; R. Heller, "Where Dunlop Is Driving," *Management Today,* May 1969, pp. 58–67, 136, 140; R. Geddes, "The Development and Organisation of the Dunlop Rubber Co. Ltd.," private paper given at the London School of Economics, January 1965; D. Thomas, "Dunlop-Pirelli's Squeezed Start," *Management Today,* November 1971, pp. 63–71.

seemed to depend on the ultimate evolution of management dedicated to the overall new corporate institution. It seemed problematical whether the rapid change in market pressures expected during the 1970s would allow sufficient time for this evolution to proceed at the leisurely pace intended. Rather, it seemed more likely that the merger might fail, or that one of the two partners would emerge as dominant, to force through the strategic and structural integration vital for success.

The remaining chemical companies were engaged in the production of pharmaceutical products which were much less capital intensive than general chemical products. In pharmaceuticals product differentiation was prevalent and frequently protected by patent coverage, thus permitting high price tolerance.

The first of these companies, the Glaxo Group,[13] became prominent initially in the 1920s as a supplier of powdered milk (for baby foods) which was produced in the United Kingdom, New Zealand, and Australia. Following the evolution of nutritional science, the company began to develop vitamin preparations for sale separately and incorporated in the company's baby food. Glaxo Laboratories was founded in 1935 and, following the development of vitamins, diversified into other pharmaceutical products. During World War II the company became the main British manufacturer of antibiotics and, after the war, undertook major developments in vaccines and corticosteroids. Overseas activities in pharmaceuticals began prior to the Second World War, and expanded geographic coverage came in the postwar period primarily for secondary production of pharmaceuticals based on raw materials exported from the United Kingdom.

Following sharp declines in the price of antibiotics, Glaxo decided it needed other marketable products and, thus, in 1955, acquired the Murphy Chemical Company, manufacturers of veterinary products. Further acquisitions of Allen and Hanbury's (1958), Evans Medical (1961), and Edinburgh Pharmaceutical Industries (1962), led to the formation of the Glaxo Group. These latter companies were acquired to build up the Group's technological abilities, as the pharmaceutical industry became more dependent on the development of new complex products and less a compounding industry. These acquisitions also brought the Group into drug wholesaling activities and, following some internal reorganization, in 1966 a joint wholesaling company was set up with the British Drug Houses. This latter company, which was partially owned by the American company, Mead Johnson, was acquired by Glaxo in 1968 and thus added two major new product lines: steroid oral contraceptives and a thriving business in laboratory chemicals.

The Glaxo Group's growth was thus largely a result of acquisitions, although it did successfully develop some major new products internally. Structurally the Group remained a holding company, with the larger acquired companies still remaining primarily independent, although there was consolidation among the multiplicity of overseas subsidiaries that were obtained as a result of the U.K. acquisition program.

The second British pharmaceutical company, the Wellcome Foundation,[14] was

---

[13] Sir Alan Wilson, "The Development and Organisation of Glaxo Group Ltd.," private paper for the London School of Economics, December 1964; see also Monopolies Commission, *Report on the Supply of Infant Milk Foods*, H.M.S.O., 1967; *Bulletin International*, company publication, various editions.

[14] A. Lumsden, "Why Wellcome Wants Profits," *Management Today*, May 1967, pp. 86–90, 150, 156; see also M. W. Perrin, "The Development and Organisation of the Wellcome Foundation Ltd.," private paper given at the London School of Economics, November 1953.

unusual in that it was made a charity after the death of its co-founder, Henry Wellcome, an American citizen who with his partner, Burroughs, formed the company. These two men set up an ethical drugs company in Britain in the late nineteenth century, the company's shares being held privately by the founders until a charitable trust was set up after Wellcome's death in 1936. The Trust used the profits, much as Wellcome had used his personal wealth, for the support of research in the areas of medical and veterinary science.

Due to its charitable status, little was published on the company until just before the 1965 Companies Act came into effect. Wellcome became one of the world's largest manufacturers of biological drugs and, apart from its British operations, developed significant overseas investments including the largest interest of any British pharmaceutical company in the United States.

A reorganization with the help of the consultant firm, Urwick Orr, divided the company into two main areas: human medical products and veterinary products. These two areas were supervised by two of the three deputy chairmen. These two deputy chairmen were also responsible for liaison with two main acquisitions: Calmic, acquired in 1967 and mainly concerned with household aerosol products; and Cooper McDougall and Robertson, acquired in 1959 when it was engaged in veterinary products. This latter company had subsequently diversified into household products. The large number of overseas subsidiaries had begun to be coordinated with the appointment of senior regional management, and research and development came under centralized control. In 1968 the company moved another step closer to a multidivisional system with the integration of the Wellcome and Cooper sales forces, and consolidation of the acquired subsidiaries seemed to be proceeding.

Beechams,[15] the third British pharmaceutical company, was primarily engaged in proprietary pharmaceuticals, toiletries, and health foods, and only entered the area of ethical drugs relatively recently. All other products were branded specialties developed with a heavy emphasis on consumer promotion, the advertising budget initially being well in excess of the research budget.

Beechams, guided for many of its formative years by H. G. Lazell, was one of the few British companies encountered that seemed to set out a consistent corporate strategy and then implement it. Building from the base of proprietary toiletries, coupled with extensive marketing, the company grew rapidly during the 1950s and maintained a high level of profitability. Activities which did not meet the high profit requirement were rapidly discarded. Beechams entered the U.S. market initially with its Brylcreem hairdressing and gradually increased its national coverage, using the revenues generated in one market area to support the advertising inputs required to develop the next. By 1959 Brylcreem was the market leader in the United States, and the same strategy was then successfully employed with other

---

[15] "An Outfit that Raises British Eyebrows," *Business Week*, November 7, 1970, pp. 96–101; R. Edwards and H. Townsend, *Business Growth*, pp. 75–76; H. G. Lazell, "Development and Organisation of Beecham Group Ltd.," private paper given at the London School of Economics, February 1960; H. G. Lazell, "The Years with Beechams," *Management Today*, 1968, pp. 67–77, 142–146; R. Hill, "How to Invade the U.S. Market," *International Management*, May 1967, pp. 37–40; H. Johannsen, *Company Organisation Structure*, pp. 15–17; Evely and Little, *Concentration in British Industry*, pp. 189–90.

toiletry products. Following this success in the United States, during the late 1960s a similar strategy was employed in Europe.

Beechams entered the field of ethical pharmaceuticals and veterinary medicine by setting up a small research team which, in 1959, successfully developed the first synthetic antibiotics. These products quickly became the fastest growing items in the company, and direct marketing was being introduced to replace the initial series of licensing arrangements whereby local manufacture was to be started in the United States.

Structurally, Lazell began the formation of product divisions in the early 1950s. He eliminated minority interests in the large number of subsidiaries forming the group, and incorporated the smaller businesses into major units which became operating product divisions. Overseas expansion of toiletries led to a geographic split in toiletries between the European Area and the North American Area in 1964–65. Subsequent product additions in North America resulted in the formation of geographic divisions, with increasing territorial responsibilities being given to the North American operations. In the late 1960s U.K. operations were regrouped from a product divisional system into Beecham Products (U.K.) which contained functional production and marketing directors for each of the main activities: drinks, food, toiletries, and proprietary medicine. Pharmaceuticals remained a separate product division, although operations in North America were controlled by the North American Division which held geographic responsibility for all activities in the Western Hemisphere. Increased activities in Europe then led to the formation of a separate European Division which initiated Beecham's entry into the new product area of cosmetics.

The final company in the chemicals group, Fisons,[16] had interests in both pharmaceuticals and heavy chemicals. A family company for several generations, Fisons was one of the first companies to develop synthetic fertilizers. Until the Second World War the company grew by expansion and acquisition, going public in 1933, and by 1944 was the dominant British fertilizer manufacturer producing mainly phosphate fertilizers. Overseas interests were developed in the White Commonwealth, and limited production of nitrogen fertilizers was started.

After World War II, Fisons remained predominantly engaged in fertilizers. The company, still managed by Sir Clavering Fison, embarked on a program of modest diversification, which took it into the fields of chemical intermediates, pharmaceuticals, and agricultural chemicals. The expansion of the petroleum-based nitrogen fertilizers brought Fisons into increased competition with I.C.I. and Shell and, lacking a suitable base in heavy organic chemicals, profits declined. Further, decontrol of the fertilizer industry by the government meant that Fisons was forced to develop its still rudimentary marketing skills. A commercial director was appointed to integrate the sales and purchasing functions, and a marketing staff was built up under the commercial director.

---

16 Sir Clavering Fison, "Development and Organisation of Fisons Ltd.," private paper delivered at the London School of Economics, February 1957; see also Lord Netherthorpe, "Fisons Limited—Ten Years On," private paper delivered at the London Graduate School of Business, April 1969; "Fisons Fertile Facelift," *Management Today,* December 1968, pp. 50–57; J. Poole, "Can Intal Cure Fisons's Profits Wheeze," *Sunday Times,* November 23, 1969; "New Look at Fisons," *Times Review of Industry,* March 1966, pp. 18–21; R. Spiegelberg, "Fisons—A Company in Metamorphosis," *The Times,* London, February 19, 1970.

In 1957 the functional management system was broken down into a series of five operating divisions which decentralized the production and research functions, although research was coordinated by a central functional director. The commercial director, however, retained his executive responsibilities, was also in charge of one of the product divisions, and was represented in the other divisions. The divisions were supervised mainly by a number of operational directors, four of whom had responsibilities in the fertilizer division, the fifth supervising all three other divisions.

The pace of diversification increased following an investigation by the Monopolies Commission, which resulted in accusations of price-fixing and monopolistic actions by Fisons. As the nonfertilizer activities grew, it became impracticable for one director to handle the day-to-day workings and, in 1960, further decentralization took place which resulted in the formation of a holding company with central coordination by the group managing director. In 1966, with the appointment of a new chief executive, a full-fledged multidivisional system was introduced based mainly on product boundaries, but which also took account of the location of the principal production units. Loughborough Division, for example, incorporated the rapidly growing pharmaceutical interests, together with ethical products, toiletries, industrial chemicals, and scientific apparatus. The overseas operations were managed through an international division formed in 1962.

The evidence shows, therefore, that strategically the chemical companies were, in the main, less diversified in the immediate postwar period than the electrical concerns. There was, however, generally some internal research capability which was extended by entry into new market segments often by the process of acquisition. Such acquisitions were usually complementary and attempted to capitalize on whatever internal skills were available. However, the potential gains from acquisition were frequently difficult to achieve due to a failure to implement structural reform, for the structural transition of the chemical companies had not yet proceeded as far as with the electrical concerns. When it came, organization reform was frequently introduced by outside consultants and occurred shortly after changes in leadership, as was the case at I.C.I., Dunlop, Fisons, Beechams and, more recently, at the Wellcome Foundation.

THE ENGINEERING COMPANIES

The engineering industry was the largest employing industry in Britain. It had a vital role to play in the economy and represented a key resource for Britain as a high added-value contributor in a country whose economy depended on the conversion of low-cost raw materials into high-value export commodities. Unfortunately, the industry, and especially the heavy engineering concerns, had been slow to adopt modern managerial practices. The goal of engineering excellence was too often allowed to override commercial sense. Companies had been, and in some cases still were, managed by men thinking as engineers rather than as managers; marketing skills were often neglected, and products had frequently not been designed to fulfill market needs.

Like the technologically based chemical and electrical industries, engineering skills were readily transferable to a wide variety of products and markets. This led to high diversity, but too frequently the result was a failure to develop new profitable product lines internally. This was due partially to a lack of awareness of market needs and the limited use of research and development.

There were twelve engineering companies in the population, seven of which were engaged in heavy engineering such as processing plant and machinery, while the remainder were active in light engineering usually producing components for other manufacturers. By 1950, six of the engineering concerns were already diversified, four were dominant product concerns, and two were still single product firms. By 1970 all of the engineering companies had diversified to the related product category.

Overall concentration of production within the industry was low due to the wide range of possible engineering products. All firms specialized to a degree but, while concentration was high in specific segments, there were no significant barriers to new entry in many areas.

The level of family influence was quite low among the large concerns—only four companies were still being managed by families in 1950. However, the industry could be characterized as traditional because there was a degree of father-to-son continuity both among the management and the workforce. This might have been a partial cause of the slowness to adopt modern managerial techniques and the emphasis on production and engineering excellence rather than market needs.

There were significant product changes in many areas of the industry brought on by technological development. However, the traditional production methods tended to remain largely unchanged. The industry had been somewhat slow to adjust to innovations such as automated equipment and numerically controlled machine tools. Capital investment per employee was low by international standards. This might reflect the low level of research and development expenditure frequently found in the industry. A further symptom of this was the tendency for growth by acquisition often aimed at expanding or renewing the product range of the acquiring companies.

During the early part of the period under study, there had been many restrictive agreements between manufacturers in the industry. These had broken down somewhat later, however, and made way for some limited concentration and consolidation. Competition generally increased, especially from overseas, and the balance of, trade deteriorated. This was particularly true in the heavy engineering sector where imports of contractors, plant, office machinery, and mechanical handling equipment all grew by over 200 percent between 1963 and 1968.

Structurally the companies in this industry were relatively slow adopters of the multidivisional form. In 1950 only one company had adopted such an organization. Many of the engineering concerns, particularly the large diversified groups in heavy engineering, were holding companies in the early years. Growth for these concerns usually involved the acquisition of a number of small family firms, which were allowed to continue their independent operations. Central offices were very small, and each subsidiary firm went its own way despite the fact that many produced the same products. The decline of restrictive agreements and increased competitive pressures made consolidation necessary. Consequently, the 1960s brought a significant increase in the number of multidivisional firms, many of them using consultants to reform their structures. By 1970, nine engineering companies had adopted multidivisional structures, six of these transitions occurring since 1960.

The level of multinational activity was moderate—in 1970 six firms were classified as multinational. Much of the overseas investment, however, was small relative to domestic activities and was often restricted to former colonial territories, especially the White Commonwealth. As a result of the limited scale of overseas operations, most of the multinational concerns had not developed their structure beyond the stage of the international division.

Six of the engineering companies were engaged in heavy engineering and were concerned mainly with the fabrication of ferrous metals into a wide variety of products. These companies generally had a long history dating back to family concerns in the nineteenth century, and traditional products still made up much of their production.

The Babcock and Wilcox Company,[17] which was independent of the U.S. company of the same name, was formed around the patents of George Babcock and Stephen Wilcox for water tube boilers. A worldwide organization was built up to manufacture and service boilers, and the British company became independent of its American parent company in 1891 with the rights to the Babcock and Wilcox patents for the world outside the United States and Cuba. Agreements were still maintained with the U.S. company subject to the Sherman Antitrust Act. Other boiler and ancillary equipment manufacturers were acquired before the Second World War. These manufacturers were allowed to continue operating as independent units, and an extensive series of overseas companies was set up. In the initial period after the war, profits rose, reaching a peak in 1955 of £4.7 million before taxes. Since then, despite attempted diversification after the market declined for steam plant, profits also declined to about 2 percent of turnover and about 4 percent of assets (fixed assets had not been revalued recently). In 1964 modest structural reform was attempted by the formation of three new companies to aid coordination. An operations company was set up to supervise the parent company activities, a holdings company became responsible for the coordination of the affairs of the U.K. subsidiaries, with a similar overseas company to perform the same role for the overseas interests.

John Brown appeared slightly more successful. It, too, was a holding company still chaired by Lord Aberconway, a third generation descendant of the founder of the John Brown Steel Company. The company, which was originally engaged in steel manufacture, integrated backward into coal mining and iron ore in the late nineteenth century and, in 1899, acquired the Clydebank Engineering and Shipbuilding Company as an outlet for its drop forgings. In 1931 it combined its steel works with those of Thomas Firth. Then, after World War II, the steel and coal assets were both nationalized. The company was left as a shipbuilder and marine engineering concern with other subsidiaries engaged in engineers tools, and railway carriage construction.

With the money received from nationalization, the company diversified by acquisition into machine tools and attempted to develop its established engineering interests with the criterion of the highest standards of engineering excellence. A

---

[17] Sir Kenneth Hague, "The Development and Organisation of Babcock and Wilcox Ltd.," private paper given at the London School of Economics, November 1958.

formal holding-company format was adopted in 1953. All trading activities were then conducted through subsidiary and associated units administered by their own boards, consisting of the principal subsidiary company executives and representatives of the parent board. Machine tools proved relatively profitable but many of the diversification moves such as landboilers, portable electric tools, and chemical engineering were disappointing. The unprofitable shipbuilding interests were finally divested in 1967, after the Geddes Report, and merged with Clydebank Shipyard. In the late 1960s the company was engaged mainly in machine tools, engineers tools, marine engineering, plastic machinery, and chemical engineering. Profits since 1950 had been erratic and disappointing, fluctuating between a loss of £2.2 million in 1966 and a peak profit of £4.5 million achieved in 1961 and 1969.

Simon Engineering [18] had a similar poor record of performance during most of the 1960s. Until 1960 it remained as two companies, both formed by Henry Simon and managed by his son for over 40 years. Henry Simon Limited was engaged primarily in the production of flour milling machinery and mechanized handling equipment; while Simon Carves was engaged in contracting for power plants, coke ovens, and, more recently, chemical plants. The two companies and their subsidiaries were run as independent autonomous units. They came together only as the result of a threatened take-over of Henry Simon in 1960.

Following the amalgamation and the relatively poor profit performance of the new Simon Engineering Company, a process of centralization was begun in 1965–66 in order to allow top management to sort out the profitable from the unprofitable activities. Urwick Orr (the consultant firm) was used initially in the Henry Simon subsidiary and that group was broken up into clearly defined sections, each under the control of a chief executive. Following the introduction of this structure a similar process was applied to Simon-Carves, despite internal reluctance. Systematic corporate planning was introduced, and activities were examined to ascertain their potential for profit; some activities were subsequently sold off. Research and development was centralized, and the company was broken down into a series of operating groups each engaged in specific areas of manufacturing or contracting. Some profit improvement had occurred since 1966, but an attempt by the Industrial Reorganisation Corporation to merge the company with another heavy engineering group was resisted.

Three of the four remaining heavy engineering companies were all at one time engaged in steel production basically as a source of raw material for captive usage. They were all relatively large, old, established companies which, although exhibiting high initial postwar growth, generally performed unimpressively during the 1960s. There were signs that these companies were now waking up. All had exhibited recent adoption of at least a partial multidivisional structure.

Guest, Keen and Nettlefold [19] dated back to 1902 when it was formed as a

[18] Simon Engineering, *The Simon Engineering Group,* private publication, 1947; see also Lord Simon "The Development and Organisation of the Simon Engineering Group," private paper given at the London School of Economics, November 1956; J. Poole, "Simons New Broom Can Sweep Back the Profits," *Sunday Times,* February 15, 1970.

[19] G. Bull, "The Restless Years at G.K.N.," *The Director,* September 1968, pp. 376–81; see also R. Edwards and H. Townsend, *Business Enterprise,* pp. 20–22; Sir Anthony Bowlby, "Problems Associated with the Manufacture and Sale of Bolts, Nuts, and Screws," in Edwards

merger of three family businesses engaged in the production of iron, fabricated steel rods and screws, and nuts and bolts, thus creating a vertically integrated business. Subsequent acquisitions before the Second World War added John Garrington, a major producer of steel forgings, and John Lysaght, a steel-making concern with sheet steel interests in Australia and a subsidiary, Joseph Sankey, a major producer of automobile wheels and chassis components. Several other producers of screws and fasteners were also acquired as the company built up a powerful position in this market with a monopoly in woodscrews, as well as involvement in a large share of the bolts and nuts market. Competition was restricted by industry-wide cartels between G.K.N. and other screw manufacturers; these cartels did not break down until the mid-1950s.

As a result, a multiplicity of independent subsidiary companies existed with virtually no central control, each company having its own board with direct access to the chairman of the group. The parent company board itself consisted largely of descendants of the acquired family companies.

In 1950 the company's steel interests were nationalized, but they were reacquired as soon as possible after denationalization. In 1953 a new chairman, Kenneth Peacock, was appointed. He continued the previous style of management, sitting on the board of each of the 40 odd subsidiaries. A strategy of increased participation in automobile accessories was followed, especially after the Restrictive Practices Act made the fastener cartels illegal. Further acquisitions increased the number of subsidiaries, and Peacock was intimately involved in the operating decisions of them all. Profits expanded, however, due to a seller's market and the rapid expansion of the motor industry. One significant centralization move did take place during this period, namely, the establishment of central cash accounting in 1956 which, although resisted by the subsidiaries, was eventually accepted.

Profits declined sharply in 1961 and 1962 and, by 1963, when Raymond Brookes was appointed as managing director, it was painfully obvious that structural reform was long overdue. In conjunction with consultants, the company was divided into product oriented subgroups in the United Kingdom and, where possible, overseas. Where subgroup divisions were not practicable, an alternative geographic grouping was adopted for overseas activities. Brookes took over from Peacock as chairman in 1965, and strategic planning was introduced; some build-up took place in the central office services. In 1967 the first active recruitment of graduates for management began; new acquisitions were made aggressively and increased expenditure was made on research and technology. In 1968 the company's steel interests were absorbed into the British Steel Corporation, but the company announced in 1969 it would build a new integrated steel works in Australia.

The company structure, although classified as multidivisional, still seemed a far cry from the American multidivisional structure. These product subgroups,

and Townsend, *Studies in Business Organisation;* A. Sampson, *Anatomy of Britain Today,* p. 537; G. Turner, *Business in Britain,* pp. 304–307, 342–50; Monopolies Commission, *Guest Keen and Nettlefold Ltd., and Birfield Limited, A Report on the Merger,* H.M.S.O., 1967; R. P. Brookes, "The Development and Organisation of G.K.N. Ltd.," private paper given at the London Graduate School of Business, December 1969; R. Sanders, "Guest Keen Goes for Growth," *Management Today,* May 1967, p. 60.

each of which had its own subgroup functional staff reporting both to the group chairman and the functional specialists at the head office, were still essentially composed of the multiplicity of subsidiary companies. These in turn retained their own boards. The result was in effect to sandwich another layer of management between the central office and the subsidiaries. Each of the subgroups was not itself an operating company, but merely a policy maker for the subsidiaries within it.

Tube Investments [20] was in many ways very similar to Guest, Keen, with tubes instead of screws as its mainstay; it had evolved as a comparable collection of companies with diverse engineering interests put together mainly by acquisition and left to run in a virtually autonomous fashion. Like Guest, Keen, Tube Investments integrated backward into steel production but much later in time. It acquired the British Aluminium Company in 1959 to protect its steel tube business from a possible threat from aluminum, and integrated forward into tube-using industries, especially bicycles, a declining industry where the company rapidly achieved a near-monopoly. A restrictive agreement with its major competitor, Stewarts and Lloyds, effectively divided the tube market and protected both concerns from serious competition until the early 1950s. The breakdown of this agreement led to some increase in competition, which was generally to the advantage of Tube Investments, for Stewarts and Lloyds was completely absorbed into the British Steel Corporation in 1967.

Tube Investments also extended into electrical products. The Simplex Company formed part of the original Tube Industries Company, and the nationalization of steel in 1968 made funds available for the purchase of Radiation, a major gas and electric appliance manufacturer. The company also produced capital goods, such as rolling mills, and in 1966 it entered the machine tool industry by acquisition.

The company was built up largely by Sir Ivan Stedeford, the son-in-law of the company's first leader. Stedeford dominated the company between 1939, when he became managing director, and 1962, when he retired as chairman. He was succeeded by Lord Plowden, an ex-civil servant, who set about rationalizing the complex system of subsidiaries into well-defined product divisions.

By 1970 the company was divided essentially into product divisions, together with an overseas division. The structure was in this sense very similar to Guest, Keen's in that the divisions were still composed of a multiplicity of subsidiaries, many of which produced similar products, as in the tubes division. The divisional management concerned itself with planning, commercial policy, major new investments, new products, and monitoring subsidiary performance; it reported to the main Tube Investments Board. Except in those cases, for example aluminum, where the division was composed of one major company, operations were conducted by the subsidiaries each with its own board. The central office was small,

---

[20] R. Hodson, "The Five Men Who Run T.I.," *The Director,* February 1969, pp. 226–29; see also G. Turner, *Business in Britain,* pp. 303–05, 342–44, 355–60, 371–78; I. A. R. Stedeford, "Management and Control of the Tube Investment Group," paper given at the London School of Economics, January 1952; A. Lumsden, "Testing Time Inside Tube Investments," *Management Today,* July 1967, pp. 55–61, 116; Evely and Little, *Concentration in British Industry,* pp. 249–53; Lord Plowden, "Tube Investments Limited," private paper given for the London School of Economics, May 1967; *This Is T.I. Today,* company publication, 1966–67.

and central control was exercised through the executive committee of the board. Although not directly responsible for the divisions, the committee members took a special interest in specific divisions. The central functions were fewer than in Guest, Keen. They consisted of financial control over capital expenditure, the approval of budgets and plans, control of senior appointments, control over central research and development (much of this was delegated within the divisions under the guidance of the director of research), and control of legal, public relations, and purchasing negotiations (actual buying was done at the divisional level).

The performance of Tube Investments was very variable during the 1960s (after rapid expansion during the seller's market of the previous decade), with a return on capital generally less than 10 percent before taxes. There were some signs, however, that performance during the 1970s might improve, reflecting the managerial reforms instituted during the late 1960s.

The third of the major heavy engineers, Vickers,[21] had been forced to undertake the most drastic strategic changes of all, in the post-World War II period. For much of its life, the company had had one major customer, the British government, for whom Vickers performed the role of chief "armourer." By 1950 the company was engaged mainly in steel, shipbuilding, railway rolling stock, aircraft and armaments, virtually all of which rapidly became declining markets during the late 1950s along with cutbacks in defense expenditure. Steel, which was nationalized in 1950, was reacquired in 1954, and one chance to escape was thus lost. Sales began to fall in 1958 and by the early 1960s the company was in serious trouble, brought about partly by an initial diversification into heavy tractors which had ended in disaster. In 1960 the company's aircraft interests were absorbed into the British Aircraft Corporation, although Vickers continued to carry the heavy cost burden and later the losses of the V.C.10 airliner. This cost, coupled with heavy investment in steel plant, proved a massive cash drain and forced the company deeply into debt by 1963.

In 1965 a new strategy and structure were formed, with help from McKinsey & Company. The holding-company structure became a series of product divisions, each with its own board which supervised the activities of subsidiaries, and each of these with their own local boards. Four new growth areas were selected for investment: printing machinery, office equipment, chemical engineering, and medical engineering. By a program of acquisitions, these were built up rapidly between 1965 and 1969 to nearly 40 percent of sales. Government was indirectly responsible for the salvation; the Geddes Report allowed Vickers to sell part of its shipbuilding interests to Swann Hunter and the nationalization of Vickers English steel subsidiary brought cash compensation to pay for the diversification program.

The McKinsey reorganization introduced detailed corporate planning with each division preparing an annual management plan for central scrutiny and review. The personnel function was expanded to provide a source for future management, and

---

[21] Sir Charles Dunphie, "The History and Organisation of The Vickers Group," private paper given at the London School of Economics, March 1960; see also Sir Leslie Rowan, "Vickers Ltd.—Ten Years On," private paper given at the London Graduate School of Business, November 1970; "Why Vickers Misfired," *Management Today,* March 1970, pp. 70–81, 138; G. Turner, *Business in Britain,* pp. 303–05, 342–44, 355–60, 372–78; *Vickers News,* company publication, various editions.

some improvements were made in the rudimentary marketing skills of the company. The actual corporate office was drastically reduced and, by 1970, consisted of less than 200 people. Control over divisional operations was based primarily on financial performance against the management plan.

Some improvement in performance took place after the mid-1960s, but profits had still not returned to the peak reached in 1960. In 1971 the company was again fighting for its life since some of the new growth areas had not done as well as expected and the chemical engineering interests were divested. Major stockholders, with the encouragement of the Industrial Reorganisation Corporation, forced management changes on Vickers in an effort to improve the company's fortunes and it remained to be seen what their impact would be.

The fourth and final concern engaged in heavy engineering was the Hawker Siddeley Group,[22] a holding company formed by a rapid program of acquisition leading to extensive diversification in the late 1950s. The company was then primarily engaged in aircraft production and, anticipating the decline of the British aircraft industry, chose to diversify as a protective strategy. Acquisitions were made in a wide variety of industries, primarily in Canada and the United Kingdom. Initially the company acquired interests in various heavy industries including electrical engineering, mechanical engineering, diesel engines and locomotives, steel manufacture, shipbuilding, coal mining, iron ore, steel castings, and railway rolling stock. This mix gave the company a product scope reminiscent of Vickers and, in addition, the group served as one of the focal points for the concentration of the British aircraft industry. Well-known airframe manufacturers such as DeHavilland, Blackburn, and Folland were acquired and combined into an aircraft division in 1963.

The company was still seemingly an aircraft company in spirit; aerospace engineering made up the bulk of Hawker Siddeley's profits and formed the primary interest of management. Some of the less profitable diversification moves were divested during the 1960s with concentration occurring on a more limited range of mechanical and heavy electrical engineering activities.

The light engineering companies were generally smaller than the heavy ones, and their performance was substantially better. These companies were usually of more recent origin and, in the main, their rapid postwar development resulted from the initial rapid growth of the automobile industry, often followed by acquisitions. For some, diversification had come during the 1960s, but when it came the companies had all adopted the multidivisional structure quite quickly without allowing the build-up of power in autonomous subsidiaries.

Delta Metal [23] was one of the largest nonferrous metal fabricators in Europe having expanded rapidly since the Second World War from a base in extruded nonferrous metal products. Expansion had occurred since the late 1950s by the acquisition of small firms engaged mainly in aluminum fabrications and sanitary and

---

[22] Sir Roy Dobson, "The Development and Organisation of Hawker Siddeley Group Ltd.," private paper delivered at the London School of Economics, January 1962; see also R. Heller, "How Hawkers Stayed Aloft," *Management Today*, May 1966, pp. 68–74, 134, 136; G. Turner, *Business in Britain*, pp. 370, 373–78.

[23] "What Management Did When a Company Doubled in Two Years," *Achievement*, July 1965, pp. 7–8.

water fittings, the latter being users of the company's primary product. In 1963 Delta Metal acquired the Enfield Group, which took the company into cables and extended overseas interests substantially. Forward integration proceeded somewhat further by the acquisition of distributors of copper tubes and fittings, and protective investments were made into plastics fabrication. Initially, in the early 1960s, divisions composed of subsidiary companies were set up, but following a profit recession a full multidivisional structure was adopted in 1967 by concentrating the activities into six divisions, each the specific responsibility of an executive chairman.

Associated Engineering [24] was not formed until 1946 and was initially a loose cartel-like association of companies making piston rings for the automobile industry. Subsequent acquisitions diversified the product line into radiators and pressed metal work, castings for the automobile and aircraft industry, metal packings, and specialized machine tools. In 1959 this growth forced a reexamination of the corporate structure. A multidivisional system was imposed dividing the company into three product divisions. Subsequent acquisitions in the early 1960s led to a significant increase in size and product diversity. Structural revisions accompanied these changes, increasing the number of product divisions and adding an international division. A group research and development center was set up, and a policy committee was formed to examine future policy; a five-year planning schedule was started in 1967. A stock option scheme had been introduced in 1965, but was terminated by the 1966 Finance Act.

Birmid Qualcast [25] was formed in 1967 as a merger between Birmid Industries, a large manufacturer of castings primarily for the motor and aircraft industries, and Qualcast whose main product was lawnmowers, and who held 90 percent of the British market. Following the merger a product-divisional structure was introduced in 1969, and this structure combined the like activities in each of the two companies. The three main product divisions were divided internally further into smaller product groups all with clearly defined areas of responsibility. The central office had relatively few functions, but was responsible for finance and accounting, corporate and financial planning, secretarial, and administrative functions.

Joseph Lucas [26] and Smiths Industries were also heavily engaged in automobile components and were the market leaders in the products they produced. These companies were investigated by the Monopolies Commission as part of an inquiry into the supply of automobile instruments and electrical components. Until 1956 a restrictive agreement was in effect whereby each company avoided competition with the other by concentrating on exclusive market segments. These two companies were somewhat different from the other engineering firms, and relied more on the technological skills which their engineers had developed.

Joseph Lucas was founded in the late nineteenth century for the manufacture of

---

[24] H. Johannsen, Editor, *Company Organisation Structure*, pp. 6–8.

[25] "Where Tom Cooper Is Leading the World's Biggest Lawnmower Makers," *Achievement*, July 1966, p. 5.

[26] "Some Aspects of General Management Practice at Joseph Lucas Ltd.," presentation to British Institute of Management, September 1966; see also N. Faith, "Can Lucas Fly Out of Its Traffic Jam," *Sunday Times*, London, March 15, 1970; Monopolies Commission, *Report on the Supply of Electrical Equipment for Mechanically Propelled Land Vehicles*, H.M.S.O., 1963.

pressed metal goods including coach lamps. With the coming of the automobile, the company moved readily into the role of an electrical components manufacturer. In the interwar period a rush of acquisitions led to the establishment of a dominant position, protected by a series of restrictive agreements with other competitive manufacturers.

In the post-World War II period, further acquisitions consolidated Lucas' position, although the expansion of the General Motors' and Ford component subsidiaries led to some competition in specific areas. Since the Second World War, Lucas had diversified its product line substantially, but was still primarily concerned with the manufacture of automobile and aircraft components. Recession in these industries caused Lucas to open new areas of interest in instruments, electronic components, and hydraulics, but these industrial activities were still small. In addition, competition, which increased somewhat with the breakdown of the cartel, was being further increased by the automobile manufacturers adopting a policy of multisourcing after a series of strikes among component manufacturers in the late 1960s. Similarly, changes in distribution channels for replacement components were increasing competition from new market entries and threatening the Lucas dominance of the automobile component market for the 1970s.

Lucas adopted a form of multidivisional structure early. In 1951 the company was divided into a series of operating divisions based on the main subsidiary companies in the group. A central office set policy and monitored the performance of the subsidiary company divisions which operated in a decentralized manner through local boards. An element of the former subsidiary identities remained, but generally the company operated as a consolidated divisional system. Central control was retained only on finance and personnel matters.

The main board was composed of executives and nonexecutive directors and was served by two committees, a finance and audit committee which dealt with overall finances, and an appointments and salaries committee which made recommendations on senior appointments. Below the main board was a group executive committee which provided the link between the main board and the divisions. This body was composed of central staff members and the heads of the main divisions. It performed a coordinating role between line and staff functions but its main role was policy formation and monitoring the implementation of policy. The central services (covering major areas such as manufacturing, research, industrial relations, engineering, and overseas activities) were functional staff specialists with no executive authority. These specialists served the whole group in an advisory capacity.

One apparently anomalous element remained in that a separate sales company was responsible for the marketing of much of the replacement market equipment. Some subsidiaries did possess their own sales force such as Batteries, C.A.V., and Girling, but the main division, Joseph Lucas (Electrical), sold only to the original equipment market.

Smiths Industries [27] was in many respects similar to Lucas. Due to the restrictive agreements, Smiths concentrated on instruments and Lucas on other electrical com-

---

[27] Monopolies Commission, *Report on the Supply of Electrical Equipment for Mechanically Propelled Land Vehicles;* Evely and Little, *Concentration in British Industry,* pp. 210–13; H. Johannsen, *Company Organisation Structure,* pp. 82–87.

ponents. Smiths diversified from this base into clocks and watches, appliance controls, and industrial instruments in the prewar period and just after the Second World War adopted a form of multidivisional system to cope with product diversity. After the breakdown of the agreement with Lucas, Smiths did well with car heating systems and entered the market for spark plugs.

In the 1960s the company faced setbacks due to the changes in government aviation policy, loss of business in instruments, especially at Ford due to its self-manufacture, and competition from cheap imported clocks and watches. Further diversification was attempted to reduce dependency on these markets, and interests were being developed in building supplies, medical equipment, and industrial ceramics.

In 1967 a further major structural amendment took place which broke up the large divisions into a series of smaller product divisions in order to depress profit responsibility to lower levels in the hierarchy. These smaller divisions were formed into four groups supported by a small central service function which provided guidance to the divisions in the areas of purchasing, legal affairs, organization and methods, and data processing. In addition, there were a small number of special directors who formed a corporate staff for the managing director. Although they had no line authority, they acted on behalf of the managing director to ensure that his policies and objectives were implemented.

In summary the strategies of the engineering concerns could be divided roughly between the heavy engineers engaged in producing finished products and the light engineering concerns producing components and sub-assemblies. The heavy concerns had been generally slow to adapt to their environment, and only the impact of declining economic performance triggered strategic change. The light engineers had been perhaps more responsive in that they were producing assemblies for more market-oriented and cost-conscious producers, especially the automobile makers. Nevertheless, both groups by and large had been weak exploiters of research and development resulting in the fairly extensive use of acquisition as a route to strategic change.

The common pattern of structural change found elsewhere was also in evidence in some of the engineering concerns. Consultants had often been used to assist in developing the multidivisional structure. At both G.K.N. and Tube Investments, structural change was observed to follow rapidly upon a change in leadership. However, many of these multidivisional structures were far from the theoretical concept of the structure and often resembled some form of hybrid between a holding company and the multidivisional form.

CONCLUSION

The early diversifiers were identified as belonging to the electrical, chemical, and engineering industries. These firms grew by relating their product range to a common technology or skill which proved highly adaptable for a variety of market needs. While initial diversification was often the result of acquisition, many of the companies in these industries institutionalized the strategy by the process of research and development. A number of the companies, however, still appeared weak in the initiation of new products, and had been forced to rely on licensed technology or acquisition, for generating product innovations. This was especially true of the engineering companies, which had generally invested less in product development and were forced to diversify more by acquisition when faced with decline in traditional markets. Growth rate in all three industries, however, had been above average and sustained by the constant development of new markets.

The wide range of markets served resulted in low barriers to new competitive entry, despite concentration and high capital intensity in some market segments. Most companies could not attempt to cover the full scope of each industry and, therefore, a strategy of specialization in specific segments was common.

Competition generally increased in all three industries due to the breakdown of restrictive agreements, the entry of new domestic competitors, and the growth of international trade. Changes in competition resulted in some increased concentration and the rationalization of resources in many companies. This occurred especially during the 1960s when there was a considerable growth in acquisition activity, partly as a means of adding new products, but primarily as a way of reducing competitive threats.

These concerns commonly adopted a multidivisional structure, especially during the 1960s. The process of structural reform was frequently associated with a change in leadership or declining profits. Thus, change did not come at G.E.C. until Weinstock, at G.K.N. until Brookes, and at I.C.I. until Chambers. The new leaders were usually men of force who did not hesitate to use their formalized power of executive office in order to redirect the enterprise. Structural change tended to be resisted since it usually transformed the existing power system. Rapid change often necessitated the departure of older executives unwilling or unable to adjust to the new managerial roles required in the multidivisional system. In functional organizations the marketing function often proved a focus of resistance. Thus at I.C.I., G.E.C., and Fisons, full adoption of a multidivisional system had to wait until marketing could be broken down to the division level. Consultants were again frequently used as change initiators.

Two of the early diversified industry groups were identical to those identified by Chandler in his study of U.S. enterprise. The engineering industry, which was not included in Chandler's sample, reflected many similar characteristics. The U.S. companies, however, were earlier to adopt a divisional system and to combine their activities. This can, perhaps, be attributed to the presence of strong antitrust legislation, prohibiting the use of cartels and restrictive practices, which tended to inhibit efficiency and consolidation. Further, many of the British companies, especially those engaged in engineering, appeared to have only partially adopted the U.S. form of multidivisional organization. The clear demarcation of individual responsibilities usually experienced in American firms was often missing in British companies which had retained intermediate executive boards or committees in the management of divisional and/or subsidiary operations.

CHAPTER 6
The Acquisitive Diversifiers

INTRODUCTION

THE WIDESPREAD ADOPTION OF THE STRATEGY of diversification in the post-World War II period was pronounced in a number of industries where companies were previously quite narrowly specialized. These industries, namely, food, textiles, paper and packaging, and printing and publishing, were generally low-technology segments where few resources were devoted internally to generating new products that would lead naturally to diversification. The firms in these industries, together with a number of firms engaged in metals and materials, diversified into areas related to their original interest. In addition, there were a few firms with disparate backgrounds which diversified right away from their original activities into unrelated or conglomerate areas. The form of diversification was generally of two types in the related product firms. First, there was market-related diversification in which new activities were added to service the same general market, as in the food and packaging companies. Second, there was diversification by vertical integration in which new markets were entered by the addition of further stages in the processing of materials, as in the textile and paper companies.

In most cases diversification was a protective strategy used to escape from activities exhibiting decline, low growth, and increased competition. The means of achieving this strategy provided the common thread uniting these concerns. Nearly all of these firms chose to diversify almost entirely by acquisition or merger.

The transitions within the related product industries and among conglomerates can be observed in Table 6–1. Excluding the metals and materials companies, which remained predominantly undiversified, only 9 of the remaining 32 firms were diversified in 1950. By 1970, including additions to the population, 29 of the 36 firms had diversified beyond the dominant product stage. Although, by 1960, 21 firms were already in the related or unrelated product class, most of the diversification activity did not start until the late 1950s. It then continued unabated throughout the 1960s.

TABLE 6–1

THE ACQUISITIVE DIVERSIFIERS

Industry	1950				1960				1970			
	S	*D*	*R*	*N*	*S*	*D*	*R*	*N*	*S*	*D*	*R*	*N*
Food	3	8	4	—	4	5[a]	7	—	1	4	11	—
Textiles	3	2	—	—	2	3[a]	1	—	—	1	5	—
Paper, Packaging, and Publishing	1	4	2	—	1[a]	1	6	—	—	1	7	—
Metals and Materials	5	4	—	—	2[a]	6	2	—	—	7[a]	4	—
Unrelated Product Companies	1	1	1	2	—	—	1	4	—	—	—	6[a]
Other	18	18	15	—	9	20	22	—	5	21	27	—
Total	31	37	22	2	18	35	39	4	6	34	54	6

[a] Denotes the addition of one new company to the sample.

NOTE: S = Single product.
    D = Dominant product.
    R = Related product.
    N = Unrelated product.

While mergers and acquisitions were important in other industries examined, they were the primary mechanism for diversification in the firms discussed in this chapter. Much of this activity began in the late 1950s as the postwar seller's market began to fade, as competition increased, and as demand patterns changed with increasing affluence. Many companies sought to break out of their original narrow product diversity by entering new markets, in order to maintain growth and profits. Most chose to continue within the same industry. In 1950 concentration was relatively low in textiles, food, paper and publishing. The expansion of the major firms in these industries did cause concentration to increase at the industry level by 1970. However, this increase seemed to be due primarily to concentration of diverse activities within the same broad industry classification into fewer large firms, rather than to horizontal concentration of like activities.

These low-technology industries all had, and in some cases still have, a high level of family influence. Most of the food, textile, paper and publishing concerns were family companies in 1950. Although family management declined overall in the British companies, it remained relatively strong in these industries. Diversification frequently took place shortly before, and especially after, a change from family management. In some cases, though, it occurred with a change in the ruling family generation.

The breadth of the product markets served by these industries widened during the period from 1950 to 1970. Many new product markets were developed in food, paper, textiles and, to a lesser extent, publishing. These changes were brought about largely by developments in processing and raw materials, many of which originated in the United States. The low order of development expenditure in many British companies caused them to import innovations; few were generated indigenously.

The level of competition increased in all these industries. In food, the growth of new market segments, new retail institutions, new competitive entries, especially from the United States, and the decline of resale price maintenance, all increased competition. In paper and textiles, increased competition came mainly from imports, which enjoyed economic advantages denied to the British producers. In publishing, competition increased by substitution: the development of commercial television had a significant effect on newspaper and magazine advertising revenue.

The postwar diversification of the food, textile, paper and publishing firms in turn led to widespread structural change. This was also true of the metals and materials industry and unrelated product firms. In all cases, the most significant change was the rapid and widespread adoption of the multidivisional structure. This occurred especially during the 1960s. Multidivisional structures in 1960 were found in six food, two textile, one paper and packaging, and one unrelated product firm. By 1970 the numbers of such structures had risen to fourteen food, three textile, four paper and packaging, two printing, and three unrelated product firms. Multidivisional structures were also found in two of the four diversified metals and materials firms.

Elsewhere strategic change was managed mainly by holding-company structures. Many of those companies with multidivisional structures initially adopted a holding-company structure, but subsequently amended it, frequently with the aid of management consultants.

THE FOOD COMPANIES

There were sixteen food companies among the largest 100 British companies as of 1970. The five firms which were still primarily engaged in one activity were discussed in Chapter 4. The remaining eleven companies diversified almost wholly by acquisition during the period from 1950 to 1970. This was especially true of the British-owned concerns since, of the four diversified food firms in 1950, only one, Unilever, could be termed British. Two of the remaining three were American-owned and the third was Swiss.

The post-World War II period saw substantial changes in the food market. There was substantial growth in processed and convenience foods, such as frozen and freeze-dried products. These served to increase the level of technology of the industry and to improve the scope for product differentiation. Rising consumer affluence led to increased demand for more sophisticated products, resulting in a decline or stable demand for more traditional items such as confectionery and flour products.

The level of competition in the food industry increased due to a widening range of product choice, the decline of resale price maintenance, new competitive entries, and new channels of distribution. While concentration was high in specific market segments, it remained relatively easy to enter many narrow market niches. Product differentiation was used more and more as a competitive device.

Products were significantly increased in value by processing. Thus, for example, the common potato was freeze-dried, frozen, canned, and converted into chips. Investment in product development could, therefore, be profitable, but among British concerns the level of research expenditure remained very low. Many of the innovations in food preparation were imported, especially from the United States; British-owned companies were found more commonly in undifferentiated, nonspecialty markets.

A high level of family ownership or control still persisted in 1970 among the British-owned food companies, and this seemed to explain, at least partly, their late diversification. Structurally, the diversified food companies had all adopted a multidivisional organization by 1970. Frequently, this was done with the aid of management consultants who were used to resolve the management problems associated with the holding companies that were built by acquisition.

Four of the food companies (Associated British Foods, Rank Hovis McDougall, Spillers, and J. Lyons) were among the five largest bread and flour confectioners in Britain. These four large plant bakers accounted for some 70 percent of bread sold, the remainder of the bread manufactured coming from smaller, local concerns. The growth strategy of one of these bakers, Associated British Foods,[1] had had a profound effect on the other baking companies, two of which had become bakers by integrating forward from the production of flour.

Associated British Foods, owned and controlled by the Weston family, formed part of the family's larger interests which originated in Canada and spread not only to Britain, but to the United States, West Germany, and the other White Commonwealth countries. The British company was a separate legal entity with its own market quotation, although the majority of its shares were held indirectly by the Weston family. In addition to British operations, the firm was also the holding company for Weston's Australian and South African activities.

Garfield Weston came to Britain in the 1930s, having already laid the foundation for a food manufacturing and retailing empire in North America. In 1935 he formed Allied Bakeries to acquire control of six bakery concerns. The company grew rapidly by the acquisition of old established bakeries and, by the outbreak of World War II, had expanded geographically to incorporate 28 bakeries and 217 shops. By 1951 Weston controlled the largest bakery group in Britain. Expansion continued into the 1950s, and between 1953 and 1956 Weston acquired about 10 more major bakeries. This strategy of concentration within a relatively fragmented industry had a significant effect on the baking industry and its main supplier, the flour milling industry.

In addition to bread, Weston entered the biscuit market and again left his mark on the whole industry. Starting with one factory in 1935, he began to produce cheap good-quality biscuits distributed through low-priced chain stores. This strategy allowed Weston to open up and capture an immense new market. Economies of scale were such that none of the traditional smaller biscuit manufacturers was able to compete with Weston on price. By 1938, when low-priced biscuits had begun to cut deeply into the established trade, price-cutting and lower profits were being experienced in many of the traditional family-owned biscuit companies.

With the coming of the Second World War, controls were imposed on both bread and biscuit manufacture, and these were not lifted until the early 1950s. However,

---

[1] "The Western-Loblaw Complex," *Financial Post* (Canada), December 6, 1966; see also R. Eisenstein, "Yeast at A.B. Foods," *Inventors Chronicle and Stock Exchange Gazette*, August 14, 1970, pp. 641–43; National Board for Prices and Incomes, *Bread Prices and Pay in the Baking Industry*, Report No. 144, H.M.S.O., 1970; Evely and Little, *Concentration in British Industry*, pp. 253–59, 288; A. Lumsden, "Fine Fares Recovery Diet," *Management Today*, June 1969, p. 78; W. S. Rukeyser, "The $4-Billion Business Garfield Weston Built," *Fortune*, June 1967, pp. 117–21, 140, 142.

Weston began acquiring other biscuit manufacturers immediately after the war, and by 1950 was operating 75 biscuit and bread factories in the United Kingdom, together with subsidiaries in Australia and South Africa.

The removal of restrictions on bread and biscuits helped Weston's operations. He continued to expand rapidly by internal growth and acquisitions, but as consumer affluence increased, demand for flour products began to decline. Associated British then embarked on a diversification strategy into other food areas. A research laboratory was opened and retail stores, acquired with the earlier bakery acquisitions, were developed into general food retailing outlets.

By 1960, a divisional structure had been adopted dividing the company into three product divisions: bakery, biscuits, and groceries. Grocery operations were extended by acquisitions in retailing and wholesaling, and new products introduced. In 1965 the group acquired a major tea packer and distributor; other smaller entries into related food products occurred in soft drinks, preserves, and meat products. The retail stores were developed into a major supermarket chain and, after a period of financial difficulty, this operation became a profitable venture.

The operations in South Africa and Australia followed a very similar pattern of flour milling, bakery products, other foodstuffs, and retail food distribution. The growth rate was high in all three countries and sustained by numerous acquisitions. Peripheral operations which were unprofitable, such as ice cream and frozen foods, tended to be sold off.   •

There was substantial product flow between some of the divisions, especially flour milling and bakeries, but there was also a significant flow external to the organization allowing the concept of profit-center responsibility to be applied. Despite its size and extensive interdivision, product flow central staff throughout the entire Weston group was very small, and the complex system of holdings was monitored mainly by a system of tight financial controls. Because of the secrecy surrounding much of the group's operations, designed to produce tax shields for the family holdings, many integration opportunities had been foregone especially in North America. In the United Kingdom, the burden of monitoring and administration fell heavily on Garfield Weston himself, and, in North America, on George Metcalf, who had become associated with Weston in the 1920s. Obviously succession loomed as a major problem facing the group, as Weston's son was in the process of succeeding his father. However, the lack of a corporate staff to coordinate the integration opportunities present within the group indicated some continued structural inconsistency and deviation from what might have been expected.

Weston's operations had a major influence on the strategies of Rank Hovis McDougall [2] and of Spillers.[3] These two family companies controlled some 50 per-

---

[2] A. Robertson, "Organisation Adds the Yeast," *The Manager*, February 1965, pp. 32–34; see also G. Nuttall, "Will Indigestion Prove Too Much for Rank Hovis?" *Sunday Times*, London, March 15, 1970; Joseph Rank Ltd., *The Master Millers*, Harley Publishing, London, 1956; Evely and Little, *Concentration in British Industry*, pp. 281–89.

[3] R. Winsbury, "Spillers Market Move," *Management Today*, April 1969, pp. 59–64, 136; E. Hennessey, "Spillers: Twice As Big By '75," *The Director*, February 1969, pp. 244–46; W. M. Vernon, "The Development and Organisation of Spillers Ltd.," private paper given at the London Graduate School of Business, December 1970; Evely and Little, *Concentration in British Industry*, pp. 281–89.

cent of the output of the flour milling industry in 1944, and exhibited only limited by-product diversification in animal feedstuffs. Flour consumption remained controlled after the Second World War, until 1953, so the millers did not attempt to diversify, being content to rebuild their milling capacity, which had been seriously damaged by wartime bombing. In 1953 Allied Bakeries (the early name of Associated British Foods), the largest British baker, requested a special quantity discount for flour, which the millers refused. Allied, therefore, began importing flour from Australia and Canada to supply about half of its needs and, subsequently, in the early 1960s, acquired its own milling capacity in Britain.

As a result of this action, the flour millers were faced with overcapacity for flour. Moreover, Allied's continued acquisition of plant bakeries was an ever-increasing threat to the remaining market. The millers therefore sought to safeguard their position. Spillers began to integrate forward into bakeries in 1954 to protect it from market fluctuations, and Rank followed in 1955. A period of intensive acquisition ensued throughout the 1950s as the millers and Allied acquired many of the medium-sized, local plant bakers. The millers did little to combine their holdings initially. Spillers set up a holding company, United Bakeries, and Rank formed a baking "division" to manage their baking subsidiaries, which were left largely to run autonomously as before.

In the 1960s the declining profitability and low growth of flour and bakery products forced Spillers and Rank to diversify further. Spillers spent most of its effort developing its animal and pet food business by acquisition, which extended its interests in biscuit and meal and added canned pet foods. Other acquisitions in the late 1960s added canned meats, fresh meat, spices and flavorings, and prepared meats to the product line.

Structurally, Spillers had originally been formed as a holding group of family milling companies. In 1926 a major amalgamation occurred placing the original subsidiaries under the direct control of four area general managers, who had complete executive authority for the activities in their respective regions. Scotland was later added as a fifth region. This organization, coupled with the United Bakeries holding company, persisted until 1966. The development of national branding of bread, the growing importance of central buyers, and the increasing product market scope then brought structural change. McKinsey & Company was called in for advice concerning reorganization. A divisional structure was adopted dividing the company into four product divisions, namely, feed, groceries, flour, and bakeries. Aggressive use of marketing, especially in grocery products, then successfully enabled the company to make progress toward decreased dependency on its traditional activities.

Rank followed a similar strategy. The company initially acquired specialist flour users such as Energen, makers of starch-reduced food products, and Hovis, a specialty bread manufacturer. In 1962, it acquired McDougalls, another major flour miller. The animal feedstuff interests were developed into wider agricultural trading in the early 1960s, and subsequently became a separate division. A specialized trades division, covering the embryonic interests in grocery wholesaling and other interests, was formed in 1964. In 1968, in an attempt to break into grocery products rapidly, the company acquired Cerebos, a firm engaged in a variety of food products. This acquisition gave Rank an entry into seasonings, pet foods, cereals, sauces, and meat products. It also brought new problems, since Cerebos was a weak competitor in most of these markets, and Rank had few marketing skills to withstand the confrontation with other major producers in these areas.

A traditional family milling company, Rank initially did little to administer the companies it acquired. These concerns continued as virtually independent operations and, since some, especially McDougalls, in turn had family management, any attempt at increased central controls was strongly resisted. Nevertheless, in 1964, consultants were used to reorganize the company into product divisions. The purchase of Cerebos later brought a subsequent reorganization of the grocery interests which were acquired in 1969.

The fourth baking company, J. Lyons,[4] grew from a family-owned catering company by integrating backward into food preparation. First came tea and coffee and, during the 1920s, Lyons began the mass production of cakes and bread for consumption and sale in its catering establishments. Ice cream was added in 1926, followed later by the development of frozen foods. Sales of food products were not restricted to the company's own outlets, and the food production side of the company soon outgrew the catering interest. This ultimately led to a split in the activities and, in the 1950s, a divisional structure was introduced dividing the company into six divisions.

The role of the company's two founding families had gradually diminished. Throughout its early history the senior executive body was essentially composed of family members, but in 1968 the executive management was made the responsibility of two nonfamily managing directors, and the different divisional activities were grouped under these men. In the past, the divisional general managers had reported directly to the board, consisting largely of family members. This change in internal structure in 1968 resulted in a review of activities, and concentration was placed on the more profitable activities. Less profitable areas, such as Lyons's overseas investments in Canada and South Africa, were sold. The interests in hotels, catering supplies, cakes and ice cream, were to be extended, and in 1969–70 the company integrated back into flour milling with the acquisition of its principal flour supplier.

Two other food companies included a significant element of vertical integration. The first of these, Unigate,[5] was formed in 1959 and was engaged in dairy products. The British dairy industry, like flour milling, was dominated by family concerns. It was also stabilized to a high degree, again like flour, by the impact of government which intervened in the supply of milk and controlled the level of retail and wholesale prices. In a sense government virtually guaranteed income, and prices were decided not only by reference to the largest, most economic producers but also with consideration for the margins of smaller units.

---

[4] J. Salmons, "The Development and Organisation of J. Lyons and Company Ltd.," in R. Edwards and H. Townsend, *Business Growth*, pp. 163–77; see also "Lyons Is Still a Family Concern," *Times Review of Industry*, April 1963, pp. 76–79; K. Van Musschenbroek, "The Strange Levitation of Lyons," *Management Today*, May 1970, pp. 86–93.

[5] "Unigate: Bigger Profits Ahead," *Investors Chronicle and Stock Exchange Gazette*, August 28, 1970, pp. 828–30; see also E. Ganguin, "How Unigate Picks the Creme de la Creme," *Financial Times*, London, December 18, 1970; Monopolies Commission, *Report on the Supply of Infant Milk Foods*; "The Unveiling of Unigate," *Management Today*, February 1971.

The two largest dairy concerns prior to the formation of Unigate were United Dairies and Express Dairies which were both formed by the same family. Initially United, then known as the Dairy Supply Company, was an equipment supply company for the milk retailing activities of Express Dairies. Wholesaling activities were added in 1917, due to the pressures of World War I, and United Dairies was formed. In 1920 United, led by the younger son of its founder, attempted to acquire the Express retailing interests run by his elder brother. This resulted in a split whereby both companies began to expand by the acquisition of other family dairy companies.

In 1959 United merged with Cow and Gate, another large family dairy products company with extensive interests in baby foods, cream, and cheese. The new corporate entity of Unigate was thus formed. Although United was the larger of the two concerns, there was little or no combination of the respective interests, and each company continued a virtually independent existence. A series of multiple managing directors divided the administration of the enterprise, and overlapping activities persisted. The subsequent major acquisition of the large Midland Counties Company compounded the situation. There was virtually no central staff or head office save for a secretariat for the chairman. As in many other British companies, the apparent synergy of acquisition was not achieved due to the failure to implement the necessary structural reform.

In 1968 declining profits, slow growth, and the complex allocation of responsibility eventually led to recognition of the need for reform. The solution adopted was to call in McKinsey & Company who recommended the introduction of a multiproduct divisional system, together with an international division to supervise overseas interests. This advice was implemented. Four product divisions, milk, food, grocery, and transport and engineering, were formed, and the international division was added later. The size of the board was halved and a single managing director, drawn from Schweppes, was appointed to sweep away the old system of divided responsibilities.

The second integrated concern was Brooke Bond Liebig.[6] This company was formed in 1968 as a result of the merger of two integrated family concerns: Brooke Bond, a tea grower, blender, and packer run by the Brooke family; and the Liebig Extract of Meat Company, engaged in cattle ranching, meat packing, and meat extracts run by the Carlisle and Gunther families. These two concerns were both integrated back into agricultural production, mainly overseas. Brooke Bond had extensive tea plantations in Asia and Africa, while Liebig had extensive ranching operations in South America and Southern Africa. Liebig was perhaps the more international of the two, with extensive overseas manufacturing operations for meat packing in South America and for other products in Western Europe.

Neither company had well-developed managerial systems although Liebig had undertaken fairly extensive structural change during the early 1960s, expanding the scope and size of its central office. There had previously been a highly personal system of supervision of the various geographic subsidiaries. This was replaced with

---

6 P. Hobday, "The Evergreen Topic at Watling House," *The Director*, April 1968, pp. 87–91; see also B. Moynahan, "Brooke Bonds Better Brew," *Management Today*, March 1967, pp. 74–77, 128, 130, 132; "Blending Brooke Bond Liebig," *Management Today*, October 1969, pp. 83–85, 162, 166, 168, 170, 174.

a more formalized system, recommended by outside consultants, incorporating a number of central executives charged with coordinating the efforts of the overseas subsidiaries, while at the same time allowing them to develop as fully as possible. After the merger the combined group adopted the Liebig structure whereby the local geographic subsidiaries, incorporating the assets of both parents, reported to a specific central divisional control group. These groups guided the operating companies within a specific geographic area and provided a link with a system of corporate functional departments. Some divided responsibility persisted, however, since the members of divisional control groups were also the heads of the functional departments.

The foregoing concerns, although possessing characteristics similar to the remaining food concerns, were primarily engaged in the production of staple products, such as milk, bread, flour, and tea. They found product differentiation difficult to achieve, and hence were perhaps forced to rely to a considerable extent on vertical integration in order to reduce market exposure and ensure captive outlets for production. Nevertheless, even this policy had proved ultimately unsatisfactory, and product market diversification was then attempted by acquisition.

By contrast the remaining five food manufacturers were more concerned with the processing of food products, thus substantially increasing value added and aiding product differentiation, and reducing problems of commodity price fluctuations. At the same time, this strategy provided the margins necessary for the extensive promotion of branded products. While all the first group of companies were British, these five concerns included subsidiaries of three foreign parent concerns, two American companies, one Swiss, and the Anglo-Dutch Unilever Company.

The first of the U.S. manufacturers operating in Britain was H. J. Heinz,[7] founded by Henry J. Heinz and based in Pittsburgh. Heinz began operating in Britain in 1905 and by 1970 had local sales of over £90 million. After successfully developing in Britain, Heinz later extended its geographic activities to Canada and Australia, prior to the Second World War. During the late 1950s further geographic expansion occurred; by 1970 the company manufactured in 13 countries and marketed its products in 150 countries.

Increasing complexity in the diverse product range, together with the growth of international operations, led to structural change. The company had retained its family tradition, including a functional structure inappropriate for meeting the competitive challenge. Thus, in 1964, Henry Heinz II came to the conclusion that change had to be made. He appointed R. Burt Gookin, who was then vice president for finance, to reawaken the company and revitalize its management.

The functional structure of the company was replaced with a system of geographic divisions with operating responsibility delegated to the chief executives of the national operating companies. In 1971 Gookin again reshuffled his senior management with the result that four of the five senior vice presidents were essentially outsiders. Considerable freedom was permitted to the overseas subsidiaries and little

---

[7] F. G. Crabb, "Heinz in Retrospect and Prospect," private paper delivered at the London School of Economics, December 1968; see also "The Good Steward," *Forbes,* March 1, 1971, pp. 24–32; K. Van Musschenbroek, "Heinz's New Variety," *Management Today,* February 1970, p. 100; J. Gooding, "Heinz Battles for Space on a World Wide Shelf," *Fortune,* October 1971, pp. 77–81, 178–79.

attempt was made to coordinate activities across national boundaries. There was some difference in product ranges, methods of raw material supply, and marketing methods, all dependent upon local conditions. The lack of central product coordination seemed somewhat different from what might be expected, and an increased central direction seemed a possible structural development for the future.

The second U.S. concern, Mars Limited,[8] was founded in Britain by the American, Forest Mars, who was given the foreign rights to "Milky Way" chocolate bars by his father and sent off from the U.S. family confectionery company. He began operations in Britain in 1932, and the business grew rapidly. Diversification followed into processed pet foods, where Mars acquired the majority of the market, convenience and snack foods, and industrial catering services.

After the successful development of his British interests, Mars returned to the United States where he built another highly successful business in candy and convenience foods. Following a long struggle, he eventually obtained control of his father's company in 1964 and retired shortly thereafter as chief executive. A caretaker chief executive was then brought in to manage operations until Mars's sons were ready to succeed their father. This highly successful company epitomized the divisional structure with strong financial controls coupled with a variable reward and sanction system to monitor product divisions. Division managers were highly motivated to meet their targets by the firm imposition of the reward and sanction system directly related to profit performance.

Cadbury/Schweppes [9] had developed market interests similar to Mars, although the British firm diversified mainly by acquisition rather than internal growth. Starting from a base in chocolate confectionery in Britain and several Commonwealth countries, Cadbury began to diversify in the 1960s. This was in response to low growth, increased competition in the confectionery market, and vulnerability to commodity price fluctuations. The Cadbury Company acquired interests in sugar confectionery, began to make cakes, and started the development of convenience foods based on North American technology. A change in the generation of family leadership in 1966 brought a structural reorganization from a functional holding-company form to the multidivisional structure. This was accomplished with help from McKinsey & Company.

Unable to generate sufficient product diversity internally, Adrian Cadbury, the new leader of Cadbury's, merged his company with Schweppes in 1969. Schweppes itself was a family company until 1950. It began by producing soft drinks and mixers in the United Kingdom and expanded overseas to the White Commonwealth coun-

---

8 A. W. McIntosh, "The Economies of the Confectionery Business," L.S.E. discussion paper, January 1953; see also J. Bugler, "Mars—Bringer of Peace," *The Times,* London, May 27, 1969; "The Man from Mars," *Duns Review,* February 1971, pp. 40–42, 90; H. B. Meyers, "The Sweet Secret World of Forest Mars," *Fortune,* May 1967, pp. 154–57, 208, 210, 212.

9 Cadbury Bros., *Industrial Challenge,* Pitman, London, 1964; see also P. Cadbury, "The Development and Organisation of Cadbury Bros. Ltd.," private paper delivered at the London School of Economics, February 1955; "A Fruit and Nut Case," *Times Review of Industry,* June 1965, pp. 22–24; "Why Cadburys Had to Change," *Management Today,* July 1968, pp. 83–87, 118, 122; G. Foster, "The Cadbury/Schweppes Mix," *Management Today,* April 1970, pp. 64–73; F. C. Hooper, "The Development and Organisation of Schweppes Ltd.," private paper delivered at the London School of Economics, October 1952; R. W. Cooper, "The Strategy Behind the Schhh," *International Management,* July 1968, pp. 28–30.

tries. In 1948 Sir Frederic Hooper was appointed as managing director. He quickly expanded the mixer drink interests, both in the United Kingdom and overseas, where franchise operations were extensively developed. The management system was decentralized into geographic areas where branch managers were placed in charge of sales and production. These men reported directly to Hooper, and they were paid commensurate to their output. The central office was divorced from line control and divided into four functional departments: production, sales, accounting, and personnel.

Expansion by acquisition into other soft drink products brought the emergence of four trading companies, similar to product divisions, each charged with specific responsibilities. In 1959 the company began to diversify by acquisition into food products.

Hooper died in 1963 and was replaced by Lord Watkinson. Hooper's personal style had become increasingly unworkable, and management consultants were used to consolidate the corporate structure into three market-oriented divisions. Further, substantial acquisitions followed, including Typhoo Tea and Kenco Coffee in 1968.

In 1969 the new Cadbury/Schweppes Company was formed with Watkinson as chairman, and Adrian Cadbury as managing director. The structure adopted remained based on the product divisions of the two prior companies. Some of the overlapping interests, such as international operations, were merged into larger divisions and, by 1969, each division was already operating against formally approved financial targets.

The two remaining food companies, Nestle and Unilever, were both diversified in their product mix and by geography. There was, therefore, continuous latent conflict between product and geographic responsibility. Nestle,[10] a Swiss company, originally developed multinational interests in dairy products. Diversification began with the introduction of instant coffee just prior to the Second World War, and further extensions of the product line since the war added soups, frozen foods, preserves, and bouillons. Despite the increased diversity, Nestle was still managed by a system of geographic divisions each supervising a number of national companies which were sometimes also broken into product divisions. The central office contained four geographic general managers and three functional directors who controlled marketing, production, and finance and accounting throughout the group. Nestle seemed to manage without a system of product coordination at the central office despite its diversity, and such an innovation might be anticipated in the future.

The Anglo-Dutch concern, Unilever,[11] was formed in 1929, as a merger between the Dutch Margarine Union and the British soapmaker, Lever Brothers. These were

---

[10] J. Heer, *World Events 1866–1966—The First 100 Years of Nestle*, J. Heer, 1966; see also A. Sampson, *Anatomy of Europe*, pp. 97–98; "Nestle's Multinational Mode," *Management Today*, pp. 86–93, 152, 158; "Running Nestle's Global Empire," *International Management*, January 1970, pp. 40–42; H. Johannsen, *Company Organisation Structure*, pp. 69–77.

[11] C. Wilson, *The History of Unilever* (3 Vols.), Praeger, New York, 1969; see also A. Sampson, *Anatomy of Britain Today*, pp. 489–97; Monopolies Commission, *Unilever Ltd. and Allied Breweries Ltd.*; A. D. Bonham-Carter, "Centralisation and Decentralisation in Unilever," in *Business Enterprise*, pp. 335–41; B. William-Powlett, "Unilever," *The Times*, London, January 6. 1970; Monopolies Commission, *A Report on the Supply of Household Detergents*, H.M.S.O., 1968; "Unilever Takes Bumps in Its Stride," *International Management*, June 1966, pp. 36–38; G. Turner, *Business in Britain*, pp. 123–39; G. Foster, "The Colossal Cares of Unilever," *Management Today*, June 1967, p. 40.

both family companies, the first formed by a merger between the continental margarine producers, Van Den Berghs and Jurgens, after a period of intense and exhausting competition. The second, Lever Brothers, was built up by the entrepreneurial genius of Lord Leverhulme, and was the dominant British soapmaker with extensive overseas interests. The main products of both companies used natural oils as raw materials, and their paths had crossed in the search for sources of vegetable oils. The partial vertical integration of the British company into plantations to obtain oil supplies also developed a general trading company, the United Africa Company.

Unilever's interests in soaps and margarine led it in two directions. The soap interests developed into detergents and toilet preparations, and the margarine interests, coupled with some personal investments by Lord Leverhulme, founder of the British company, developed into a highly diversified food group, with interests in quick frozen foods, soup mixes, canned and dehydrated foods, jam, tea, coffee, dairy products, and other convenience foods. A large animal feed business developed as a by-product of the oil milling interests and recently, from bases acquired to service internal requirements, the company had extended into packaging and chemicals.

Like Nestle and Heinz, widespread geographic interests initially led Unilever to adopt a multigeographic divisional organization with considerable local autonomy, supported by a large central office containing a number of service functions. As markets became more homogeneous, especially in Western Europe, and as the product line became more diversified, product coordination was required at the center. This was started initially in the United Kingdom in 1949 where widespread diversification came first. In 1965 the system of product coordination was extended throughout the organization and by 1970 there were twelve product coordinators and four regional coordinators. This structure was best described by Stopford's concept of a grid, namely, that responsibility was shared on a geographic and product basis. As a variant of the multidivisional system, it was rare and was only found associated with companies engaged in widespread product and multinational markets. Unilever's 1970 structure which contained inbuilt conflict between product and area responsibilities was, in 1971, being reviewed by McKinsey & Company, who might well recommend a product division system in preference to the present area divisions.

The food companies clearly portrayed a high level of family influence. There had often been some diversification initially by vertical integration, but this had usually been followed by market-related diversity. Much of the change in the scope of the British companies came by acquisition (these companies were still often closely associated with commodity markets), while the foreign companies, such as Heinz and Mars, tended to develop new products internally and relied more on processing to increase value-added and product differentiation.

The structure of many of these concerns had changed in the late 1960s and early 1970s, frequently with help from consultants, especially McKinsey & Company. Reorganization sometimes followed a leadership change as in the case of Cadbury, Schweppes, and Heinz. A number of the multinational concerns, especially Heinz, Nestle, and Unilever, had adopted geographic divisional structures where product-oriented divisions or at least substantially more product coordination seemed theoretically predictable. Unilever, in the early 1970s, was undertaking a major structural review which might lead to such a change. To some extent reliance on local suppliers of raw materials, and a low degree of intergroup transnational trading, meant that international coordination of production was less necessary than more capital intensive industries such as automobiles and chemicals. As a result, geographic subsidiaries enjoyed greater autonomy. It was the changing character of marketing and the form of brand advertising in particular which was placing increased demands on these companies for additional central coordination.

THE TEXTILE COMPANIES

The presence of a number of large textile companies in the sample did not seem surprising in view of Britain's long tradition in this industry. However, large integrated textile companies were very recent phenomena, having been born in the 1960s. The British textile industry, which played such a significant role in Britain's industrial development, was basically of two types: the cotton industry centered in Lancashire, and the woolen industry located on the other side of the Pennines in Yorkshire. Both industries were built up as a system of small, usually family-managed, units, each concentrating on a specialized single process in the chain of textile production. These processes were frequently geographically separated, with whole districts concentrating on a single activity. There had been virtually no consolidation since the Industrial Revolution, except for the amalgamation of groups of specialist producers such as the thread makers, the spinners and doublers, and the printers. Marketing was almost totally undeveloped, with each link in the chain of processes producing what was ordered by the next.

Overseas industrialization, especially in Asia, was often initiated by the development of indigenous textile industries ironically built up with Lancashire-made processing machinery. This led to intense competition, particularly in cotton textiles, which cost the British industry its lucrative overseas markets and caused recession in the domestic market. The more enterprising British companies moved overseas to obtain the cheap labor advantages enjoyed by competitors, but during most of the twentieth century the domestic cotton industry was declining.

Government action was taken in an attempt to rationalize the cotton industry, an action which, although successful in reducing capacity, did not affect any major change. The main post-World War II consolidation occurred in the 1960s due to the activities of the major synthetic fiber producers, I.C.I. and Courtaulds, who wanted large integrated textile units to ensure a constant market for their capital intensive fibers plants. These two companies sought out promising small users of synthetic fibers, especially in the cotton industry, and injected funds in them to set off a program of acquisitions to build large multiprocess, multifiber, integrated textile units. Courtaulds also went one step further and integrated forward—a disconcerting move to the other British, American, and European fiber makers who had traditionally refrained from entering the processing markets.

In this way Carrington and Dewhurst, Viyella International, and English Calico were all built up. The same strategy was basically adopted independently by J. & P. Coats who chose to concentrate on integration within the woolen industry, which in 1970 was still much more fragmented than cotton. Integration led to diversification of products and processes, with the majority of the product flow between integrated units going directly to outside markets rather than being consumed internally.

In 1950, Carrington and Dewhurst [12] was a small family-owned manufacturer of lining materials made of viscose fiber. The growth of competition caused profits to decline during the 1950s, but an initially small-scale development of bulked polyester yarns led to profit improvement in the early 1960s. In 1963 I.C.I. and Courtaulds took up part of the company's shareholding, thus providing funds for a program of acquisitive expansion. Between 1963 and 1969 a series of acquisitions extended the company's activities into woven cotton fabrics, worsteds, warp and weft knitted fabrics, prints, furnishing and industrial fabrics, and a wide variety of garments. Sales rose from £9.6 million in 1962 to £69.1 million in 1969.

The acquisitions did not, however, lead to new injections of managerial skills. Until 1967–68 the chief executive was still the former managing director of the single product linings company. The acquisitions were grouped into "divisions" from 1965–66 but only limited consolidation occurred within the subsidiary companies in each division, and there was little attempt to coordinate and integrate the differing product needs of each division.

Viyella International [13] had a similar history except for one significant difference —Mr. Joe Hyman. He entered the textile industry in 1957, acquiring a small textile company, Melso Fabrics, which employed 30 people. Melso Fabrics suffered a loss of £8,000 in Hyman's first year. Hyman had two convictions: that warp knitted nylon fabrics would take over much of the garment market, and that the Lancashire cotton industry was ripe for rationalization. He was right on both counts. His small company grew rapidly and merged with the much larger William Hollins in 1960 to form Viyella International. The rapid success of warp knitting lifted profits to £0.5 million by 1963 when I.C.I. decided to back Hyman with the capital needed to fulfill his strategy of reorganizing the Lancashire industry.

Hyman began a rapid program of acquisition, building a large vertically integrated group controlling interests in spinning, dyeing and finishing, warp knitting, and garments. These interests were rapidly combined, old managements removed, inefficient or extraneous operations closed down and sold, and the remainder grouped into independent profit-centered divisions with freedom to buy and sell in the best markets. Despite a strategy of vertical integration, therefore, Hyman did not structure his company to achieve it nor did he encourage the divisions to adopt this strategy. The central office was deliberately kept very small, and no central coordination was attempted, despite an increasing interdivisional product flow.

In 1967 Hyman severed his relationship with I.C.I. by repaying the loan. Sales had grown from £5.9 million in 1960 to £70.2 million in 1968, but profits did not match up to expectations. Hyman was a difficult man to live with and, in December 1969, after a further decline in profits, he was removed from Viyella in a boardroom putsch. In January 1970, despite a government embargo on further tex-

---

[12] D. Thomas, "What Went Wrong in Textiles," *Management Today,* May 1970, p. 102.

[13] J. Hyman, "The Development and Organisation of Viyella International Ltd.," private paper for the London School of Economics, May 1965; see also E. Cummins, "Combined English Mills: A Case Study in Rationalisation," private discussion paper given at the London School of Economics, December 1966; "The Viyella Man," *The Times,* London, December 11, 1969; "Viyellas Vertical Weave," *Management Today,* January 1969, pp. 44–51, 100, 102, 104; G. Turner, *Business in Britain,* pp. 407–09, 412, 415–16; D. Thomas, *What Went Wrong in Textiles.*

tile mergers, I.C.I. bid for both Viyella and Carrington and Dewhurst, and the two were subsequently merged. New management was being introduced in an attempt to improve performance. It seemed that the interdivisional trading might well necessitate more central coordination and structural reorganization in the new combined Carrington Viyella group.

To go back to Hyman's regime, English Calico [14] came into being in 1968, after Hyman had bid for English Sewing Cotton. This company, not caring to become part of Hyman's empire, opted for a protective merger with the Calico Printers Association thus linking the last two major Lancashire textile groups. Courtaulds Limited was to make a subsequent bid for the combined group in 1969. This resulted in a government-imposed ban on further textile mergers, and this ban remained in force until I.C.I. was permitted to acquire Carrington Viyella in 1970, subject to a number of antimonopoly safeguards.

English Sewing Cotton was formed in 1897 by the combination of a group of thread manufacturers in response to the amalgamation between J. & P. Coats, the largest thread maker, and its three largest rivals in 1896. After the Second World War, English Sewing Cotton was essentially a single product business. It had built up the American Thread Company in the United States, which had subsequently outgrown the parent company and provided much of the total profits. English Sewing did not even do its own marketing, which was handled by the J. & P. Coats selling organization, and the company had no access to its own customers. Some strategic change was initiated in that the company initially began to build up its overseas thread interests especially in the Commonwealth countries, while in the United Kingdom it acquired additional spinning and weaving capacity.

These activities were grouped into divisions, but operations were still largely controlled from board level until 1961. Declining profits and the threatened take-over of Courtaulds by I.C.I. prompted increased diversification within textiles supported by funds from I.C.I. and Courtaulds. In 1963 the company acquired Tootal, a major cotton textile company with other interests in paper products and plastics. This acquisition led to the adoption of a decentralized divisional structure, each division being run by a management committee composed of interlocking directors. Other acquisitions followed, but only limited merger and integration of these took place. In 1967, following Hyman's bid, came the merger with Calico Printers Association. This latter company had discovered polyester fibers and, until the early 1960s, its profits were composed mainly of royalty payments from this discovery. Diversification took Calico Printers increasingly into textile retailing, and the combined English Calico formed a chain of vertical integration from spinning through to retailing. The same divisional management committee system was still in operation and again more coordination and structural reform seemed warranted.

Coats Patons [15] was formed in 1960 as a merger between J. & P. Coats, the main

---

[14] Sir Cyril Harrison, "The Development and Organisation of the English Sewing Cotton Company Ltd.," private paper given at the London School of Economics, January 1964; G. Turner, *Business in Britain*, pp. 402–08, 412–16; D. Thomas, *What Went Wrong in Textiles;* R. Winsbury, "English Sewing in America," *Management Today*, February 1967, p. 64.

[15] M. O'Neill, "How Coats Patons Bought a Future in Textiles," *Financial Times*, July 24, 1970; see also P. A. Wright, "The Development and Organisation of Patons and Baldwins Ltd.," private paper given at the London School of Economics, February 1959; G. Turner, *Business in Britain*, pp. 402–03, 409, 412–16; Evely and Little, *Concentration in British Industry*, p. 118; A. Sampson, *Anatomy of Britain Today*, p. 545.

British thread company, and Patons and Baldwins, a company primarily engaged in the production of wool yarn. Coats had built up an international thread business but, by the end of the 1950s, profits were seriously declining and diversification became essential to reduce the dependency on thread.

A strategy of diversification into wool textiles was chosen. This was initiated by the acquisition of Patons and Baldwins in 1960, followed by further acquisitions particularly into wool garments and retailing. The company did not seek to become vertically integrated like the other textile groups but concentrated on the purchase of specialist garment manufacturers. Structurally the operating subsidiaries were essentially still autonomous but they were required to conform to board policy. All the chief executives of main subsidiaries sat on the board of Coats Patons (U.K.), which handled the entire U.K. operations and was chaired by the group chairman. Overseas subsidiaries were engaged mainly in thread and wool yarns and were controlled through a separate overseas area organization.

Courtaulds [16] was very different from the other textile companies in many respects. It was a fiber producer with an origin in textile processing which it rapidly outgrew. It was not until after the Second World War that it became heavily engaged in direct textile processing. Formed by the Courtaulds family in 1891 as silk throwsters, it grew into a major producer of mourning crepe. As this market declined, the company integrated backward into the manufacture of artificial silk—viscose fibers —in 1905. In 1910 a U.S. subsidiary, the American Viscose Company, started operations and, in 1913, the present company, Courtaulds Limited, was formed. The rapid development of viscose fibers, in the period between the two world wars, was initially an extremely profitable period for Courtaulds in both Britain and the United States. Courtaulds grew rapidly, extending overseas into Canada and France, forming a joint venture in Germany, and taking a share of Snia Viscosa in Italy. During the 1930s the company introduced viscose "staple" fiber and tire viscose, and began to produce transparent cellulose wrapping materials. Competition became intense in Britain due to the entry of many other manufacturers, and Courtaulds had to depend heavily on the profits from its U.S. subsidiary.

The Second World War proved very costly to Courtaulds; in 1941 the company was forced to sell the American Viscose Corporation for a ridiculously low price, and most of its British and European operations were severely damaged. In 1940 a joint company was formed with I.C.I. to develop nylon, based on Du Pont technology—a move that marked Courtaulds's entry into synthetic, as distinct from viscose, fibers.

After the Second World War the company attempted to rebuild its rayon interests, at first unconcerned by the potential threat of the new synthetic fibers. The first

---

[16] G. Turner, *Business in Britain*, pp. 403–08, 412–16; see also D. C. Coleman, *Courtaulds— an Economic and Social History* (2 Vols.), Clarendon Press, Oxford, 1969; A .H. Wilson, "The Organisation and Planning of Research and Development in Courtaulds Ltd.," in *Business Enterprise*, pp. 317–24; A. Sampson, *Anatomy of Britain Today*, pp. 536–37; Monopolies Commission, *A Report on the Supply of Man-Made Cellulosic Fibres*, H.M.S.O., 1968; "Weft and Warp of a Man-Made Success," *Times Review of Industry*, August 1963, pp. 48–50; A. Robertson, "A New Look at Courtaulds," *The Manager*, January 1965, pp. 25–27; C. F. Kearton, "Courtaulds Today and Tomorrow," private discussion paper for the London School of Economics, December 1965; *Newsline,* company publication, various editions.

nonfamily chairman was appointed in 1947, and the initial postwar seller's market caused management to remain complacent about the future. A dominant position in viscose fibers was built up by the acquisition of other producers in the United Kingdom including Courtaulds's main rival, British Celanese. Restrictive agreements were developed with continental suppliers to prevent competition from imported viscose.

However, by the mid-1950s it became apparent that synthetic fibers were taking over and cutting into the markets formerly held by viscose. Nylon began to do well, but Courtaulds was tied up with I.C.I. in the British Nylon Spinners (B.N.S.) venture and, from 1952 on, B.N.S. had separate management. Both I.C.I. and Courtaulds were then completely excluded from the B.N.S. technology. I.C.I. had acquired the patents to polyester fibers, and Courtaulds belatedly began research into acrylics. Profits had begun to fall seriously by 1958, and diversification was sought outside of fibers. Courtaulds, therefore, began to acquire companies that manufactured paint, packaging, plastics, and foundation garments.

Then, in December 1961, I.C.I. made a take-over bid for Courtaulds and, following a major battle, Courtaulds defeated the bid. This event had a traumatic effect on the company, and a serious battle was fought internally between the old guard, who wished to surrender to I.C.I., and the younger, militant directors led by Mr. (later Lord) Frank Kearton, who emerged as the new leader of the company. The shares acquired by I.C.I. were subsequently exchanged for Courtaulds's 50 percent participation in British Nylon Spinners.

Kearton set out to revitalize Courtaulds and to change its strategy dramatically. He convinced the board that Courtaulds's future lay in textiles, and proposed a grand design of putting together a giant textile group, incorporating five of the largest Lancashire companies. This failed, but did lead to the capital injections by Courtaulds and I.C.I. in Carrington, Viyella, and English Sewing Cotton.

Courtaulds itself embarked on a massive acquisition program developing major interests in spinning, dyeing and finishing, weaving and knitting, hosiery and garments, and smaller interests in wholesaling and retailing. Research was expanded. From a small research unit that had been attached to British Celanese, Courtaulds was soon able to launch its own nylon fiber. Between 1962 and 1970 Courtaulds spent £176 million on acquisitions, £146 million of which was on fiber-using capacity. At the same time Courtaulds spent £227 million on expanding and re-equipping its activities, of which £137 million was used for developing its fiber-making capacity. Between 1962 and 1969 sales grew from £173 million to £627 million and profits from £9.6 million to £26.7 million, after taxes.

Structurally Courtaulds's organization revolved around the figure of Kearton. He disbanded the plethora of committees which had previously provided the link between the operating units and the board. Two main committees were retained: the policy executive committee, comprising the chairman and three deputy chairmen, and an operations executive committee consisting of the members of the policy executive committee together with three other Courtaulds executive directors. The first of these committees was responsible for all matters of general policy and planning, and for trade investments, while the second supervised all the group's main trading activities. Elsewhere the operations of the company were divided into a mixture of over 70 divisions and subsidiary companies, each of which was a profit center. Each operating unit prepared, annually, financial plans and budgets which extended three years ahead and which covered the expected development in profits, capital employed, and return on capital. These figures, together with a more important written explanation of the unit management's plans, were submitted annually by each profit center to the operations executive. Internal product flows were made at market prices, and there was a central office with responsibility for the supervision of finance, administration, personnel, overseas relations, labor relations, and legal matters. In addition, there were several functional departments that were not just advisory. The marketing department supervised the direct sales operation and merchandising activities for fibers. Research was controlled centrally, although none of this was charged directly to the operating units, and a group purchasing department purchased all the main raw materials for the group, as well as coordinating buying done directly by the operating units. Lord Kearton remained intimately linked with all major policy decisions, and there was little delegation of authority in these matters.

Structurally, therefore, Courtaulds was somewhat of a mix between a holding company and a multidivisional concern. This apparent structural defect was justified by the company on the grounds that the textile trade still required the existence of a large number of small corporate units each with its own independent brands and character. Despite the probable truth of this, it was still considered that significant structural reform would probably become necessary in view of the extensive degree of internal product flow.

Nevertheless, the strategy of Courtaulds played a major role in the rapid reconstruction of the British textile industry which took place during the 1960s. Further change seemed likely, especially in woolens which remained fragmented; and with the continued threat of competitive imports, further consolidation seemed necessary in cotton.

The development of diversified corporations which did take place in textiles was quite different from that which occurred in most industries. The primary strategy was one of vertical integration, and it was the deliberate or accidental managerial failure to coordinate integrated activities accumulated rapidly by acquisition which made the strategy actually one of diversification. All the textile companies examined had adopted a partial multidivisional structure yet still containing many features of a holding company. Those structures were especially ill-suited to coordinated integrated operations, since great autonomy was permitted to the operating units, and very few central office services had been developed.

The continued pressures of competition seemed to point toward increased specialization, concentration on differentiable products, and a much greater emphasis on the use of marketing skills. New management seemed necessary to achieve the necessary coordination and integration of operating units and the close involvement of the fiber producers seemed to foreshadow the development of an oligopoly of large integrated textile producers.

THE PAPER, PACKAGING, AND PUBLISHING COMPANIES

There were eight firms engaged in paper, packaging, and publishing in the sample population. With one exception, these companies were engaged primarily in the production or conversion of paper. The eighth company, although engaged in paper packaging, was mainly a producer of metal containers. In 1950 only two of these firms were diversified, but by 1970 the number had grown to seven.

Family influence was again high in these concerns in 1950, but had diminished substantially by 1970. Growth and diversification were achieved in large measure by acquisition. The level of competition for the paper and publishing firms increased markedly over the period. In the paper companies this was caused by increased foreign competition, especially during the 1960s. The publishing firms experienced competition for a major part of their revenue from the growth of commercial television. In packaging, the growth of competition was mainly by product substitution. New processes and the growth of plastics caused considerable change in the pattern of demand.

Adoption of a strategy of diversification again brought structural change. In 1950 none of the companies in these industries had a multidivisional structure but, by 1970, six of the eight concerns had adopted it. Consultants, as the initiators of structural change, were again in evidence in some cases. Whereas, in several cases, structural change followed closely after a change in corporate leadership.

The first of these concerns, Wiggins Teape,[17] was a specialty paper maker. Wiggins Teape started originally as a firm of wholesale stationers in 1761 and continued these operations until 1890, when it integrated backward into the production of high-grade papers. Photographic base papers were added between the world wars, and other specialty grades were added with the acquisition of Alex Pirie, the company's largest competitor in 1922. Further acquisitions extended the company's merchandising interests and also added to its paper-making capacity. During the 1930s, following the imposition of import duties on some paper grades, Wiggins entered the market for greaseproof and parchment papers. These innovations were made in conjunction with continental partners who were subsequently bought out.

After the Second World War other specialty products were added, such as tracing paper, tissues, and carbonless copy paper, the latter in association with National Cash Register. Pulp mills were built to supply part of the company's pulp requirement, and conversion operations were started. These ventures were only partially successful and some were later sold. An association with British American Tobacco began in 1960, with the formation of the Millbank Paper Company, to manufacture materials for British American's cigarette production. This association ultimately led in 1970 to the total acquisition of Wiggins Teape by British American as part of the tobacco company's diversification program.

Structurally, Wiggins Teape managed its diversified business with a functional organization until 1966. The increasing complexity of the business, coupled with declining profits, led to a McKinsey-sponsored reorganization in 1966. This divided the company into three product and geographic groups: United Kingdom/Europe paper operations, overseas operations, and converted product operations. Product divisions were in turn set up within these groups each of which was the responsibility of an overall general manager.

Dickinson Robinson was also a producer of specialty paper but, in addition, was engaged in packaging products. This company resulted from a merger between the

---

[17] L. W. Farrow, "Production and Marketing Problems of the Wiggins Teape Group," private paper given at the London School of Economics, May 1959.

family-controlled E. S. & A. Robinson Group and John Dickinson in 1966. The first of these concerns had developed as a manufacturer of specialty wrappers and packagings. Other converted products, together with printing inks and packaging machinery, were added later. When Sir Foster Robinson retired as chairman in 1961, he was succeeded by John Robinson. Shortly thereafter the new chairman divided the company and its many subsidiaries into product divisions with an overseas division to supervise foreign investments. By contrast John Dickinson was primarily engaged in the production of stationery products. Right after the merger, the two concerns continued to run as independent entities, but by 1969 the like activities of both had been combined mainly into an enlarged multiproduct divisional structure.

Apart from the specialty paper makers two companies developed primarily around the production of bulk low-value-added paper grades. The first of these, Bowater Paper,[18] was the largest newsprint manufacturer in the world. It was built up by the acumen of Sir Eric Bowater, the grandson of the company's founder. The company was originally engaged in paper merchandising, but integrated backward into production during the 1920s. In 1936 Kemsley Mill was acquired, at that time the largest newsprint mill in Europe. Shortly thereafter, in 1938, Bowater acquired large timber rights in Newfoundland, together with the integrated pulp and paper mills at Corner Brook. Subsequently other mills were acquired in Sweden and Norway and, after World War II, major new newsprint mills were opened in southern United States.

Little diversification took place outside of newsprint until the 1950s, when conversion activities were added primarily in the United Kingdom. In 1955, in conjunction with Scott Paper, the company made an entry into the U.K. tissue market. This was later extended elsewhere with Scott providing the marketing skills sorely lacking in Bowater.

Sir Eric Bowater died in 1961 leaving the company facing world overcapacity of newsprint and a new competitive threat from Scandinavia after the formation of the European Free Trade Association (EFTA). He had managed the company in a highly centralized fashion, making all the major planning decisions. Each mill, sales group, and even the purchasing group, was incorporated as a separate company under Bowater's direct supervision.

Bowater was succeeded as chairman by Sir Christopher Chancellor who, with Martin Richie, a former packaging man from Eburite, one of Bowater's diversification acquisitions, set about reorganizing the corporate structure. Control was decentralized by combining local activities into groups in the United Kingdom. Each had its local board and control over sales, production, purchasing and finance, leaving the central office to perform a coordinating role. Controls at the center were basically financial, calling for the monthly monitoring of performance, capital expenditure limits, control over acquisition policy, and approval of senior executive

---

[18] Bowater Paper Corporation, *Bowater Built a Mill in Tennessee,* company publication, London, 1956; see also R. Sinclair, *Bowaters in North America,* Bowater Paper Corporation, London, 1962; A. Sampson, *Anatomy of Britain Today,* pp. 538–59; "Bowaters Paper Chase," *Management Today,* November 1969, pp. 66–75, 158, 160, 162; "Getting Quick Decisions in a Big International Company," *Achievement,* September 1965, p. 5; "Bowater Paper Corporation," Case Study, Manchester Business School, 1971.

appointments. Overseas, management companies were formed. In North America, for example, a management company was set up. This company was composed of the presidents of the Canadian and U.S. holding companies, and the New York sales company, in an effort to reduce the heavy production orientation of the company. In the United Kingdom, marketing was improved by the introduction of outside executives, and a corporate planning director was appointed. Further diversification was being urgently sought due to the increasing threat from bulkgrade paper imports in the United Kingdom. Moreover, low profitability made it difficult to negotiate acquisitions and, by 1970, nearly 40 percent of sales was still made up of newsprint operations. In addition, the serious managerial weaknesses left behind after the death of Sir Eric Bowater still seemed apparent, increasing the difficulties of launching a diversification program which would reduce the company's dependence on the declining bulk paper markets.

Like Bowater, Reed Paper [19] was also heavily engaged in newsprint in its early years. It did not expand overseas until the post-World War II period, but diversified within the United Kingdom into packaging products. The company was run by Sir Ralph Reed, the son of the founder who, until his retirement in 1954, had been chairman for 34 years. In 1954–55 the company embarked on diversification into tissues in conjunction with Kimberley Clark and International Cellulose Products Company, both U.S. concerns. Other diversifications in the 1950s took Reed into plastics, packaging, and pitch fiber pipes. The first overseas investment was made in 1958 in the Tasman Pulp and Paper Company in New Zealand, a company formed to exploit local timber for newsprint production.

The formation of the European Free Trade Association opened the way to intense competition from low-cost Scandinavian produced newsprint and bulk paper grades. This began to have a serious effect on Reed. In 1961, in an attempt to obtain low-cost production, it acquired the Anglo Canadian Pulp and Paper Mills from *Daily Mirror* newspapers. A shareholding was taken in a Norwegian mill in 1962 and, in 1963, competition forced Reed to abandon the U.K. production of kraft paper.

Daily Mirror newspapers and its associate, *Sunday Pictorial* newspapers, owned the majority of the stock in Reed from the early 1950s. Lord Rothermere, who led the *Daily Mirror* for many years, acquired a substantial stake in Reed in 1920 when the shares of the company were put on the market by the executors of Albert Reed. He bought two-thirds of the common stock without realizing that the preference shares had voting rights. Thus, the *Mirror* group held about 30 percent of Reed until the early 1950s. On the death of Reed's managing director, a dispute arose between Reed and the *Daily Mirror,* and the shareholding was increased.

The *Daily Mirror* group did not take an active part in Reed's management, how-

---

[19] E. Foster and G. Bull, "What Makes Ryder Run?" *The Director,* May 1970, pp. 260–65; see also S. T. Ryder, "Diversification, Decentralisation, and Decision—The Management Philosophy of Reed International," private paper delivered at the London Graduate School of Business, December 1970; S. T. Ryder, "How To Make Rationalisation Work," *Achievement,* May 1966, pp. 9–10; "Can Reed Paper Over the Cracks in IPC," *Sunday Times,* January 25, 1970; A. Sampson, *Anatomy of Britain Today,* pp. 543–44; P. Coldstream, "Reed's New Pattern for Wallpaper," *Management Today,* April 1966, p. 88; "Reed International," Case Study, Manchester Business School, 1971.

ever, until the early 1960s. Faced with the serious threat to Reed's long-term viability, Cecil King, the leader of the *Daily Mirror,* took over its management in 1963. A *Daily Mirror* man, S. P. Ryder (later Sir Don Ryder), was appointed as chief executive, his objective being to save Reed from overseas competition. Ryder sought to achieve this by diversification and overseas expansion.

A concerted effort toward acquisitions began. In 1963 Spicers, a specialty paper producer and a good Reed customer, was acquired. Packaging was built up by acquisition. Major expansions were made in Canada, Australia, New Zealand, and South Africa. Research and development was reduced, duplication was cut out, and uneconomic units were closed down. Separate companies were formed to direct the affairs of the individual product groups, each responsible for its own profitability.

Further major acquisitions followed in 1965 with the purchase of Wall Paper Manufacturers, another major customer, and a combine controlling about 80 percent of the British wall covering market, and Polycell Holdings, a company producing specialized building products. These acquisitions, together with the subsequent addition of plastic building products, made Reed less dependent on paper. By 1969 building products represented some 35 percent of sales. In 1970 Reed ironically acquired the International Publishing Corporation (formed out of the *Daily Mirror* and *Sunday Pictorial* newspaper groups), which still held some 27 percent of Reed's stock. This stockholding could have been used to block Reed's future expansion, and I.P.C. itself was in serious financial difficulty. As a result of its acquisition program, by 1970 Reed appeared to be moving rapidly into the unrelated diversified category, although the tenuous link of paper usage still ran through the group.

The aggressive acquisition policy of Sir Don Ryder, therefore, transformed Reed. Thus, unlike Bowater, its dependence on bulk grade papers was substantially reduced. Despite the market transformation and rapid growth of sales and assets, however, profits in terms of earnings per share showed little or no tendency to grow. In reality many of the acquisitions did little more than transfer problems to a somewhat later stage in an integrated chain, and the relative failure to grasp the need for structural reform meant that potential advantages achievable from the strategic moves undertaken had still to be obtained.

The managerial requirements for the different enterprises Reed had become engaged in were very different, and structurally a form of multidivisional system had been adopted. In reality, however, this structure still contained elements of a holding company structure. The central office remained very small containing only about seven key executives providing specialist services, such as finance, technical, legal, and corporate planning functions. Operations were delegated to four divisions: the Reed Group, International Publishing, Wall Paper Manufacturers, and Reed Overseas. These divisions were in turn each composed of a number of subsidiary companies, and the rationalization of the like activities of acquired concerns had often taken a considerable time to implement. An operations executive committee, consisting of Ryder and the heads of the finance and technical functions, monitored divisional performance and considered short-term policy. A similar small executive committee carried out the same function at division level, with Ryder acting as chairman of each of these committees. The structure of the group was thus highly dependent on the personality of Sir Don Ryder who, apart from his corporate responsibilities, was, by his highly personal style, heavily engaged in operational decisions, often at the level of detail of the smallest subunits.

The International Publishing Corporation,[20] which was acquired by Reed in 1970, was one of the largest publishing concerns in the world. It was formed from the twin bases of the *Daily Mirror* and *Sunday Pictorial* newspapers, two newspaper publishing companies with interlocking shareholdings which shared the same chairman, managing director, deputy chairman, editorial, and finance directors. These two companies long held a significant holding in Reed Paper and owned the Anglo Canadian Pulp and Paper Mills. Neither of these interests was subject to managerial control. They also made investments in commercial T.V. as a protective move against the potential threat from television to newspaper circulation.

Led by Cecil King, a member of one of the great newspaper families, the International Publishing Corporation was put together in four years between 1958 and 1962 by the major acquisitions of Amalgamated Press and Odhams Press. These groups were themselves collections of companies: Amalgamated was an ailing magazine group founded by relatives of King, and Odhams a newspaper and magazine company which had responded to King's purchase of Amalgamated by buying two other periodical publishers.

This collection of companies with interests in newspapers, television, periodicals, book publishing, trade magazines, advertising, directories, and exhibitions was initially allowed to run as a series of independent companies with virtually no central coordination. Profits began to decline due to restrictive union practices, competition for the same markets between the subsidiaries, duplication of effort, and loss of advertising revenues. In two years earnings per share dropped by over a third and, in 1968, King was fired following a special meeting of the board. McKinsey & Company was called in to sort out the structural problems and, in 1968, a divisional structure was adopted. The lack of adequate central management, however, was so serious that by 1970 I.P.C. was again in serious financial trouble and was acquired by Reed Paper—the *Mirror* group's own former subsidiary.

One of I.P.C.'s major rivals was the Thomson Organisation.[21] Roy Thomson, a Canadian, came to Britain, after building a newspaper empire in Canada and the United States, and obtained the franchise for Scottish Television. In the early, lucrative years of British commercial television Thomson prospered and, in 1959, acquired the ailing Kemsley Newspapers. Using this base, Thomson revitalized the *Sunday Times,* and subsequent diversification took place into regional newspapers, book publishing, magazines, and package holidays.

In 1966 Thomson was permitted to purchase *The Times* of London, which was in serious financial difficulty, and he proceeded to lavish much of his personal wealth in an attempt to revive its fortunes. However, *The Times* remained a millstone for the Thomson group in Britain, and its continued losses had a significant impact on

[20] R. Winsbury, "IPC's Giant Solution," *Management Today,* October 1966, pp. 64, 69, 126, 128; see also R. Winsbury, "The Attack on IPC," *Management Today,* November 1968, pp. 94–99, 156, 162; C. H. King, "Organisation and Management of the Daily Mirror Newspapers Ltd.," private paper given at the London School of Economics, November 1955; W. Mennell, *Takeover,* Lawrence and Wishart, London, 1962, pp. 80–85.

[21] D. Norton-Taylor, "Into Britains Parlour With His Hat On," *Fortune,* February 1967, pp. 137–39, 168, 170, 172, 174, 176; W. Mennell, *Takeover,* pp. 80–85.

earnings per share. Thomson always sought to make his enterprises profitable apart from his personal whim to own one of the world's great newspapers, *The Times.* Structurally Thomson adopted a series of product divisions to administer the group, although this structure was not achieved until 1969, when the marketing function was decentralized and the marketing director resigned.

The final company in this group was primarily engaged in metal containers and not paper products. The Metal Box Company [22] originated in 1921 as the amalgamation of four family companies engaged in tin box manufacture and paper printing. Further subsidiaries were acquired in the interwar period and, following an attempted invasion by American Can which was successfully repelled, Metal Box was left a near-monopoly of the British can market. The struggle with American Can was won largely due to an agreement reached with Continental Can which gave Metal Box the exclusive rights to Continental's technology in Britain. The relationship between these companies still existed in the early 1970s. The company bought its own tinplate works in 1935, acquired engineering works to produce can machinery, and formed a central research laboratory in 1937. A central office was built up and a central sales force was created out of the subsidiary company's independent forces. In 1944, however, the company still consisted of 20 independent manufacturing units; at that time a functional organization was therefore set up to improve coordination.

The postwar period brought rapid growth in packaging, diversification into plastics, and increased paper and board interests. The central sales organization system became increasingly unworkable, and in 1956 the company was broken down into distinct product divisions. The overseas operations, which were initially built up during the period between the world wars and expanded subsequently, were broken away into a separate organization in 1950.

The present structure was very similar in some respects to the old established U.S. multidivisional systems, such as Du Pont, with a series of autonomous product divisions each with a full set of functional responsibilities, a well-developed central office with a wide range of services, financial controls, and sophisticated planning procedures.

The paper, packaging, and publishing companies thus repeated the pattern observed in the food and textile companies. The companies, often with family managements initially, found increasing competition in their traditional markets posing a serious financial threat in the early 1960s. Having stayed too long in their original product market niches, the companies, often with new management, belatedly attempted to break out with extensive acquisition activity. Those acquisitions, while creating a strategic transformation, seldom produced the anticipated advantages re-

[22] "Metal Box," *Times Review of Industry,* February 1964, pp. 23–25; see also R. Winsbury, "The Reshaping of Metal Box," *Management Today,* September 1967, pp. 58–67, 130; D. Ducat, "Growth of a Company: Metal Box," *The Manager,* August 1964, pp. 25–30; Monopolies Commission, *A Report on the Supply of Metal Containers,* H.M.S.O., 1970; "General Management Practice Employed at the Metal Box Co. Ltd.," company presentation for British Institute of Management, January 21, 1966; H. Johannsen, *Company Organisation Structure,* pp. 59–68; D. Ducat, "The Development and Organisation of the Metal Box Co. Ltd.," private paper given at the London School of Economics, February 1964; Evely and Little, *Concentration in British Industry,* pp. 230–33.

quired due to inadequate structural reform. Indeed, the strategic moves sometimes compounded earlier difficulties until correct structural reorganization was undertaken.

THE METALS AND MATERIALS COMPANIES

Only four of the metals and materials companies had diversified beyond the dominant product category. Like the other industries described above, these companies accomplished their initial diversification mainly by means of acquisition. Unlike the other metals and materials concerns, only one of the four exhibited a high degree of integration. Family influence was found in only one of these firms in the post-World War II period. Two of the concerns were engaged mainly in building products where capital intensity was low, while the other two were heavily engaged in mining, rather than large-scale production.

Structurally, only two of the four had adopted the multidivisional structure, and one of these was divided geographically. Of the other two, one had surprisingly retained a functional structure, while the other was still a holding company.

The company most like the undiversified concerns in this industry group was Turner and Newall.[23] This company was formed in 1920 to amalgamate the interests of four companies, each of which had an interest in asbestos. Turner Brothers' Asbestos, who led the merger, first entered asbestos textiles after the manufacture of cotton packings for steam engines. It later added asbestos, cement, and other products while integrating backward to asbestos mining in Rhodesia. J. W. Roberts and Newalls Insulation Company were both engaged in insulation, using asbestos as an insulating material. Newalls was an associate of the Washington Chemical Company which was primarily engaged in the manufacture of magnesia, a product with a variety of uses including that of an insulating material.

In 1925 the company acquired Ferodo, manufacturers of brake linings produced from asbestos, thus assuring a captive market for much of Turner Brothers' output of asbestos textiles. In 1926 a large asbestos mining source was acquired, followed in 1929 by the acquisition of Bell's United Asbestos Company, a similar vertically integrated asbestos producer. The duplicate interests of the two companies were merged and the asbestos cement activities combined into a new specialist company. Smaller acquisitions of insulating companies occurred, and a dominant position in mining African asbestos was obtained by the acquisition of the Rhodesian and General Asbestos Corporation. Further overseas expansion took place in India and the United States prior to the Second World War, whereby Turners acquired the Bell Asbestos Mine in Canada, another major raw material source.

After the war the company continued to operate much as it had before, holding a near-monopoly in asbestos products in the United Kingdom. Profits rose rapidly in the early postwar years but, after the mid-1950s, growth became slow. Minor acquisition of asbestos products manufacturers occurred in the United Kingdom and over-

---

[23] R. G. Soothill, "The Development and Organisation of the Turner and Newall Group," private paper given at the London School of Economics, February 1962; A. Sampson, *Anatomy of Britain Today,* p. 546; *Turner and Newall Ltd.: The First Fifty Years,* company publication, 1970.

seas and, in 1954, a small diversification was made into glass fibers. In 1961 the company acquired British Industrial Plastics which took it into the production of resins and plastics, and further developments took place in glass fibers.

The organization of Turner and Newall remained that of a holding company. A central office was gradually built up in the 1960s but, by 1970, maximum responsibility was still left with the original operating companies. The central office services had no executive authority, and links between the operating units and the main board remained essentially on a personal basis.

By contrast, Tarmac Derby grew to become a sizable company in the postwar period. Initially it was a very small company engaged primarily in the manufacture of roadstone materials and road contracting. Roadstone plants were built adjacent to steel or other slag-producing units, and growth followed the expansion of the government road-building program. Geographic expansion was achieved partially by acquisition, and in 1959 a system of geographic divisions was set up. Declining profits led to a need for more central organization, and a group managing director was appointed following resignations of several subsidiary company directors. An acquisition program followed which extended the group's quarrying interests, and in 1965 Derby began to build a bitumen refinery as a joint venture.

Diversification of the construction interests led to entry into industrialized building and the rental of heavy equipment for contractors, and in 1966 the company reorganized into a series of product groups. A major merger in 1968 with Derbyshire Stone led to the adoption of the 1970 corporate identity. The combined activities were organized into five divisions, four of which were product divisions while the fifth supervised the expanding overseas interests. Within the divisions, subsidiary companies did continue to operate with duplication and a full multidivisional system remained to be achieved.

The Marley Company [24] was again very much a postwar phenomenon built up by the Aisher family who continued to manage it. Started by the first Owen Aisher in the early 1920s, there were seven Aishers in senior management positions by 1970 and they held about a third of the share capital. Growing from a base in concrete roof tiles, which gained rapid acceptance in the postwar housing reconstruction boom, the company diversified rapidly into a wide variety of building and plastics products. Overseas expansion also occurred not only in the White Commonwealth areas but particularly in Western Europe. Vertical integration took place to tap the do-it-yourself market and, during the 1960s, a chain of retail and wholesale stores was developed. Structurally, the company was divided into a series of product markets. With the exception of plastic foams (polyurethane) and system-built (prefabricated) homes, however, marketing remained separate from manufacture. The manufacturing subsidiaries sold to the marketing function and both attempted to meet the corporate goal of a 25 percent return on capital before taxes.

The Rio Tinto Zinc Company [25] was an exception to the generalization that the

---

[24] D. Thomas, "How Marley Made Millions," *Management Today*, pp. 83–89.

[25] *RTZ Explained*, company publication, September 1965 and 1970; see also V. Duncan, "The Development and Organisation of the Rio Tinto-Zinc Corporation," private paper for the London School of Economics, February 1967; G. Foster, "RTZ's Unparalleled Prospects," *Management Today*, September 1970, pp. 74–81, 138–40.

diversified metals and materials companies were not engaged in the more traditional heavy metal and material industries. Rio Tinto Zinc had interests in heavy metals but it was engaged in a wide range of such products at the same time, and was also widely diversified geographically. Starting as a mining company, it had become a highly diversified manufacturing, as well as mining, concern in a very short space of time, by the adoption and implementation of an impressive strategy of diversification.

The present company was formed in 1962 as the result of a merger between the Rio Tinto Company and the Consolidated Zinc Corporation. The Rio Tinto Company owed its name to a copper/pyrites mine in Spain, acquired in 1873 and, apart from investments in copper mines in Rhodesia, this was the sole asset of the company. In 1954 a two-thirds interest in the Rio Tinto mine was sold to the Spanish government and, with the proceeds of the sale, the company under its managing director, Mr. (later Sir) Val Duncan, embarked on the strategy of forming a world-wide mining company. The Consolidated Zinc Company (then called the Zinc Corporation), was founded on the rich deposits of lead and zinc at Broken Hill in Australia and was the largest Australian producer of such ores. Following negotiations between the British and Australian governments during the First World War, long-term agreements were made by Britain to purchase concentrates of Australian zinc; and the National (later Imperial) Smelting Company was set up to produce primary zinc in Britain as a strategic necessity. The Zinc Corporation and the smelting company merged in 1949 to form the Consolidated Zinc Company. By 1962, Imperial Smelting had diversified into sulphuric acid and fluorine chemicals. At the time of the merger, Consolidated Zinc was about to develop, in conjunction with Kaiser Aluminum, newly discovered bauxite deposits in Australia.

From 1954 on, Rio Tinto began to diversify fast, moving first into uranium mining in Canada and Australia and then adding small interests in oil production. At the time of the merger with Consolidated Zinc, Rio Tinto was about to develop a massive copper deposit discovered in South Africa. The merger increased both geographic and product spread together with the new prospects in Australia and South Africa. The Australian bauxite project was broadened to include Alcan and Pechiney to construct a large aluminum plant, and an aluminum smelter was acquired from the Tasmanian government. A third major project was soon added to open up, in conjunction with Kaiser Steel, vast iron ore deposits discovered in Western Australia.

In 1967–68, two major acquisitions were made. One was Capper Pass, a U.K. company specializing in the treatment of low-grade tin materials; the other was Borax (Holdings), a major borax mining and products company with extensive U.S. interests. Manufacturing interests outside of metal refining were also developed in specialty steels, potash, chemicals, alloys, metal fabrication, building materials, and hydroelectric power. Turnover grew from £60 million in 1960 to £372 million in 1969 and no more than 20 percent of assets were in any one product area.

After the Rio Tinto/Consolidated Zinc merger, the group called in McKinsey & Company to examine its structure. As a result, R.T.Z. adopted a decentralized system partly because it wanted to, and partly because of necessity, since it frequently engaged in joint ventures and had several subsidiaries with substantial local shareholdings. The overseas interests were managed locally by national management companies, which supervised the company's local interests, and by a new British subsidiary recently formed to supervise all the British interests. Control over these operations was exercised by central approval of financing, predetermined capital expenditure limits, approval of senior appointments, and agreement on dividend policy. The central office was very small, consisting of about 300 people with staff functions concerned with exploration, personnel and public relations, and research. A separate profit-center company, R.T.Z. Consultants, was formed to offer management consulting services to the other group companies, but they were not forced to use R.T.Z. Consultants, which in turn did work outside the group. The key central services were the finance and planning departments which dealt with profit and financial planning and the evaluation of new major projects. While much of the present system apparently grew in a rather ad hoc fashion, the company appeared to have developed a sophisticated managerial system and a strategy which provided considerable safeguard against the decline of any one product or threat of annexation by local political intervention.

These four concerns, while classified in the metals and materials industry, did exhibit some differences from the less diversified firms in this group. In particular, they were less integrated and did not require such large ongoing capital injections to maintain their present business. They had generally broken out of the lower categories of diversification, at least initially, by acquisition, a characteristic which related them to the other enterprises discussed in this chapter.

THE UNRELATED DIVERSIFIED COMPANIES

There was no real emergence of the acquisitive conglomerate form of manufacturing company in Britain. Of the six companies in the sample population, however, five had diversified in the postwar period. Only two of the four British companies bore a real resemblance to the American conglomerates (the fifth company was American), although all had relied heavily on acquisition as part of their growth strategy. Two of the companies diversified as a response to either a declining market or the traumatic shock of nationalization. Two companies were opportunistic diversifiers, while the fifth was the result of a merger of family firms with disparate product lines. The last company was one of the major American conglomerates.

Four of these firms had adopted a multidivisional structure, while two remained as holding companies. By 1970 family influence was almost extinct; only one firm was found to be family controlled. However, three of the firms were still largely owned or managed by the original entrepreneurs who built them, and a fourth diversified as the result of the impact of new leadership.

The first such firm was Sears Holdings.[26] This company was rapidly built up, in the 1950s, by Charles Clore, ably assisted by a few close advisers, and achieved the reputation of being a corporate raider. Clore, the son of a Russian Jewish refugee,

---

[26] W. Mennell, *Takeover,* pp. 31–32; see also A. Sampson, *Anatomy of Britain Today,* pp. 550–53; G. Turner, *Business in Britain,* pp. 70–71, 251, 272; W. Davis, *Merger Mania,* Constable, 1970, pp. 18–27; G. Bull and A. Vice, *Bid for Power,* Elek Books, London, 1961, pp. 113–29.

made his first major deal at the age of 22 when he bought the Cricklewood Ice Rink for its property development potential. In 1948 he bought a substantial interest in New Century Finance, the largest shareholder in Investment Registry, a West End issuing house. Clore obtained control of Investment Registry and became a director in 1951.

From this base, Clore began a spectacular series of bids. After two abortive attempts, Clore bid for and won J. Sears & Company, a vertically integrated boot and shoe concern with some 900 stores in prime high-street locations. Clore perceived that the property assets shown on the balance sheet were drastically undervalued, furthermore conservative management had restricted dividends, thus further depressing the share price. Clore was therefore able to purchase the company for considerably less than its true worth.

Clore sold and leased back a number of the footwear stores and used the cash flow generated, for further acquisitions. He quickly added a number of other footwear companies which were acquired for their property assets. Other interests were also acquired in engineering, shipbuilding, department stores, and automobile distribution, and blended together into a holding company under the Sears name. By 1960, Clore had built a large holding company and a personal fortune by concentrating primarily on corporations with undervalued property assets. An attempt by Clore to buy Watneys was rebuffed but served as one major force to restructure the brewing industry.

Sears Holding was less active during the 1960s, by which time most companies were more aware of the value of their property. Further acquisitions were made in stores, and in laundries and knitwear in the United States, while the ailing shipbuilding activity was divested. The company remained a highly diversified holding company still largely controlled personally and financially by Clore and a few close associates with no real corporate headquarters at all.

The Rank Organisation [27] also retained elements of the original entrepreneurs who built it. The voting shares were closely held in a trust set up by J. Arthur Rank and his family, and the company (in the early 1970s) was still led by John Davis, who managed the company throughout the Second World War and afterward.

The Rank Organisation exhibited phenomenal growth during the 1960s resulting from a diversification program which fortuitously gave it the world rights to xerography outside the Americas. The company was formed in 1935 by J. Arthur Rank, the flour miller, a religious man who was annoyed to find that he could not gain distribution for a religious film he had helped finance. As a result he bought a West End cinema, founded a film distribution company and bought film production companies and more cinemas. By 1942 he had built up a chain of 600 cinemas and owned 60 percent of the British movie production industry.

After World War II the company fell into dire financial straits with falling cinema attendance and severe losses on film production. To support his film production and cinema interests Rank had acquired companies making cinema equipment, cameras,

---

[27] G. Bull, "The Next Man In At Rank," *The Director,* December 1968, pp. 434–41; see also Monopolies Commission, *The Rank Organisation Ltd. and the De la Rue Co. Ltd.,* H.M.S.O., June 1969; "Tying Job Appraisal Into the Business," *International Management,* July 1970, pp. 31–32; G. Foster, "The Rank Xerox Boom," *Management Today,* February 1969, pp. 55–59, 118, 120.

and lenses and furnishings, and those companies together with acquisitions provided the basis for a major diversification program which converted Rank into a highly diversified enterprise. The company was still engaged in movies but had diversified into radio and television appliances, audio-visual products, scientific instruments, hotels, bowling alleys, leisure activities, and the extremely profitable Xerox operation which produced over 75 percent of net profits.

Rank was organized into product divisions each under a managing director and separate board. The chairman and chief executive of Rank, John Davis, was, however, the main driving force of the company and had been so since the 1940s when Rank withdrew to supervise his flour interests.

The final firm still managed by its founders was Slater Walker.[28] This company was perhaps most like the U.S. conglomerates. It had only a very recent history in its present form dating back to 1964 when Mr. James Slater in partnership with Mr. Peter Walker, backed by a number of institutional investors, acquired a small almost defunct textile and property concern.

Slater, trained as an accountant, worked for a truck manufacturing company acquired by Leyland Motors, where he was spotted by Donald Stokes and then was appointed as Stokes' assistant. Good at detecting investment opportunities, Slater built himself a small personal fortune while at Leyland and offered advice to that company's pension fund. In 1964 he decided to enter business on his own and acquired a small property company, H. Lotery. The company's name was changed to Slater Walker Securities and, like Charles Clore before him, Slater used this as a vehicle for a vigorous acquisition program by selecting companies with underutilized asset positions.

He soon built up a large industrial and finance group in Britain and Australia serving a variety of unrelated product markets with profit before taxes rising from £0.14 million in 1964 to £10.4 million in 1969. The industrial group was organized into divisions with a director in charge of each. The divisions operated on a strict system of budgetary control and each director had clearly defined responsibility for management and profits. The small yet strong central executive director system provided policy guidance, assisted with organization improvements, and was available to deal with major problems.

Slater Walker grew very fast, buying medium-sized companies, injecting new management, selling them off, or liquidating loss-making activities while building up profitable ventures, and turning out impressive increases in profitability. In 1968, however, the company began a second transformation which seemed destined to turn it from an industrial conglomerate into a multinational investment bank with other interests in investment management and insurance. The investment banking function was to continue to include the purchase of poorly managed companies, turning them around, and selling them off at a profit. The primary strategy, however, seemed to be to develop the group as a diversified international financial concern offering a comprehensive range of financial services, and taking an extremely active role in dealing with its investment clients.

---

[28] R. Winsbury, "Slater Walkers Non-Conglomerate," *Management Today*, August 1969, pp. 82–87; E. Foster and G. Bull, "Jim Slater's Six Fat Years," *The Director*, August 1970, pp. 228–32.

One interesting new tactic increasingly being adopted during the company's new phase was the spinning off of satellite ventures led by former employees identified as having entrepreneurial flair. Slater Walker via its investment activities provided the necessary financial backing for these ventures in return for a minority shareholding, some control over development, and appointment as financial advisors to the satellite. This tactic provided interesting possibilities for concerns that did not wish to lose potential entrepreneurial managers completely, offered an unusual motivation to internal management, and reduced the level of risk associated with portfolio investment. At the same time it proliferated the activities Slater Walker could become involved with and provided a significant market for the internal financial services of issuing, insurance, and investment.

Thomas Tilling,[29] on the other hand, was a holding company moving slowly toward the model of the managed U.S. conglomerate. Tilling was originally engaged in bus transportation, which was largely nationalized during the first postwar Labour administration. Rather than repay all the shareholders's funds, the management decided to form an industrial holding company. During the 1950s, acquisitions were made in the areas of building products, glassware, textiles, insurance, light engineering, publishing, vehicle distribution, and wholesaling. Although further acquisitions were made in the 1960s, these tended to reinforce the original product market interests rather than extend the degree of diversity.

Initially Tilling built up its diverse interests by acquiring small companies still managed by owner entrepreneurs who wished to sell to avoid death duties. The original managements were left intact, and no acquisitions were made which were not voluntary. However, this policy began to change, and the independence of the member companies became increasingly challenged. By the early 1970s, for example, the building materials companies began regrouping into what was essentially a product division. The small central office executive team was extended, tight financial controls applied, and the new central management was beginning to fulfill the role of the group executives frequently observed in U.S. multidivisional conglomerates.

Reckitt and Coleman [30] was the oldest established British "conglomerate," although its present corporate form was not established until 1954 as a full paper merger between Reckitt and Sons, J. & J. Coleman, and Chiswick Products. The Reckitt and Coleman companies were both old, established family concerns engaged in starch products. Coleman's was engaged primarily in mustard, and Reckitt entered this market in the United States in 1926 with the purchase of R. T. French,

---

[29] A. Parker. "How Tillings Rule the Roost," *The Director*, May 1969, pp. 266–70; R. Edwards and H. Townsend, *Business Enterprise*, pp. 67–68, 471; P. H. D. Ryder, "The Method of Control in a Holding Company," *Achievement*, March 1966, pp. 10–11; "The Tilling Group," company reprint from Sir Roger Falk, *The Business of Management*, Penguin Books, 1970; T. Lester, "Tillings Three Way Testing," *Management Today*, August 1971, pp. 39–47, 86.

[30] B. Reckitt, *The History of Reckitt & Sons*, A. Brown, London, 1952; "A Panoply of Products," *Times Review of Industry*, February 1967, pp. 30–32; B. N. Reckitt, "The Development and Organisation of Reckitt and Coleman Ltd.," private paper delivered at the London Graduate School of Business. February 1970; Evely and Little, *Concentration in British Industry*, pp. 266–69, 127; D. Thomas, "How Reckitt Married Coleman (At Last)," *Management Today*, April 1971. pp. 51–59; Reckitt and Coleman *Newsletter*, company publication, various.

the largest U.S. mustard manufacturer. Both companies developed substantial overseas interests, and competition in laundry blue led to a profit pooling arrangement
in South America. In 1921 this arrangement was extended to cover all world trade
outside the United Kingdom and, by 1938, after both companies had increased their
range of household products further, a merger of all trade was agreed upon, although the companies retained their original independence. Chiswick Products was
formed in 1929 and manufactured shoe and floor polishes. Reckitt had entered this
market by acquisition during the 1920s, but rather than compete with Chiswick it
exchanged its interest for a shareholding in Chiswick.

The three companies finally merged completely in 1954 to form Reckitt and
Coleman Holdings, a highly diversified company with interests in polishes, shoe
accessories, food and beverage, toiletries, pharmaceuticals, and a wide variety of
household products. Despite some divestitures by 1970, the combined company's
diversification had been increased by the introduction of new products and further
acquisitions. The 1954 merger remained essentially a paper transaction, however,
since structurally the main component companies retained their independence until
1969–70. Then the complexities of the business finally led to a McKinsey-inspired
reorganization. This divided the business into five product divisions in the United
Kingdom, with three overseas divisions to supervise the extensive foreign interests.

The final unrelated diversified company was one of the major U.S. conglomerates,
the International Telephone and Telegraph Company (I.T.T.).[31] This company and
its British subsidiary Standard Telephones and Cables was primarily engaged in
telephone equipment production and operations until 1959. Eighty percent of
corporate earnings came from extensive foreign operations especially in Western
Europe, and total sales were some $750 million.

At this point a new chief executive, Harold S. Geneen, was appointed. He
quickly transformed the company into what by 1970 had become perhaps the most
successful multinational conglomerate. Geneen undertook a huge number of acquisitions, over 100 in ten years, which took I.T.T. into a wide range of new markets
primarily in service industries. By 1969 sales had grown to some $5.5 billion and
profits to $234 million, of which 55 percent were generated in the United States.
Profits from newly acquired service industries represented 60 percent of total North
American profits and 15 percent of overseas revenue.

Geneen increased the growth of I.T.T. by acquisitions especially in car rental
(Avis), home construction (Levitt), foods (Continental King), insurance (Hartford
and Abbey Life), mutual funds (Hamilton Management), and hotels (Sheraton).
Many of these acquired concerns which had operated principally in the United
States were then developed in Western Europe. At the same time, other acquisitions
were made and internal growth was fostered in the traditional electronic business of
the group.

A system of multiproduct divisions was introduced in the United States in 1960,

---

[31] "How I.T.T. Manages Itself By Meetings," *International Management*, February 1970,
pp. 22–25; "The Creative Habit," *Times Review of Industry*, August 1965, pp. 18, 20; "I.T.T.
Plans To Stay Ahead," *International Management*, September 1967, pp. 79–82; "Inside the
I.T.T. Empire," *International Management*, July 1963, pp. 37–39; J. Thackray, "I.T.T.'s One
Man Machine," *Management Today*, December 1966, p. 78; H. Stieglitz and C. D. Wilkerson,
Corporate Organization Structures, pp. 79–81.

while overseas subsidiaries were also reduced to measurable product divisions in the local geographic subsidiaries which, in Western Europe, reported to a European headquarters.

An elaborate system of tight business planning and financial controls was built up to administer the diversified group operations, the managers of which were personally examined at frequent intervals by Geneen and his central staff of some 400 administrative, technical, and financial experts. Local operating unit managers were called upon to prepare an annual business plan forecasting every aspect of the business they controlled including sales, earnings, capital requirements, working capital, cash requirements, inventory, receivables, and new products. This plan was scrutinized by headquarters for realism and for judging whether it would work. The scrutiny enabled the 16 general product-line managers to assess the unit managers, who were called to headquarters to review their plans. Once accepted, this plan formed the basis for managerial assessment, with any deviations calling for immediate remedial action.

The success of I.T.T. owed much to the power and personal impact of Geneen, who took a close interest in the assessment of his operating managers. The system he built up was an extreme example of the use of the multidivisional system to manage the diversified enterprise. Nevertheless, the fact that it depended so much on Geneen personally might prove a problem for the future, except that the pressure system had already produced an impressive list of other general managers who had left I.T.T. to successfully lead other large American enterprises.

There were few British companies that had consciously adopted a strategy of conglomerate diversification in the same way as the American conglomerates. Apart perhaps from Tilling and Slater Walker, there were only a few smaller manufacturing companies which were not in the population under study together with a group of concerns which were engaged in nonmanufacturing activities such as services and international trading. In general, a conglomerate movement had not materialized. This might have been partially due to a shortge of the general management skills necessary to run such a concern. Further, since the late 1960s, there had been some government disfavor of such concerns following the collapse of some financial conglomerates in the United States.

CONCLUSION

This chapter has been concerned with those industries and firms which have diversified in the 1950s and 1960s mainly by acquisition. The communications, and food and packaging companies diversified in response to changes in processes, materials, and markets. They were not heavily committed to technology, and the internal development of new products was difficult, thus resulting in the need to acquire the diversity required for sustained growth. These industries were related by the market needs they served, producing a variety of products to meet a particular need, and diversification was often a quick means of obtaining new products which could not be developed internally.

The paper and textile companies, which were relatively recent diversifiers, were much concerned with a range of products based on specific raw materials. In this

sense they were the closest to the low diversity industries, which also tended to concentrate on a material such as steel, oil, or tobacco. They were less attuned to meeting new market needs than sustaining their existing market, and diversified only
when placed at a competitive disadvantage. Diversification into new markets was
often a strategy secondary to that of vertical integration and came only after integration had failed to protect existing markets.

The diversified metals and materials concerns, and some of the unrelated product
concerns, also tended to diversify in an effort to escape overdependency on a narrow product range. Other unrelated concerns were primarily opportunistic, but there
was no major trend toward a conglomerate movement like that in the United States.

Growth rates and profitability, within the main industry groups discussed, tended
to be low. In specific segments, however, there were high growth areas such as convenience foods, plastic packaging, and synthetic fibers. Despite some increased concentration, competition probably intensified for most of these concerns. This was
due, especially to new competitors, both in the United Kingdom and overseas, to
substitution competition, and changes in legislation to break down restrictive practices. In many cases, the broad scope of the industry, coupled with low entry barriers, eased competitive entry.

In many of these concerns there was, until the early 1970s, a high level of family
influence which might well have retarded diversification. This had diminished but
remained strong, especially among the food companies. As a result, perhaps, the
British-owned companies in particular had largely found themselves engaged in
relatively narrow product markets where the products themselves were difficult to
differentiate, or late in their life cycle, or subject to competitive forces based on more
economic natural resources or production procedures. The onset of competition produced declining financial returns, a worsening stock market position, and increased
vulnerability. Thus, these companies tried to break out from their traditional markets by acquisition. Many grew substantially in a short space of time in both sales
and assets managed. Improved profitability in return on assets or earnings per share
rarely followed, however, since the managerial and structural reorganizations that
were needed to achieve the potential benefits from acquisitions were rarely made.
Deficiencies in management skills, inadequate financial controls, and poor rationalization actually often compounded the earlier difficulties. Much of the acquisition
strategy of the 1960s, therefore, probably had little real benefit for stockholders or
the British economy as a whole.

Structural change, especially to the multidivisional structure, thus followed the
strategic change when it became a necessity brought on by recognition of the inadequacy of the holding-company structures built up by acquisition. The use of
consultants, in particular McKinsey & Company, was again widespread in introducing reorganization. Change in some cases also took place shortly after a change in
leadership, but this was less common than among the technologically diversified
concerns. It was noticeable that many of the companies adopting the multidivisional structure had still not developed a large central office as had many of the
early diversified technological concerns. This might be attributed to the recent nature of the change, for some older diversified firms, such as Metal Box and Unilever, had developed large central staffs, and this was the common experience among
U.S.-related product firms from these industries. The full features of the multidivi-

sional system were actually rare and only really found among the U.S. subsidiary concerns. Most of the British companies still appeared to be in an intermediate phase between a holding company and a divisional system, with loose control and planning systems, and a poorly developed central office. This latter failing was sometimes especially noticeable in those firms led by a dominant personality such as Weston at Associated British Foods, Hyman at Viyella, and Ryder at Reed. However, it was not obvious that a very large central office was necessary to manage the diversified enterprise, and the American experience which developed before improved communication and information systems were available could possibly be superfluous if firms combined to diversify toward the conglomerate form.

CHAPTER 7

The Internal Characteristics of British Corporations

INTRODUCTION

THIS CHAPTER DEALS WITH THE INTERNAL characteristics of a number of the 100 companies studied. A stratified sample of 25 companies was visited in order to interview directors of senior executives for establishing the validity of the conclusions reached using published data. The sample is briefly discussed, together with the validation results.

Structured interviews were conducted, which enabled some tentative comparisons to be made concerning specific internal characteristics, and which differentiated managerial systems in the dominant product and related product companies that had extensively adopted a form of multidivisional structure. The data presented deal with research and development, performance measures, reward systems, control systems, objectives, central services, the composition of top management, and investment procedures. The basic hypothesis regarding the internal characteristics of multidivisional structures was considered and amended in the light of the data. Other relevant research was considered regarding the socioeconomic background of the senior management in British corporations.

The chapter concludes with a comparison between the internal characteristics of British corporations and their U.S. equivalents. As the trend in both diversification and structure had been remarkably similar, a comparison between the internal characteristics of companies with similar structures shows whether these concur and, if not, where they differ.

THE VALIDATION SAMPLE

The first purpose of the sample of 25 [1] British- or European-owned companies visited was to check the validity of the structural and product-market categories as-

---

[1] Subsequent to these formal research interviews, discussions with a further 15 or so companies were conducted on a more random basis. The results of these additional interviews tended to corroborate the findings obtained from the 25 original companies.

signed to the British corporate population. The sample chosen was stratified as far as possible along three dimensions:

(1) The companies interviewed were stratified according to size and weighted to include more of the larger companies. Seventeen companies were chosen from the top 50 and 8 from the bottom 50 corporations.

(2) The sample was stratified by industry group, and 25 percent of the British-owned companies in each industry sector were interviewed.

(3) Stratification was made according to the categories of diversification, using the 1970 numerical breakdown. Twenty-five percent of the companies in each category were interviewed: 2 from the single product, 9 from the dominant product, 13 from the related product, and 1 from the unrelated product categories.

In addition to the above criteria, the companies interviewed tended to be chosen to check those corporations about which there were the least published data.

A structured interview was conducted which, in addition to discussion of the degree of diversification and the corporate structure, covered the following topics:

(1) Degree of product integration and methods of internal pricing.

(2) Research and Development—location, expenditure (as a percentage of sales), and type.

(3) Performance measures.

(4) Reward system for senior management.

(5) Control systems—including financial, strategic, and personnel.

(6) Corporate objectives.

(7) Composition of top executive management.

(8) Investment criteria and procedures.

(9) Central office responsibilities.

(10) The extent, responsibilities, and composition of senior executive committees.

The degree of product integration was assessed as the percentage of divisional production flowing into other divisions as a primary input for a further stage of the manufacturing process. The executives interviewed were asked to assess the extent of this product flow as a percentage of overall divisional output and, based on the evidence, interdivisional flows of more than 50 percent were treated as "high," between 25 and 50 percent "moderate," and below 25 percent "low." Such definitions were crude and empirical, but did seem important in terms of the other managerial characteristics of organization. For example, the level of interdivisional product flow seriously affected the method of interdivisional transfer pricing used. This was determined by three principal methods, namely, interdivisional bargaining, market prices, and central office imposed.

Research and development expenditures were also measured crudely at the level of both the industry and the enterprise as a percentage of gross sales revenue. Empirically it was determined that such expenditure could be divided into three classes: high (over 4 percent of sales), medium (2 to 4 percent of sales), and low (less than 2 percent of sales). In addition, the location and control of research effort was ascertained between the central office and divisions. Similarly, companies were questioned concerning the type of research undertaken in order to determine if the thrust of expenditure was toward the development of new products for new markets or continued development of existing products.

Executives were asked which measures of performance were used in their respective organizations. The most commonly experienced measures were return on investment, and return on sales and market share, although others such as gross turnover, overall costs, and cash flow were sometimes used in conjunction with one or more of the more common measures.

Corporate reward systems were assessed principally in terms of direct and indirect rewards. Direct rewards were taken as straight salary, salary plus a bonus, or stock option plan related to performance, or any other such variants. Indirect systems centered on continuous employment and fringe benefits, such as status rewards, pension schemes, loans for house purchase, and the like.

Control systems were assessed in several dimensions. First, executives were questioned on whether an annual budgetary system was used. Initially it was automatically assumed that such a rudimentary control would be in force; however, this did not always turn out to be the case. When such a control was used, the precise makeup of the budget was elicited to determine what financial and nonfinancial variables such as costs, sales, cash flow, market share, and the like, were covered. In addition, the frequence of monitoring was established, together with some understanding of central office actions on budget discrepancies.

Second, other controls were assessed, such as the presence or absence of long-term plans, the duration and composition of such plans, the presence or absence of decision rules, such as discretionary expenditure at division level, division recruitment, salary policy, and the like; the procedures for the appointment of senior executives and the location of management development policies were also discussed.

Executives were questioned about corporate objectives. First, it was ascertained if such objectives formally existed and, if so, in what terms were they stated, were they quantified or not, and how had they been formulated—as part of a logical planning process or by some less rational method.

The composition of top executive management was taken as the role of the executive members of the main board. It was established if these individuals were operationally responsible for a specific division, a specialized function, such as marketing or finance, or some combination of such activities.

Investment criteria and procedures were examined first as to method, and second as to the location of decision making. The financial methods used, such as payback and discounted cash flow, were established together with other requirements, such as cutoff rates of return, nonfinancial or strategic justification required, and the like. Apart from the frequent use of discretionary decision rules for minor capital expenditure, major items were usually considered centrally, and the location and makeup of central decision-making bodies were established. Most commonly such bodies consisted of the managing director alone, the finance function, an investment committee the composition of which might or might not include division general managers, and the company board.

The exact nature of central office services was established together with the jurisdictional limits of such central functions. For example, could a central office marketing department import policy on divisional marketing activities, were all acquisitions determined centrally, and so on.

Finally, the extent, responsibilities, and composition of all senior executive committees were identified together with any other significant comments about corporate procedures.

Obviously much of this information was considered confidential and, therefore, in discussing the corporations interviewed, no identification was made of individual concerns. The sample size and the small numbers of single and unrelated product concerns in the population precluded any significant consideration of specific characteristics for these corporations, but it was possible to compare and contrast the characteristics of the dominant and related product concerns; and this was done.

The interviews conducted confirmed the categorizations of both diversity and structure in all except one case. The exception was one of degree of diversity where the concern had been incorrectly categorized. All structural categorizations were confirmed by the interviews. These results suggested a high probability of accuracy in the classification of those companies not interviewed.

THE INTERNAL CHARACTERISTICS OF BRITISH COMPANIES

The internal characteristics of the sample companies were expected to differ according to the degree of diversified activities. The single product companies, for example, were nearly all found to exhibit a functional form of organization, or, in the case of British American Tobacco, a series of multigeographic divisions reflecting geographic diversity, but little product diversity.

The dominant product concerns were basically of two types: First, those companies which diversified their product line to a small degree as an ancillary to their main activity (the downstream secondary chemical operations of the oil companies was an example); second, those companies which entered new secondary product market areas where there was little similarity to the primary product line (the entry of a tobacco company into food manufacture, for example). Where there was a high degree of product flow between the primary and secondary activities, it was expected that although a multidivisional system might exist, the secondary activity would enjoy less autonomy than in the case where there was little relationship between the primary and secondary activities. The autonomy of the primary division was likely to be least overall, since this division would be the main concern of senior management, which would be composed largely of executives with experience within the primary division.

The related product companies were also expected to vary in the degree of central coordination and control required. Thus, a full line chemical company such as I.C.I. might well exhibit a high degree of product flow between divisions, since the product of some divisions would be raw materials for others. Whereas a specialized chemical concern such as Fisons, which was engaged in a series of diverse market segments, would not exhibit such product flow between divisions. The controls of the central office and divisional autonomy might, therefore, be expected to vary, with more central control needed in the first case than in the second. However, overall there was likely to be more autonomy in the divisions of related product companies than in the primary division of a dominant product concern, in view of the greater contact with the market, and a top management less dedicated to one major product market.

The unrelated product companies were engaged in a variety of different product markets where interdivisional activity was minimal, hence there was little need for a large central coordinating function. Thus, there was more likelihood of a holding-company structure or multidivisional structure with a very small central office, controlling divisional activities primarily by the use of financial measures.

The observations reported broadly supported these arguments as summarized in Table 7–1, which reveals the internal characteristics associated with the dominant and related product concerns in the limited sample. It will be observed that different characteristics were found in dominant concerns (where diversification was closely associated with the primary product) from those in firms where diversification was less related. Second, the diversified firms related by technology or skill (the early diversifiers) had different characteristics from those that were related by market or vertical integration. These latter concerns had, in general, diversified more recently primarily by acquisition, and the small size of their central office could reflect a shortage of time to build up a multifunctional specialist staff.

THE DOMINANT PRODUCT FIRMS

The dominant product companies interviewed had all adopted a form of multidivisional structure. They, therefore, possessed a central office which provided a number of staff monitoring and service functions for a set of operating product or geographic divisions. The divisions were nominally responsible for their own profitability and performance, the responsibility resting with a division general manager or a collective divisional committee or board.

Four of the nine dominant product companies reported a high percentage (greater than 40 percent) of product flow between the divisions, and appeared correspondingly more centralized than the five companies which had a low percentage of interdivisional product flow.

The main differences seemed to occur in the control of interdivisional transactions and control of research and development, new products, marketing, and production. Two of the four companies with high interdivisional product flow said they imposed transfer prices centrally and two allowed bargaining between the divisions, whereas the companies with little interdivisional product flow, tended to rely on bargaining or market prices where such flows existed.

The reported degree of central control over research, new product introductions, marketing, and production was much greater in the four highly integrated dominant product companies than in the five with low integration. Three companies in moderately technological industries, had developed centralized research organizations, and each of these was subject to control from the central office. In three cases there were also substantial central office marketing departments, which were said to have considerable powers of intervention over the operating divisions' activities. Two companies had central production departments which supervised divisional production operations. In all four cases product-market strategy was determined centrally, and all new product introductions were subject to approval from the central office.

These positions were nearly reversed in the five nonintegrated divisional dominant product companies, although one was substantially increasing its degree of divisional integration and was moving toward more centralization. The level of research expenditure was moderate in one concern, below the overall industry average in two firms, and very low in the remaining concerns. Overall, the research intensity was somewhat lower than in the integrated concerns. Research and development was decentralized within the divisions in four companies and partially so in the fifth. Only two companies had central research and development departments or directors to coordinate activities across the divisions. All five companies possessed a central marketing staff function, but these were basically divorced from operations and tended to be specialists in such fields as market research or advertising. None of the companies possessed a central production staff, and only one maintained other than financial controls over divisional product-market strategy.

The size of the general office reflected these observed differences. In three of the four integrated concerns, a large multifunctional general office had been built up basically to coordinate flows of product between the various product-market activities. In those companies with little integration, the central office tended to be small and concerned with fewer functions. The adoption of a multidivisional structure had meant that frequently many of the central services that had formed the central office function were transferred to the dominant product division, leaving a relatively small central corporate staff.

There were, it seemed, two basic forms of dominant product company, therefore: those which diversified by developing ancillary activities closely related to the original dominant product, and those which expanded into new products and markets usually by acquisition. The distinguishing characteristic of the dominant product group as a whole, however, seemed to be that the emphasis of each company was on the continued development of the dominant activity, and little interest in diversification was reported. Thus, eight of the nine firms said they devoted by far the greater part of their research expenditure to the development of the existing product-market area (the ninth firm did not have a significant research program). Only one of these eight firms had institutionalized a search for new products and markets, and this appeared due to its entry into a high technology industry. The senior management and central staff were composed almost entirely of personnel from the dominant product activity. Despite the adoption of a multidivisional system, senior management continued to play an active role in operations, especially in the affairs of the dominant product activity. The top executive management were divorced from operations in only two companies, both of which were attempting to diversify by acquisition.

Corporate objectives were seldom clearly specified but generally tended to focus on growth of return on investment (reported in five companies). Three companies said they had turnover growth as an objective and for two of these, this appeared to be the primary objective in a situation where return on assets or investment was not even a secondary objective. Only three companies had earnings per share growth objectives, and these were of very recent origin. The use of earnings per share as a measurement was not found in six companies. Indeed, the finance director of one company did not understand the meaning of the measurement when it was explained.

Apart from the chairman, who was also frequently the chief executive, top executive management was usually composed of a managing director, functional spe-

TABLE 7–1

The Observed Characteristics of British Dominant and Related Product Companies

Diversification Stage Characteristic	Dominant Product		Related Product	
	Integrated	Nonintegrated	Technical	Nontechnical
Organization Structure	Multidivisional		Multidivisional	
Research and Development: Type	Centralized	Decentralized Search Mainly for Improvements to Existing Product Lines	Centralized Institutionalized Search for New Products	Undeveloped
Internal Product Flow: Level	High	Low	Low	Moderate
Pricing	Imposed	Bargaining or Market	Bargaining or Market	Imposed or Market
Performance Measures	Return on Investment Return on Sales Costs		Return on Investment Market Share	
Rewards	Straight Salary Continuous Employment		Straight Salary Continuous Employment Few Bonus/Stock Option Schemes	

Control System	Annual Budget Long-Term Financial Plans Central Cash Accounting Central Appointment of Top Executives Capital Expenditure	Annual Budget Central Cash Accounting Central Appointment of Top Executives Capital Expenditure	
		Strategic and Financial Long-Term Plans	Financial Long-Term Plans
Corporate Objectives	Return on Investment Growth Turnover Growth Market Share Growth Few Earnings per Share Growth	Return on Investment Growth Diversification Market Share Growth Few Earnings per Share Growth	
Central Office Size Most Common Functions	Large Small Finance and Corporate Planning Accounting Legal Personnel Purchasing Line and Staff Marketing Research and Development Production	Large Finance Small Accounting Corporate Planning Legal Personnel Staff Marketing Research and Development Management development Production Services	Acquisition
Division Responsibility	Operations	Operations Product Strategy Product Market Scope	
	Dominant Product Operations Other Products Operations Product Strategy Product Market Scope		

cialists, particularly the finance and marketing directors, and the divisional general managers.

The occurrence of group level general managers was uncommon, being reported in only two of the largest companies with extensive overseas operations. Policy was frequently set by an executive policy committee usually composed of the chairman, managing director, and finance director, and frequently including the divisional general managers. The board was usually composed of the senior executive directors, together with a small number of nonexecutive directors. Some policy committees also reviewed operations and allocated resources, but separate operating committees were found in three companies, and the allocation of resources was more commonly reported to be a responsibility of the chief executive alone (two cases), a separate investment committee (two cases), or the whole board (two cases).

The active involvement of the division general managers in these top committees meant they were in part responsible for measuring themselves and for setting the policies against which they were to be measured. As a result, it was not clear to what degree or extent careful performance appraisal was practiced at the top levels of these corporations. Return on investment criteria were used by seven companies that adopted discounted cash flow methods of assessing return in the allocation of resources. Payback was used as an additional check in three companies. Two companies had yet to establish such financial criteria, and investments were influenced by more intuitive criteria based on interaction between the chief executive and the divisional general managers. For example, in one of these concerns an outside finance director had recently been appointed. He was attempting to introduce economic measurement criteria but he found that when challenged on the economic justification of some capital requests, divisional general managers tended to make a personal approach to the chief executive. He usually granted their requests without calling for formal economic justification.

Strategic or nonfinancial criteria were uncommon, being reported in only three cases. This seemed to reflect a general attitude of maintaining the dominant product position, rather than a search for new markets where returns might be better. It was interesting that in several companies where investments were made against a corporate return on investment objective, the overall performance of the corporation was considerably below the stated objective, yet there was no post-audit examination of investments.

A number of central services were common to practically all the dominant product companies. These included legal, finance and accounting, personnel, and corporate planning functions, the last two being of recent origin in most cases. The personnel function was also usually responsible for formal management development where this existed (found in only four of the nine companies). A formal management development function was generally a very recent innovation, and only one company reported it had developed a comprehensive program for anticipation of its future management needs. Corporate planning was also very new, being introduced mainly within the last five years, although seven companies had added planning functions. These were frequently attached to the finance department and were mainly concerned with the development of long-term financial plans. Most companies considered their procedures were still somewhat primitive, being mainly extrapolations of past data, and they were working on improving their systems.

Strategic ingredients, other than financial forecasts, were only observed in the long-term plans of three companies. The strategic implications of such financial characteristics as debt/equity ratio, and divided payout ratio, were usually missing, and executives not specifically charged with financial responsibilities seemed largely ignorant of these matters. Those companies with multinational interests usually had some form of central coordination to set the policy and monitor performance of overseas activities. In two cases, where worldwide product divisions existed, this task was performed at the divisional level, however, and the degree to which such services had been developed, depended largely on the extent of the overseas activity. Where overseas activity was less well-developed, international subsidiaries tended to be allowed considerable autonomy reporting in a relatively informal, personal manner to a specific executive who was also responsible for other duties. These concerns had not developed consistent multinational strategies —rather, they seemed opportunistic in approach.

The main control system in all companies was reported to be the annual budget and this appeared to be almost entirely a financial document. Surprisingly, even here some companies had only recently introduced an annual budgetary system.

One recently appointed managing director reported that his company was currently in the first year of its annual budget and he was still unable to obtain results more frequently than bi-monthly. He had found on his arrival that there was no central management accounting system save for the annual visit from the auditors. In two other companies, which had recently changed from a holding-company structure, a budgetary system had only been introduced within the last four years, when standardized accounting procedures covering all the subsidiaries had been introduced.

The budget documents usually included projections of sales, costs, gross profits, and capital expenditure with less frequent coverage of cash flow and return on investment. Other strategic measures such as product strategy, market share, and new products were rarely included and some companies reported that these criteria were not even formally considered. Systematic analysis of competitors' strategies was rarely, if ever, undertaken. Rather, policy was more usually determined as a short-term response to competitive actions.

Other control mechanisms most frequently used were central control over senior appointments, central cash accounting, and decision rules governing expenditure and personnel policies. These controls tended to be quite stringent. For example, the managing director of one company said he had to approve all appointments of salaries over £1,500 and spending discretion at the divisional level appeared to be of similar scale in several cases. Eight of the companies had central cash accounts, and the same number had central control over senior appointments. Decision rules did vary, but eight companies had controls on capital expenditure, and most imposed tight controls on salary structure and cash expenditures.

The performance of the divisions was most commonly measured by a return on investment criteria (reported in seven companies), frequently in conjunction with other criteria, especially return on sales, costs, and market share. However, performance was rewarded or sanctioned indirectly via promotional prospects, rather than by some more direct form of incentive compensation. All nine of the dominant product companies rewarded executives by a straight salary system, which was not tied directly to either divisional or corporate performance. Two companies did have, in addition, a bonus system unrelated to performance and not normally variable, thus becoming merely a part of the salary. Six of the nine companies also said they practiced a system of continuous employment and did not, under normal circumstances, fire their executives. None of the dominant product companies granted stock options to senior executives and, save in the case of one family company interviewed, the equity participation by senior executives and directors was minimal.

When questioned on their attitude toward rewards linked directly to performance, many of the executives considered such rewards unfair and inappropriate to their companies. The concept also seemed personally distasteful. All executives considered their pension rights to be very important, and most were proud of the schemes developed by their companies. Most did not consider the lack of transferability of pension rights to be over-important, but these men were virtually all long-service employees who had frequently been with their company all or nearly all their working life.

The interviews tended to indicate the presence of two distinct forms of dominant product company. In the first of these, the ancillary activities were closely related and were often vertical extensions of the dominant product line. This strategy led to an administrative system that consisted of a large central coordinating staff which severely restricted divisional decision-making capability, especially in the dominant product division. In contrast, the second dominant product strategy reflected management's desire to reduce dependence on the dominant product by the entry, usually by acquisition, into new, often unrelated markets. Firms adopting this strategy tended to transfer many former control service functions to divisional responsibility thus permitting substantially greater autonomy to division general managers.

Nevertheless, with both these strategies, there appeared to be a significant direct involvement by senior control management in operational activities especially in the dominant product division. This could create difficulties in measuring the objective performance of the division general managers and this was compounded by the active role played by many such managers in policy formulation, both as participants in executive committees and as main board members.

THE RELATED PRODUCT COMPANIES

The related product companies interviewed had also adopted multidivisional structures and, while exhibiting a number of common characteristics, there seemed to be a significant difference between the technological and skill-related companies, which were usually early diversifiers, and those low technology firms that had diversified more recently. The six technological and skill-related companies all had research programs which, although variable in size, were in every case at least partially oriented toward the discovery of new products to permit growth in new or existing markets. The process of continued product diversification appeared deeply institutionalized, and five of these companies stated that continuous diversification was a clearly defined corporate objective. This was apparently less true of the seven nontechnological diversified companies. Funds allocated to research and development were reported to be very low in these concerns (less than 1 percent of sales in five cases), and no research was conducted in one case. R&D was said to be related mainly to developing the existing product-market scope. Four of these companies did have an objective of increased diversification but, for the present, it seemed that this would be achieved mainly by acquisition or imitation, since little had yet been done to build up their research capabilities.

The other main difference that was observed between the two groups lay in the role of the central office. The technological companies had usually built up a large multifunctional general office, which coordinated corporate activities and performed a series of monitoring functions. Five of the six technological companies had such a structure, whereas only two of the nontechnological companies had built a large central staff. Despite greater potential complexity in the technological companies, which serviced a wide variety of markets, the product divisions apparently had less autonomy and were more closely monitored than the nontechnological companies. This could well have been a function of time, since the newly diversified companies had had less time to build up a general office and in many cases had only recently adopted a multidivisional structure, which they were still adjusting to.

None of the technology-related companies reported a high degree of internal product flow (all were 25 percent or less), but in two companies some self-manufacture of components had led to special cases of limited high internal product flow. Here transfer prices were imposed centrally. Elsewhere transfers were settled by interdivisional bargaining. While some research was decentralized in five companies, in four companies there were central research laboratories which handled general or fundamental research. All research, however, was reported to be coordinated centrally by a corporate level research executive and his staff (found in five of six companies). There were centralized control and coordination of purchasing in three companies, which negotiated companywide contracts for major items with buying being conducted at the divisional level. Four companies said they exercised central control of the divisional product-market scope, and new products could not be introduced at the division level without prior approval. The central personnel functions usually appeared well-developed, and specialist functions such as labor relations were also found. Management development was of more recent origin in some companies and was still not in evidence in two concerns. A specialized marketing staff was observed in four central offices, and two companies reported they had central line marketing functions, which had executive authority over divisional policy. The role of top management in divisional operations varied by area and by company. Although it was hard to generalize, top management did seem to be less involved than in the dominant concerns.

The financial control systems in the technology-related concerns generally appeared to be well-developed and of long standing. Annual budgets had been used for many years in all companies, and these had enabled long-term corporate planning to become relatively sophisticated, despite its newness. In most cases the planning function was not started until the mid-1960s. Five companies had well-established, forward-planning systems generally covering five years, and the sixth had just begun long-term planning but considered its results still primitive. The plans, which always contained financial elements, also contained more detailed strategic inputs in four concerns. In one company, for example, a division general manager reported that he was asked to prepare rolling four-year forecasts, incorporating full financial forecasts for operations, anticipated pattern of capital expenditure for replacement, growth of present product lines, and capital requirements for new ventures. He was also asked to predict market share, impact of new products on market share, and detailed business plans as to forward strategy. All this was required centrally on a worldwide basis for each product division. Monitoring of divisional performance against annual budgets was generally conducted monthly, although one company had instituted weekly monitoring.

The investment criteria also reflected the sophistication in the control system. All companies reported the use of return on investment criteria, usually calculated on a discounted cash flow basis, coupled with sensitivity analysis. Nonfinancial criteria were also often required, including impact on the existing product line, on corporate cash flow, and on market share. One company also stated that it consciously considered the past performance of the division managers in assessing capital expenditure requests.

The nontechnological concerns had all diversified and divisionalized during the period under review, mainly during the 1960s, and by a process of acquisition. Perhaps, consequently, their central offices tended to be smaller and their procedures in monitoring divisional performance less sophisticated. Similar companies, such as Metal Box or Unilever, which diversified earlier, had developed strong research functions, a large central office, and sophisticated management techniques.

The companies interviewed tended to exhibit somewhat greater interdivisional product flow than the technology-related concerns, and in two companies the reported internal flow was over 50 percent. This reflected, to some extent, the number of integrated concerns that had recently diversified and also some attempts at vertical integration. Three companies with high internal flows imposed transfer prices centrally, but the remainder relied more on market prices than on bargaining. In all but one case, research expenditures were reported to be less than one percent of sales. Further, the research tended to be more concerned with development of the existing product line, than in producing new products. Three companies had central research laboratories which were now working on the development of new products, but there was little divisional research activity. Perhaps because of this only one company exercised close control over divisional product-market scope, since it seemed unlikely that anything other than modification of existing products would be forthcoming. The will to diversify was strong, however, and four companies reported they had further diversification as a conscious corporate objective, while one company wished to integrate its diverse activities more closely.

As mentioned earlier, the central offices of these companies tended to be smaller than the technology-related concerns, although three had developed central purchasing and staff marketing functions. The remainder generally had central service functions which played no part in day-to-day operations and were essentially advisory; these were legal, personnel, finance and accounting, and corporate planning. Two companies had developed small acquisition departments to further their objective of growth by this means but, in view of the high level of acquisition these firms had engaged in, their attention to selection and screening of acquisition opportunities seemed relatively undeveloped. The two concerns with acquisition departments had indeed only added them long after diversification by acquisition had been

initiated and a number of early acquisitions had not achieved the results anticipated.

The control systems employed were usually centered on the annual budget.
Long-term planning, as in the dominant product companies, was also basically
financial and appeared less well-developed than in the technological diversified concerns. It tended to consist of five-year financial forecasts, often largely extrapolations, and one company still did not have any long-term plans, while another had
recently forecast three years ahead. Similarly, investment criteria were basically
financial, six of the companies using a return on investment criterion (one company
had not developed clear criteria), usually calculated by a discounted cash flow
method. Nonfinancial justification were rarely required, and the impact of investments on the company's composition position was not normally considered in conjunction with a detailed evaluation of the external environment.

Top management was less divorced from operations but tended to concern itself
with the original area of interests of a company perhaps reflecting recent diversification by acquisition. In one company, for example, top management actively intervened in the division embracing the original activity, which represented less than
25 percent of sales, but relied on divisional management in the remaining divisions.
The transition from being an operating manager in a low diversity firm to becoming a corporate policy maker in a diversified enterprise appeared difficult, especially for entrepreneurs who had built up the original corporate activity.

The senior executive management was more likely to be composed of the chief
executive, and divisional general managers alone (apart from the finance director)
in the nontechnological companies, than was the case in the technological companies where there were more central staff directors. The smaller central staff led
also to fewer coordinating committees, although there were still four companies
with an executive committee and/or an operating committee composed of the chief
executive and the divisional general managers. The primary task of such committees, however, was not coordination, although active intervention in divisional
operations, as well as in monitoring, was usually a valid function.

The senior general officers and divisional general managers frequently made up
the executive director representation on the main board of the related product companies, as had been the case with the dominant product concerns. Little use was
made of nonexecutive directors to act as monitors of executive performance in
British companies. Few companies reported the presence of a level of general managers within the central office to supervise the activities of divisions. In one company, where such executives were observed, these men were also charged with
specific functional operating responsibilities thus confusing the demarcation of
responsibility. The group executive function found in many American companies,
appeared to be notably missing in most British concerns.

Eleven of the thirteen related product companies stated that a major corporate
objective was the continued growth of return on investment, while four had recently introduced earnings-per-share objectives. These objectives were seldom
quantified or considered within the overall context of the corporation's skills and
resources but were mainly generalized blue sky goals drawn out in discussion. Sub-
objectives, such as turnover growth and market share, were also found in a number
of cases, and continued diversification of the product-market scope was consciously

sought in nine companies. A consistent strategy toward these ends, however, appeared to be usually lacking.

Apart from budgetary and financial controls, the other most common central controls were over the appointment of senior executives and central cash accounting. Twelve companies retained central control over senior appointments and eight companies exercised central control over corporate cash balances. Decision rules appeared to be less in evidence, and wide freedom was permitted in some cases, although there were controls on capital expenditure in nearly all companies.

Divisional performance was reported to be most frequently measured by return on investment or similar criteria (used in nine companies), although the calculation of the divisional investment base was variable. Two companies were more concerned with return on sales, and two companies had yet to develop clear measurement systems.

Performance was generally rewarded on the basis of straight salary alone (found in nine companies), but four firms had bonus or stock option plans in addition. Two of these were stock option plans unrelated to either corporate or divisional profits; while the other two were recently introduced schemes whereby bonuses or stock options were given related to overall corporate performance. A similar scheme was about to be introduced in a third company.

The concept of continuous employment was reported to be much less common among the diversified companies than it had been among the dominant product concerns. Only six companies admitted that this was consciously followed, while a seventh stated that the policy varied between divisions. Apart from companies with a high degree of family interest, equity holdings by senior executive management remained very low in most cases, thus reflecting the general lack of availability of stock option plans. The related product company executives found the idea of variable reward systems, based upon performance, generally distasteful. All firms provided extensive pension schemes for management, and most executives considered these to be very important.

The hypothesis that British multidivisional companies would adopt variable reward systems based on performance was therefore not supported on the basis of the evidence from both the dominant product and related product companies. Rewards were found to be more commonly on the basis of straight salary, often coupled with employment security. Performance was only reflected indirectly in promotion prospects, although the control systems and review procedures adopted in many companies, coupled with problems of objective measurement, seemed to make this somewhat arbitrary. Fringe benefits were extensively used, especially status rewards and pension schemes. The rights to pensions were generally not transferable—a factor which restricted executive movement especially at senior levels. Since the tax system militated against high salaries, pension rights became an increasingly significant factor in an executive's career, as he had no other way to accumulate capital to make him independent. There was, therefore, pressure especially at more senior levels of management to avoid undue risks and, while performance-related rewards were generally considered distasteful by top management, some limited evidence suggested that younger managers held the opposite opinion.

The control systems used in British multidivisional companies did tend to emphasize return on investment as the main criterion for measuring divisional and corporate performance. However, performance frequently did not seem to match the generally high corporate goals allegedly in force, post-audit examinations did not appear evident, nor was success or failure directly rewarded or penalized.

The development of a general office was found to be variable, with large multifunctional central offices developing in the case of the integrated dominant product and technologically related concerns. Other firms had small general offices, attributed in the nonintegrated dominant product concerns to the transfer of central functions to the dominant division, with the buildup of a new, unrelated secondary activity, and in the nontechnological related concerns to the recent nature of the diversification.

The main differences between the dominant product and related product concerns was in the degree of autonomy allowed the divisions, and the will to continue to diversify. In the dominant concerns there was more central intervention, especially in the dominant activity and integrated secondary activities, even down to operations. In the related product concerns, top central management was more likely to be divorced from operations, especially if diversity was long established, and the central office provided a series of staff advisory service functions with no powers over the operational activity of the divisions. The related concerns also tended to institutionalize the process of continuous diversification, whereas the dominant companies showed little desire to continue to diversify unless this was part of the development of the dominant product line, or a response to environmental pressures.

A disconcerting feature of the British companies, in general, was the frequent occurrence of the divisional general managers in the policy-making process and as executive members of the main board. It created doubt as to the objective measurement of these same divisional managers. Likewise it raised doubts as to objective appraisal of the profitability of various resource allocation possibilities. Overall it tended to prevent the development of internal competitive pressures between the divisions, which could lead to increased internal efficiency as well as more effective distribution of capital.

Finally, the failure of British companies to use a performance-related reward and sanction system meant there was little direct incentive for general managers to improve divisional performance. The British companies, therefore, were probably not making full use of the multidivisional organization form, which permitted pressure for performance to be distributed deep down into the organization and allowed the organization to distribute its resources to those managers best able to use them. While this phenomenon was perhaps socially less abrasive, limited evidence suggested that the performance of more aggressive companies using variable rewards was better.

SOCIOECONOMIC CHARACTERISTICS OF BRITISH SENIOR MANAGEMENT

A number of recent studies had been made on the socioeconomic background of the senior management in British companies. Since these studies included the sample companies and contained more information than was available from published reports, it seemed superfluous to attempt a similar detailed study of the population and detract from the main thrust of the research. However, since this evidence may well be of significance in considering the internal management style of British companies, it has been reported here. Two studies conducted by *Management Today,*[2] in 1967 and 1970, on the boardroom anatomy of Britain's largest companies (including nonmanufacturing concerns), revealed that the average company director was 56 years old, not particularly mobile, most likely educated at a public school and, having only a 50 percent chance of a university education, most likely graduated from Oxford or Cambridge. In 1967 a negligible number of directors had received a business education but, by 1970, 9 percent had received some such training. In addition, a considerable number of British directors had received other professional training, mainly as accountants. Apart from family connections, which were diminishing but still remained strong (15 percent of directors had such links in 1970), the vast majority of British directors had little or no significant equity participation in the companies they managed. Rewards were essentially by straight salary with an average of £11,000 per annum in 1970.

A change which may well have reflected the spread of the multidivisional system and the drive to amend administrative structures in the face of competition, was a move to more clearly defined executive hierarchies. In 1968, in another survey, *Management Today*[3] observed that 66 percent of the top 120 British companies had no hierarchy other than the chairman and managing director, but by 1970 this was down to 25 percent. Multiple managing directors were also less common, declining from 33 to 23 percent. In 52 percent of the cases the chairman was also chief executive, a decline from the 65 percent observed two-and-a-half years before. A further change in the same direction was the increased number of companies with a third or more nonexecutive directors up from 20 percent to 40 percent; but *Management Today* commented "there is no sign of increasing use of part-timers in their most effective role . . . to represent shareholders by badgering the executives and keeping them up to scratch"[4]—a phenomenon also observed in the 25 companies interviewed.

Other researchers tended to confirm these results. A study by Hall and Amado-Fischgrund[5] added some additional sociological data. They pointed out that almost 20 percent of the managing directors in Britain were born overseas, that their social origin was predominantly upper class and that Cambridge clearly dominated Oxford and all other universities as the main source of graduates. Since these studies were concerned with managing directors only, they obtained a higher average salary (of approximately $37,000) from that observed by *Management Today.*

Comparative studies[6] with other European nations and America revealed that

[2] R. Heller, "Britain's Top Directors," *Management Today,* March 1967, pp. 62–65; R. Heller, "Britain's Boardroom Anatomy," *Management Today,* September 1970, pp. 82–85.

[3] R. Heller and G. Foster, "Managers At the Top," *Management Today,* January 1968, pp. 80–85.

[4] R. Heller, "Britain's Boardroom Anatomy," p. 85.

[5] D. J. Hall and G. Amado-Fischgrund, "Chief Executives in Britain," *European Business,* January 1969, pp. 23–29.

[6] L. A. Brua, "Directors Compared," *The Director,* November 1969, pp. 260–65; see also D. J. Hall, H. de Bettignies and G. Amado-Fischgrund, "The European Business Elite," *European Business,* October 1969, pp. 45–55.

British chief executives were internationally the least formally educated, with only 40 percent having attended university compared with 89 percent of French, 83 percent of American, and 78 percent of German and Italian chief executives. In addition, only 5 percent of the British chief executives had ever received any kind of training at a business school.

Thus, British managers were lower paid at all levels in the hierarchy, not merely at the top. Further, the British progressive tax system took more of the gross salary at higher levels than any other system. The British tax system also penalized the use of stock options, had a capital gains tax, a high tax on investment income, and high death duties. For British executives, it was very difficult to accumulate the capital necessary to maintain an independent posture. There was, therefore, a progressive tendency to become locked in to the corporation, a significant disincentive to take risks for fear of loss of a stable income, and pension rights, and low financial reward for success.

It was true that for the top executives there was a high level of satisfaction in running a large organization. However, with the multidivisional system, where profit responsibility could be depressed down into the organization, there was little incentive for division and profit center managers to take risks. The evidence suggested that there was a noticeable opting out of the promotion race by executives over 35 who had reached salary levels of £3,000 or more.[7]

This evidence tended to suggest that the British senior executives and the managerial system were not well suited for the transition from a single product company existing in a stable protected environment, to a diversified concern in a competitive environment. The average age of all directors in 1970 meant that their early formative experience was most likely spent in a single or dominant product concern, organized in either a functional or holding-company structure, and existing in a cartelized, noncompetitive environment. They had a relatively low level of overall education and almost no business education. They were used to an internal environment of continuous employment and were unaccustomed to competing internally for financial rewards.

Much of the change observed in strategy and structure was forced upon the system by environmental forces, particularly changes in the marketplace and increased competition, especially from aggressive U.S. concerns accustomed to competition. From the observed characteristics of British managers, it did not seem so surprising that so many British companies sought the advice of management consultants to restructure their organizations when forced to adopt new strategies in the face of increased competition. Nor did it seem surprising that such companies balked at possible proposed changes in their management reward systems.

British companies thus widely adopted the multidivisional structure during the past 20 years as the organizational form best suited to manage the diversified enterprise. However, the observations indicated that while companies accepted the need to divide their organizations into logical multifunctional units, many of the internal characteristics of the corporations adopting multidivisional structure reflected prior structural forms. In particular, there was little evidence of change in the reward system, especially as a mechanism to apply pressure and *internal* competition for

---

[7] H. Roff, "What Makes Managers Work?" *Management Today*, February 1968, p. 67.

divisional performance. Further, the features of the present system, which reflected the system of taxation, made change difficult.

The British and American Systems—A Comparison

The strategy and structure of large enterprises, in both Britain and the United States, have been shown to be clearly moving in similar directions, toward the diversified corporation administered by a multidivisional organization structure. The United States corporations have gone further than their British counterparts in this respect and in the United States a new breed of corporation, the conglomerate or unrelated diversified company, appeared, managed by a multidivisional structure with a small general office devoted to the formation of a strategic posture for the total organization within which the divisions could formulate their own local strategic decisions.

The dominant product and related product concerns were represented in both industrial systems, the single product companies having become rare. Since the two main organization forms were present in both systems in roughly similar proportions, and as they accounted for the bulk of the large corporations, a comparison of management practices between the British and American firms seemed of value.

In both countries the dominant product and the related product concerns showed many similarities. In particular, there appeared to be significant differences in the managerial characteristics associated with the degrees of product-market diversity in the United Kingdom as in the United States.

Wrigley [8] examined three large U.S. multidivisional concerns drawn from the dominant product, related product, and unrelated product categories. These three companies, General Motors, General Electric, and Textron, were all large and therefore perhaps not wholly representative of the other companies within these categories, since they could represent extreme examples of sophisticated managerial systems. On the other hand, these concerns were formed into multidivisional structures longer than most British concerns and, therefore, could represent the future shape of the British population.

General Motors and General Electric both developed large multifunctional general offices which tended to be more sophisticated and covered more functions than any, save a very small number, of the largest British companies interviewed. Textron, which had a very small central office, was a multidivisional unrelated product company in which the central office performed the role of setting a broad corporate strategy, allocated resources between the divisions, and monitored the divisional performance. The central office acted essentially as a small and very efficient capital market in its allocation of resources on a competitive basis between the divisions, rapidly intervening when performance did not meet the planned level, maintaining strict financial controls, and determining what businesses to be in. Within these limits, product strategy was a function of the divisions which exhibited little or no interdivisional product flow.

General Motors exhibited similarity to both the dominant product concerns with

---

[8] L. Wrigley, "Divisional Autonomy and Diversification," Chapter 5.

integrated and nonintegrated activities. The automobile divisions were closely supervised by the central office, and autonomy within these divisions was reduced almost
to routine operations. This was similar to the .trends observed in the British integrated dominant product concerns. However, the controls, methods, and procedures
in General Motors appeared more developed and sophisticated in both financial and
nonfinancial systems than in the British companies. Despite a close supervisory
role, the central management was divorced from operations which were left to divisions whose performance was measured accordingly. Performance was measured
along a number of dimensions. Like the British companies, measurement heavily
emphasized return on investment, but growth, market share, and costs measures
were also used, and the reward system contained a large variable element based
on performance.

The nonintegrated areas of General Motors, such as Frigidaire appliances, enjoyed greater autonomy than the automobile divisions, but were again subject to
relevant central controls on such items as product styling as well as finances. Performance was measured mainly by return on investment and was rewarded accordingly. These divisions of General Motors resembled the nonintegrated British dominant product concerns in that there was apparently greater autonomy granted to the
subsidiary activities. The main differences appeared to be in the breadth of the performance measures and the use of a variable reward system.

The General Electric Company conformed closely to the British technological
and skill-related diversified companies. All divisions dealt directly with the market,
and only the components and materials division exhibited significant internal product flow with prices set at ruling market levels. Each division acted within a policy
framework laid down by the chief executive and the central staff, and its performance was measured along eight key criteria with a variable reward system based on
performance. Research and development was mainly decentralized within the divisions, but a central research unit was responsible for developing new ideas. The
central office was very involved in the question of supplies to the divisions, not
merely in terms of raw materials, but in a host of service functions. Management
development was centralized, and some control was exercised over divisional product strategy and product market scope. Within General Electric the continuous
development of new products was deeply institutionalized, and a key role of the
central office was continuous, but controlled, diversification by the use of corporate
planning.

These characteristics were very similar to those exhibited by the British technology-related product companies. These concerns appeared to have developed relatively sophisticated internal systems, with the exception of the heavy engineering
concerns. Significant differences were found in the emphasis on management development, the less detailed nature of British corporate planning, and a tendency to
have more central control over marketing. The British financial monitoring and
measurement systems were perhaps somewhat less sophisticated; performance was
certainly not measured in as many dimensions, and there were few performance-
related reward systems.

The nontechnological British companies in the early 1970s seemed somewhat
more like Textron than General Electric. They were characterized by a small central
office concerned primarily with financial monitoring and resource allocation, but

with much less sophisticated procedures, a greater degree of intervention in operations, and a much less developed strategic posture. Again the lack of a variable reward system stood out as did the lack of a corporate general management cadre. Textron, which had grown and diversified to a considerable extent by acquisition, had also developed sophisticated methods of screening and evaluating potential acquisitions compared with comparatively ad hoc methods adopted by the British concerns.

In general, collective responsibility was more common in British concerns, where committees including divisional executives were frequently involved in the policy-making process. Management development, corporate planning, and financial measurement tended to be less sophisticated. Again there was little evidence of rewards based on performance.

While the U.S. concerns, examined by Wrigley, may not have been wholly typical, other evidence suggests that they were at least partially so. For example, more U.S. multidivisional companies gave incentive awards based on the performance of the division or profit center than on total company performance.[9] Ninety percent of the top 100 industrial U.S. companies employed executive stock option schemes and about 81 percent used incentive awards. Seventy-three percent used both these incentive methods.[10] Formal corporate planning was more widespread and had been used longer than in Britain—a Stanford research inquiry reported that 60 percent of the 500 largest U.S. firms had organized formal corporate planning programs by 1963, and a further 24 percent were intending to introduce them.[11] Finally, the evidence accumulated by Stieglitz [12] from a wide variety of U.S. corporations strongly supported Wrigley's findings.

Conclusion

A stratified sample of 25 British companies, chosen from the largest 100 population, was interviewed in order to validate the strategy and structural data presented in earlier chapters. At the same time the internal characteristics of these companies were discussed, and the results have been presented in this chapter in an attempt to distinguish specific managerial characteristics of the dominant and related product concerns. These results revealed that the hypothesis that British multidivisional companies would possess performance-related reward systems was not supported.

An examination of other research indicated the socioeconomic characteristics of British top management and, relative to European standards, they were less formally educated, less mobile, and less well-paid. Social class mobility, although low, was high relative to most West European countries. British management tended to come

[9] J. P. Kensey, "An Incentive Formula for Divisionalized Companies," *McKinsey Quarterly,* Fall 1970, p. 52.

[10] "Sixth Annual Executive Compensation Report," *Business Management,* March 1971, pp. 15–29.

[11] G. Steiner, *Top Management Planning,* Macmillan, London, 1969, p. 15.

[12] H. Stieglitz and A. R. Janger, *Top Management Organization in Divisionalized Companies,* National Industrial Conference Board, Inc., New York, 1965.

from an upper class background, to be educated at public schools, and lack higher education, especially training in business techniques other than accounting. The age characteristics, coupled with this information, suggested British top management was possibly ill-suited to manage the rapid transition from a nondiversified firm in a noncompetitive environment to a diversified company facing intensified competition.

The chapter concluded with a brief comparison between the British dominant and related product concerns and their U.S. equivalents. Although similarities existed, the British firms tended to be less developed than the U.S. concerns in their planning, control, and management development techniques, had not divorced policy and operations to the same degree, did not directly reward performance, and had not developed the widespread U.S. practice of a cadre of central staff general executives to monitor the activities of the division general managers.

CHAPTER 8

The Strengths and Weaknesses of British Industry

INTRODUCTION

BRITAIN, ALTHOUGH DECLINING AS A WORLD economic power during the greater part of the twentieth century, underwent its greatest relative decline in the post-World War II period. The loss of the Empire, with its protected markets, the failures in world trade, the crises in the balance of payments partially offset by the sale of industrial and commercial assets to others, especially the Americans, were all signs of weakness.

This study has been essentially concerned with the evolution of the strategy and structure of the largest British manufacturing enterprises during this postwar period. The methodology used has, therefore, not been that of traditional economic methods which survey an economy or industry in macro terms without generally considering the role of the individual enterprise; rather, it has focused primarily upon the economic decision-making units, the individual enterprises, and upon the industries of which they form a part. The study does permit some evaluations to be made which may be of value in assessing economic prospects. For it will be these great corporations and the men who manage them which make the strategic decisions that can affect the whole economy, and their performance will in large part determine the economic outcomes. Without their success Britain will not achieve the economic growth and material wealth it seeks during the 1970s.

The analysis of 100 corporations studied, together with the environmental pressures and trends examined, permitted the observation of a number of strengths and weaknesses existing in British manufacturing enterprises. The purpose of this chapter is to attempt to identify those strengths and weaknesses using as comparison what is perceived, despite short-term recession, as perhaps the greatest economic threat, that of the American challenge. Other challenges will also have to be met both in world markets, especially from Japan, and within Europe when Britain enters the enlarged European Economic Community. British enterprises must build upon their strengths and correct their weaknesses if they are to develop successfully in the increasingly competitive world market system.

The strengths and weaknesses of British industry have been strongly influenced by the changes in the environment that have occurred, especially during the post-World War II period. It is, therefore, appropriate to review briefly the basic changes that have occurred in the past 25 years. Four trends were of particular note.

First, Britain emerged from the war as an economy of shortages. Its industrial and financial resources were seriously depleted by the years of conflict. Its major industrial problems were initially those of reconstruction and the relief of shortages. In a few short years, Britain was transformed to an economy of relative abundance, and its problems changed to those of growth in a competitive marketplace.

Second, the great depression and the Second World War left Britain with a relatively protected economy. At home, cartels and restrictive practices covered much of industrial production; in overseas markets, British industry was largely dependent upon the protected markets of the Empire. As a result, there was little need for efficient and effective economic performance. There was little rationalization of production; small inefficient units could survive and prosper. British industry operated in a relatively closed system. The introduction of new legislation, the coming of the American challenge, new trends in world trade, and the dissolution of the Empire reintroduced the necessity for effective economic performance and recreated the need for competitiveness in order to survive. The economic system was no longer closed in splendid isolation, and British industry was forced to compete with the corporations of other nations in world markets.

Third, changing social conditions in postwar Britain changed the pattern of supply and demand. Successive governments undertook to redistribute the wealth of the nation and to play a greater role in the management of the economy. Consumer aspirations rose with growing affluence, and government undertook to fulfill these aspirations by seeking economic growth; it also sought to remove the specter of unemployment, and thus became an increasingly important consumer of production.

Fourth, rapid change in technology in the postwar period brought significant industrial change. New products and processes were developed, frequently changing the pattern of competitive advantage. Traditional industries were transformed by technological changes, often developed in other sectors of the economy. The scale of development costs forced the consolidation of research intensive industries, such as aircraft and computers.

Given these changes, this chapter attempts a preliminary analysis of the strengths and weaknesses of British industry. The analysis, based upon a methodology developed by Scott,[1] begins with a study of the individual enterprise which is the decision-making element of the industrial sector of the economy. It then progresses to consideration of industries, and ultimately to the macroeconomic environment, indicating how the strengths and weaknesses of succeeding strata affect the performance of the enterprise.

---

[1] B. R. Scott, "The Strengths and Weaknesses of French Industry," Unpublished Paper, Harvard Business School, Boston, 1971.

THE ENTERPRISE

The 100 enterprises examined formed the essential core of Britain's manufacturing capability. Between them they accounted for approximately 60 percent of the net assets used, 45 percent of the workforce employed, and 60 percent of goods sold from this sector of the economy. Furthermore, the economic importance of this small number of large corporations was growing. Their future success in an increasingly competitive world was therefore vital to Britain's economic well-being. These corporations possessed a number of important strengths which, if successfully exploited, could lead to improved performance. At the same time, a number of weaknesses were apparent, and these would need correction if those enterprises were to survive and prosper in the competitive environment of the 1970s.

The first significant strength observed in British enterprises was the response adopted in the face of new competition. The majority of the large corporations chose to diversify as a response to competitive and market pressures. In addition they had, in more recent times, adopted the multidivisional structure to enable them to manage their newly found diversity. The choice of diversification, apart from reducing the risk associated with a narrow product scope, institutionalized the search for new products and markets. The enterprise thus became more oriented toward market needs and was more flexible and open to changes in the competitive environment in which changing technology was playing an increasingly important role. Instead of decline or even extinction as the product life cycle reached maturity, the enterprise was made to regenerate itself and continually evolve.

Second, the adoption of the multidivisional structure permitted the more efficient use of resources. The careful measurement and monitoring of divisional performance allowed the enterprise to choose its investments in the light of expected future prospects for the business or businesses it chose to be in. It enabled the enterprise to put pressure on the divisional managers to deliver results that would best serve the strategic goals of the total corporation. In addition, the adoption of the new structure helped to develop the new general management skills which had been lacking in British enterprises. As they became more available, diversification proceeded at greater speed.

Third, technological development already strong in the chemical, electrical, and some engineering concerns, was potentially enhanced within the newly diversified corporations. This was suggested by the fact that some longer established diversified concerns in lower technology industries, such as food and packaging, had developed research capabilities. In the past, British industry had been technically proficient but was slow to capitalize on the stream of innovations flowing from basic research. The narrow product ranges of many companies may well have led to overspecialization, to a degree that developments outside the existing product line were neglected as not being relevant. Further, product maturity often led to decline. The diversified concern with its broader product scope seemed much more able to perceive new opportunities, and its flexible organization structure eased problems of adding new areas of activity.

Fourth, the very size of British enterprises was potentially a strength by comparison with the fragmented state of much of Western European industry. Although many British corporations were smaller than comparable American concerns, they were usually of sufficient size and financial strength to allow the employment of sophisticated managerial skills. They could afford to employ the latest managerial techniques, to maintain management development and establish the research and development functions necessary to the continued evolution of the enterprise. Their size also improved their competitive prospects against new market entries, especially from large American concerns, and reduced the risk of outside take-over.

Fifth, the number of family-owned firms which tended to be slower to adopt the strategy of diversification had diminished. Those that survived were proving more ready to change and the restrictions of the past were giving way to less paternalistic progressive concerns.

Finally, British enterprises had had long experience operating in overseas markets and, already, many of them could be classified as multinational. By comparison with Western European corporations, and even to some degree American, the experience of British firms could be considered a strength capable of greater exploitation. The adoption of the new strategy and structure could be expected to assist in the capitalization of this strength.

Correctly exploited, these strengths offered British companies and the national economy a significant opportunity for progress during the 1970s. However, no less important were the weaknesses also apparent which, unless corrected, posed a significant threat to future British progress in a competitive environment.

The first of these weaknesses concerned the overall profitability of British companies. A study published by *Management Today* [2] showed that approximately 80 percent of the largest corporations had failed to double their profits in real terms throughout the decade of the 1960s. Indeed, 15 percent even failed to maintain the real value of their 1960 earnings. Profitable growth was thus extremely low in British companies. Without considerable improvement in profit performance, therefore, many companies will not generate enough internal funds nor be sufficiently attractive to external financial sources, to provide the capital necessary for investment for long-term growth. In addition, the low rate of profitability in many companies threatened to lower stock market prices and thereby increase the risk of takeover by stronger competitors.

Second, in comparative terms, British companies had performed notably worse than their American counterparts. Table 8–1 provides details of the 1968 performance of the largest British corporations and their nearest U.S. equivalents, in each of the industries observed in the study. Although it is perhaps somewhat unfair to make such criticism on the basis of a single year's performance, and the choice of the specific year is perhaps especially unfair to particular corporations, examination revealed that similar results could be reproduced for any year in the 1960s.

All three measures of profitability revealed that British corporations generally performed worse than their U.S. counterparts engaged in similar product markets. There were several reasons for Britain's weakness, but two were especially evident: managerial deficiencies and the fact that high profits were considered somehow immoral. Not only was Britain's comparative performance worse, but there was little pressure to do better either from internal management or the values of society.

Third, it could be argued that the relative size of the domestic market forced the British corporations to cover a wider variety of product markets, some of which

---

[2] "Real Growth in British Business," *Management Today*, December 1970, pp. 90–94.

TABLE 8-1

BRITISH AND AMERICAN CORPORATE PERFORMANCE, 1968

Corporation	Sales [a]	Net Profit [b]	Total Assets [c]	Invested Capital [d] (In Thousands of Pounds)	Sales Assets	Profit Sales	Profit Assets	Profit Inv. Cap (In Percent)	Employees	Sales per Employee (In Pounds)
Undiversified Industries										
Drink										
G.B. Distillers	275	28.4	365	284	97	10.7	7.8	10.0	19,100+	14,400+
U.S. Anheuser-Busch	271	18.6	220	119	124	6.8	8.5	15.6	10,500	25,000
U.S. Nat. Distillers & Chemicals	238	13.8	330	180	72	5.8	4.2	7.7	14,000	17,000
G.B. Bass Charrington	212	13.3	376	211	56	6.3	3.5	6.3	55,700	3,800
G.B. Allied Breweries	210	16.2	368	211	57	7.6	4.4	7.7	45,700	4,600
U.S. Seagrams	189	9.8	306	185	62	5.2	3.2	5.3	7,000	27,000
Tobacco										
G.B. British-American Tobacco	590	63.2	783	488	75	10.7	8.1	12.9	95,000	6,200
U.S. Reynolds Tobacco	527	62.5	499	391	106	11.9	12.5	16.0	21,300	24,700
U.S. American Brands	465	38.7	630	297	74	8.3	6.1	13.0	40,500	11,500
G.B. Imperial Tobacco	275	34.9	632	478	43	12.7	5.5	7.3	49,000	5,600
Metals and Materials										
Steel										
U.S. United States Steel	1,890	106	2,663	1,395	71	5.6	4.0	7.6	201,000	9,400
U.S. Bethlehem Steel	1,193	66.9	1,275	785	94	5.6	5.2	8.5	131,000	9,100
G.B. British Steel	1,071	−9.3	1,349	829	79	—	—	—	254,000	4,200
Cement and Glass										
U.S. Owens-Illinois	480	23.0	484	246	99	4.8	4.7	9.3	61,400	7,800
U.S. PPG Industries	435	20.1	457	264	95	4.6	4.4	7.6	39,300	11,100
U.S. Corning	200	19.5	193	130	103	9.8	10.1	15.0	26,100	7,700
G.B. Associated Portland Cement	137	8.6	213	118	64	6.3	4.1	7.3	23,900	5,700
G.B. Pilkington	113	10.0	133	86	82	8.8	7.2	11.6	34,000	3,300

U.S. Standard Oil (N.J.)	5,870	531	6,990	4,110	84	9.1	7.6	13.0	151,000	38,900
G.B./D. Royal Dutch-Shell	3,840	390	5,960	3,385	64	10.1	6.5	11.5	171,000	22,500
U.S. Mobil	2,592	179	2,863	1,695	91	6.9	6.2	10.5	78,300	33,100
U.S. Texaco	2,275	349	3,620	2,258	63	15.3	9.6	15.4	78,500	29,000
G.B. British Petroleum	1,358	101	2,107	1,211	64	7.4	4.8	8.4	68,000	20,000

Power Machinery

Automobiles

U.S. General Motors	9,480	721	5,838	4,065	162	7.6	12.4	17.8	757,200	12,500
U.S. Ford Motor	5,865	261	3,730	2,060	157	4.5	7.0	12.7	415,000	14,100
U.S. Chrysler	3,102	121	1,833	860	169	3.9	6.6	14.1	231,100	13,400
G.B. British Leyland	907	19.2	628	248	145	2.1	3.1	7.7	188,200	4,800

Aerospace

U.S. McDonnell Douglas	1,505	39.5	556	191	269	2.6	7.1	20.6	124,700	12,100
U.S. Boeing	1,365	34.6	912	338	150	2.5	3.8	10.2	142,400	9,600
U.S. Lockheed Aircraft	924	18.6	391	155	236	2.0	4.7	12.0	95,400	9,700
G.B. Rolls-Royce	320	8.9	349	162	92	2.8	2.5	5.5	88,300	3,600
G.B. British Aircraft	191	4.2	99	24	193	2.2	4.3	17.6	36,800	5,200

Diversified Industries

Food

G.B./D. Unilever	2,306	86.5	1,435	800	160	3.8	6.0	10.8	312,000	7,400
U.S. Kraftco	1,012	31.8	395	266	257	3.1	8.0	11.9	47,000	21,500
U.S. Armour	874	5.0	234	123	374	0.6	2.1	4.1	32,800	26,600
U.S. General Foods	725	43.1	435	265	168	5.9	9.9	16.3	37,000	19,600
U.S. Consolidated Foods	508	21.8	237	129	214	4.3	9.2	16.9	45,000	11,300
G.B. Associated British Foods	503	9.4	221	66	228	1.9	4.3	14.3	107,300	4,700
G.B. Unigate	301	5.5	138	89	218	1.8	4.0	6.2	38,000	7,900
G.B. Rank Hovis McDougall	300	10.0	186	109	161	3.3	5.4	9.1	58,500	5,100
G.B. Cadbury/Schweppes	243	10.6	234	152	104	4.4	4.5	7.0	45,200	5,400
G.B. Tate and Lyle	229	6.3	185	84	123	2.8	3.4	7.5	42,000	5,400
G.B. Brooke Bond Liebig	209	5.7	139	69	149	2.7	4.0	8.2	75,000	2,800

TABLE 8–1 (Continued)

Corporation	Sales[a]	Net Profit[b] (In Thousands of Pounds)	Total Assets[e]	Invested Capital[d]	Sales/ Assets	Profit/ Sales (In Percent)	Profit/ Assets	Profit/ Inv. Cap	Employees	Sales per Employee (In Pounds)
Electrical Engineering and Electronics										
U.S. General Electric	3,492	149	2,393	1,038	146	4.3	6.2	14.3	400,000	8,700
U.S. I.B.M.	2,870	363	2,810	1,904	102	12.7	12.9	19.1	242,000	11,000
U.S. I.T.T.	1,695	80.2	1,677	688	101	4.7	4.8	11.6	293,000	5,800
U.S. Westinghouse	1,373	56.3	946	531	145	4.1	5.9	10.6	138,000	10,000
G.B. G.E.C./E.E.	898	30.8	1,050	431	86	3.4	2.9	7.2	233,000	4,200
G.B. Thorn	267	17.2	223	111	120	6.4	7.7	15.5	70,000	3,800
G.B. Plessey	179	11.2	208	130	86	6.3	5.4	8.6	72,000	2,500
G.B. ICL	22	2.7	130	57	71	3.0	2.1	4.8	34,200	2,700
Chemicals and Pharmaceuticals										
U.S. Du Pont	1,450	155	1,371	1,058	106	10.7	11.3	14.6	114,100	12,700
G.B. Imperial Chemical Industries	1,237	85.9	1,828	1,008	68	6.9	4.7	8.5	187,000	6,600
U.S. Goodyear	1,219	61.8	990	484	123	5.1	6.2	12.8	119,700	10,200
U.S. Union Carbide	1,119	65.3	1,337	709	84	5.8	4.9	9.2	100,400	11,100
U.S. Firestone	888	52.9	784	421	113	6.0	6.7	12.6	102,400	8,700
U.S. Monsanto	746	45.3	790	469	95	6.1	5.7	9.7	59,800	12,500
U.S. Dow	688	56.7	964	421	72	8.2	5.9	13.5	47,400	14,500
G.B. Dunlop	450	11.3	363	129	124	2.5	3.1	8.8	102,500	4,400
U.S. American Cyanamid	426	35.8	406	285	105	8.4	8.8	12.5	35,400	12,100
U.S. Merck	243	38.8	203	159	120	15.9	19.0	24.3	18,900	12,900
G.B. Glaxo	136	10.8	105	54	131	7.9	10.4	20.5	26,900	5,200
G.B. Beechams	134	12.6	133	72	100	9.4	9.5	17.6	20,500	6,500
G.B. British Oxygen	134	5.6	184	88	73	4.2	3.1	6.4	31,600	4,200
G.B. Albright and Wilson	112	2.9	133	61	84	2.6	2.2	4.8	14,800	7,600
Engineering										
U.S. Bendix	579	18.3	378	185	153	3.2	4.8	9.9	68,200	8,500
G.B. Guest Keen and Nettlefold	434	17.6	402	240	108	4.1	4.4	7.3	100,800	4,300
U.S. Borg-Warner	406	19.6	326	211	124	4.8	6.0	9.3	38,000	10,700
U.S. Eaton Yale and Towne	371	20.5	260	151	143	5.5	7.9	13.6	41,200	9,000

U.S. Studebaker Worthington	296	10.0	251	121	118	3.4	4.0	8.3	27,700	10,700
U.S. Combustion Engineering	277	9.2	209	89	133	3.3	4.4	10.4	25,900	10,700
G.B. Joseph Lucas	251	9.0	169	96	149	3.6	5.3	9.4	76,000	3,300
G.B. Tube Investments	250	7.1	260	135	96	2.8	2.7	5.3	70,000	3,600
G.B. Vickers	182	4.1	165	94	110	2.3	2.5	4.4	40,700	4,500
G.B. Delta Metal	157	4.2	119	58	132	2.7	3.5	7.2	22,000	7,100
Textiles										
U.S. Burlington Industries	674	32.9	497	263	136	4.9	6.6	12.5	83,000	8,100
G.B. Courtaulds	576	25.6	571	259	101	4.4	4.5	9.9	151,000	3,800
U.S. Celanese	523	32.1	690	231	76	—	—	—	38,700	13,500
U.S. Genesco	420	13.3	186	103	226	3.2	7.2	12.9	66,000	6,400
G.B. Coats Patons	210	10.9	230	123	91	5.2	4.7	8.8	72,000	2,900
G.B. English Calico	157	4.9	124	63	127	3.2	4.0	7.8	37,100	4,200
G.B. Viyella International	70	3.2	72	38	97	4.6	4.5	8.5	24,100	2,900
G.B. Carrington and Dewhurst	69	3.2	61	32	114	4.6	5.2	9.8	17,000	4,100
Paper and Packaging										
U.S. American Can	680	32.3	556	296	122	4.8	5.8	10.9	54,000	12,600
U.S. International Paper	651	41.6	714	451	91	6.4	5.8	9.2	53,700	12,100
U.S. Continental Can	628	34.8	447	273	141	5.5	7.8	12.7	48,400	13,000
U.S. Crown Zellerbach	362	27.2	391	226	93	7.5	7.0	12.0	27,100	13,300
G.B. Reed International	282	8.6	346	171	82	3.1	2.5	5.1	53,500	5,300
G.B. Bowater	214	8.4	311	144	69	3.9	2.7	5.9	29,500	7,200
G.B. Metal Box	177	8.1	145	77	120	4.6	5.6	10.4	50,100	3,500
Printing and Publishing										
U.S. Time Inc.	237	13.4	214	92	110	5.7	6.2	14.5	10,400	22,800
G.B. International Publishing	156	8.2	158	96	99	5.2	5.2	8.6	32,000	4,900
U.S. McGraw-Hill	153	11.6	128	71	120	7.6	9.1	16.5	12,900	11,900

[a] Including service and rental revenues and sales of subsidiaries if consolidated; excluding intercompany transactions, customs duties and excise taxes.
[b] Less depreciation, loan interest, tax, minority interest, etc.
[c] Total assets employed in the business at year end less depreciation.
[d] U.K. definition: preference and ordinary capital plus net reserves and intangibles.
  U.S. definition: net worth.

SOURCES: *Fortune* Annual Reports.

were less profitable, whereas their U.S. counterparts were able to concentrate on more profitable market segments. This argument was only partially valid, however, since the U.S. corporations, as examined by Wrigley, were generally more diversified than the British. The difference most likely stemmed from the fact that the U.S. corporations tended to avoid products which were not differentiable in the market-place. The U.S. corporations were more oriented toward marketing their products than the British, and concentrated their efforts on the development of products with differentiable features which permitted market segmentation. There was a conscious effort to avoid the price competition that frequently followed when competitive products were readily interchangeable. By comparison, many British concerns were production- or quality-oriented, without due regard to the needs of the market. While this was permissible in the period of cartelization and a closed economy, it was a significant disadvantage in increasingly open world markets where British corporations were forced to compete equally with the most efficient firms from other nations.

Fourth, despite the production orientation of some concerns, the production efficiency of British corporations did not compare favorably with their American equivalents (see Table 8–1). The sales per employee ratio revealed that U.S. corporations managed to sell much more for each member of their payroll than did British concerns. While there were some mitigating circumstances, such as price differences and the fact that British firms may have performed more of their own services, the differences were too great to be accounted for in this way. Some of the studies referred to in Chapter 2 revealed that British concerns used up to twice as much labor in similar-sized plants to do the same job. Dunning's studies (see Chapter 2) revealed that even among American firms operating in Britain, the differences still persisted.

Causes of this inefficiency included the low ratio of capital to employees and the deficiencies in the system of industrial relations at the level of the firm. While part of the deficiency in industrial relations was attributable to the Trade Unions, it was found that managerial deficiencies were also present within the enterprise which tolerated and contributed to the inefficient use of labor. In large measure management got the industrial relations it deserved.

Fifth, weakness was discernible in strategic planning. While British companies had long-established overseas investments, the location of these assets reflected the strategic choice of concentrating in the former colonial markets which were traditionally easy to exploit. Despite the changing pattern of trade, British enterprises avoided the largest and richest world markets of North America and Western Europe. Instead of early capitalization of their strength in overseas operations, many British concerns had only recently made a belated effort to enter the developed economies. Some companies remained in the declining product markets until virtually forced to diversify in an attempt to maintain their position. They had not created the strategic opportunities by scanning their environment and adjusting to it, but rather had belatedly responded in order to survive.

In addition, even when a strategy of diversification had been belatedly adopted, it was implemented primarily by acquisition. There was evidence that many of the acquisitions made had been poorly planned in that insufficient screening had been conducted prior to the acquisition. Further, management had often not achieved the results hoped for from acquisitions, since as well as poor pre-bid screening, which had led to incorrect or overexpansive acquisition choices in some cases, post-bid integration and/or rationalization was often slow, inadequate, or nonexistent. This was due primarily to managerial deficiencies unable or unwilling to undertake the necessary reforms of organization, capital structure, and control systems. As a result, much of the extensive growth in acquisition activity probably did little more than perpetuate a number of mediocre firms without producing much improved efficiency for the economy as a whole.

Sixth, there was weakness in both the will and the level of knowledge among managers to correct the earlier deficiencies. Little attention had been paid to management education and development. Internationally, British managers were less qualified in formal education than their overseas contemporaries and, specifically, they lacked training for business. In many cases, as reported in Chapter 2, British companies considered such education to be of little value and their own problems unique. Even the growing numbers of young, business-school educated potential managers were not sought after by many companies. Instead a disproportionate number of Britain's new MBAs were being employed by international subsidiaries of North American concerns anxious to enhance their managerial advantages.

Seventh, such business education as existed was devoted more to the education of functional specialists than to the development of general management skills. The widespread adoption of a strategy of diversification and a multidivisional organization highlighted the need for a large number of general managers without which the potential advantages offered by strategic and structural change could well be lost.

Finally, and most important, there appeared to be weakness in those who performed the leadership function. Poor performance and the other weaknesses could survive only if they were tolerated by those who ran the great corporations. The reward system built around a system of progressive taxation in most British concerns made the senior executives heavily dependent upon their pension rights for future security. This may have been a major factor in the rationale for tolerating poor performance, risk avoidance, and maintenance of the status quo. Leaders anxious to aggressively pursue a program of increased performance were often noticeable by their absence.

For improvement in the level of performance, it was necessary to have strong corporate leaders who possessed both the will and the strategic ability to direct the enterprise toward the achievement of higher goals. That dramatic transformation was possible was evident from the success of the few who had achieved it. Britain truly needed more such men as Weinstock at G.E.C./E.E., Lazell at Beechams, Kearton at Courtaulds, and Slater at Slater Walker.

THE INDUSTRY SECTOR

The largest 100 companies occupied a key role in most industry branches of the British economy. These companies often accounted for the majority of the production in an industry and their prospects, together with some consideration of trends in the environment, and permitted some analysis of the strengths and weaknesses of the main industrial sectors in the British economy. The analysis was made comparative by the inclusion of data on the distribution of U.S. industry as shown in Table 8–2, which indicates the level of net output and employment in the sectors of

TABLE 8-2

THE DISTRIBUTION OF BRITISH AND AMERICAN MANUFACTURING INDUSTRY, 1968

Characteristic Industry	BRITAIN						UNITED STATES					
	Employed (In Thousands)	Percent of Total	Net Output (In Thousands of Pounds)	Net Output Percent of Total	Output per man (In Pounds)	SIC Code	Employed[b] (In Thousands)	Percent of Total	Value Added[c] (In Thousands of Pounds)	Value Added Percent of Total	Value Added per man (In Pounds)	SIC Code
Food	621	7.7	1445	9.0	2325	III−(231, 2,9,240)	1426	7.3	9620	8.1	6760	20−208
Drink	143	1.8	557	3.5	3884	231,2,9,239	223	1.1	2153	1.8	9667	208
Tobacco	41	0.5	172	1.0	4169	240	74	0.4	896	0.8	12,060	21
Oil Refining and Products	25	0.3	134	0.8	5381	IV−261	115	0.6	2400	2.0	20,930	2911 299
Metal Manufacture	561	6.9	1098	6.8	1958	VI	1273	6.5	8774	7.4	6882	33
Mechanical Engineering	1010	12.5	2027	12.7	2008	VII−342	1743	8.9	11,024	9.3	6326	35−3573
Metal Fabrications	566	7.0	999	6.2	1764	XII	1423	7.3	8435	7.1	5920	34+391
Instrument Engineering	170	2.1	277	1.7	1636	VIII	398	2.0	2867	2.4	7210	38
Shipbuilding and Repairs	180	2.2	285	1.8	1587	X	173	0.9	682	0.6	3942	373
Aerospace Equipment	229	2.8	490	3.1	2141	383	806	4.1	5200	4.4	6454	372
Transport Equipment	560	6.9	1149	7.2	2054	XI−383	915	4.7	7977	6.7	8710	37−(372, 373)
Electrical Engineering	767	9.5	1403	8.8	1827		2009	10.2	12,035	10.1	6020	36+3573
Textiles	701	8.7	1104	6.8	1574	XIII	1231	6.3	5440	4.6	4419	22+(239, 2823−4)
Clothing	374	4.6	383	2.4	1024	XV−450	1183	6.0	3991	3.4	3370	23−239
Bricks, Pottery, Glass, etc.	307	3.8	610	3.8	1986	XVI	591	3.0	3846	3.2	6583	32
Timber and Wood Products	112	1.4	196	1.2	1755	471,479	554	2.8	2430	2.0	4390	24
Furniture and Fixtures	159	2.0	285	1.8	1790	XVII−(471,479)	437	2.2	1910	1.6	4367	25

BRITAIN

Characteristic Industry	Employed (In Thousands)	Percent of Total	Net Output[a] (In Thousands of Pounds)	Net Output Percent of Total	Output per man (In Pounds)	SIC Code
Leather and Leather Goods	151	1.9	218	1.4	1442	XIV+450
Paper and Allied Products	239	3.0	459	2.8	1923	XVIII−(486,489)
Printing and Publishing	375	4.6	793	5.0	2112	486,489
Chemicals and Allied Products	538	6.7	1653	10.3	3074	V+491
Miscellaneous Manufactures	248	3.0	433	2.6	1744	XIX+261, 342
Total	8077	100.2[d]	16,021	100.7[d]	1982	

UNITED STATES

Employed[b] (In Thousands)	Percent of Total	Value Added[c] (In Thousands of Pounds)	Value Added Percent of Total	Value Added per man (In Pounds)	SIC Code
335	1.8	1213	1.0	3626	31
648	3.3	4373	3.7	6438	26
1037	5.3	6450	5.4	6220	27
1318	6.7	1283	10.8	9740	28+30−(2823−4)
826	4.2	4475	3.8	5417	39+19
19,587	95.7	119,120	100.2[d]	6087	

[a] Net output defined as: Value added to materials by the process of production and includes the gross margin on any merchanted or factored goods sold. It is derived from value of sales and work done + change in inventory − purchases + payments for work given out + transport, and adjusted for duties, etc.

[b] Employment by industry does not include central administrative office and auxiliary unit employees totaling some 834,000.

[c] Value Added: Derived by subtracting cost of materials, etc., and contract work from value of shipments for products manufactured plus receipts for services. This result is adjusted by addition of value added by merchandising, plus net change in inventories.

[d] Errors due to rounding.

SOURCES: *Board of Trade Journal* 12/31/69; U.S. Dept. of Commerce.

British and American manufacturing industry. Corrections were made to reduce, as much as possible, the effects of different industrial classification schemes used in each of the countries. Slight differences remained, but the profiles presented did provide a crude measure of national differences which were useful for comparison purposes.

The first and major strength observed was the wide distribution of British industry. It was distributed in a very similar fashion to that of American industry and, at this level of aggregation, was clearly not deficient in any major industrial sector. This broad distribution meant, therefore, that the British economy was not over-dependent on any particular narrow product range, but rather offered a wide variety of activities where skills and resources could be deployed.

Second, the high growth industries, such as chemicals and electrical engineering, were well-developed and these areas had resisted competitive U.S. invasions in large measure. Although foreign ownership was high in specific segments of the economy, overall British industry remained remarkably free of foreign domination by comparison with many other developed economies.

Third, British industry had developed an extensive technological capability. Britain spent more of its gross national product (2.7 percent in 1967–68) on research than most other industrialized nations. It was the United States's nearest rival in technological spending. This expenditure had led Britain to develop all the major technological industries, and, for its size as a nation, to produce a disproportionate number of the major technological discoveries.

Fourth, British industries did not suffer greatly from disadvantages of scale by comparison with U.S. industry. By comparison with other nations, British industry possessed a considerable advantage in economies of scale.

Notwithstanding the presence of these great strengths and the potential they offered, however, progress toward their successful exploitation was threatened by a number of discernible weaknesses.

First, the differences in the British and American industrial profiles were generally sources of weakness in the British system. Britain still obtained a greater percentage of her net output from the traditional industries such as textiles, shipbuilding, building materials, leather products, and food, drink, and tobacco. In the United States the new technological capital intensive industries with higher growth potential, such as chemicals, instrument engineering, electrical engineering and aerospace, represented a larger portion of value added than did their British counterparts. The United States was thus in a better position to remain internationally competitive despite a high wage cost economy, since more of its production capability was based in industries where the ratio of capital to labor was high. Britain, also a relatively high wage cost economy, especially in view of relatively low productivity, exhibited a relative weakness in failing to move its industry base more rapidly away from the older more labor-intensive industries.

Second, while the traditional industries were declining in Britain, the actions of government tended to sustain them and slow the rate of such decline. The distribution of public funds had not been made on the basis of expected growth of return on investment, but rather in terms of high technical content and high employment, and often for short-term political rather than long-run economic reasons. Thus, public funds were channeled into shipbuilding, textiles, aerospace, and metal manufacture, all of which were industries where the growth and profit potential for British concerns appeared to be low. This use of resources could be expected to have slowed the overall economic growth rate, and reduced the overall national competitiveness, while in turn it had reduced the prospects for the newer industries, such as chemicals and electrical engineering.

Third, the use of investment grants, which had not been geared to economic performance, tended to generate plant investment, which was not viable except for the use of public funds. These grants aided capital intensive industries such as chemicals but, in some cases, the returns generated by such plants were negligible, and they would not have been erected had it not been for the injections of public funds. Government support needed to be channeled into profitable investments which would produce returns for the community as a whole rather than to subsidize uncompetitive ventures.

Fourth, there is a significant difference at the industry level in the productivity of the workforce between the U.S. and British industries. On average the U.S. worker was producing over three times the value added of his British counterpart. This was partly to be expected, due to the different factor costs of capital and labor in the two societies. However, the difference was so great that it also seemed clear that British industry was just not as efficient as U.S. industry. This was seen partially as a failure by industry to invest in capital equipment, and partially as the result of deficiencies in the system of industrial relations. It was observed in Chapter 2 that compared not only with the United States, but with other industrial nations, British workers were supported by a low level of capital per man. Further, the system of industrial relations had serious deficiencies both at the level of the firm and at the level of the industry. The structure of the Trade Union movement led to inefficient use of labor, restrictive practices and disruptive wildcat strikes. These deficiencies were also partially condoned by managerial failures to develop new institutions for collective bargaining and to resist including many productivity features in industry-wide agreements.

Fifth, while the level of technological development in Britain was high, deficiencies were observed in the distribution of technical effort and the conversion of discoveries into commercial innovations. By comparison with other nations, Britain was heavily committed to basic research and to expenditure on aerospace. Much of this expenditure was provided from government funds. In view of the limited resources available, it would have been appropriate to question this expenditure and redistribute it on the basis of the expected return on investment. The poor success rate on the conversion of discoveries to innovations was attributed to deficiencies in the supply of engineers as distinct from basic scientists, the level of capital investment by industry, and managerial deficiencies leading to the pursuit of technology for its own sake.

Sixth, efforts by government, aimed at restructuring industry have led to the formation of a number of concentrated industries created by a series of acquisitions. While some concentration and consolidation were clearly necessary, there was no guarantee they would provide efficiency without the necessary managerial skills. Furthermore, the building of narrow product-scope concerns increased the vulnerability of such industries and, if it was later decided they were not viable, produced serious social and political difficulties for remedial action to correct the situation.

Rather than the perpetuation of some increasingly uncompetitive labor intensive industries, government policy might have been better directed toward real improvements in both financial payments and facilities for workers needing retraining as a result of product-market obsolescence.

Finally, British industry still seemed to dislike competition. Although government legislation had broken down most of the former cartels and restrictive practices, and forced the abandonment of resale price maintenance, there still seemed to be a lack of competitive drive. Information agreements appeared in place of cartels. Marketing was found to be underdeveloped in some industries. Restrictive practices were still present in some industries, such as metal containers and viscose fibers. Vertical integration had been used in some industries, notably brewing and petroleum, to obtain control of the channels of distribution. Government monopoly policy remained somewhat obscure, and no strictly enforced system, such as the U.S. antitrust laws, had yet materialized.

THE MACROECONOMIC ENVIRONMENT

While the role of the state has been observed as it affected the individual enterprise and industry sectors of the industrial system, the state's role in the macroeconomy impinged on the system overall. Several aspects of public policy seemed to have had a detrimental effect on the development of business enterprise.

First, the macroeconomic performance of government had generally been to inhibit business confidence by the continual use of stop-go economic policies which were frequently poorly timed and sometimes in a direction that inhibited growth and productivity. The emphasis of the government treasury was centered on goals related to the balance of payments and the level of unemployment. Movements of these indicators had resulted in the continuous use of short-term policy measures to control demand without sufficient regard for their long-term consequences to the industrial system and general business confidence.

Second, the choice of policies was consistently aimed at specific industries, such as automobiles and consumer durables. This made planning most difficult for these industries and may well have affected their capacity for future growth and development.

Third, the system of personal taxation related to egalitarianism did little to provide either incentives for saving and investment or for improved economic performance, especially among the key strata of senior industrial management. Entrepreneurial risk taking was not encouraged and there was little opportunity in Britain to build capital wealth before retirement. The result of this policy was to reinforce the maintenance of the status quo, the avoidance of risk, and the reduction of executive movement. Progressive income taxation led to narrowing the range of net remuneration between the lowest and highest paid in British industry with improved affluence for all. At the same time it prevented the use of executive rewards based on performance and forced executives to rely upon future pension rights for their long-term security. The lack of transferability of pension rights forced the executive to maintain his existing position and avoid risks. It does seem odd that while productivity- and performance-related rewards were advocated for operating personnel, such rewards were heavily penalized for managers.

Fourth, while the two main political parties in Britain held similar viewpoints on many important issues, there was some dichotomy on economic issues. It had been Labour Party policy, in particular, that advocated heavy taxation for high incomes and corporate profits. While this was not inappropriate where gross exploitation was evident, it seemed unjust to penalize honest effort. Labour also advocated major government intervention in industry and when in office had been responsible for the nationalization of several sectors of the economy. It is arguable whether this had always been successful since it seemed guided more by doctrinaire than economic reasoning. Further, once nationalized, industries became subject to political whim and their managements more subjected to conflicting economic and political pressures, often by ministers ill-equipped to understand the complexities of the management task.

While it may have been necessary for the state to take a direct role in industry for the good of the community, it would perhaps have been best served by the use of economic rather than political criteria. The Conservative Party, on the other hand, was more committed to a policy of reliance on the market system for the determination of its economic policy. In office, however, its management of the nationalized industries seemed little different from that of its Labour counterpart. Indeed, although Tory governments were generally preferred by businessmen, this preference was possibly due as much to such governments' attitude of nondirect intervention as to superior economic management.

As a consequence of the dichotomy between the political parties, however, there was fluctuation in business confidence every few years at the prospect of national elections. On the evidence it would seem that the Labour Party's industrial policies needed most reorientation if British industry was to grow and prosper. It was unfortunate that this party had been particularly slow to adjust its industrial policy, for it had also been a great innovator in social policies, which had done much to contribute to the development of civilized humanity in Britain. In an international competitive system, however, it was no longer possible to maintain isolationist domestic policies divorced from an outside environment, which was predominantly based on the market system, yet this seemed to be what the Labour Party had implicitly been attempting. Their industrial policy should be rewritten in the light of the economic facts of life in an open economy of the second half of the twentieth century rather than on the closed economic system operating at the end of the nineteenth century.

Fifth, the state was also manager of the educational system, and the level of and type of education in Britain had a significant impact on the industrial system. The significant lack of higher education among the leaders of British industry was evident and probably a cause of poor performance. Further, the efforts devoted to the type of education needed by management were insignificant compared with those made in the United States. The output of trained managers in Britain would certainly not meet the demand in the coming decade and, far from narrowing, the management gap seemed likely to increase.

Finally, governments of both main parties and the bureaucracy which served them had shown little to demonstrate great competence in managing the long-run strategy of a complex economy. To some extent this was inevitable, since long-term economic strategies necessarily took second place to short-run political expediency in a democratic system with elections every few years. Government was most effective when it did not seek to manage directly but provided the legislative framework protecting the community as a whole. Within this framework those professional managers charged with the responsibility for the long-run future of great corporations could get on with their task.

Apart from the role of the state, the capital market in Britain had been a source of both strength and weakness to the industrial sector. The capital market was highly developed and as such presented a source of great strength to the potential growth of British industry. There was no shortage of capital funds caused by lack of a suitable financial market to hold back the development of the profitable enterprise. Unfortunately, however, many of the great institutional investors had been unwilling to use their great financial strength to force British corporations into improving their performance. Since World War II the institutional investors had become the prime force in the ownership of share capital and, apart from the relatively recent appearance of the more performance-oriented unit trusts, the large insurance and many pension fund investors had been generally complacent on corporate performance. As the holders of the funds of small investors, the institutions, it would seem, should assume the obligation to apply pressure for results and, if necessary, to use their financial power to remove managements incapable of performing.

The consumer market infrastructure in Britain was also highly developed, especially in food and some other areas of multiple retailing. It still lagged behind the United States in the development of discount retailing, the development of suburban shopping, and in the hours of shopping convenience. More aggression, however, was needed from this sector to force improved industrial efficiency and concentration on market needs, in order to build up competitive strength in the industrial enterprises. To some extent the failure to develop more competitive retailing institutions lay with government, who had consciously restricted the development of suburban shopping centers by the use of planning controls. Britain lacks land for indiscriminate urban growth, but the efficient use of resources should permit the development of new institutions to reduce urban congestion and improve retail efficiency.

CONCLUSION

This chapter has sought to identify those strengths and weaknesses observed within the population and the environment in comparison with the United States industrial system. As such the analysis draws together many of the sub-conclusions which can be obtained from the research. The analysis built from the bottom up, commencing with an analysis of the strengths and weaknesses observable at the enterprise level, and progressing upward in aggregation to the industry level and those forces which influenced the enterprise within the macroeconomy.

Overall, the British industrial enterprises have been seen as basically strong, and the total system seems capable of much better performance in the next decade than had occurred in the past, if it can rapidly correct its deficiencies. Time is of the essence, however, since competitive pressures are increasing. Unless the industrial sector can meet and withstand these pressures, the overall British economic performance will continue to be poor. Furthermore, British entry into the wider European Community will increase the level of competitive pressure. However, in addition to an increased level of risk, the prospect of an enlarged European trading bloc brings a great new opportunity which the British industrial enterprises should be well placed to exploit if they focus on their strengths and eliminate their weaknesses.

CHAPTER 9
Conclusions

THE PATTERN OF CHANGE

THE STUDY OF THE STRATEGY AND STRUCTURE of the 100 largest British manufacturing enterprises over the past two decades (1950–70) provided much, although still insufficient, data on the evolution of the new economic institution, the large corporate enterprise. It was this relatively new institution that provided the driving force for the continued prosperity and economic growth in Britain. Large-scale enterprises have mainly superseded their original entrepreneurial founders and now represent the dominant base for the generation of economic wealth within the industrial society.

The 100 companies studied represented some 60 percent of the assets of Britain's manufacturing industry, provided employment for much of the workforce engaged in manufacturing industry, produced most of the goods, and, by the wealth they generated, supported a major portion of the services which go to make up the quality of life we have come to enjoy. The continued growth and development of the large enterprises, therefore, has a profound impact on the whole society. In conclusion it seemed appropriate to consider some of the implications of this growth for the managers charged with the responsibility for running corporations, for government with its responsibilities to the wider society, and for teachers of business administration.

The post-World War II period saw a dramatic transition in the major British manufacturing corporations. These firms became much larger, and more of the nation's industrial assets were concentrated under their control. This did not, however, generally result in the decline of market forces or a reduction in the level of competition, indeed the reverse seemed to be the case. The use of legislation, the changes in market demand, the growth of international trade, and the coming of the "American Challenge" led to a much higher level of competition in the marketplace. This was a primary cause of the transition in the corporate population. Clearly other factors, notably the role of government and the rapid growth of technology, also played a significant part in strategic development; however, the evidence of the 100 companies reviewed showed that the overwhelming reasons for growth and change were responses to market and competitive pressures.

The early postwar period allowed the continuation of the protected, cartelized prewar industrial system which had emerged following the great depression. These conditions did not remain for long, however, and despite resistance by many businessmen competitive pressures rapidly began to build up. At home, government legislation broke the power of the cartels and new competitors entered the British market, especially American enterprises, who were accustomed to a competitive environment. Finally, domestic production experienced new competition from imported manufactures. Overseas, the dissolution of the great colonial empire caused British manufacturers to lose their protected position in traditional markets. This brought them into direct competition with local fledgling industries in the developing countries, and with the other industrialized countries, especially the revitalized West Germany and Japan. Apart from the change in competitive pressures, other market forces were at work in the environment. Newly found affluence and the improved distribution of income led to rapid growth of the mass-consumption society changing the pattern of demand and supply. The rapid growth of technology led to the formation of new product markets and changed patterns of competitive advantage. New financial institutions appeared which began to place emphasis on corporate performance. These environmental pressures led to change, and the pattern of response was clear.

The main reaction in some industries, notably aircraft, automobiles, shipbuilding, cables, brewing, newspapers, steel, and computers was to reduce the new competitive pressures by concentration into larger groups. This concentration was often achieved by the largest and strongest concerns acquiring the weakest, frequently with encouragement from government. The result of these actions was to build a series of highly concentrated industries, often increasingly buttressed against outside competition by high entry barriers or government protection. The companies engaged in these industries thus joined another group of highly concentrated industries such as tobacco, glass, cement, aluminum, distilling, and petroleum where frequently similar concentrations had occurred in earlier times. These industries remained concentrated and sufficiently immune to competitive pressure to avoid undertaking new strategies. The lack of growth and profitability in many of the industries was also a barrier to new competitive entry and to the further development of the firms already engaged in these activities.

Elsewhere the response of enterprises to the changing environment was distinctly different. While some concentration and amalgamation certainly occurred, again often prompted by government action as in textiles and electrical engineering, the predominant strategy was one of diversification. During the postwar period the trend to product-market diversification was increasingly widespread and, by 1970, the diversified concern represented the majority of the largest British corporations.

In 1950 the diversified firm represented approximately 24 percent of the population of the largest 100 firms. This minority was composed essentially of those enterprises engaged in technological or skill-related industries where the technology required to compete, naturally led to the evolution of a wide product line. By 1970 the minority had become the majority and no fewer than 60 percent of the population was relatively highly diversified. This majority included many industries with a wide variety of technological requirements, such as food, chemicals, paper and packaging, textiles, electrical equipment, and electronics and engineering.

Furthermore, once adopted, the strategy of diversification tended to become institutionalized, leading eventually to the formation of corporate scanning functions in order to continuously search for new profitable ventures. This process of institutionalized search for new products and markets was of the greatest significance to the development of the British economy, and of far greater importance than the increased production of basic industries, such as metals and materials which would be continuously threatened by competitive pressures from other, more economic sources outside the United Kingdom. It ensured the continuous evolution of corporations and, through them, the nation's economy in response to the changing events and opportunities presented by the environment.

In many industries in Britain, however, a strategy of diversification had only recently been adopted. The initial method of broadening a firm's product-market scope had usually been by acquisition, as internal processes for developing new products for new markets were absent or weak. In these newly diversified industries and those that had still to broaden their product lines, the internal initiation of innovation had yet to become institutionalized. Indeed, this was also true for some of the long-established diversified firms which had still to organize themselves adequately to generate new opportunities.

The adoption of the new strategy also brought a dramatic change in the administrative structure of the large corporate enterprise. The multidivisional structure provided the administrative mechanism to control, consolidate, and institutionalize the new strategy. In the postwar period the new structure swept through the British-owned corporations. From a small nucleus of 8 percent of the population in 1950, most of which were subsidiaries of foreign parent companies, the multidivisional structure was found in over 70 percent of the population by 1970.

In 1950 the most common structural form was that of the functional organization, but as new firms began to diversify, the adoption of the strategy of diversification led to increasing managerial complexity and to the decline of the functional form. Since much of this early diversification was by acquisition, it was common initially to adopt a holding-company structure. The subsidiaries were left to continue formulating their own independent strategies as a way of resolving the problems of managing the diversified enterprise. Thus, by 1960, the holding-company structure was the most common in large-scale British enterprise. However, neither the functional nor the holding-company structure proved adequate to the task of managing the diversified enterprise.

The addition of new markets, products, and processes made it increasingly difficult to control and coordinate the multiplicity of operating decisions with the functional system. The flow of information and the structure of authority proved inadequate, as the senior executives were now called upon not merely to supervise operations but to determine a program of strategic decisions involving many variables. The task of rational resource allocation became one of deciding between alternatives for investment in different businesses rather than what investment should be made to expand the existing product line. The increased complexity made it difficult to measure the performance of the different activities with the frequently primitive control systems. The functional system was, therefore, increasingly abandoned, many firms moving initially to a holding-company structure with a smaller number of others moving to a multidivisional system.

Similarly the holding companies proved inadequate as a structural response to diversity. The late 1950s saw the end of the postwar seller's market in most industries. In addition, greater international competition and an increasingly open domestic economy meant that firms were forced to become more competitive and efficient. The complacency born of a protected domestic and overseas market began to give way to concern. The lack of central guidance and control over the strategy of the holding-company subsidiaries frequently resulted in wasteful duplication, internal rivalry, and inefficiency. The impact of the new competition led to declining profits, slow growth and, in some cases, financial crisis. The executives responsible for the guidance of the enterprise were forced to reconsider their primary role and plan for the future.

In many firms new leaders were called upon to consolidate the empires built by earlier men. The lack of adequate controls and suitable internal skills led to the frequent use of outside consultants to assist in restructuring. No fewer than 32 of the largest 100 firms were known to have called in management consultants to assist in the revision of administrative structure. In 22 of these cases the consultant firm called upon was McKinsey & Company. The consultants almost always recommended the adoption of a form of the multidivisional organization that had been tried and tested in the competitive American environment. In some firms the leaders evolved new structures by their own efforts, but overall the response was usually the same.

The multidivisional system called for the enterprise to be divided into logically autonomous units based upon either products or geography. Ideally, each division was to be managed by a general manager responsible for the operating decisions of his division and for its performance. A general office was set up to monitor performance and provide specialist services to the divisions. Dependent upon the degree and form of interrelationship between the divisions, the size and role of the general office varied. Where the diversification was long established and where there was a considerable degree of internal transaction, or a technological interrelationship, the general office tended to become large and multifunctional, establishing a wide variety of policies and services with which to control and assist the divisions. Where the diversification was more recent or the divisional interrelationship was low, the general office was concerned mainly with financial monitoring, and delegated control of not merely operations but also product-market strategy to the divisions. The autonomy of the divisions also varied according to the level of diversification of the enterprise. Where there was little diversification, the central office and the senior officers intervened more in the affairs of the major product line, and the autonomy of the senior division was restricted.

Despite the widespread adoption of many features of the new structure, however, British general executives had not wholly emulated their American counterparts in adopting certain characteristic mechanisms associated with the system. In Britain, management was still using some of its traditional techniques in managing the multidivisional form. Notably there was little use of performance-related rewards or sanctions, except through the indirect link of promotional prospects. The divisional general managers were participating in the formation of central policy in a way that made monitoring and performance measurement difficult. The general officers of many corporations had not yet divorced themselves from the operations of the divisions in order to concentrate on their entrepreneurial role of strategic decision making. In some corporations transformation to a formal divisional system was incomplete, with parts of the business still run as a holding company, or specific functions, especially marketing, still centrally managed. Finally, there was little generation of internal competition between divisions, to allow the enterprise to allocate its resources as a small, but highly effective, capital market.

These differences between the American and British systems are expected to decrease in time as market competition increases. Some firms will doubtless become more performance-oriented. By their success their presence will in turn apply pressure for others to change, in order to compete and to avoid the threat of take-over. Over time, therefore, the population can be expected to become increasingly similar to its American counterpart unless outside influences intervene.

IMPLICATIONS FOR MANAGEMENT

The policy of diversifying to control competition during the postwar period was frequently not the result of a deliberately planned strategy but more a sequence of ad hoc opportunistic moves almost in desperation to gobble up potential sources of entry into related product markets. As a result many acquisitions failed to achieve the hopes their purchasers intended. Expected similarities and complementarities did not materialize. Apparently related product markets turned out to be much more unrelated than had been foreseen.

While it often seemed easier and more economic to make an initial entry into a new product market by acquisition, most British firms seemingly made little attempt to rationalize their purchases. Very few had even developed such skills by 1970. The analysis of potential acquisitions remained largely opportunistic despite some recognition that companies would consciously adopt this route to further diversification. Such a situation represented a managerial failure. For the firm which intended to continue to diversify by acquisition it was essential that it set up a small specialist function to screen and continuously monitor the environment for the most suitable candidates which might match the overall corporate strategy.

Even acquisitions which were clearly related or complementary to existing operations often failed to produce the synergistic effect anticipated, and in many cases reduced earnings actually resulted. This again was caused largely by managerial failure. Synergy as a concept is meaningless without a theory of implementation and administration to achieve it. Frequently, acquired concerns were allowed to continue along much as before without real influence from the parent. The acquisition was in name only, not in managerial action. For those who would argue that it was not possible to enforce rapid change in a newly combined system, others would agree that some limits should be set. If an impossible situation should arise, then this is evidence of further failure in the screening process prior to the acquisition, but it could still be divested. There were extremely few cases where managements had recognized acquisition mistakes and had divested.

The newly diversified enterprises in many cases had still to institutionalize diversification by internal development. For many of the concerns rapid growth by acquisition brought great size, but this growth rate was increasingly difficult to sustain merely by acquisition. Yet internal development was still weak in many of the concerns. The active search for new products to meet new needs was often poorly supported with resources, if this search existed at all, and certainly was subordinate in the hierarchy to other functions. As a result many British firms had relied heavily on imported technology for new products or were still engaged in semi-commodity markets where product differentiation and margins were low.

The research indicated that the adoption of a strategy of diversification called for the introduction of a multidivisional structure. This would permit top management to delegate the detailed management of operations and would allow them to concentrate on the strategic decisions of the enterprise. The role of top management is thus to determine the strategic objectives of the enterprise, to decide what the enterprise is, or is to become, based on its distinctive competences, and to determine progress toward the firm's objectives by measured criteria. Resources are then allocated on the basis of the strategy of the enterprise and the competence of the divisional management. As diversification increases, the top management becomes increasingly divorced from operations and does not necessarily possess the detailed knowledge to determine the product strategies of the divisions. To an increasing degree management must rely on the institutionalization of corporate strategic objectives and policies both to constrain and to guide the decisions delegated to the divisional general managers.

The role of top management is thus that of the strategist and policy maker and not of the operations manager. For many chief executives this is a difficult role to fulfill, if their previous experience has been operational. Further, the multidivisional structure calls for another stratum of general managers within the enterprise, and management must take conscious steps to build for future managerial succession. Once institutionalized, however, the depth of general management experience becomes a source of great strength to the enterprise and permits the ready addition of new activities.

Although adopting the multidivisional structure nominally many concerns had not implemented it completely. For many it was still very new and they were undergoing the often painful period of adjustment to the new system.

Indeed, the initial structural transition of the enterprise to the multidivisional system will frequently be both painful and difficult. This is especially so for the functionally organized concern where the executive power of the enterprise is divided and allocated to a number of functional specialists and the only level with general management responsibility is the office of the chief executive. These concerns possess neither the general management competence nor the control systems necessary to manage the multidivision structure. Furthermore, to introduce it necessitates the destruction of the power base of the specialist functional managers—a move these managers are unlikely to accept willingly.

Within the holding-company structure, executive power is delegated to the general managers and boards of the subsidiary operations. The central office staff is typically small and only fragmentary control systems are usually used. However, the subsidiary companies may well provide the general management skills required for structural change. Further, the imposition of controls and constraints upon the autonomy of subsidiaries will not necessarily result in as much opposition as the destruction of the power base of functional specialists. However, where divisionalization calls for the rationalization of subsidiary activities, a high degree of internal resistance can be anticipated from the executives whose position is weakened.

There are no simple solutions to these problems, which probably explains in large part why firms postpone structural change until a crisis arises, and why management consultants have been so widely used. For a successful transition there appears to be one vital ingredient, however, a strength of leadership. The leadership function within the enterprise is vested with the legitimate power of the hierarchical position but those assuming the role do not necessarily make use of it. It is essential that the leader or leaders of the enterprise should use the power of the executive office in order to achieve a speedy and successful structural transformation. If this does not occur, the goals of the enterprise will be subordinated to the goals of those resisting the transition. Furthermore, the evidence suggests that difficulties of transition may be greater for established leaders who have either built or maintained the existing system. This may help to explain the great number of structural transitions which occurred shortly after changes in leadership in the various companies.

In Britain, although nominal acceptance of the multidivisional structure was widespread, its full potential was not being achieved; because, in general, there was a lack of desire on the part of the leaders of enterprises to install some of the essential characteristics of the system. This is understandable since the system is clearly not always benevolent to those engaged in it. Further, other factors militate against the use of financial rewards and sanctions, the close measurement of performance, and the prospect of loss of employment security as a penalty for failure. The introduction of these characteristics implies no less than a dramatic change in the system of social values in the society at large.

British enterprises had consciously adopted the new structure but, as late as the 1970s, many did not wish to adopt all that it implied and they were, therefore, retaining the less achievement-oriented systems of previous structural forms. However, already a number of concerns were using the complete multidivisional system; some were American subsidiaries, such as Mars and Standard Telephones; some were British, such as General Electric/English Electric and Slater Walker. These concerns were achieving superior economic performance, a fact that was lauded, although their methods were frequently considered distasteful. There seemed little doubt that more and more companies would adopt features such as stock options and increasingly these would be directly related to corporate and divisional performance. As more firms adopt the achievement-oriented system in toto, competitive pressures will make it increasingly difficult to avoid; and the opportunities for those who dislike such pressures will become fewer. The national goal remains one of economic growth and, while this is generally desired by all, it is important to realize that the achievement of this goal will transform present values—a fact that will almost certainly not be universally approved.

IMPLICATIONS FOR GOVERNMENT

The role of government in British industry had become increasingly evident during the past two decades (1950–1970). After an initial return to the market system in the immediate postwar period, government involvement in industry had grown, building to a climax in the Labour administrations of 1964–70. This role had an impact both directly and indirectly on the strategic development of British industrial enterprises. The overall impact was probably to slow the transformation of British industry by sustaining the weak and holding back the strong. The basis for this judgment is that government seemed to be using the wrong model of modern corporate enterprise, being concerned more with concentration as a means of meeting competitive pressure than with diversification, which was generally adopted by many enterprises themselves.

Direct government intervention was mainly concerned with the undiversified industries where the actions of the state led to concentration in the aircraft, automobile, shipbuilding, and steel industries. The state-sponsored Industrial Reorganisation Corporation was also active especially in the electrical and engineering industries. Here the model used was clearly one of consolidating existing resources into a new organization of a size comparable to international competitors; product diversity was something to be consciously avoided. Nationalization concentrated on single product industries or services such as transportation, coal, gas, electricity, steel (and recently aero-engines) and, although there were plans for the nationalization of diversified industries such as chemicals, these did not materialize. In other nondiversified industries such as sugar and cement, government largely controlled the environment through the pricing mechanism which helped to constrain the advent of new competition.

The creation of such narrow-product base enterprises led and can lead to a series of problems. First, the combination of smaller, similar concerns in order to create a viable large one implies that the sought-after synergy would indeed materialize. This reflects the same naiveté which many corporate managements experienced in their own acquisition programs. Synergy requires administration and implementation, and frequently government neglected this aspect of modernization. Second, once-created, large single product enterprises become much more difficult to effectively intervene in, where such intervention implies reorganization or rationalization. If such concerns continue to be uneconomic as a whole, remedial action becomes very difficult because of the political pressures created. To close down an uneconomic enterprise employing an organized labor force of 50,000 men is politically very visible compared with similar action against even 5,000. Third, such large enterprises can be even more vulnerable than the series of smaller concerns from which they were created. Overheads are necessarily much greater, and their product-market scope, labor, investment, and pricing policies are frequently politically constrained. The synergy of such groupings may, therefore, be greater by combining dissimilar but complementary concerns in order to add strength where once there was weakness rather than compounding weaknesses in the hope they can be converted into strengths.

In managing the economy, major impact was also focused on the nondiversified industries with fiscal measures being heavily concentrated on appliances, automobiles, tobacco, and alcohol. Here the frequent use of fiscal controls probably had an adverse effect on industrial development especially of the automobile and consumer durable industries. Government spending on research and development and financial aid was concentrated in the undiversified industries, notably aircraft, and such spending was seldom made on the basis of a significant expected return on the resources allocated. Investment grants had more widespread usage, but this method of financial incentive to industry further permitted the development of uneconomical investments paid for in large part with public funds. The system of personal taxation geared to the laudable goal of egalitarian income distribution served to block the development of entrepreneurial risk taking via the use of incentive rewards and favored retention of the status quo. These actions all tended to support the judgment that government was using an obsolete model of corporate enterprise and both main political parties need to reappraise their policies of resource allocation to meet the needs of modern enterprise in an open, competitive economy.

The continual intervention in narrow product-market scope industries most of which were in decay, tended to slow the natural process of corporate evolution and sustain low growth industries whose manpower could have been better employed elsewhere. Government should address its policies toward smoothing this process and relieving the social problems it creates rather than attempting to hold back the inevitable. The modern corporate enterprise exists within an open system unbounded by national frontiers and where international competitive pressures created outside narrow national boundaries are often outside the control of individual national governments. Any attempt to operate policies which imply a closed national industrial system will almost certainly fail. This is especially true for a trading nation such as Britain.

Some actions, however, were in favor of the growth of competitive enterprise, notably the legislation which tended to break down cartels, restrictive practices, and resale price maintenance. It was, in particular, the postwar Labour administrations that had been concerned mostly with the policy of direct intervention in the undiversified industries. Their industrial policy still seemed more appropriate for the latter half of the nineteenth century than for the twentieth. However, Conservative administrations were involved in the transformation of the aircraft industry although they were responsible for many of the other actions cited and attuned to the market system.

The implications for government, therefore, are centered on the realization that the goal of economic growth means the continued development of profitable corporate enterprise. Further, if Britain intends to remain an open economic society, it must be realized that the form of the new institution will be different. The multidivisional enterprise permits corporate management to more readily pursue profitable growth, and the diversified concerns are rapidly coming to account for the bulk of manufacturing industry. Reform of the taxation system and/or transferability of pension rights are necessary to permit the use of incentives for individual executives and to encourage individual enterprise. Government funds should be placed where they will produce economic returns; there is no point in spending the bulk of government industrial expenditure in industries such as aerospace, steel, and coal mining, if it can be better spent elsewhere; there is no point in propping up declining industries if they are unable to compete in world markets.

The real function for government is to recognize and ease the problems continuously created by this evolution. As industry applies the criteria for performance more rigorously, especially in the multidivisional concerns where profit responsibility is delegated to general managers (who are accountable for their profitability), the level of unemployment can be expected to rise considerably as the inefficiencies of the past are corrected. This will occur in both declining industries and in those that are presently significantly overmanned. In many cases workforces appear to be twice as high as needed by comparison with U.S. concerns. Competitive pressures leading either to narrower profit margins and/or increased internal demands for performance can be expected to lead to a considerable narrowing of the gap which in turn means a drastic shake-out of excess labor. Initially, those firms which had really begun to use the high performance criteria of the multidivisional system could be expected to lead, but their presence will no doubt produce a growing influence on competitors to follow suit. Nor will this unemployment be confined to blue collar workers but will include increasing numbers of white collar workers and executives unsuited or unable to perform according to the standards of the new system. Government will be called upon to deal with this growing social problem—to relocate, retrain, support, and placate Trade Union pressure. There will be a drastically increased need for such government action. Further, it will almost certainly be continuous, although the peak will be during the 1970s as the new system becomes operative. Men can expect to be retrained more frequently and become more mobile, thus creating severe social problems which government and industry must make adequate provisions for, if the change is to be acceptable.

Clearly the political choices involved in such strategies involve some transition of the values presently held by the society. An alternative model of industrial society, such as that of the Japanese, also seems to work well, but Britain has chosen to use the American model. If economic growth is to remain a major national objective, and it surely is, the full implications of that model must be realized and acted upon. The benefits achievable from sustained progress require personal sacrifice as part of the price.

IMPLICATIONS FOR THE TEACHING OF BUSINESS ADMINISTRATION

The development of the diversified corporation and of the multidivisional structure has great significance for those who would teach the skills of business administration.

Presently business education in Britain is still very much in its infancy by comparison with the United States. It was not until the mid-1960s when, stimulated by government and industry, the universities began teaching business administration. The early pioneering work which began after the Second World War was done by polytechnics on a part-time basis. Today a number of British business schools have been formed but they are generally very small by comparison with those in the United States, with an average postgraduate capacity in the university sector in 1968–69 of little more than 40 students.[1] This number is clearly too low to sustain

---

[1] National Economic Development Office, *Management Education in the 1970's*, p. 40.

an adequate diversity of faculty, and the critical problem in British schools is indeed the production of suitable faculty. The primary course in the British schools is still for only one year, and there are only some 300 students presently engaged in Master's courses compared with over 19,000 in the United States in 1968–69.[2]

In addition, the British schools suffer from their curriculum which tends to emphasize the academic at the expense of the empirical. Many of their faculties strive to maintain their linkages with traditional academic disciplines and view multidisciplined business from the vantage point of the academic specialist. The structural system reinforces this viewpoint with its emphasis on academically respectable research rather than that designed to assist the practitioner.

In addition to its emphasis on academic specialisms, the present curriculum in the British schools and, indeed, many American schools, is centered on the model of corporate enterprise with a functional form of organization. As such, the system tends to train functional specialists for either divisional operations or staff roles. While many specialists are required in the multidivisional organization, the key need is for those with general management skills. The curriculum used in these schools, therefore, needs to be amended in order to provide for this demand.

Further, the needs of specialists in the multidivisional firm are somewhat different from those in the functional firm. For example, the control systems used need to measure divisional performance in addition to the measurement of specific functions. While marketing specialists teach that the senior marketing executive must sit on the right hand of the chief executive, in the multidivisional organization, line marketing is delegated to the divisions while only staff service functions remain in the central office.

The academic institutions need to adjust their research and teaching to the requirements of modern business enterprise. At present they are not teaching in a manner wholly relevant to the large diversified corporation. The complexities of the large diversified enterprise seem to have been neglected, while research and teaching have been concentrated in the narrow functional or academic disciplines best suited to divisional subunits. This may partially explain the business community's criticism that the business schools are too "academic." At the same time, however, many such critics would do well to demonstrate, before they criticize, that they are indeed capable of leading and producing the best managerial performance possible with the assets for which they are responsible.

SUGGESTIONS FOR FUTURE RESEARCH

This study clearly established that a close parallel existed between the development of corporate enterprise in Britain and in the United States. The model survived the transference from one culture to another, although the process of corporate evolution came somewhat later. From the corporate data collected, several fruitful areas for future research became evident.

First, there were many obvious similarities in the cultural backgrounds of Britain and the United States which might explain the similarities in the process of cor-

---

[2] *Ibid.,* pp. 40, 137.

porate evolution. Further studies, conducted in less culturally similar industrial societies, would therefore be useful in order to test the more general acceptability of the model. Such work is now proceeding, and the results should soon be available for similar studies conducted in France, West Germany, and Italy.

Second, this study has dealt with the strategy and structure of firms engaged in the manufacturing industry. To date little similar research has been conducted on firms engaged in the growing service sectors of the economy. Do these firms evolve strategically and structurally in a similar way? Does the model tested apply generally to business organizations, or are the problems of the service industries sufficiently different to cause modifications? Further study of the strategy and structure of firms engaged in retailing, finance, insurance, and the like, would seem a useful adjunct to studies of the manufacturing industry.

Third, the widespread use of management consultants in introducing major structural change and especially the multidivisional system offers some scope for further empirical study. It is known that they were widely used in the United States but their actual impact has not been traced. This would be useful as would similar studies in other industrial societies. Why were they used so frequently and how often was their use associated with a leadership change in the client concern? The problems of transition from other structural forms to the multidivisional system have been suggested as being related to the changes required in the personal power system and perhaps consultants serve as a catalytic mechanism to enable these changes to take place. Alternatively the client organization may use consultants because it is often incapable of developing a realistic appraisal of its developing structural needs, and this reflects the embarrassing problem of managerial inadequacy. How different are the executives before and after such a transition? Empirically it seemed that effective introduction of a new system often required significant executive replacement. Further detailed studies to reveal the clinical workings of such transitions, the roles and interrelationships of leaders, outside consultants, and the existing executive structure would lead to greater understanding of this specific process and the wider area of organizational dynamics.

Fourth, differences were observed in the internal characteristics of British and American concerns with special regard to internal motivation systems and the board participation of British division general managers. Further clinical studies to reveal the exact nature and effect of these variations would serve to establish what differences, if any, can be anticipated over the long term due to cultural differences between the multidivisional systems in the two environments.

Fifth, the present teaching of specialist business disciplines seems more attuned to the functional organization than the multidivisional system. Further interdisciplinary, clinical research would seem useful to understand the nature of the role of functional specialists within the new structure. In addition, research is needed into the tasks and role of the general manager in the multidivisional system in order to produce academic programs better suited to the managerial requirements of the diversified enterprise.

Sixth, the concept of relating organization structure to the strategy of the enterprise has significant implications for other social sciences. The development of the sociotechnical system approach in recent years bears some similarity to the strategy model but takes the strategy of an enterprise, largely as a given and tends to overemphasize the role of production technology and size. This study has clearly demonstrated that size is not the key determinant of structure and, while production technology is significant, it is only its relationship to the strategy of the enterprise which is more market- than production-oriented, that partially determines structure. Studies which use strategy as an independent variable permit structure to be used as the dependent variable in order to produce normative concepts on the form of organization best suited to particular strategies. Such studies would do much to clarify the apparent dichotomies between the classical and participative schools of management thought, each of which might be appropriate for specific strategies.

Finally, the study revealed a number of insights on the nature and role of leadership which suggest future avenues of research into the psychology of management. The successful entrepreneurs observed tended to come from socially outcast sectors of society, tended to run their organizations autocratically, tended to find it difficult to delegate responsibility (even for operations), and tended to hold on to the organization even when age or product-market complexity would seem to indicate structural change was necessary. By contrast, organizations which successfully underwent the transition from entrepreneurial leadership to managerial control tended to adopt leadership by what might be called administrative personalities who consolidated, restructured, and institutionalized into the organization the original purpose determined by the entrepreneur. The contrasting styles of these two extreme cases suggest they might be ends of a spectrum perhaps embracing small-sized to medium-sized entrepreneurs and less dedicated managerial personalities on the middle ground. Differences would seem to be apparently some function of personality, and studies of such personalities might reveal meaningful generalizations on the type of leadership required by enterprises at various stages of their evolution.

Index